THE HOLY BLOOD

This is the first extended study of relics of the Holy Blood: portions of the blood of Christ's Passion supposedly preserved from the time of the Crucifixion and displayed as objects of wonder and veneration in the churches of medieval Europe.

Inspired by the discovery of new evidence relating to the relic deposited by King Henry III at Westminster in 1247, the study proceeds from the particular political and spiritual motives that determined this gift to a wider consideration of blood relics, their distribution across western Europe, their place in Christian devotion and the controversies to which they gave rise among theologians. In the process the author advances a new thesis on the role of the sacred in Plantagenet court life as well as exploring various intriguing byways of medieval religion.

NICHOLAS VINCENT is Professor of Medieval History, Christ Church College, Canterbury. His previous books include *Peter des Roches: An Alien in English Politics, 1205–1238* (1996).

THE HOLY BLOOD

King Henry III and the Westminster Blood Relic

NICHOLAS VINCENT

CAMBRIDGE
UNIVERSITY PRESS

CAMBRIDGE UNIVERSITY PRESS
Cambridge, New York, Melbourne, Madrid, Cape Town, Singapore, São Paulo

Cambridge University Press
The Edinburgh Building, Cambridge CB2 2RU, UK

Published in the United States of America by Cambridge University Press, New York

www.cambridge.org
Information on this title: www.cambridge.org/9780521571289

First published 2001
This digitally printed first paperback version 2006

A catalogue record for this publication is available from the British Library

Library of Congress Cataloguing in Publication data
Vincent, Nicholas.
The Holy Blood: King Henry III and the Westminster blood relic / Nicholas Vincent.
p.   cm.
Includes bibliographical references and index.
ISBN 0 521 57128 6
1. Jesus Christ – Relics – History of doctrines.   2. Henry III, King of England,
1207–1272.   3. England – Church history.   I. Title.
BT465.V56   2001
232.96′ 6 – dc21   2001025595

ISBN-13 978-0-521-57128-9 hardback
ISBN-10 0-521-57128-6 hardback

ISBN-13 978-0-521-02660-4 paperback
ISBN-10 0-521-02660-1 paperback

For Juliet

'Beware those who do not blush to write books about the circumcision of the Lord.'

Guibert of Nogent, De pigneribus (c. 1120), claiming to quote from Origen

'We are sending you a portion of the most precious Blood of the Lord Jesus Christ shed at Calvary within the church of Jerusalem . . . and know most certainly and without doubt that this is truly that Blood which flowed from Christ's side.'

Robert Patriarch of Jerusalem, writing to King Henry III of England (1247)

'[William Buckland (1784–1856), Oxford's first Reader in Geology, later Dean of Westminster, visited] a foreign cathedral where was exhibited a martyr's blood – dark spots on the pavement ever fresh and ineradicable. The Professor dropped on the pavement and touched the stain with his tongue. "I can tell you what it is; it is bat's urine." '

William Tuckwell, Reminiscences of Oxford (London 1900)

Contents

Illustrations

Maps

Acknowledgements

This study developed out of an attempt to explain the circumstances of a letter from the Patriarch of Jerusalem, discovered purely fortuitously amongst the archives of Westminster Abbey. Originally, I intended, in collaboration with Simon Lloyd, to publish no more than a brief commentary on the letter, but as work progressed it became apparent that the lack of a reliable history of blood relics necessitated a far more extensive survey than had originally been planned. Since it was Simon Lloyd who first encouraged me to publish the patriarch's letter, and since this study developed along very different lines from those that he had been led to expect, I owe him a very great burden of thanks, not only for his patience and forbearance, but for his detailed commentary upon the finished piece. For help with particular points, and for commentary upon earlier drafts I am indebted to Julia Barrow, Peter Biller, Paul Binski, Christopher and Rosalind Brooke, James Carley, David Carpenter, Henry Chadwick, Richard Cross, Bill Davies, Eamon Duffy, Michael Gervers, Lindy Grant, Bernard Hamilton, Barbara Harvey, John Hirsh, Brian Kemp, Simon Keynes, Peter Linehan, Roger Lovatt, John Maddicott, Henry Mayr-Harting, James King, Colin Morris, John Osman, Nigel Ramsay, Sean Ramsden, Miri Rubin, Richard Sharpe, Jonathan Shepard, Alison Stones, Robert Swanson, Deirdre Webber, Björn Weiler, Brian Wormald and Patrick Zutshi. In particular Henry Mayr-Harting provided enormous assistance and advice, whilst Peter Biller persuaded me to make substantial changes to the structure of the final chapter. Richard Mortimer at Westminster and Kate Harris at Longleat provided expert guidance to the archives in their care, whilst for permission to reproduce original material, I am grateful to the Marquess of Bath, the President and Fellows of Magdalen College, Oxford, and the Dean and Chapter of Westminster Abbey. The staffs of the Bodleian, Cambridge University and British libraries, and of the Bibliothèque nationale in Paris, coped with a plethora of bizarre requests and, on occasion, must have wondered whether they were dealing with a historian or a close cousin of Jack the Ripper. Written and accepted for publication several years ago, this book has since languished in my files, unpublished, the delay being attributable in equal measure to my own sloth and to King Henry II. That it has at last been wrenched into the light of day, checked and updated, I owe in large part to the generosity of the British Academy in electing me to a research readership, to my employers at Christ Church Canterbury for allowing me leave of absence and to the hospitality provided by the Warden and Fellows of All Souls College, Oxford, and the Master and Fellows of Peterhouse, Cambridge.

Cambridge, September 2001

Abbreviations

Acta SS	*Acta sanctorum*, ed. J. Bollandus *et al.* (Antwerp, Tongerloo and Paris 1643–)
BL	British Library, London
CCCM	Corpus christianorum continuatio mediaevalis
CM	Matthew Paris, *Chronica majora*, ed. H. R. Luard, 7 vols., Rolls Series (London 1872–84)
Mansi, *Concilia*	*Sacrorum conciliorum nove et amplissima collectio*, ed. J. D. Mansi, 53 vols. (Florence, Venice and Paris 1759–98)
MGH	*Monumenta germaniae historica*
Migne, *PG*	*Patrologiae cursus completus: series Graeco-Latina*, ed. J.-P. Migne (Paris 1857–66)
Migne, *PL*	*Patrologiae cursus completus: series Latina*, ed. J.-P. Migne, (Paris 1841–64)
PRO	Public Record Office, London
SA	*Sangue e antropologia*, ed. F. Vattioni, 8 vols. in 21 parts, Centro studi sanguis Christi (Rome 1981–)

CHAPTER I

Introduction

In his *Chronica majora*, Matthew Paris supplies us with an eye-witness account of a ceremony conducted by King Henry III at Westminster on Sunday, 13 October 1247, the feast of the translation of the relics of St Edward the Confessor. Falling midway between Henry's birthday on 1 October, and the anniversary of his accession on 28 October, the feast of St Edward's translation had long been celebrated as one of the highpoints of the royal year, coinciding conveniently with the Michaelmas sessions of exchequer and the Bench, a busy time for King and courtiers, drawing many hundreds of people to attend at Westminster. The Confessor himself was a saint for whom Henry III felt keen, even fanatical, devotion. The pious, demilitarized Edward of legend served as a model for Henry's own preferred style of kingship. There were more personal resonances too, between the Confessor's early life, deprived of both father and mother, and the insecurities of Henry III's own orphaned childhood.[1] For many years past Henry had lavished money and attention upon the Confessor's shrine and upon the monks of Westminster who served it. In 1228 he had written to the Pope requesting Edward's inclusion in the Roman calendar of saints, and in 1239 he had named his first-born son Edward, in the Confessor's memory.[2] In 1245, he had set about the demolition of the east end of the Abbey church in order that the whole might be sumptuously rebuilt. As a result, the relics of St Edward had been removed to a temporary site and Henry had taken the opportunity to obtain further support from the Pope, soliciting a papal indulgence that offered a year and forty days' remission of enjoined penance to all who attended the proposed movement of

---

[1] P. Binski, *Westminster Abbey and the Plantagenets* (New Haven 1995), 3–6, 52–89; P. Binski, 'Reflections on "La Estoire de Seint Aedward le Rei": Hagiography and Kingship in Thirteenth-Century England', *Journal of Medieval History* 16 (1990), 333–50; N. Vincent, 'Isabella of Angoulême: John's Jezebel', *King John: New Interpretations*, ed. S. D. Church (Woodbridge 1999), 215–16.
[2] Binski, *Westminster Abbey*, 52.

Edward's bones.[3] A year later he had established an independent financial office at Westminster for the furtherance of his building projects there.[4] More recently still, in October 1246, he had decreed that his own body was to rest at Westminster after his death; the clearest sign of devotion that a king could bestow upon any religious house.[5] At much the same time he had obtained licence for the abbots of Westminster to offer pontifical blessing to the congregation during the celebration of Mass, Matins and Vespers.[6] Hence, in the autumn of 1247, when he ordered his nobles to assemble at Westminster on 13 October, 'to hear the most agreeable news of a holy benefit recently conferred upon the English', the summons may have been greeted with lively anticipation. Certainly, it was sufficient to draw the chronicler Matthew Paris and at least three of his fellow monks from St Albans to Westminster, possibly at the King's own invitation, to record whatever events might unfold.[7]

---

[3] Westminster Abbey Muniments MS Domesday fo. 386v, letters of Innocent IV, dated 31 July 1245: *Eius licet immeriti . . . idem rex devotionis ardore succensus corpus beati Edwardi regis Anglie gloriosum de loco ad locum honorifice ac sollempniter transferre proponat*, and see also fo. 406r for another papal indulgence, of 26 July 1245, directed to the inhabitants of the dioceses of London, Lincoln and Winchester, offering twenty days' remission of enjoined penance to all contributing to the Abbey's fabric. The best general accounts of Henry's work at the Abbey are those provided by H. M. Colvin in *The History of the King's Works I: The Middle Ages*, ed. R. Allen Brown, H. M. Colvin and A. J. Taylor, 2 vols. (London 1963), I 130–57, and, in much greater detail, by Binski, *Westminster Abbey*.

[4] *Calendar of Patent Rolls 1232–47* (London 1906), 478, and for the special Westminster exchequer see in general E. F. Jacobs, 'The Reign of Henry III. Some Suggestions', *Transactions of the Royal Historical Society* 4th series 10 (1927), 33–41, esp. 38–9; *King's Works*, I 135–6.

[5] Westminster Abbey Muniments 6318A, enrolled in *Calendar of Charter Rolls 1226–57* (London 1903), 306. The chancery enrolment survives only in a mutilated version. See also B. Harvey, *Westminster Abbey and its Estates in the Middle Ages* (Oxford 1977), 391, for the King's foundation of chantries in the Abbey in 1245–6 for his father-in-law, Raymond-Berengar count of Provence, and for his mother, Isabella of Angoulême.

[6] *CM*, IV 589; *Les Registres d'Innocent IV (1243–54)*, ed. E. Berger, 4 vols. (Ecole française de Rome 1884–1921), I no. 1866. The abbots had for many years been allowed to dress themselves in pontificals: *Westminster Abbey Charters 1066–c. 1214*, ed. E. Mason, London Record Society XXV (1988), nos. 173–5.

[7] For what follows see *CM*, IV 640–5. The gift of the Holy Blood is briefly mentioned in various later chronicles, for the most part derived from Matthew Paris: *De antiquis legibus liber. Chronica maiorum et vicecomitum Londoniarum*, ed. T. Stapleton, Camden Society XXXIV (1846), 13; *Eulogium (historiarum sive temporis) . . . a monacho quodam Malmesburiensi exaratum*, ed. F. S. Haydon, 3 vols., Rolls Series (London 1858–63), III 138 (under the year 1248); *Chronica Johannis de Oxenedes*, ed. H. Ellis, Rolls Series (London 1859), 178 (under the year 1247); *Chronicon Henrici Knighton vel Cnitthon, monachi Leycestrensis*, ed. J. R. Lumby, 2 vols., Rolls Series (London 1889–95), I 218; *Polychronicon Ranulphi Higden, monachi Cestrensis*, ed. C. Babington and J. R. Lumby, 9 vols., Rolls Series (London 1865–86), VIII 238–9 (misdated 1248); *Flores historiarum*, ed. H. R. Luard, 3 vols., Rolls Series (London 1890), II 343–4, III 241. This last account, although derived from Paris, states that the blood was brought to England by a Hospitaller. In the *Chronica majora* it is said to have been delivered by a Templar.

According to Matthew Paris, on the day appointed, the King announced that he had come into possession of a most precious relic; a portion of the blood of Jesus Christ, sent to him under the seals of the patriarch of Jerusalem, the masters of the Templars and the Hospitallers and various bishops from the Holy Land. From the time of its arrival in England, the relic is said to have been kept a closely guarded secret, stored at the London church of the Holy Sepulchre.[8] Having spent the previous night in fasting and prayer, early in the morning of 13 October Henry led a solemn procession from St Paul's Cathedral to Westminster. Dressed in a simple cloak, he carried the crystal vase containing Christ's blood in his own hands, supported by two attendants and walking beneath a pall borne upon four spears. For the two miles of his journey he is said to have kept his gaze fixed upon heaven and the relic he held in his hands. At the bishop of Durham's house in Whitehall, he was met by the monks of Westminster and by a great congregation of bishops, abbots and other prelates. The King then continued on his way, carrying the relic in procession around the church, the palace and the royal apartments of Westminster, before presenting it to the monks and to their patron saints, St Peter and St Edward. Mass was then celebrated and a sermon preached by the bishop of Norwich, who extolled the virtues of the relic, comparing it in flattering terms to the relics of Christ's Passion that had been acquired a few years earlier by the French King Louis IX. The bishop announced that indulgences totalling six years, one hundred and sixteen days had been granted to all who should come in future to venerate the Holy Blood. After this, crowned and dressed in cloth of gold, the King bestowed knighthood upon his half-brother, William de Valence, and upon a number of William's associates. Matthew Paris tells us that he himself was then summoned to the throne and questioned by the King on what he had seen. The King commanded Matthew 'to write a plain and full account of all these events, and indelibly to insert them in writing in a book, that the recollection of them may be in no way lost to posterity'. The chronicler and three of his companions were invited to dine with the King, whilst a splendid feast was arranged in the monks' refectory for the whole convent of Westminster.

---

[8] The secret storage of the relic is not mentioned by Paris, but appears in the London chronicle printed in *Chronicles of the Reigns of Edward I and Edward II*, ed. W. Stubbs, 2 vols., Rolls Series (London 1882–3), I 44 *sub anno* 1246: *ante festum sancti Michaelis venit sanguis domini nostri Iesu Cristi Londonias et occulte depositus in hospitali Sancti Sepulcri*. For the reference here to a hospital of St Sepulchre, see below p. 28.

Not surprisingly these events have found a place in most accounts of the reign of Henry III. The procession from St Paul's to Westminster was later depicted by Matthew Paris in one of his better known drawings, whilst his interview with the King has been justly regarded as an indication of the close relations that bound the chronicler to the court.[9] However, to date no attempt has been made to investigate the background to the gift of the Holy Blood to Westminster. Historians have been content to recite Paris' description, without searching for further evidence.[10] As will become apparent, the archives of Westminster Abbey yield important new material relating to the affair, including a letter from the patriarch of Jerusalem that describes the relic of the Holy Blood in some considerable detail. The present study is intended both as a commentary upon this rediscovered letter, and as an attempt to provide an overview of the history of relics of Christ's blood, their origin, distribution and place in popular devotion, essential if we are to understand the particular blend of scepticism and reverence with which the Holy Blood of Westminster was regarded from the moment of its arrival in England. Remarkable as it may seem, there exists no comprehensive account of the history of such relics, a fact that is all the more extraordinary given the attention that historians have lavished upon relics in general, and in particular upon Corpus Christi, the more solid counterpart to relics of the Holy Blood.[11]

The present study begins with the immediate circumstances behind the gift of the blood to Westminster. This in turn will carry us on to the letter from the patriarch of Jerusalem and an attempt to explain its rather peculiar contents by reference to the wider relations between England and the church of Jerusalem. Thereafter we shall turn back to investigate the history of blood relics prior to 1247, posing one question above all others: why was it so difficult for the Westminster relic to find acceptance as a genuine relic of Christ's blood? This question requires an answer, since, as we shall see, the Holy Blood of Westminster, unlike similar relics elsewhere in Europe, was not destined to serve as the object of

---

[9] The drawing is variously reproduced by S. Lewis, *The Art of Matthew Paris in the Chronica Majora* (Aldershot 1987), plate 10 between pp. 290 1; M. E. Roberts, 'The Relic of the Holy Blood and the Iconography of the Thirteenth-Century North Transept Portal of Westminster Abbey', *England in the Thirteenth Century: Proceedings of the 1984 Harlaxton Symposium*, ed. W. M. Ormrod (Harlaxton 1985), figure 8; *The Illustrated Chronicles of Matthew Paris: Observations of Thirteenth-Century Life*, ed. R. Vaughan (Stroud 1993), 38.

[10] The one honourable exception being Harvey, *Westminster Abbey and its Estates*, 44 n. 3, who notes the existence of letters from the patriarch of Jerusalem, treated in greater detail below.

[11] For the few general accounts of blood relics which I have been able to trace, see below pp. 51 3 n. 76. For works on related topics, see M. Rubin, *Corpus Christi* (Cambridge 1990).

any popular cult or devotion. In seeking to explain this failure, we shall look to the schools and to scholastic opinion, specifically with regard to the relic of Westminster and more generally in respect to the wider problems associated with all relics of Christ's bodily presence on earth. Finally we shall consider the aftermath of the events of 1247, the grant of indulgences, the pictorial representation of Henry III's relic and the cult that developed, or rather that *failed* to develop, around the blood of Westminster in the later Middle Ages. To appreciate the full extent of this failure, we shall compare the Westminster relic with its rivals elsewhere, and in particular with the cult of the Holy Blood at Hailes. Here too, new evidence will be brought to light, suggesting that the blood of Hailes enjoyed a more respectable pedigree than the Westminster blood, sufficient, perhaps, to explain its greater attractiveness to pilgrims.

In what follows, I have been able to do no more than touch upon some of the more important themes associated with relics of Christ's blood. My enquiry will not please all readers. To certain critics, it will no doubt appear hopelessly 'old-fashioned'. In particular, I have made little or no attempt here to incorporate the findings or to adopt the methods of many of those historians now engaged in the study of the medieval 'body'. The best of such studies are excellent: none better than those of Caroline Walker Bynum, cited frequently below. For the rest, however, I find myself unimpressed by the mixture of crude Freud and over-ripened Derrida that too often passes for 'body history'. The authors of such studies too often appear to be as ignorant of the learned languages of the Middle Ages as they are incapable of coherent expression in the modern vernacular. 'Misdirected' is perhaps the politest term that can be applied to much of this sort of writing. The pursuit of 'mentalities' is a valuable scholarly exercise. Indeed, much of what follows can be read as a study in the medieval mentality – political, religious, cultural and otherwise. I have held back, however, from what I regard as some of the wilder attempts by historians to superimpose modern terminology upon the thought-processes of the past. Such themes as sacrality, 'the holy' and the interplay of scientific and theological belief-systems will be found here in abundance. I plead guilty, however, to a charge of attempting to rob such themes of much of the numinous aura with which they have on occasion been invested.

The students of another variety of 'misdirected' research will likewise be disappointed by my findings. No one who ventures upon the study of relics, and in particular the relics of Christ, can avoid an encounter with the world of esoteric publishing. There are any number of studies, populist or arcane as the case may be, devoted to such themes as masonic blood sacrifice, or the Druidic mysteries of the Grail. In pursuing the story of the Holy Blood, I have met with more than my fair share of such stuff. Its authors – worthy men and women no doubt – can claim at least one distinction from the gnostics of academe. For the most part they write in pursuit of some private obsession, or merely to put money in their pockets. The gnosis to which they lay claim is of a different, and for the most part more innocent, order to that claimed by tenured university scholars. The writers of esoteria, through personal psychosis or healthy commercialism, are preconditioned to detect conspiracy behind even the most innocent of facts. Academics, by contrast, have no excuse for burdening their readers with that which is sloppy or fraudulent. Those in search of 'body' language, or esoteric enlightenment, should look elsewhere. I make no claim here to have discovered the whereabouts of the Holy Grail, or to have unearthed the treasure of the Templars, and I leave it to others to apply 'bodily' or 'mental' spin to my findings. By drawing attention to a rich new vein of source material I hope none the less, that my enquiry may encourage, rather than pre-empt, further research into a fascinating and altogether remarkable aspect of medieval spirituality.

CHAPTER 2

The ceremony of 1247

King Henry III was neither a devious nor a calculating man.[1] His taste was for spontaneous emotional display. In particular he had a love of grand public ceremony, all the better if it could be combined with pious acts: the feeding of paupers, pilgrimage, the celebration of masses. Such religious observances followed in a much longer tradition of royal piety that even as late as the thirteenth century can be regarded as an expression, albeit a much diluted expression, of the Plantagenet claim to both royal and sacral authority. The reception afforded by Henry to the Holy Blood represents an entirely genuine display of devotion to an important relic. It would be wrong to think of it as a calculated political act, still less as a cynical exercise in propaganda. Yet, whilst the King may have been lacking in guile, there was guile in plenty at his court. Even if we admit that the gift of the Holy Blood to Westminster was a spontaneous, heartfelt gesture, it was a gesture from which the King might hope to reap numerous incidental benefits. To this extent, it is only natural that we should look for worldly motives behind the veneer of other-worldly piety. But precisely what motives?

To begin with, the ceremony of 1247 can be represented as an attempt to emulate, indeed to better, the splendid reception afforded by King Louis IX to the relics of Christ's Passion. Purchased from the bankrupt Latin Emperor of Constantinople, these had been brought to France in several instalments after 1239, and finally ceded to Louis in legal title as recently as June 1247.[2] Obvious comparisons can be drawn between Matthew Paris' description of the reception of the Holy Blood of Westminster and his account of the ceremony conducted by Louis IX in

[1] In what follows I have benefited greatly from discussion with David Carpenter.
[2] For the grant of legal title, see *Exuviae sacrae Constantinopolitanae*, ed. P. E. D. comte de Riant, 2 vols. (Geneva 1877–8), II 134–5 no. 79. The comparison between Henry III's gift of the Holy Blood to Westminster and Louis' earlier acquisition of the Passion relics is well drawn by S. Lloyd, *English Society and the Crusade 1216–1307* (Oxford 1988), 203–5.

I　King Louis IX of France displaying the True Cross and the Crown of Thorns as depicted by Matthew Paris *c.* 1250 (Cambridge, Corpus Christi College MS 16 fo. 141r)

March 1241, in which the Holy Cross was paraded through the streets of the French capital.[3] Just as the rebuilding of Westminster Abbey appears to have been planned in conscious competition with Louis' patronage of the Sainte-Chapelle, so the Holy Blood may have been intended to rival the sanctity of Louis' collection of Passion Relics.[4] Although by 1247 Henry had yet to view the Sainte-Chapelle in person, he had undoubtedly been made aware of its splendours: according to a later satirical poem, so impressed was he after his first sight of it in 1254 that he expressed his desire to have the entire building transported on a cart from the Seine to the banks of the Thames.[5] Matthew Paris refers explicitly to the French relics in his account of the Westminster blood. Both in his summary of the sermon preached by the bishop of Norwich and in a short tract on the Holy Blood that he attributes to bishop Robert Grosseteste of Lincoln, Matthew suggests that the blood deposited at Westminster was in its way a far greater treasure than the relics acquired by Louis IX:

If the True Cross [one of the Passion relics brought to France] is sanctified on account of its contact with the body of Christ, and the Crown of Thorns, the Lance and the nails likewise; so much more holy is the blood of Christ, the price of man's redemption, since it is because of and through the stain [of that blood] that the Cross and the other relics are sanctified, not the blood that is sanctified by the Cross.[6]

It is also worth noting that earlier in 1247 Henry III had been upstaged by King Louis in respect to another set of relics that by rights should have been brought to rest in England. On 7 June 1247 it had been Louis, not Henry, who presided over the translation of the relics of St Edmund of Abingdon at the Cistercian Abbey of Pontigny.[7] It was at Pontigny that St Edmund, archbishop of Canterbury (1234–40), had spent his final days in exile following a bitter quarrel with King Henry. In exile, Edmund

[3] *CM*, IV 90–2.

[4] For the stylistic similarities between the new work at Westminster and Louis IX's projects in and around Paris, see R. Branner, 'Westminster Abbey and the French Court Style', *Journal of the Society of Architectural Historians* 23 (1964), 3–18. Binski, *Westminster Abbey*, esp. ch. 1 pp. 7, 29, 33–5, 39, 44, 46, 106, suggests that the element of copying at Westminster from Paris was relatively slight, and that the entire idea of a 'court style' is badly in need of revision.

[5] Binski, *Westminster Abbey*, 46.

[6] *CM*, IV 642, VI 143.

[7] For the translation of 1247, see *CM*, IV 631, VI 128–30; L. Carolus-Barré, 'Saint Louis et la translation des corps saints', *Etudes d'histoire du droit canonique dédiées à Gabriel le Bras*, 2 vols. (Paris 1965), II 1089–91; *The Life of St Edmund by Matthew Paris*, ed. C. H. Lawrence (Stroud 1996), 99, 166–7. Under the year 1241 Paris refers to France's acquisition of the Holy Cross and the relics of St Edmund as twin, related, blessings; *CM*, IV 91–2.

had deliberately followed the example of Thomas Becket and Stephen Langton, his predecessors in the see of Canterbury, who had sought sanctuary at Pontigny during their own disputes with the English court. The breach between Edmund and the King had been widely reported in England, not least in the papal bull of canonization of January 1247 which draws an explicit comparison between Edmund's exile and that of St Thomas.[8] We would do well to remember that in 1247 the Pope himself was living as an exile at Lyons, on neutral territory between France and the Empire, effectively under the protection of the French King, Louis IX. It must have been all the more humiliating to Henry III that the relics of the first English saint to be canonized in twenty years should have been honoured more by the French than by the English court, much as a few years earlier Henry is said to have been disappointed in his attempts to entice the Pope to take up residence under English rather than French protection.[9] At much the same time that the Holy Blood was being carried through London, Henry's brother Richard of Cornwall was endeavouring to make good his earlier neglect of St Edmund with a pilgrimage to the saint's shrine in France.[10] In the manuscript containing Matthew Paris' verse life of St Edmund, Matthew's poem ends with what may originally have been an independent metrical account of the Holy Blood of Westminster, as in the *Chronica majora* compared in flattering terms to the nails and the Crown of Thorns acquired by King Louis.[11] In this way, the gift of the blood relic can be regarded as a response by Henry III to the triumphs scored by Louis IX over the past few years, both in respect to the Passion relics of the Sainte-Chapelle and to the relics of St Edmund at Pontigny.

Secondly, the ceremony of October 1247 must be set in the context of Henry III's wider devotion to Westminster Abbey. Clearly, the King hoped that his gift would attract pilgrims to the Abbey church that he was in the process of rebuilding. Since the time of his official

---

[8] For the canonization pronounced on 16 December, and for the bull of 11 January 1247 see *CM*, IV 586, VI 120 5, which also announces an indulgence of a year and forty days to all visiting the saint's shrine each year on the newly instituted feast day, 16 November. Paris reports that Richard of Croxley was elected abbot of Westminster on the same day as Edmund's canonization, 16 December 1246, and that as a former friend of St Edmund he set about building a chapel in Westminster Abbey in the saint's honour: *CM*, IV 589, and see *Flores historiarum*, II 320 1 and *The History of Westminster Abbey by John Flete*, ed. J. A. Robinson (Cambridge 1909), 109 10, for Richard's burial in the chapel of St Edmund.

[9] *CM*, IV 32, 631 2, VI 128 9.

[10] *CM*, IV 632, 646 7, and see *CM*, V 228 for the King's sense of remorse.

[11] A.T. Baker, 'La Vie de saint Edmond archevêque de Cantorbéry', *Romania* 55 (1929), 335, 380 1 verses 1888 2020, noticed by P. Binski, 'Abbot Berkyng's Tapestries and Matthew Paris's Life of St Edward the Confessor', *Archaeologia* 109 (1991), 94.

canonization in 1161, neither St Edward the Confessor nor his shrine at Westminster had captured the popular imagination in the way that, for example, the cult of St Thomas Becket had brought money and pilgrims flooding into Canterbury.[12] To rectify this situation, in 1236 Henry had obtained a bull from Pope Gregory IX, recommending that the feast of St Edward's translation be observed by the English church as a *festum feriandum*, or solemn holiday; a request that was publicized at a legatine council convened in London in November 1237.[13] In time, the King sent out further requests that the Confessor's feasts be observed by other English churches. In 1243, at Henry's suggestion, the prior and convent of Christ Church Canterbury agreed that in future they would celebrate the Confessor's translation (13 October) with all the solemnities reserved for the feast of the Ascension, whilst in July 1246 the bishop of Salisbury commanded his dean and chapter to hold special celebrations on the feasts of both the translation and the deposition of St Edward (5 January).[14] Despite this, there is little to suggest that either of these feasts achieved much popularity beyond the confines of Westminster.[15] Undaunted, the King continued in his devotion to Westminster and its relics. Judging from an almoner's roll that survives for the year 1238–9, whenever he was in the vicinity of Westminster Henry offered special weekly oblations to the Abbey's relics.[16] In 1241 he began the rebuilding of the shrine of St Edward.[17] Seen in this context, the Holy Blood was but one of a large number of relics with which the King sought further to adorn the Abbey. It may even be that the King had come to look upon Westminster as a great multifarious reliquary, akin to the Sainte-Chapelle in Paris, built by Louis IX to house his unrivalled

[12] For the cult of St Edward and its apathetic reception beyond Westminster and the court, see *The Life of King Edward who Rests at Westminster*, ed. F. Barlow, 2nd edn (Oxford 1992), 150–63.

[13] *Les Registres de Grégoire IX*, ed. L. Auvray, 4 vols., Bibliothèque des Ecoles françaises d'Athènes et de Rome (Paris 1896–1955), II no. 3330; *CM*, III 418, and in general see Harvey, *Westminster Abbey and its Estates*, 43–4.

[14] Westminster Abbey Muniments MS Domesday fos. 388v–9r (also at fo. 409v), both orders being made specifically at the King's request. For the celebration of the feast of the translation at Salisbury, where there was an altar dedicated to St Edward, see *Ceremonies and Processions of the Cathedral Church of Salisbury*, ed. C. Wordsworth (Cambridge 1901), 203, 225, 227–8, 304. Both the translation and the deposition of St Edward were included in the Salisbury calendars; *ibid.*, 3, 12; *Breviarium ad usum insignis ecclesiae Sarum*, ed. F. Proctor and C. Wordsworth, 3 vols. (Cambridge 1882–6), I pp. iii, xii, III 909–14.

[15] Harvey, *Westminster Abbey and its Estates*, 43 n. 3, which notes a mandate of Pope Innocent IV, *Mirabilis Deus in sanctis suis*, 10 January 1249 (Westminster Abbey MS Domesday fo. 406r), re-iterating the earlier papal injunction that the feast (according to the rubric, the feast of the translation) be generally observed.

[16] PRO C47/3/44 mm. 1–2.

[17] *CM*, IV 156–7.

collection of Passion relics.[18] According to the lists preserved in the chronicle of John Flete, prior of Westminster *c.* 1457–65, Henry's gifts to Westminster included a head relic of St Maurice, probably acquired from the Savoyard kinsmen of Henry's queen, Eleanor of Provence; parts of the head of St Christopher, an arm of St Silvester, a tooth of St Athanasius, various unspecified relics of St Leonard and parts of the clothing, blood and the ebony comb of St Thomas Becket.[19] In the 1240s Henry is known to have paid for the refurbishment of arm relics of St Bartholomew and St Thomas the apostle, supposedly given to the Abbey by St Edward.[20] In 1249 he gave the monks a stone bearing the imprint of Christ's footstep, brought from the Holy Land by a group of Dominican friars.[21] Flete also credits him with the gift of a spine from the Crown of Thorns, and

[18] See Branner, 'Westminster Abbey and the French Court Style', 17–18.

[19] Flete, *History*, 71–2. The gift of the head of St Maurice is probably to be dated to the abbacy of Richard of Croxley (1246–58), in whose time the King persuaded the monks to introduce special celebrations in the saint's honour: *ibid.*, 109. For the cult of St Maurice, of whom relics were broadcast far and wide in the aftermath of the translation of his remains in Savoy in 1225, see L. Dupont Lachenal, 'A Saint-Maurice au XIIIe siècle: l'abbé Nantelme (1223–1258) et la "révélation" des martyrs de 1225', *Annales Valaisannes* 2nd series 31 (1956), 393–444. In 1246 the King's uncle by marriage, count Amadeus IV of Savoy, had rendered homage to Henry for a series of feoffs guarding the Alpine passes, including St-Maurice near Martigny (Switzerland, canton Valais), the saint's supposed resting place; *CM*, IV 550, and see N. Vincent, 'Frederick II, Henry III and the Council of Lyons (1245)' (forthcoming). Since the German church claimed that the saint's body had been translated to Magdeburg in 960, Westminster was by no means alone in claiming St Maurice's head, rival claims being advanced, for example, by the church of St Paulinus at Trier; E.-J. Heyen, *Das Erzbistum Trier I: Das Stift St Paulin von Trier*, Germania sacra neue folge VI (Berlin and New York 1972), 342, 346, and in general for the German cult of St Maurice, see D. Claude, *Geschichte des Erzbistums Magdeburg bis in das 12. Jahrhundert*, 2 vols. (Cologne 1972–5), I 25–31, 39–40. For a gift of the saint's ring to Peter of Savoy, another of Henry III's uncles, and for a later gift of relics to Louis IX of France, see E. Aubert, *Trésor de l'abbaye de Saint-Maurice d'Agaune* (Paris 1872), 55, 57. For images of St Christopher at Westminster and elsewhere painted from 1240 onwards, possibly related to the head relic, see *Calendar of Liberate Rolls 1240–5*, 15; *ibid.* 1245–51, 177; P. Tudor-Craig *et al.*, *The New Bell's Cathedral Guides: Westminster Abbey* (London 1986), 112–13.

[20] *Close Rolls 1242–7* (London 1916), 270, 276, 286; *Calendar of Liberate Rolls 1240–5*, 288–9; H. F. Westlake, *Westminster Abbey: The Church, Convent, Cathedral and College of St Peter, Westminster*, 2 vols. (London 1923), II 499. For the supposed gift of these relics by Edward the Confessor, see Flete, *History*, 70. The arm of St Bartholomew was possibly a portion of an arm relic of the saint purchased by Cnut's wife, Emma, from the bishop of Benevento, and granted to the monks of Canterbury, as recorded in *Eadmeri historia novorum in Anglia*, ed. M. Rule, Rolls Series (London 1884), 107–10, a reference that I owe to Christopher and Rosalind Brooke.

[21] *CM*, V 81–2 and see Flete, *History*, 69, where it is described as having been made at the time of Christ's Ascension. As such it may be identified as one of the miraculous footprints from the summit of the Mount of Olives referred to by several early Jerusalem pilgrims: J. Wilkinson, *Jerusalem Pilgrims before the Crusades* (Warminster 1977), 100–1, 166b. In February 1251 the King ordered that it be enclosed in silver, ready for the solemnities of Good Friday; *Close Rolls 1247–51* (London 1922), 413, drawn to my attention by Paul Binski. It is further referred to in numerous indulgences, the earliest of them dated 1287; Westminster Abbey MS Domesday fos. 398v–9v, and see Westlake, *Westminster Abbey*, II 499.

[Medieval Latin text in abbreviated Gothic script]

scpulis relinqueret: cum ibi ipsum ultimo
uiderunt. Dūs aū rex illis ecce Westm̄
cōtulit. sicut nup sanguē z gratias. z sic
o̅ q̅d̅ iacat nobile donatiuū. De hoc uul
Compil̄; q̅ sub eisdē lulo z Sigillatulo
q̅ida hōmūcio. n̄ aū nanus q̅a me
bra huic sibi ꝓpor cōnalia. etat seq̅ hūs ei
exbui. inuent̄ z i illis a nocte: ueluti n̄ p̅
icrementi suscepturis. statue q̅ fuit uir
ipedar. noie Johis. Que q̅si prodigiū regi
na secū ceudurit. Eodem̄ tempe Quida
puer a q̅da demone ieuba n̄ di gnatus
i gsinio Wallie apparuit. Cl ista dimidi
um annus plene denrat: ad statam as

Xpe ascendens relinqit suis discipulis pro
memoriali. ultimo passus sui impressi
one i marmore candido. q̅m dūs rex
hūr. in. cōtulit ecce Westm̄

2 Stone imprinted with Christ's footstep as depicted by Matthew Paris
c. 1250 (London, British Library MS Royal C vii p. 146)

'a great portion of blood from a miracle', this last being distinguished
from the Holy Blood bestowed in 1247.[22] Such gifts were clearly intended
to enhance the Abbey's prestige and to increase its revenue from pilgrims.
They demonstrate the piety of a king who throughout his life chose to
surround himself with relics and sacred objects.[23] To make Westminster
a more attractive destination, it was important that the Abbey's relics
be accompanied by the grant of indulgences, and here too the King
appears to have done his best to oblige the monks. It may well have been
Henry who encouraged a series of episcopal indulgences intended to
promote veneration of a portion of the True Cross, supposedly given to
the Abbey by Edward the Confessor.[24] In September 1250 Pope Innocent
IV was persuaded to offer a year's indulgence to all who contributed to
the Abbey's fabric, whilst after 1247 the Holy Blood was to be directly
responsible for the award of numerous episcopal indulgences intended to
encourage pilgrimage to Westminster.[25]

Thirdly, the reception afforded to the Holy Blood can be seen as one
aspect of a wider series of contacts between Henry III and the Holy Land
that were to culminate in 1250 with Henry's taking vows as a crusader.
Between 1228 and 1244 the city of Jerusalem had reverted briefly to
Christian lordship, but in 1244 it had fallen once again to a seemingly
invincible alliance between the Khwarizmian Turks and as-Salih Ayub,
Sultan of Egypt and Damascus. The Christian patriarch of Jerusalem,

---

[22] For the spine from the Crown of Thorns and the *magnam partem sanguinis de miraculo*, see Flete,
History, 69, and below pp. 48–9.

[23] See for example *Calendar of Patent Rolls 1232–47*, 39; *Calendar of Liberate Rolls 1251–60*, 90, for a
list of relics received from the monks of Norwich in 1234 to be kept for the remainder of Henry's
life, and for the installation in 1252 of a bench in the King's wardrobe at Clarendon *ad reliquias
nostras desuper ponendas*. In general, for the royal relic collection, see N. Vincent, 'The Pilgrimages
of the Angevin Kings of England, 1154–1272', *Pilgrimage: The English Experience*, ed. C. Morris
and P. Roberts (Cambridge 2001).

[24] Fourteen indulgences directed to pilgrims visiting the relic of the True Cross are preserved in Westminster Abbey MS Domesday fos. 399v–402v, the earliest of them dated 1230. It is presumably
to be identified as the *magnam partem sanctae crucis in quadam cruce bene ornata et cognita cum multis
aliis partibus eiusdem*, which according to Flete, *History*, 69, had been given to the Abbey by the
Confessor. Described as 'a grete parte of the holy crosse', it was still at Westminster in the 1520s;
Westlake, *Westminster Abbey*, II 499.

[25] *Reg. Innocent IV*, II no. 4852. In addition, see the papal indulgences of one year and forty days
to all attending the feast of St Peter each year (6 April 1248); one year to all attending the
consecration of the new Abbey with a further forty days to all attending the anniversary of
the consecration in future (12 April 1251); one year and a hundred days to all attending the
translation of St Edward's relics to their new resting place (3 June 1251); and one year and forty
days to all attending the feast of St Edward's translation (31 May 1254): *Reg. Innocent IV*, II
no. 5238; Westminster Abbey MS Domesday fos. 386v, 388r; PRO SC7/36/4, printed in
T. Rymer, *Foedera*, new edn vol. I part I, ed. A. Clark and F. Holbrooke (London 1816), 101
as a bull of Innocent III. For the episcopal indulgences see below pp. 159–66.

a Breton, Robert of Nantes, lived at Acre, an exile from his see. Over the next few years it was he more than anyone else who was responsible for bombarding England and the rest of Christian Europe with requests for assistance in the launching of a new crusade.[26] The papacy appears to have made no sustained effort to secure Henry III's participation in this venture. Given that Louis IX had taken the Cross immediately after the fall of Jerusalem in 1244, it may be that Innocent IV was anxious that Henry remain behind, to counter any attempt by the Hohenstaufen Emperor, Frederick II, to exploit Louis' absence in the East. After 1244 the chief thrust of papal diplomacy seems to have been directed more towards securing peace between England and France than towards any attempt to recruit Henry as a crusader in his own right. None the less, by 1247 many Englishmen had taken the Cross, the most prominent being the King's cousin, William Longespée, claimant to the earldom of Salisbury, and the bishop of Worcester, Walter de Cantiloupe.[27] Although Henry had levied no specific taxation for the crusade, the bishops of England and Scotland had pledged themselves at the Council of Lyons in 1245 to provide subsidies for the reconquest both of the Holy Land and of the Latin Empire of Constantinople. As a result, a large number of papal and eastern envoys were dispatched to England, to preach the Cross, to collect papal taxation and arrears of earlier crusading taxes, and to secure the monetary redemption of vows from crusaders unable or unsuited to make the journey to the East. The six months to October 1247 had witnessed missions to England by a series of papal agents whose demands for clerical subsidy had been conceded by a council held at Oxford in April.[28] There had also been a visit to court by the Emperor of Constantinople, Baldwin II, who in May 1247 had received cash subsidies of 1,000 marks and the cost of his journey home.[29] In addition the bishop-elect of Bethlehem, Goffredo de Prefetti, had spent several weeks in England in May and June 1247, issuing indulgences for at least three English monasteries, including Matthew Paris' own Abbey

---

[26] For what follows see Lloyd, *English Society and the Crusade*, 210–17. Here and elsewhere I have benefited enormously from discussions with Simon Lloyd.

[27] *CM*, IV 629–30, 635–6.

[28] In general see *Councils and Synods with Other Documents relating to the English Church II: 1205–1313*, ed. F. M. Powicke and C. R. Cheney, 2 vols. (Oxford 1964), I 388–90; *CM*, IV 599–602, 617–23. For the redemption of crusader vows in 1247 see *CM*, VI 134–8.

[29] *CM*, IV 625–6; *Close Rolls 1242–7*, 510; *Calendar of Liberate Rolls 1245–51* (London 1937), 119, which are here assumed to cover two separate payments of 500 marks, contrary to Lloyd, *English Society and the Crusade*, 254. Baldwin's expenses in returning to the continent are listed together with those of nuncios to the Infanta of Castile, estimated at just over £41; PRO E272/92 (Pipe Roll 32 Henry III) m. 3.

of St Albans.[30] In this way the envoys who brought the Holy Blood to Henry III were but the latest in a whole series of such visitors from the East, all of them, directly or indirectly, associated with preparations for the forthcoming crusade. As we shall see, the relic of the Holy Blood itself was clearly intended as a means of focusing men's minds upon the sufferings of Christ and hence upon the need for a crusade to deliver the land of Christ's birth and Crucifixion. In the immediate term, the blood relic may have encouraged a particular association between the projected crusade and the monks of Westminster Abbey. Around the year 1250, the relic appears to have been rehoused in a splendid new reliquary, at much the same time that the King himself was preparing to take vows as a crusader.[31] It was to be at Westminster in March 1250 that Henry publicly took these vows. Two years later, Henry summoned the men of London to Westminster to hear him repeat his vows, and to listen to sermons preached by the bishops of Worcester and Chichester and the abbot of Westminster, Richard of Croxley, exhorting them to follow the King's example.[32] Abbot Richard was to serve as one of the chief commissioners of the crusade during the 1250s, acting together with bishop Walter Suffield of Norwich – the very man who had preached on the occasion of the delivery of the Holy Blood – preaching the Cross and arranging for the collection of crusader taxation.[33]

Finally, we should not forget that the delivery of the Holy Blood to Westminster was but one in a series of ceremonies over which the King presided on 13 October 1247. According to Matthew Paris, the King's summons to his nobles to attend him at Westminster had referred only in the most mysterious terms to the relic of the blood. The avowed purpose of the summons had been to assemble the great men of the realm for the feast day of St Edward and so that they might witness the knighting of Henry's half-brother, William de Valence.[34] St Edward's feast day, it should be noted, also marked the anniversary of the eve of the Battle of Hastings (13/14 October 1066), which may have made it a particularly appropriate occasion for the ceremonial conferment of knighthood.

[30] *CM*, IV 602. The indulgence for St Albans is referred to in BL MS Cotton Nero D vii (List of St Albans' benefactors) fo. 88v, and in general, see N. Vincent, 'Goffredo de Prefetti and the Church of Bethlehem in England', *Journal of Ecclesiastical History* 49 (1998), 213–35.

[31] Below pp. 171–5.

[32] *CM*, V 100–1, 282.

[33] *CM*, VI 296–7; *Calendar of Patent Rolls 1247–58*, 164, 370, 377, 396, 411, 462, and see *CM*, VI 217–18 for the use of crusading language in letters of the abbot of Westminster, summoning other Benedictine heads of houses to a general chapter at Oxford in 1252.

[34] *CM*, IV 640.

Certainly, in 1247 it is the knighting of William de Valence that occupies a considerable part of Paris' narrative. William and his three brothers, Aymer, Guy and Geoffrey de Lusignan, were the offspring of Henry III's mother, Isabella of Angoulême, by her second marriage to the Poitevin Hugh de Lusignan, count of La Marche. William, Guy and Aymer had all come to England by the early summer of 1247 and had immediately been showered with favours.[35] In August, William had been married to Joan, daughter of Warin de Mountchesney, heiress to a portion of the great earldom of Pembroke. William's sister, Alice, was betrothed to the young earl Warenne, very much at the King's command.[36] Although the records of the royal chancery and exchequer are entirely silent about the King's gift of the Holy Blood to Westminster, they preserve numerous details of the ceremony of knighthood and its accompanying feast: the gift to William de Valence of thirty silver dishes and a dozen silver cups to be engraved with his coat of arms, the provision of wine and candles for the feast and the names of at least seven of the men, most of them Englishmen, who were to be knighted at the same time as William.[37] Clearly, the King placed great importance upon William's knighting, and by combining it with the ceremonial reception of the Holy Blood afforded it a prominence that it might not otherwise have achieved. Why were two such spectacles combined in this way?

From the moment of their arrival in England, William de Valence and his brothers had excited the suspicions of several factions at court: not only the native English baronage whose opinions are trumpeted by Matthew Paris, but the King's Savoyard uncles who for the past ten years had enriched themselves from the stock of royal patronage. As sons of Hugh count of La Marche, the Lusignan brothers were tainted by their association with one of the most fickle politicians in the whole

---

[35] *CM*, IV 627–8. Aymer had been promoted rector of the church of Tisbury (Wiltshire) as early as June 1246 and by the summer of 1247 appears to have been resident at the Oxford schools; *Calendar of Liberate Rolls 1245–51*, 87, 96, 121, 134; *Calendar of Patent Rolls 1232–47*, 483–4, 496, 503, and see 312 for an unsuccessful attempt to promote him as rector of Northfleet as early as 1242. Early in 1247 Henry may have attempted to secure his promotion as provost of Beverley Minster; *CM*, IV 601. Guy was in England by early July 1247, when he was promised an annual fee of £900. William is first mentioned on 20 July, and on 31 July received an annual pension of 500 marks as well as lands and wardships estimated at a further £500; *Calendar of Patent Rolls 1232–47*, 505–6, 508–9; *Calendar of Liberate Rolls 1245–51*, 126, 130–1, 135, 142; *Close Rolls 1242–7*, 524.

[36] *CM*, IV 628–9; *Close Rolls 1242–7*, 527, 529.

[37] *Calendar of Liberate Rolls 1245–51*, 147; *Close Rolls 1242–7*, 539–40. The liberate roll for the autumn of 1247 survives only in fragments, so that it is conceivable that details relating to the reception of the Holy Blood have been lost. Likewise, the charter rolls, whose witness lists might have provided details of attendance at the ceremony, have been lost for the period August–November 1247.

of Europe, a man who since the reign of King John had blighted every attempt at a Plantagenet reconquest of northern France. As recently as 1242 Hugh had conspired with the French to bring about the collapse of Henry III's Poitevin expedition: one of the greater diplomatic and financial *débâcles* of Henry's reign.[38] Not surprisingly, Hugh's sons were suspected of inheriting their father's treacherous nature. The collapse of the Poitevin expedition of 1242 had dealt a serious blow to royal finances. For the next fifteen years, Henry III was to lurch from one financial crisis to another, drawing upon a dwindling supply of money, lands and heiresses with which to purchase support. Patronage was in short supply. The lavish gifts bestowed by the King upon his half-brothers could be made only at the expense of other men, already established at court, who not surprisingly resented the Lusignans' promotion.[39] Yet to Henry, the Lusignans were beloved kinsmen who provided a vital link to Poitou and the long dreamed of reconquest of the Plantagenet lands in France. Their arrival in 1247 coincided with a mission to France by the King's brother, Richard of Cornwall, during which Louis IX was once again petitioned for the restoration of Normandy. Louis is said to have referred the matter to the Norman bishops, who inevitably pronounced against the Plantagenet claim.[40] None the less, Henry still treasured hopes of a Plantagenet reconquest in which his Lusignan half-brothers would have an important role to play. What better way of reconciling the Lusignans to a suspicious court than by combining the knighthood of William de Valence with the splendid welcome afforded to the Holy Blood? At one and the same time Henry would greet and honour his half-brothers and extend welcome to a most precious relic: a relic, moreover, directly associated with the forthcoming crusade in which count Hugh and his eldest son had already vowed to participate.[41] A similar reception had been mounted in January 1241 when, shortly after his arrival in England, the King's uncle, Peter of Savoy, had been knighted at Westminster on the feast of St Edward's deposition.[42]

---

[38] *CM*, IV 211-18, 252-4, 633, and for the general after-effects of the Poitevin expedition of 1242, see R. C. Stacey, *Politics, Policy and Finance under Henry III 1216-1245* (Oxford 1987), esp. 198-200, 237-59.

[39] In general see H. W. Ridgeway, 'Foreign Favourites and Henry III's Problems of Patronage, 1247-1258', *English Historical Review* 104 (1989), 590-610.

[40] *CM*, IV 645-7.

[41] For the crusading vows taken by Hugh count of La Marche and his son, Hugh the younger, see *Œuvres de Jean sire de Joinville comprenant l'histoire de Saint Louis*, ed. N. de Wailly (Paris 1867), 75. Guy and Geoffrey de Lusignan also sailed with the French contingent to the East, but it is unclear when they had taken the Cross: Lloyd, *English Society and the Crusade*, 84n.

[42] *CM*, IV 85-6. It should be noted that Henry had already established chantries at Westminster for his father-in-law and for Isabella of Angoulême, the mother both of the King and of his Lusignan half-brothers; above p. 2 n. 5.

In this way the ceremonial reception of the Holy Blood in October 1247 served many functions. It was intended to boost the prestige of Westminster Abbey by supplying the monks with a relic fit to rival those of the Sainte-Chapelle in Paris. With Europe on the brink of a crusade, it served to focus men's minds upon the Passion of Christ and hence upon the recent sufferings of the Holy Land. As an exercise in pomp and circumstance it appealed to the taste of Henry III and to his love of public demonstrations of piety, a demonstration that in this instance could be combined with a display of welcome to a new, and potentially controversial, group at court. In processing the relic of Christ's blood around the Abbey and the royal apartments at Westminster, walking beneath a pall borne on four spears, Henry was also, either deliberately or subconsciously, re-enacting the pious ceremony of his own coronation, in which the King processed to Westminster walking beneath a pall carried on four spears.[43] For all of these reasons, the ceremony of 1247 should have proved a towering success. Certainly, the King did his best to ensure that it was recorded, requesting the chronicler Matthew Paris to set down the day's events in writing.

To date, it has been Paris who has served as our only guide to the reception of the Holy blood. But Paris himself tells us that the blood was sent to England under the seals of the patriarch of Jerusalem and numerous other bishops and archbishops. Presumably these seals were appended to some sort of written guarantee of the relic's authenticity. A search through the muniments of Westminster Abbey reveals that just such letters are preserved, transcribed into the great cartulary known as the Westminster Domesday and accompanied by copies of upwards of twenty episcopal indulgences issued for the most part by English and Irish bishops in the aftermath of the ceremony of 1247.[44] We shall consider the indulgences in due course. For the moment, let us concentrate upon the letters, issued at Acre on 31 May 1247, addressed to Henry III by the patriarch and the chapter of Jerusalem. What do they add to our knowledge of the reception of the Holy Blood as described by Matthew Paris?

---

[43] See the account of the 1189 and 1194 coronations of Richard I as reported by Roger of Howden, *Chronica*, ed. W. Stubbs, 4 vols., Rolls Series (London, 1868–71), III 10, 247–8.
[44] The only printed reference to the patriarch's letters is to be found in Harvey, *Westminster Abbey and its Estates*, 44 n. 3.

CHAPTER 3

The patriarch's letters

The patriarch's letters, printed below as an appendix, are packed full of easily verifiable detail; so much so that forgery seems to be out of the question. Rather surprisingly, however, they deal with the gift of the Holy Blood almost as if it were a secondary issue. Much their greater part is taken up with an account of the sufferings of the Latin church in the East, an appeal for Henry to grant assistance to the chapter of Jerusalem and a blow-by-blow account of the most recent invasion of Palestine by the Sultan of Cairo. To summarize very briefly, they open with a flattering address to Henry III, praising his ancestors above the kings of all other nations as being those most devoted to the church of Jerusalem and the memory of Christ's sufferings upon the Cross. It is hoped that Henry will emulate such piety by aiding the patriarch and his church. There then follows a long passage in which the sufferings of the patriarch, his church and chapter are set out in detail and Henry is asked to assist in the recovery of various rights that have been lost. The patriarch has sent two members of his chapter, John and master Matthew, to pursue this appeal more fully in person. Only then do the letters pass on to the relic of the Holy Blood, sent in a crystal pyx (*pixide cristallina*) via the aforementioned nuncios under the patriarch's privy seal (*parvo sigillo nostri patriarch(ii) signata*), to honour King Henry and so that the King may have the memory of Christ's Passion always before his eyes. It is stressed that the relic is a genuine one, shed by Christ at his Crucifixion and preserved from ancient times amongst the treasures of the church of Jerusalem. Thereafter, rather than dwell at any length upon the relic, the letters pass on to more recent news, providing a detailed account of an attack launched by the Saracens upon the few remaining Christian outposts in the Holy Land, and in particular describing the sieges laid to Tiberias and Ascalon between 11 and 25 May 1247. Unless Henry III and his fellow princes send military support soon, the letters warn, the power of the Sultan is much to be feared.

Although they are addressed to King Henry, the fact that the letters are preserved at Westminster Abbey, rather than in the royal archives, suggests that they were deposited together with the Holy Blood at Westminster in October 1247. It may be that they represent only one of several documents that accompanied the Holy Blood to England. Matthew Paris certainly implies that the relic was supported by testimony from numerous eastern bishops besides the patriarch of Jerusalem – a relatively common phenomenon in the authentication of relics from the East.[1] Whereas earlier newsletters from the Holy Land had been shown to Paris and copied into his chronicle, the contents of the present letters do not appear to have been widely broadcast.[2] For example, the attack upon the crusader castles launched in May 1247 goes unnoticed in the *Chronica majora* or indeed in any other chronicle, although Paris was undoubtedly interested in the fate of the castle of Ascalon and had devoted part of his annal for 1246 to the preparations for its defence.[3] Certain details from the surviving letters may have reached him indirectly. In particular, the flattery with which the letters treat Henry III and his ancestors appears to be reflected in Paris' account of the sermon preached at Westminster by the bishop of Norwich, praising the King as *inter omnes Christianitatis principes Christianissimus*. The patriarch's letters had referred to Henry's ancestors as 'having amongst all the catholic princes of the world, pre-eminent devotion to the holy church of Jerusalem'.[4]

Such flattery was hardly justified and would no doubt have been dismissed with short shrift by the Capetian kings of France or the Hohenstaufen emperors of Germany. Indeed, the application of the title *princeps Christianissimus* to Henry III may have been part of a quite deliberate rhetorical side-swipe against the French. Already by the 1240s, the title *princeps* or *rex Christianissimus* was becoming the peculiar prerogative

---

[1] See, amongst many examples, BL MS Egerton Charter 455, a certificate from John de St-Maixent archbishop of Tyre and vicar of Jerusalem, and other eastern dignitaries, 15 May 1272, testifying to the authenticity of relics of the True Cross, of Saints Philip, Helena, Stephen and other saints, received by Alan de Lascelles from brother Thomas Berardi master of the Temple and placed in a reliquary cross. Alan, a north-country knight, was at that time with the Lord Edward's crusading army in the Holy Land: Lloyd, *English Society and the Crusade*, 111, 124.

[2] For a convenient list of eastern newsletters copied into the *Chronica majora*, see Lloyd, *English Society and the Crusade*, appendix 1 pp. 248–9.

[3] *CM*, IV 559–60.

[4] *CM*, IV 641, 643, and see appendix 1 below.

of Louis IX and the Capetian Kings of France. Its application to an English King may well have been intentionally provocative.[5] Of Henry III's immediate ancestors, only one, Richard the Lionheart, had in any way distinguished himself as a crusader. Henry's father, John, had never fought in the East and had taken the Cross, not so much out of piety as for motives of political expediency.[6] Henry's grandfather, Henry II, had persistently failed to fulfil his crusading vows and by sending money rather than men to the East had, albeit unwittingly, helped to precipitate the disastrous campaign of 1187 in which Jerusalem was first lost.[7] It is true that Henry III's great-great-grandfather, Fulk count of Anjou, and his descendants had ruled as kings of Jerusalem from 1131 to 1186. Via his mother, Isabella of Angoulême, Henry was also related to the Courtenay lords of Edessa, later Latin Emperors of Constantinople, and to the Lusignans of La Marche, two of the leading dynasties in the East.[8] Such ties were not unimportant, and would quite naturally be stressed by correspondents, such as the patriarch, anxious to recruit Henry's support.[9] Henry's own brother, Richard of Cornwall, and his brother-in-law, Simon de Montfort, had both participated in the crusade of 1240–1. Perhaps above all, however, it was the King's illustrious uncle, Richard I, who provided the strongest link between Henry III and Jerusalem. The memory of Richard's valour was to be employed directly in the 1220s and again in the 1250s, in the course of appeals to Henry.[10] With particular reference to the letters of 1247, it is intriguing to note that one of Richard's supposed acts of heroism in the East had been to ransom the relics of the Holy Sepulchre and the other churches of Jerusalem, packed into four great caskets of ebony. For this Richard is

---

[5] See, for example, the use of *princeps Christianissimus* as a title applied to Louis IX in the protest to the Pope made in 1245 on Louis' behalf, recorded by *CM* VI 99, and in general, see J. R. Strayer, 'France: The Holy Land, the Chosen People and the Most Christian King', in J. R. Strayer, *Medieval Statecraft and the Perspectives of History*, ed. J. F. Benton and T. N. Bisson (Princeton 1971), 300–14, esp. 303, 306–7; C. Beaune, *Myths and Symbols of Nation in Late-Medieval France*, trans. S. R. Huston and F. L. Cheyette (Berkeley, Calif. 1991), 172–5.

[6] Although, as Simon Lloyd has pointed out to me, there is evidence to suggest that John actually contemplated a journey to Jerusalem in the aftermath of his vow. See, for example, *Rotuli de oblatis et finibus*, ed. T. D. Hardy (London 1835), 562–3, 589; *Rotuli litterarum patentium*, ed. T. D. Hardy (London 1835), 186b; *Diplomatic Documents Preserved in the Public Record Office: Volume I 1102–1272*, ed. P. Chaplais (London 1964), no. 54, all of which references I owe to Simon Lloyd.

[7] See especially H. E. Mayer, 'Henry II of England and the Holy Land', *English Historical Review* 97 (1982), 721–39.

[8] For Isabella and the Courtenays, see N. Vincent, 'Isabella of Angoulême: John's Jezebel', *King John: New Interpretations*, ed. S. D. Church (Woodbridge 1999), 175–81, 201–4, and note Baldwin's claim to kinship with Henry III in 1247: *CM*, IV 626.

[9] Lloyd, *English Society and the Crusade*, 31–3.

[10] *Ibid.*, 33–4.

said to have parted with the enormous sum of 52,000 bezants, perhaps £5,000.[11] Presumably, this ransomed treasure included the *pignores que Dei filius in thesauris ecclesie sancte Ieroslimit' reliquit*, from amongst which the patriarch claimed to have extracted the relic of the Holy Blood. The Holy Blood was by no means the first relic which Henry III had received from the East. A unique list of gifts made to the King in the period from December 1234 to June 1235 includes, besides a great quantity of gold and silver plate, silk cloths and even an ivory chess set, a silver reliquary brought to England by a Franciscan friar containing relics of St George, St Theodore and St Pantoleon, as well as a wooden case containing a spine from the Crown of Thorns.[12] More remarkable still, on 25 February 1235 the King had taken possession of a glass vase containing oil exuded by the miraculous icon of Saidnaiya north of Damascus, together with relics of St Jerome, of the golden gate of Jerusalem, of the Holy Sepulchre, of Calvary, of the altar upon which Christ had been presented in the Temple, and of the burning bush from which God had spoken to Moses, all of them sent to England by the Knights Hospitaller.[13]

As with these earlier gifts, the dispatch of the Holy Blood and the flattery lavished upon Henry III in the patriarch's letters of 1247 were clearly intended to support a call for assistance to the church in the East. Although outwardly little more than a simple newsletter, the patriarch's brief contains two distinct requests, one of them specific, the other linked to the evil news from the East. By communicating the plight of the crusader castles and the strength of the latest Saracen attack, the patriarch undoubtedly sought to recruit military support from England. Although he voices no direct appeal for Henry to join the forthcoming crusade, such an appeal is implicit in the closing lines of his letters: unless assistance is sent soon, the power of the Sultan is greatly to be feared. The

---

[11] *Radulphi de Coggeshall chronicon anglicanum*, ed. J. Stevenson, Rolls Series (London 1875), appendix to preface pp. xxvii–viii, taken from BL MS Cotton Vespasian D x fo. 61r (58r), a loose leaf *c.* 1220, inserted into Coggeshall's chronicle. Because of its peculiar place in the printed edition, this account appears to have gone largely unnoticed.

[12] PRO C47/3/4/1: *i. almonera in qua continetur una capsa argent(i) cum relliquiis de sanctis Georg', Theodoro, Panteleun et aliis contentis et insertis eidem, et de spina corone domini in una capsa lignea.*

[13] *Ibid.: De dono Elye (?) hominis fratris Iohannis de Merc' de domo hospitali i. vasculum vitreum cum oleo de Sardenay . . . est in parva ymagine argent(i) beate Marie, i. particulam de porta aurea Ierosol', i. particulam de sepulcro Domini, i. particulam de altari in qua Cristus fuit presentatus, i. particulam de rubo quo viderat Moyses, i. particulam de Sancto Ieronimo, i. particulam de Monte Calvar'.* For the oil of Saidnaiya, see B. Hamilton, 'Our Lady of Saidnaiya: An Orthodox Shrine Revered by Muslims and Knights Templar at the Time of the Crusades', *The Holy Land, Holy Lands, and Christian History. Studies in Church History* 36, ed. R. N. Swanson (Woodbridge 2000), 207–15. I am indebted to Bernard Hamilton and to Colin Morris for their assistance here. Anglo-Norman verses commemorating the oil of Saidnaiya are preserved in Oxford, Corpus Christi College MS 232 fos. 67r *et seq.*

second of his requests is stated quite explicitly. To understand it we need to turn for a while to consider the wider relations between England and the church of Jerusalem.

Much of the patriarch's letter is taken up with a plea to Henry III to assist in the recovery of rights formerly exercised by the patriarchate over certain unnamed churches, priories and houses. Whereas 'in ancient times' the priors, rectors and brothers of these places had worn crosses on their caps and cloaks as a token of their subjection to the church of Jerusalem, they had long ago ceased to lend assistance or to communicate with their mother church, either in person or by letter. Moreover, they had abandoned the token of their subjection: 'the badge of the living Cross'. Since the patriarch names no names in his appeal, it is tempting to suggest that he was engaged in a speculative 'fishing expedition', dispatching envoys to England in the hope that they would uncover sources of revenue previously overlooked. However, there is good reason to suppose that in 1247 he had something more definite in mind.

Like the great military orders, the patriarchs of Jerusalem and their chapter, the church of the Holy Sepulchre, organized after 1112 as an Augustinian priory, had at one time possessed lands in both Outremer and the West. The most important of these estates lay in Spain and Italy. For the rest, in 1168–9 the patriarch and the prior of the Holy Sepulchre agreed to take equal shares in their revenues from England, Denmark, Germany, Poland, Constantinople, Hungary and elsewhere.[14] In order to supervise this endowment, the priory in Jerusalem served in effect as mother house to a number of western churches, grouped together as an independent order of Augustinian canons. The history of this order of the Holy Sepulchre remains somewhat obscure.[15] Dwarfed by the Templars

---

[14] *Le Cartulaire du chapitre du Saint-Sépulcre de Jérusalem*, ed. G. Bresc-Bautier, Documents relatifs à l'histoire des croisades XV (Paris 1984), no. 150, and for further references to the English lands, none of which is named, see *ibid.*, nos. 151, 170.

[15] A. Couret, *Notice historique sur l'ordre du Saint-Sépulcre* (Paris 1905), is now outdated. Pending the publication of Dr Bresc-Bautier's thesis on the western lands of the Holy Sepulchre, see the abstract in *École nationale des chartes: positions des thèses soutenues par les élèves de la promotion de 1971* (Paris 1971), 15–25, especially 18–22, and her essay 'Le Prieuré du Saint-Sépulcre de la Vinadière 1263–1498', *Bulletin de la Société de lettres, sciences et arts de la Corrèze* 83 (1980), 39–47. The leading authority on the order is Kaspar Elm, for whose studies see 'Fratres et Sorores Sanctissimi Sepulcri: Beiträge zu fraternitas, familia und weiblichem Religiosentum im Umkreis des kapitels vom Hlg. Grab', *Frühmittelalterliche Studien* 9 (1975), 287–333; *Quellen zur Geschichte des Ordens vom Hlg. Grab in Nordwesteuropa aus deutschen und niederländischen Archiven (1191–1603)* (Brussels 1976); 'Kanoniker und Ritter vom Heiligen Grab. Ein Beitrag zur Enstehung und Frühgeschichte der palästinensischen Ritterorden', *Die Geistlichen Ritterorden Europas*, ed. J. Fleckenstein and M. Hellmann. Konstanzer Arbeitskreis für mittelalterliche Geschichte Vorträge und Forschungen XXVI (Sigmaringen 1980), 141–69; 'Mater ecclesiarum in exilio. El capitulo del

and the Hospitallers and, in England at least, less significant than such crusader orders as the Trinitarians or the Lazarites, it not surprisingly underwent significant changes following the loss of Jerusalem in 1187. From 1187 until 1291, the canons of Jerusalem were exiled to Acre, being removed finally to Perugia after the final collapse of the crusader states in 1291.[16] The election of Pope Urban IV (1261–4), a former patriarch of Jerusalem, brought a temporary upsurge in the canons' fortunes and although their order was officially suppressed in 1489, individual houses continued to function under the direct supervision of Rome as late as the nineteenth century.[17] Meanwhile, their estates in England and France appear to have been lost, in practice if not in theory, soon after the fall of Jerusalem in 1187. Even so, as late as the fifteenth century the antiquary John Rous, our chief source for events in England, records that members of the order of the Holy Sepulchre had originally worn a double cross of red *in pectore capae*.[18] Here, surely, we have an explanation for the patriarch's appeal in 1247.

Santo Sepulcro de Jerusalén desde la caida de Acre', *La Orden del Santo Sepulcro: I Jornadas de Estudio* (Calatayud and Zaragoza 1991), 3–24. For an important survey of the impact of the Holy Sepulchre on church building in the West, see G. Bresc-Bautier, 'Les imitations du Saint-Sépulcre de Jérusalem (IXe–XVe siècles): archéologie d'une dévotion', *Revue d'histoire de la spiritualité* 1 (1974), 319–42, and see also C. Morris, 'Bringing the Holy Sepulchre to the West: S. Stefano Bologna from the Fifth to the Twentieth Century', *Studies in Church History* 33 (1997), 31–59.

[16] The only work on the English congregation remains that by J. C. Dickinson, *The Origins of the Austin Canons and their Introduction into England* (London 1950), 83–4, and J. C. Dickinson, 'English Regular Canons and the Continent in the Twelfth Century', *Transactions of the Royal Historical Society* 5th series 1 (1951), 72–3, although Elm, 'Mater ecclesiarum in exilio', 17 n. 21, refers to a thesis then (1991) in progress at the Free University of Berlin. E. Jones, 'Knights of the Holy Sepulchre', *Journal of the Historical Society of the Church in Wales* 26 (1979), 11–33, provides a somewhat indiscriminate list of Welshmen who may have been elected knights of the later, military, order of the Holy Sepulchre, founded only in the 1330s, but in the sixteenth century supplied with forgeries in an attempt to trace its origins to the time of Godfrey de Bouillon, for which see Elm, 'Kanoniker und Ritter', 142–7; X. de Bourbon-Parma, *Les Chevaliers du Saint-Sépulcre* (Paris 1957), and especially J.-P. de Gennes, *Les Chevaliers du Saint-Sépulcre de Jérusalem, essai critique*, 2 vols. (Cholet 1995).

[17] Especially at Miechów in Poland, Calatayud in Aragon and Denkendorf in Germany, for which houses see W. Oblizajek, 'Najstarsze dokumenty bożogrobców miechowskich (1198)', *Studia Źródłoznawcze* 24 (1979) 97–108 (with French abstract); J. G. Ayala, *Canónigos del Santo Sepulcro en Jerusalén y Calatayud* (Madrid 1970); H. Werner, *Kloster Denkendorf. Ein Gang durch seine Bauten und seine Geschichte* (Stuttgart 1965). A very distantly affiliated order of canonesses of the Holy Sepulchre survives to the present day.

[18] *Joannis Rossi antiquarii Warwicensis historia regum Angliae*, ed. T. Hearne, 2nd edn (Oxford 1745), 139–40, also printed in William Dugdale, *Monasticon anglicanum*, ed. J. Caley, H. Ellis and B. Bandinel, 6 vols. in 8 (London 1846), VI 602–3. For Rous' general reliability see A. Gransden, 'Antiquarian Studies in Fifteenth-Century England', *Antiquaries Journal* 60 (1980), 75–97, reprinted in A. Gransden, *Legends, Traditions and History in Medieval England* (London 1992), 317–22. For the significance of badges worn, not only by the members, but by the tenantry of the military orders, see PRO E326/9107, a settlement of the mid-thirteenth century between the Hospitallers of Dalby in Leicestershire and Monks Kirby priory, in which the Hospitallers admitted to having conferred *signum nostrum quibusdam hominibus dictorum prioris et monachorum in preiudicium et gravamen eorundem.*

3   Cambridge, the Round Church *c.* 1150 (London, Conway Library)

The English houses of the order were none of them of any great size. According to Rous, the priory of Holy Sepulchre Warwick served as the head of a congregation that included members at *Tetford* (presumably Thetford, Norfolk, where there was a small hospital dedicated to the Holy Sepulchre), Winchester and *Wentbryg*, this latter perhaps to be identified

as the Round Church at Cambridge, begun before 1130 as the result of
a grant by the abbot of Ramsey to a fraternity that intended building a
minster in honour of God and the Holy Sepulchre.[19] To Rous' list we
can probably add the priory of Caldwell near Bedford, small hospitals
at Nottingham and Stamford and the church of St Sepulchre Newgate,
in which the Holy Blood may have been lodged before its delivery to
Westminster.[20] By 1200 the joint revenue of all of these establishments
is unlikely to have exceeded £100 a year. None the less, the fact that
the order was endowed with numerous small plots of land, in the case
of Thetford scattered across more than twenty parishes, suggests that it
enjoyed some success, most probably in appealing to those too poor to
make the journey to Jerusalem in person.[21] At some time, the general
privileges of the order were confirmed in charters of Kings Henry II
and Richard I, mentioned but not recited in a further confirmation by
Henry III, issued in 1232.[22] Rous states that the Warwick house was
founded by the earls of Warwick, and that its prior was charged with
the collection of money for the Holy Land, a task in which he was
supported by many indulgences (*cum maximis indulgentiis*), but that, following the loss of Jerusalem, the profits of the English houses together
with their privileges were transferred to the order of the Holy Trinity.
Rous' comments here may represent a confusion between the hospital at Thetford in Norfolk, at one time almost certainly affiliated to
the Holy Sepulchre, and the small priory at Thelsford in Rous' native

[19] *VCH Cambridgeshire*, II 146; *VCH Warwickshire* II 97–9; *VCH Norfolk*, II 391–3. Nothing further is
heard of the Winchester house, although there was a chapel in Winchester Cathedral dedicated
to the Holy Sepulchre from the twelfth century onwards: D. Park, 'The Wall Paintings of the
Holy Sepulchre Chapel', *Medieval Art and Architecture at Winchester Cathedral*, British Archaeological
Association Conference Transactions VI (1983), 38–62, and see also D. Keene, *Survey of Winchester
in the Middle Ages*, Winchester Studies II, 2 vols. (Oxford 1982), I 135n for a reference in 1256 to
a church dedicated to the Holy Sepulchre, probably the result of confusion with another of the
city's churches. The place-name *Wentbryg* might in fact represent a reference to a leper hospital
at Wentbridge in West Yorkshire, whose existence is otherwise attested by a single mention in
the 1380s; *VCH Yorkshire*, III 334. For an important study of the various round churches, many
of them associated with the Templars, built in England in emulation of the Holy Sepulchre at
Jerusalem, see M. Gervers, 'Rotundae Anglicanae', *Evolution générale et développements régionaux en
histoire de l'art: Actes du XXIe congrès international d'histoire de l'art* (Budapest 1972), 359–76.
[20] *VCH Bedfordshire*, I 382–4; *VCH Nottinghamshire*, II 168; *VCH Northamptonshire*, II 165. For
St Sepulchre Newgate, see below p. 28; C. N. L. Brooke and G. Keir, *London 800–1216: The
Shaping of a City* (London 1975), 144, 165. In addition it is possible that the order was associated
with one or more of the various houses and hospitals dedicated to the Holy Sepulchre elsewhere
in England, for which see S. Thompson, *Women Religious* (Oxford 1991), 36–7 and note.
[21] *VCH Norfolk*, II 391–3.
[22] *Calendar of Charter Rolls 1226–57*, 174, which refers to no specific estates. The charter was renewed
in 1328, specifically as a concession to the priory of the Holy Sepulchre at Warwick; *Calendar of
Charter Rolls 1327–41* (London 1912), 88.

Warwickshire. Thelsford was indeed reconstituted as a Trinitarian priory at some time early in the thirteenth century, but its early charters and its dedication to St Radegund and St John the Baptist give little reason to suppose that it had ever been associated with the church of Jerusalem.[23] Elsewhere, the English houses affiliated to the Holy Sepulchre seem either to have been absorbed by richer neighbours, or to have lingered on in loose confederacy with the Augustinian order after 1187. In this way the Cambridge Round Church became a parish church annexed to Barnwell Priory, whilst Caldwell and Warwick were eventually admitted as members of the English Augustinian congregation, Caldwell accepting a prior from the nearby Augustinian foundation of Dunstable as early as 1212.[24]

Clearly in 1247 the patriarch hoped to rally what remained of the order of the Holy Sepulchre in England. Coinciding with the delivery of the Holy Blood, attempts may have been made to establish a hospital in the precinct of the London church of the Holy Sepulchre, possibly placed under the general authority of the patriarch and chapter of Jerusalem. It was in the church at Newgate that the blood relic is said to have been stored prior to its delivery to Westminster, and between November 1247 and April 1248 the King gave a series of vestments, including a costly samite chasuble, to 'the hospital' of the Holy Sepulchre London. Thereafter, nothing further is heard of any hospital at Newgate.[25] Of the patriarch's two envoys dispatched to England in 1247, John and master Matthew, John at least appears to have been received at court. In June 1248 the King issued instructions for him to be given 20 marks for his expenses besides a set of vestments and a mitre to deliver to the patriarch.[26] In 1250 John was probably once again at court when he

[23] *VCH Warwickshire*, II 106-8, following Tanner. St Radegund, it is true, enjoyed a close association with the True Cross, of which she is said to have brought a relic with her from the East to her new foundation at Poitiers before 573: A. Frolow, *La Relique de la Vraie Croix*, Archives de l'Orient chrétien VII (Paris 1961), 179-80 no. 33. An abstract of the lost cartulary of Thelsford (Oxford, Bodleian Library MS Phillipps-Robinson c77 fos. 1-19) preserves various grants to the hospital, unknown to the compilers of the *VCH*. On 21 December 1248 the Pope issued general letters of protection for the lands of the English Trinitarians, addressed to the archdeacon and precentor of York; Durham, University Library Special Collections MS D. & C. Durham Misc. Charter 5045 (*Pium esse dignoscitur*).

[24] *VCH Cambridgeshire*, III 124; *Chapters of the Augustinian Canons*, ed. H. E. Salter, Canterbury and York Society XXIX (1922), 16, 279; *Annales monastici*, ed. H. R. Luard, 5 vols., Rolls Series (London 1864-9), III (Dunstable) 39. The hospital at Stamford appears to have been under the patronage of the Benedictine Abbey of Peterborough as early as 1189: *VCH Northamptonshire*, II, 165.

[25] *Calendar of Liberate Rolls 1245-51*, 51, 152, 173, and above p. 3 n. 8. For the site of the church, see *The British Atlas of Historic Towns Volume III: The City of London from Prehistoric Times to c. 1520*, ed. M. D. Lobel (Oxford 1989), 92 and map 5.

[26] *Close Rolls 1247-51*, 60.

received letters of protection to last two years.[27] The prior of the Holy Sepulchre visited England in person in 1251, receiving a gift of 20 marks and, for the patriarch, either a mitre or, if the prior were unwilling to wait for this to be made, a ring set with a precious stone worth 10 marks.[28] Four years later, in April 1255, the King licensed the canons and brothers of the Holy Sepulchre to beg for alms.[29] Even so, these visits did little to restore either the priory or the patriarch to their lands in England. In 1252 the royal chancery could still refer to the canons of Caldwell by their former title as 'brothers of the Holy Sepulchre', but for all practical purposes Caldwell, like its fellow houses in England, had passed beyond the control of the church of Jerusalem.[30]

Ironically, whilst the patriarch's appeal seems to have fallen on stony ground, it coincided with the successful establishment in England of representatives from another of the crusader churches. Amongst the eastern envoys active in England in 1247 was the bishop-elect of Bethlehem, Goffredo de Prefetti: a Roman who for many years had been beneficed in England.[31] In October 1247 Goffredo attended the delivery of the Holy Blood to Westminster and in the same year issued indulgences for at least three other English monasteries. According to Matthew Paris, he had been sent from Rome as papal envoy to Scotland, with no other purpose than to milk the revenues of the Scottish church. In fact his mission may have been less mercenary in intent: possibly to preach the crusade in Scotland, to arrange for the collection of crusading taxation and to obtain support for the exiled church of Bethlehem.[32] On 23 October, less than a fortnight after the delivery of the Holy Blood to Westminster, Goffredo obtained a grant of property in London outside Bishopsgate, in the modern Liverpool Street. This, the original Bethlehem hospital,

---

[27] *Calendar of Patent Rolls 1247–58*, 69. Master Matthew, the envoy of 1247, is presumably to be identified with a namesake, 'canon and preceptor' of the church of the Holy Sepulchre, in 1253 appointed by the bishop of Lydda and Goffredo bishop-elect of Bethlehem, papal judges delegate, to arbitrate between the bishop of Hebron and the master of the Teutonic Order over property at Acre: *Tabulae ordinis Theutonici*, ed. E. Strehlke (Berlin 1869), 81–4 nos. 102, 104, drawn to my attention by Bernard Hamilton.

[28] *Close Rolls 1247–51*, 454; *Calendar of Liberate Rolls 1245–51*, 357.

[29] *Calendar of Patent Rolls 1247–58*, 406.

[30] Dugdale, *Monasticon*, VI 392–3, calendared inaccurately in *Calendar of Charter Rolls 1226–57*, 394. In 1267 the inmates of the hospital at Nottingham make their first recorded appearance, described in royal letters patent as brothers of the Holy Sepulchre Nottingham: *Calendar of Patent Rolls 1266–72*, 46.

[31] *The Letters and Charters of Cardinal Guala Bicchieri, Papal Legate in England 1216–1218*, ed. N. Vincent, Canterbury and York Society LXXXIII (1996), no. 55; N. Vincent, 'Goffredo de Prefetti and the Church of Bethlehem in England', *Journal of Ecclesiastical History* 49 (1998), 213–35.

[32] For the Scottish church and the crusade in the late 1240s, see A. Macquarrie, *Scotland and the Crusades 1095–1560* (Edinburgh 1985), 47–51.

was intended to serve as lodgings for the bishop and canons of Bethlehem whenever they visited England, its inmates following the rule of the church of Bethlehem and wearing the sign of a star on their caps and cloaks. For the next two hundred years, the Bethlehem hospital was to provide a tangible link between England and the crusader church in exile.[33] By contrast, after 1247, the relations between England and the exiled patriarchate of Jerusalem were to become increasingly more distant.

[33] Dugdale, *Monasticon*, VI 621–3; *VCH London*, I 495–8, and in general see Vincent, 'Goffredo de Prefetti'.

CHAPTER 4

The Holy Blood

Both of the appeals made in the patriarch's letters were unsuccessful. In 1247, Henry did little to encourage the dispatch of military aid to the East, or to support the financially embarrassed church of Jerusalem. However, in admitting the failure of the patriarch's bid for assistance, we should not forget that it was this bid alone that had justified the dispatch of the relic of the Holy Blood. For all that it may have been dressed up as a favour freely bestowed, the blood was given to Henry III in the full expectation that it would prompt the King to action. Why should it have been thought likely that a gift of the Holy Blood would encourage Henry to look more sympathetically upon the fate of the Holy Land? The time has come for us to turn from the England of the 1240s to the far wider history of blood relics, and specifically of the relics of Christ's own blood.

To begin with, it goes almost without saying that the blood of Christ, recreated daily in the sacrament of the Mass, occupied a pre-eminent place in the religious life of medieval Europe. By the shedding of his own blood upon the Cross, Christ had offered the ultimate sacrifice to God, fulfilling and at the same time far surpassing the Old Testament tradition of the blood sacrifice of animals.[1] The death of Christ, the lamb of God, had dispensed his followers from the Jewish obligation of animal sacrifice. None the less, even amongst Christians, a belief persisted that blood sacrifice could establish contact with the supernatural, not least through the use of blood to conjure demons.[2] Old

---

[1] For a vast and ongoing collection of essays on the religious symbolism of blood, see *Sangue e antropologia*, ed. F. Vattioni, 8 vols. in 21 parts, Centro studi sanguis Christi (Rome 1981). Particularly useful is *Le Sang au Moyen-Age: actes du quatrième colloque international de Montpellier Université Paul-Valéry (27 29 novembre 1997)*, ed. M. Faure (Montpellier 1999). J.-P. Roux, *Le Sang: mythes, symboles et réalités* (Paris 1988), esp. chs. 7 9, provides a populist account.

[2] V. I. J. Flint, *The Rise of Magic in Early Medieval Europe* (Princeton 1993), 52 3, 179, 335, and see the attention devoted to demons and their taste for blood by Vincent of Beauvais in the thirteenth century, as reported by M. Tarayre, 'Le Sang dans le "Speculum Maius" de Vincent de Beauvais. De la science aux "miracula"', *Le Sang au Moyen-Age*, ed. Faure, 349 50. This

Testament traditions, preserved in such passages as the Vulgate translation of Leviticus xvii. 17, 'The soul of the flesh *(anima carnis)* is in the blood',
may well have encouraged the belief, held for example by the heretics
of thirteenth-century Languedoc, that it was in the blood of man that
the soul resided.[3] Orthodox opinion rejected such crude assumptions.[4]
None the less, there was universal agreement, amongst Christian physicians and schoolsmen alike, that blood was an essential of human life.
Likewise in devotional literature it was the blood of Christ that symbol-
ized the redemptive power of Christ's Passion and Resurrection. From
a very early date, the qualifying term 'precious' *(pretiosus)* had come to
be applied to Christ's blood (1 Peter i. 19), a term that in due course
was to become inflated into the superlative *pretiosissimus*, 'the most
precious blood'.[5] To the ninth-century monk, Paschsius Radbertus of
Corbie, as to various others of the early authorities on the mass, the reception of the flesh and blood of Christ in the eucharist was essential to
the mingling of the human substance of man with the divinity of Christ,
and hence to the salvation of the individual believer.[6] Although this emphasis upon the physical necessity of communion was to be challenged
by writers who emphasized the primacy of the spiritual over the merely
bodily reception of Christ,[7] in the metaphorical language of medieval
Christianity, enshrined in Catholic doctrine in the 1340s, a single drop
of Christ's blood was deemed sufficient to wash away the sins of the

same taste may explain the medieval topos of the demon entering the body of a woman shortly
after childbirth, which itself may help to explain the far more ancient exclusion of menstruating
women from religious ceremony, and such practices as the blessing or 'churching' of women
after pregnancy. For an overview here, see C. de Miramon, 'La Fin d'un tabou? L'interdiction
de communier pour la femme menstruée au Moyen-Age. Le cas du XIIe siècle', *ibid.*, 163–81,
esp. 177–8.

3 See here the beliefs reported in *Le Registre d'inquisition de Jacques Fournier évêque de Pamiers (1318–
1325)*, ed. J. Duvernoy, 3 vols., Bibliothèque Méridionale 2nd series XLI (Toulouse 1965), I 260,
and III (index) *sub* 'matérialisme', as drawn to my attention by Peter Biller.

4 See for example Alexander of Hales, *Summa theologica* 4.3.1.2 ch. 5, ed. B. Klumper, C. Koser
et al., 4 vols. (Quaracchi 1924–48), II 680–1, with a sophisticated discussion of the various
theories linking blood to life, the heart and the soul. For specific rejections of the belief that the
soul resides in the blood, see, for example, *Avicenna latinus: liber de anima seu sextus de naturalibus
I–III*, ed. S. van Riet (Louvain 1972), 43, 57; *Iohannes Blund tractatus de anima*, ed. D. A. Callus
and R. W. Hunt, Auctores britannici medii aevi II (London 1970), 7–8.

5 E. Rasco, 'Il "Sangue Prezioso" di Cristo nella prima lettera di Pietro', *SA*, I (1981), 851–64;
M. Augé, 'Il Sangue nel sacramentario Veronese', and G. Venturi, 'Il Linguaggio liturgico del
sangue di Cristo: l'uso di "Prezioso-issimo"', *SA*, IV part 3 (1984), 1331–5, 1547–57.

6 For eucharistic theology, see G. Macy, *The Theologies of the Eucharist in the Early Scholastic Period*
(Oxford 1984), 27–8, 47–8, 66–7. Here, as in his collection of essays, *Treasures from the Storeroom:
Medieval Religion and the Eucharist* (Collegeville 1999), esp. chs. 3, 5, Macy emphasizes how slowly,
and with what great diversity, the church came to determine any sort of doctrine of the eucharist
or of 'transubstantiation'.

7 For the new emphasis upon spiritual as opposed to physical communion, see Macy, *Theologies of
the Eucharist*, 78, 93–7, 129–32, 135.

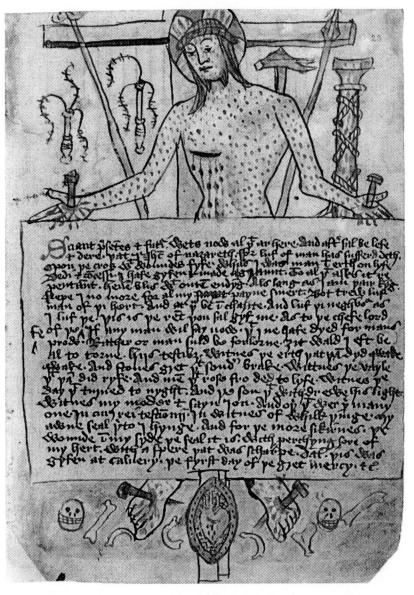

4   Charter of Christ (London, British Library MS Additional 37049 fo. 23r)

world.[8] Mankind was fed with the blood of Christ, even made drunk from this most precious liquor, flowering like a tree in spring watered with the blood from Christ's side.[9] By the fourteenth century, a pious forgery calling itself the *Carta humani generis* claimed to be written in the blood of Christ. Announcing man's redemption, the *Carta* was said to have been delivered by Christ at Calvary, using his blood as ink, the nails that pierced his body as a quill and his skin as parchment.[10] It is perhaps no coincidence that this peculiar document, in some versions witnessed by God the Father, Son and Holy Ghost, enjoyed its greatest success in England, the land of Magna Carta. Such emphasis upon the sacrificial and redemptive significance of Christ's blood coincides with an important change in the practical disposition of the eucharist. From the twelfth century onwards it became increasingly common for the laity to receive the sacrament in one kind only, being offered the consecrated host but not the wine, or at least only a cleansing draught of unconsecrated wine.[11] In the fifth century such a restriction of the communion to the element of bread alone had been fiercely condemned by Pope Gelasius I (492–6), whose opinion on the matter was still being cited in the twelfth century in the *Decretum* of Gratian.[12]

[8] See for example *Fasciculus morum: A Fourteenth-Century Preacher's Handbook*, ed. S. Wenzel (Philadelphia 1989), 200–13; *The Sermons of Thomas Brinton, Bishop of Rochester, 1373–1389*, ed. M. A. Devlin, 2 vols., Camden Society 3rd series LXXXV–VI (1954), 188–94, 157–62, II 241–7. For the doctrinal statement of Pope Clement VI issued in 1343, see below p. 110. There are illuminating discussions of the medieval attitude to blood in M.-C. Pouchelle, *The Body and Surgery in the Middle Ages*, trans. R. Morris (Oxford 1990), 72–5, 154–7, and in J. E. Hirsh, *The Boundaries of Faith: The Development and Transmission of Medieval Spirituality* (Leiden and New York 1996), 91–111.

[9] For the various metaphors here, see the writings of the fourteenth-century mystics Catherine of Siena and Margaret of Oignt, quoted with similar material by C. W. Bynum, 'The Body of Christ in the Later Middle Ages: A Reply to Leo Steinberg', *Renaissance Quarterly* 39 (1986), 400–39, esp. 408–9, 412, reprinted in C. W. Bynum, *Fragmentation and Redemption: Essays on Gender and the Human Body in Medieval Religion* (New York 1991), 79–117, an important study first drawn to my attention by Sean Ramsden, with further essays on female or mystic devotion in *Le Sang au Moyen-Âge*, ed. Faure, esp. 377–91, 405–49. In general, see *Dictionnaire de spiritualité, ascétique et mystique*, ed. M. Viller, F. Cavallera *et al.*, XIV (Paris 1990), cols. 319–33, esp. 326–33.

[10] *Fasciculus morum*, ed. Wenzel, 146–7, 212–13; M. C. Spalding, *The Middle English Charters of Christ*, Bryn Mawr College Monographs XV (Bryn Mawr 1914), esp. xiii–xxxv, 95, 97. The 'charter' is prefigured by a fable preserved in Oxford, Corpus Christi College MS 32 fo. 94v no. 24, composed in England before *c.* 1210, employing the image of Christ's body as a charter, with particular emphasis upon the various blood sheddings of the Passion.

[11] In general, see Macy, *Theologies of the Eucharist*, 75, 120; Rubin, *Corpus Christi*, 70–3; J. R. H. Moorman, *Church Life in England in the Thirteenth Century* (Cambridge 1945), 72, which refers to the conciliar decrees of archbishop Pecham in *Councils and Synods II*, ed. Powicke and Cheney, II 894–5.

[12] P. Jaffé, *Regesta pontificum romanorum*, new edn by W. Wattenbach *et al.*, 2 vols. (Leipzig 1885–8), I 93 no. 725; Gratian, 'Decretum' III.2.12, printed in *Corpus iuris canonici I*, ed. E. Friedberg (Leipzig 1879), col. 1318, drawn to my attention by Henry Chadwick. General participation in the wine of the Mass is implied by Gregory the Great, 'Letter 14', in Migne, *PL*, LXXXIX col. 525.

None the less, by 1250 or so, communion in one kind for the laity, without the consecrated wine, was becoming the norm rather than the exception. Even amongst the ruling dynasties of Christendom, only the Capetian kings of France and the German emperors continued to receive both the host and the chalice: Henry III himself may have been excluded from drinking the wine-blood of communion.[13] In all probability, this restriction sprang from the practical difficulties involved in ministering the chalice at a time when ever greater emphasis was being placed upon the transformation of the sacraments of bread and wine into the substance of the true body and blood of Jesus Christ. As any priest can testify, administering the host presents relatively few problems compared to the chalice from which it is all too easy for drops of wine to be spilled.[14] It was for this reason that from a very early date various churches had adopted the use of the eucharistic reed or 'calamus', a drinking straw, often made of precious metal, through which communicants could imbibe the consecrated wine, and which could be sucked entirely dry at the end of the communion. The 'calamus' responded to a fear, expressed by various writers, that consecrated wine might adhere to the beards and facial hairs of communicants, or become polluted by spittle.[15] Even after the restriction of the chalice to the clergy, in theory both elements of the mass, Christ's body and blood, were believed to be concomitant, or present together, in either of the sacraments of bread or wine.[16] In these circumstances, there was no need for the laity to receive wine as well as bread. None the less, the new limits placed upon the distribution of consecrated wine can only have encouraged a belief in its very special potency. The host was given to all communicants, but from the thirteenth century onwards, only the clergy, the elect, could partake of the blood of Christ.

Added to this, we know that within his own religious life Henry III placed an extraordinary emphasis upon the mass. An almoner's roll for 1238–9 suggests that Henry attended the sacrament at least once every day, and sometimes twice, when special masses were celebrated in honour

[13] M. Bloch, *The Royal Touch*, trans. J. E. Anderson (New York 1961), 119–20.

[14] A point originally drawn to my attention by Brian Wormald.

[15] T. Borenius, 'The Eucharistic Reed or Calamus', *Archaeologia* 80 (1930), 99–116, with references to bearded communicants at p. 101n.

[16] A sermon *c.* 1300 for the monks of Hailes Abbey, themselves the possessors of a relic of the Holy Blood, suggests that the sacraments should be received only in the species of the bread *tum propter periculum effusionis, tum propter periculum fidei, ne crederetur corpus esse ex sanguine dum sub alia speciem sanguinis sumeretur, tum propter periculum admixtionis et solvationis specium que per minimam admixtionem possent resolvi*; BL MS Royal 8 A.v (Hailes sermons and homilies) fo. 40r.

5   The Papal Mass, showing the use of the 'calamus' or eucharistic reed, from
A. Rocca, *Opera omnia* (1719) (Cambridge University Library)

of the Virgin Mary or particular saints.[17] This devotion to the sacraments
was widely reported. At least one chronicler claims, with exaggeration,
that Henry attended three masses a day, whilst an account of a visit that
Henry paid to the city of Paris in 1259 states that he could not bear to pass
by a church where mass was taking place without stopping to participate
in the ceremony. Whereas Louis IX favoured sermons above masses, the
chroniclers report, Henry preferred to see his God in flesh and blood.[18]
Henry's role model, St Edward the Confessor, was himself reported to

---

[17] PRO C47/3/44, covering the period 28 October 1238–30 April 1239, during which time
two masses were celebrated on at least five occasions, with three masses on Christmas day. A
later roll, for the period January–June 1265 (PRO E101/349/30 m. 2), shows certain changes
in practice: the introduction of a large number of masses for particular saints, especially for
St Edward the Confessor in whose honour mass was celebrated at least once and sometimes
twice a week; and an increase in the level of the King's monetary offerings, from the standard
3d after mass in 1238/9, to 5s in 1265. However, by 1265, a single mass each day appears to
have become the standard. We cannot be sure whether Henry received the sacraments daily. It
is more likely that he merely observed the priest's communion, although see below n. 18.

[18] *Annales F. Nicholai de Triveti*, ed. T. Hog (London 1845), 280; *Willelmi Rishanger . . . chronica et annales*,
ed. H. T. Riley, Rolls Series (London 1865), 74–5, which are related to one another and to the
longer, anonymous, account published as 'Historiola de pietate regis Henrici III, A. D. 1259',
ed. E. A. Bond, *The Archaeological Journal* 17 (1860), 318–19, taken from the lost MS Cotton
Vitellius D XIV, a reference traced with the help of David Carpenter and John Maddicott. For

have witnessed a miracle in which the Christ child had appeared in person on the altar of Westminster in place of the eucharistic host.[19] In these circumstances it is easy to appreciate why a relic of the Holy Blood should have enjoyed a strong appeal to Henry's sensibilities.

Beyond this general sense of sacramental devotion, the blood of Christ enjoyed a very particular association with the Holy Land and the church of Jerusalem. It was in Jerusalem, after all, that Christ's blood had been shed for the redemption of mankind. The church of the Holy Sepulchre, although built upon Christ's tomb, the site of his Resurrection, extended to include the rock of Calvary where Christ was crucified.[20] In 1100, immediately after Jerusalem's capture by the crusading army, Pope Paschal II had communicated the news that 'those places sanctified by the blood and presence of Jesus Christ' had been restored to the Christian faith, urging his correspondents to strengthen the enterprise: *quia vos de pretioso Christi sanguine benemeriti, operi tam praeclaro tantoque illustri facinori manus adiutrices ac strenuas apponere pro posse studuistis.*[21] William of Tyre could refer to the church of the Holy Sepulchre in the 1150s as that 'which was consecrated (*dedicata est*) by the precious blood of our Lord and Saviour upon the Cross'.[22] A preaching manual drawn up in England at some time after 1210, amidst the preparations for the Fifth Crusade, stresses the obligation of sinners to come to the defence of Christ: 'As the nails of the Cross were warmed by the blood of Christ, so ought sinners to be inflamed in charity to the service of Christ by the blood of Christ.'[23] Letters of 1215, excommunicating the rebellious English barons, refer

the persistence of this story in later sermon *exempla*, see G. R. Owst, *Literature and the Pulpit in Medieval England*, 2nd edn (Oxford 1961), 161, 581. Rishanger claims that Henry III not only assisted in the celebration of mass, but would hold and kiss the priest's hand when the host was elevated. Louis IX, although devoted to the sacrament, does indeed appear to have restricted his communion to the most solemn festivals of the year: J. Le Goff, *Saint Louis* (Paris 1996), 763 5.

[19] Binski, *Westminster Abbey*, 146, citing the life of St Edward, composed in the 1240s or 50s possibly by Matthew Paris: *Lives of Edward the Confessor*, ed. H. R. Luard, Rolls Series (London 1858), 96 8, 250 2, lines 2538 97. The vision of the Christ child attributed by Binski to Eleanor, Henry III's sister, in fact represents a misreading of the account in the annals of Waverley for 1245, in *Annales monastici*, II 336.

[20] For the layout of the church, see B. Hamilton, 'Rebuilding Zion: The Holy Places of Jerusalem in the Twelfth Century', *Studies in Church History* 14 (Oxford 1977), 105 16.

[21] *Die Kreuzzugsbriefe aus den Jahren 1088 1100*, ed. H. Hagenmeyer (Innsbruck 1901), 180 (Letter 22: *Gloria in altissimis*).

[22] William of Tyre, 'Chronicon' 18.3, in *Willelmi Tyrensis archiepiscopi chronicon*, ed. R. B. C. Huygens, H. E. Mayer and G. Rösch, 2 vols., CCCM LXIII (Turnhout 1986), II 813 lines 35 6, and see *Cartulaire du Saint-Sépulcre*, ed. Bresc-Bautier, nos. 20, 72, for grants to the church of Jerusalem referring to its association with the blood of Christ.

[23] *Quinti belli sacri scriptores minores*, ed. R. Röhricht (Geneva 1879), 15: *Sanguine Christi calesiebant clavi in cruce, sic debent peccatores accendi in caritate ad servicium Christi per sanguinem Christi.*

to the injury done both to the crusade and to King John: *rex catholicus et tam Ihesu Cristo quam ecclesie illius sanguine rubricate devotus.*[24] In writing to Henry III and his brother, Richard of Cornwall, on the business of the crusade, Pope Innocent IV made frequent reference after 1245 to the Holy Land as a place consecrated by Christ's blood: *Terra Sancta, Cristi respersa sanguine . . . cuiusque sanguine rubuit saepe sparso*, imploring the King 'by the blood of Jesus Christ' that he send aid to the East.[25] In May 1248, shortly after the delivery of the blood relic to Westminster, Innocent wrote to the patriarch of Jerusalem, announcing the intention of the count of Toulouse to join the forthcoming crusade *ad eripiendam terram de inimicorum manibus, domini nostri Ihesu Christi sanguine dedicatam.*[26] Jerusalem and the blood-shedding of Christ were immutably linked, both in crusader propaganda and in medieval writing in general.

Precisely this same association between the Holy Land and the Holy Blood is woven into the patriarch's letters to Henry III announcing the dispatch of the blood relic to England. Here, Henry III is reminded of the reverence his ancestors had shown for the church of Jerusalem, where Christ had spilled his blood and offered himself upon the altar of the Cross. The church of the Holy Sepulchre had been consecrated with the precious blood of God's son. This same blood of man's redemption, shed within the church at Calvary, had been sent to England so that Henry might glory in the Cross and remember Christ's Passion.[27] A remembrance of the Cross would have come particularly easily to a king accustomed to participate in the liturgy of Good Friday, in which, by the thirteenth century, it was customary for the congregation to prostrate themselves, not merely on bended knee but with their very stomachs touching the ground, in adoration of the Holy Cross, the instrument of Christ's sacrifice.[28] For all its apparent artlessness, the patriarch's letter

---

[24] *English Episcopal Acta IX: Winchester 1205–1238*, ed. N. Vincent (Oxford 1994), no. 100, p. 84. Simon Lloyd has pointed out to me that the phrase *sanguine rubricate devotus* is common in other papal and eastern letters.

[25] For the Pope's letters to England, which survive separately from the papal register, see *Foedera*, II 254–5; P. Sambin, 'Problemi politici attraverso lettere inedite di Innocenzo IV', *Memorie del Instituto Veneto di Scienze, Lettere ed Arti, classe di scienze, morali e lettere* 31 fasc. 3 (Venice 1955), 38–9 nos. 1–2, with further reference to Christ's blood at 51 no. 21, 60 no. 36. The crusading summons of the Council of Lyons (1245) had likewise referred to the Holy Land as that *quam Dei filius aspersione sui sanguinis consecravit*: Mansi, *Concilia*, XXIII 626.

[26] *Layettes du trésor des chartes*, ed. A. Teulet et al., 5 vols. (Paris 1863–1909), III no. 3662.

[27] Below appendix 1.

[28] See here J. D. Chambers, *Divine Worship in the Thirteenth and Fourteenth Centuries* (London 1877), appendix pp. xxvi–xxxv, esp. xxxi, as noted by Bloch, *The Royal Touch*, 92–3, where Bloch remarks that this 'creeping to the Cross' preceded the ceremony in which the kings of England, at least from the time of Edward II, made offerings at the altar later converted into 'cramp rings' for the miraculous cure of epilepsy and related illnesses.

is in fact a carefully calculated attempt to play upon the emotions of the King by linking the gift of the Holy Blood to Christ's Passion and hence to the more recent sufferings of his church at Jerusalem. In theory, no gift could have been better calculated to arouse the King's sympathy or to encourage greater reverence in the hearts of the faithful; provided, of course, that the blood given to Westminster in 1247 could win recognition as a genuine relic of the blood of Christ's Passion. The patriarch's letter is insistent that the relic was a true memorial of Christ. Yet ironically, this very insistence suggests that by no means everyone was likely to be convinced of the relic's authenticity. As we shall see, relics of the Holy Blood excited scepticism on both historical and theological grounds. In due course, we shall examine this scepticism in greater detail. In essence, however, the objections to the Westminster blood can be stated as follows: it was by no means unique, being merely the latest in a whole series of such relics to have found their way to western Europe over the past four hundred years; it came from a source, the Latin church of the Holy Sepulchre in Jerusalem, that had never before claimed to possess a portion of Christ's blood; and furthermore, like every other such relic, it appeared to involve a challenge to theological orthodoxy, and in particular to the church's teachings on the Incarnation and Resurrection of Christ. But this is to anticipate. For the moment, let us examine the history of relics of the Holy Blood prior to the events of 1247.

Relics of the saints were the object of veneration at least as early as the second century if not earlier, and a desire to possess tangible evidence of Christ and the Holy Family was as old as the cult of relics itself.[29] With the discovery by St Helena of the site of Christ's Passion, Jerusalem became the natural focal point for relic-hunters. Already in the fifth century St Augustine records the miraculous qualities ascribed to earth from the site of the Holy Sepulchre,[30] whilst by the year 800 or so, in England as elsewhere in Europe, no great relic collection was complete that did not include its fragments of stone, wood or cloth supposedly sanctified by Christ's touch. At Exeter, for example, there were preserved relics of Christ's crib, bath, Cross and tomb, of the table from which he had eaten, of the seal that had closed his tomb, and of the waters of

[29] Amongst the many outstanding studies of the cult of relics, see in particular N. Herrmann-Mascard, *Les Reliques des saints: formation coutumière d'un drôit* (Paris 1975); A. Angenendt, *Heilige und Reliquien: die Geschichte ihres Kultes vom frühen Christentum bis zur Gegenwart* (Munich 1994).
[30] Augustine, *De civitate Dei* 22.8, ed. B. Dombart and A. Kalb, Corpus Christianorum Series Latina XLVII–VIII, 2 vols. (Turnhout 1955), II 820 lines 199–205, and in general, for the earliest phase of relic-collecting from the Holy Land, see C. Hahn, 'Loca Sancta Souvenirs: Sealing the Pilgrim's Experience', *The Blessings of Pilgrimage*, ed. R. Ousterhout, Illinois Byzantine Studies I (Urbana and Chicago 1990), 85–96.

Jordan.[31] Later relic-lists testify to an indefatigable craving for fragments of Christ's raiment and his shroud, the vase from which he washed the disciples' feet, the rocks upon which he had stood at significant moments during his ministry, and especially for the instruments of his Passion: the lance that had pierced his side, the sponge from which he drank on the Cross, the nails that had pierced his hands and feet, thorns from the Crown of Thorns, and so on.[32]

It goes without saying that the relics of Christ differed in one important respect from relics of the saints. Christ's bodily Ascension into heaven, affirmed as a central tenet of the Christian faith, ensured that, at least to begin with, relic-collectors were forced to content themselves with secondary objects, wood, stone and the like, rather than with the flesh and bones left on earth by the average run of saints. In the same way, the heavenly assumption of Christ's mother Mary meant that at least until the ninth century no church dared claim any of her human remains. It is one of the more intriguing elements of our story that the first evidence of bodily relics of Christ should date from much the same time as the appearance of bodily relics of his mother.

The willingness of the faithful to believe that Christ and his mother had left behind bodily traces of their lives on earth can be linked to various wider themes in western history; a growing devotion to the humanity of Christ, and in tandem with this, a heightened awareness of his sufferings upon the Cross.[33] In general, with the relics of the saints as with those of Christ himself, the ninth century was to witness a turning away from devotion to secondary objects sanctified merely by contact with the bodies of the saints, towards a demand for primary relics, bones, hair and other physical remains of the saints' earthly bodies.[34] At much the same time

---

[31] M. Förster, *Zur Geschichte des reliquienkultus in Altengland*, Sitzungsberichte der Bayerischen Akademie der Wissenschaften 1943 part 8 (Munich 1943), 69–70, and see *Liber Vitae: Register and Martyrology of New Minster and Hyde Abbey Winchester*, ed. W. de Gray Birch, Hampshire Record Society (Winchester 1892), 147–53, listing amongst other things a fragment of the crib from which Christ's blood was wiped: *de presepe unde sanguis domini fuit tersus*.

[32] Förster, *Geschichte*, 116, 119. For other English lists which mention relics associated with Christ, see for example N. Rogers, 'The Waltham Abbey Relic-List', *England in the Eleventh Century*, Proceedings of the 1990 Harlaxton Symposium, ed. C. Hicks (Stamford 1992), 176, 178–80; *Chronicon monasterii de Abingdon*, ed. J. Stevenson, 2 vols., Rolls Series (London 1858), II 155, and from a later date J. P. Carley and M. Howley, 'Relics at Glastonbury in the Fourteenth Century: An Annotated Edition of British Library Cotton Titus D VII fos. 2r–13v', *Arthurian Literature* 16 (1998), 94–5; *Extracts from the Account Rolls of the Abbey of Durham*, ed. J. Fowler, 3 vols., Surtees Society 99, 100, 103 (1898–1901), II 428, 430, 431, 433, 435, 437–8.

[33] In general, see G. Constable, 'The Ideal of the Imitation of Christ', in G. Constable, *Three Studies in Medieval Religious and Social Thought* (Cambridge 1995), 145–248.

[34] Herrmann-Mascard, *Les Reliques des saints*, 67–70.

we find a reawakened interest in the nature of the sacraments and a growing desire to define the process by which the elements of the mass could
be transformed from mere bread and wine into the body and blood of
Christ.[35] Such themes lie beyond the compass of this study. None the less
they may help to explain why, from around the end of the ninth century,
churches ceased to be content with mere sticks and stones associated with
Christ and his mother, but came instead to claim the possession of more
personal remains; the blood of Christ and the hair and milk of Mary.[36]
Not only was the host to be treated increasingly as a relic for public
display, but devotion to the host, together with devotion to the newly
discovered physical relics of Christ and his mother, exhibit a common
devotion to the human Christ focused above all upon the eucharist as the
chief point of contact between mankind and Christ physically present on
earth.[37] The relics of the Virgin Mary lie beyond the confines of this study,
although it is significant that from the tenth and eleventh centuries they
became increasingly prominent in relic collections. According to Orderic
Vitalis, hairs of the Virgin had been preserved in the church of the Holy
Sepulchre at Jerusalem, where they were rediscovered following the First
Crusade by a man named Ilger Bigod. Bigod later bestowed individual
strands of the hair upon various churches in Normandy, and it may be
from the same source that the canons of Laon acquired the hair relic
which is said to have worked miracles when toured around England and
northern France in 1112–13 as part of a fund-raising mission for the rebuilding of Laon Cathedral.[38] Mary's milk need not detain us here, save
to note that like the Virgin's hair, but unlike the Holy Blood, portions of
the milk were claimed by the twelfth-century church in the Holy Land: in
1123 the patriarch of Jerusalem carried Christ's Cross into battle accompanied by a former abbot of Cluny carrying the Lance, and the bishop of
Bethlehem bearing a pyx containing the Virgin's milk.[39] We might note

---

[35] In general, see Rubin, *Corpus Christi*, 12–35.

[36] For relics of Mary's milk, collected in England from before the year 1000, see M. Clayton, *The Cult of the Virgin Mary in Anglo-Saxon England* (Cambridge 1990), 138–9. See also B. P. McGuire, *The Difficult Saint, Bernard of Clairvaux and his Tradition*, Cistercian Studies CXXVI (Kalamazoo 1991), 189–225, and E. Waterton, *Pietas Mariana Brittanica* (London 1879), 195–205, which, although written from a devotional standpoint with a consequent anxiety to rationalize the irrational, provides useful references. Henry of Blois is said to have given a milk relic to the monks of Glastonbury: Carley and Howley, 'Relics at Glastonbury', 116.

[37] Macy, *Theologies of the Eucharist*, 90–2.

[38] B. Ward, *Miracles and the Medieval Mind*, revised edn (Aldershot 1987), 134–9, 209. Portions of the Virgin's milk and hair were preserved at Westminster in the fifteenth century, supposedly given to the Abbey by Edward the Confessor: Flete, *History*, 69–70, and see below p. 126.

[39] 'Anselm Gemblacensis continuatio', in 'Sigeberti Gemblacensis chronica cum continuationibus', ed. D. L. C. Bethmann, *MGH Scriptores*, VI 379.

too that the milk, though common amongst medieval relic collections, was in many ways a less plausible relic than the Holy Blood. For the spilling of Christ's blood, if not for its preservation, the Gospels furnished incontestable proof. They had nothing whatsoever to say of Mary's milk. Hence, perhaps, the fact that milk relics seem to have been attended by little of the fervour that surrounded relics of the blood. For this there may have been a yet cruder explanation. To believe in the survival of Mary's milk was to believe that Mary had lactated during Christ's infancy. Since lactation was widely held to be the product of the blood of menstruation – used to nourish the foetus during pregnancy and thereafter transformed into milk – and since the menstruation of the Virgin was a highly delicate topic to medieval theologians, encumbered by age-old taboos concerning the 'impurity' of the menstrual cycle and the curse of Eve, relics of Mary's milk carried associations that were as likely to repel as to attract the faithful.[40]

By contrast to the human relics of Mary, the relics of Christ's blood could claim at least some support from scripture. Scripture leaves us in no doubt that Christ bled copiously, both during his scourging and on the Cross. Relics of the blood also followed in a long tradition of collecting the blood-stained clothing of the martyrs.[41] Blood-shedding, after all, is the pre-eminent mark of human suffering: the chief visual sign to an onlooker, be it to an actual bystander or to a much later audience faced by a pictorial representation, of violent suffering and death.[42] The blood of the early Christian martyrs was being collected, venerated and attributed with miraculous powers of healing at least as early as the fifth century, perhaps even before the rediscovery outside Jerusalem in 415 of the body and blood of St Stephen, the very first Christian martyr.[43]

---

[40] See here C. T. Wood, 'The Doctor's Dilemma: Sin, Salvation and the Menstrual Cycle in Medieval Thought', *Speculum* 56 (1981). 710–27; P. L'Hermite-Leclerq, 'Le Sang et le lait de la vierge', *Le Sang au Moyen-Âge*, ed. Faure, 145–62, with further essays in the same volume dealing with the impurity of menstrual blood.

[41] From England, see for example the blood-stained shirt of St Edmund King and martyr kept at Abingdon, or at Waltham and Shrewsbury the blood relics of St Laurence; *Chronicon de Abingdon*, II 157; Rogers, 'The Waltham Abbey Relic-List', 177; H. Owen and F. B. Blakeway, *A History of Shrewsbury*, 2 vols. (London 1825), II 43, from Cambridge, Fitzwilliam Museum MS 88 (1972) (Shrewsbury lectionary) fo. 11: *de ossibus sancti Laurentii martiris et de cruore eius.*

[42] This is a theme explored by numerous essays in *SA*. See, for example, J. Janssens, 'Il Sangue dei martiri nei carmi damasiani e in altre iscrizioni romane', *SA*, III part 3 (1983) 1505–18; J. Janssens, 'Il Tema del sangue nelle antiche iscrizioni martirologiche dell'Africa del nord', *SA*, IV part 3 (1984), 1561–71.

[43] See here the extremely useful study by U. M. Fasola, 'Il culto del sangue dei martiri nella chiesa primitiva e deviazioni devozionistiche nell'epoca della riscoperta delle catacombe', *SA*, III part 3 (1983), 1473–89, and for St Stephen, see the sermons preached by Augustine, 'Sermons

Blood-stained earth from the grave of the English protomartyr St Alban is said to have been collected by bishop Germanus of Auxerre on a visit to England as early as 429.[44] Bede records the miracles worked by earth impregnated with the blood of St Oswald (d. 642).[45] By the seventeenth and eighteenth centuries, it had become traditional, when excavating the Roman catacombs, to identify whatever glass containers might be found there as phials for the preservation of the blood of the early Christian martyrs – a fantasy to which even the great Leibnitz was prepared to lend 'scientific' support.[46] From the stoning of Stephen, via the executions of Mary Queen of Scots or King Charles I, through to the cult of the political 'martyrs' of revolutionary France, human history reveals a near irresistible urge to collect the blood-stained relics of those who die by violence. Belief in the potency of such blood is revealed by the assumption, reported into relatively modern times, that the blood of a murder victim will flow spontaneously if that victim's corpse is brought into the presence of its murderers. In much this way, Gerald of Wales claimed that the blood of the late King Henry II flowed from his nostrils when his corpse was approached by his son and betrayer, Richard I. The bones of St Thomas Cantiloupe of Hereford, although boiled down after death, are said to have bled spontaneously when carried through the lands of his late persecutors. Likewise, the corpse of Shakespeare's Henry VI

---

314 24', in Migne, *PL*, XXXVIII 1425 47; H. Delehaye, *Les Origines du cult des martyrs* (Brussels 1933), 80 2. St Stephen's blood is specifically stated to have been discovered together with his body: 'De miraculis sancti Stephani protomartyris', in Migne, *PL*, XLI 834. By the following century, a portion of the blood had reached Bazas in Aquitaine, as reported by Gregory of Tours, 'Liber in gloria martyrum' 1.33/4, in Migne, *PL*, LXXI 735, also in *Gregorii Turonensis opera*, ed. W. Arndt and B. Krusch, *MGH Scriptorum Rerum Merovingicarum*, 1 (Hanover 1885), 508. Gregory ('Liber' 1.11/12, in Migne, *PL*, LXXI 717; *MGH Scriptorum Rerum Merovingicarum*, 1 495) is likewise the authority for the tradition that a further blood relic, of St John the Baptist, had been preserved at Bazas, purchased from the Baptist's executioner and thence brought back to Gascony, supposedly as early as the first century.

44 D. Rollason, *Saints and Relics in Anglo-Saxon England* (Oxford 1989), 12. Much later, Matthew Paris records that at some time between 1214 and 1235 the monks of St Albans came into possession of a cross, once belonging to St Amphibalus, supposedly dipped in Alban's blood; Matthew Paris, 'Gesta Abbatum', in *Gesta abbatum monasterii sancti Albani a Thoma Walsingham, . . . compilata*, ed. H. T. Riley, 3 vols., Rolls Series (London 1867) 1 292.

45 *Bede's Ecclesiastical History of the English People*, ed. B. Colgrave and R. A. B. Mynors (Oxford 1969), 245.

46 Fasola, 'Il Culto del sangue dei martiri', 1473 6, citing the polemic of M. A. Boldetti, *Osservazioni sopra i cimiteri dei santi martiri ed antichi cristiani di Roma* (Rome 1720), with notice of Leibnitz at pp. 186 7. Boldetti's treatise was intended as a defence of Roman practice against Mabillon and those others who questioned the authenticity of many of the relics taken from the catacombs. Fasola, it might be noted, is himself anxious to demonstrate the antiquity of martyrs' blood relics, as a defence for the antiquity of the famous relic of St Januarius at Naples.

bleeds fresh blood when approached by the King's assassin, the future Richard III.[47]

Similar themes appear from an early date in the history of the saints. To Pope Gregory the Great, so powerful were the bones of the saints that to touch them or to attempt to move them might spell death. Instead it was better that secondary materials such as cloth and parchment, known as *brandea*, be charged with the saints' holy essence. When cut with a knife, even such cloth or parchment had been known to exude blood as a proof of its miraculous powers.[48] As early as the 390s, Victricius of Rouen had described the way in which blood, or particles of blood, could be locked away, invulnerable, within the physical relics of the saints, and in 502, when Clovis of the Franks removed a tooth from the jaw bone of St Rieule of Senlis, a martyr who had died several centuries earlier, the jaw is said to have bled fresh blood.[49] Later, in the twelfth century, we find a series of blood-related miracles in the cults of the saints which to some extent can be regarded as paving the way for the reception of the Westminster relic of the blood of Christ.

At St Martin's church in Tours, for example, then firmly under Plantagenet rule, it was claimed that St Martin himself had visited the site of the martyrdom of St Maurice and the Theban legion, from which he had carried away several phials of blood. These he kept with him for the remainder of his life, bequeathing some of his treasure to the cathedral churches of Angers and Tours where it is said to have been rediscovered around the year 1180.[50] In England, at Finchale in county Durham, the body of the local hermit St Godric (d. 1170) was discovered to exude

---

[47] For the belief in general, and for these and other specific examples, see H. Platelle, 'La Voix du sang: le cadavre qui saigne en présence de son meurtrier', *La Piété populaire au Moyen Age*, Actes du 99e congrès national des Sociétés savantes, Besançon 1974, Section de philologie et d'histoire jusqu'à 1610 vol. 1 (Paris 1977), 163–79; Shakespeare, *King Richard III*, ed. A. Hammond, The Arden Shakespeare (London 1981), Act 1 scene 2 lines 55ff, noting Shakespeare's dependence here upon the Warkworth Chronicle. For a brilliant account of the 'cruentation' and the controversy that surrounded the bleeding relics of St Thomas of Hereford, see A. Boureau, *Théologie, science et censure au XIIIe siècle: le cas de Jean Peckham* (Paris 1999), chapters 7–8.

[48] Gregory, 'Epistolae' 4.30, in *Gregorii I papae registrum epistolarum*, ed. P. Ewald and L. M. Hartmann, 2 vols., *MGH Epistolarum*, I–II (Berlin 1891–9), I 264–6; Migne, *PL*, LXXVII, 702, and see the further examples of bleeding *brandea* cited by Rollason, *Saints and Relics*, 11.

[49] For Victricius, see below p. 93. For St Rieule, see 'Vita S. Reguli', in *Acta SS: March*, III 825. A similar miracle is recorded by William of Malmesbury, writing in the twelfth century of the translation of the relics of Edgar at Glastonbury at some time between 1024 and 1053: Rollason, *Saints and Relics*, 140.

[50] S. Farmer, *Communities of St Martin: Legend and Ritual in Medieval Tours* (Ithaca 1991), 232–5, commenting upon the account in *Guiberti Gemblacensis epistolae*, ed. A. Derolez, 2 vols., CCCM LXVI (Turnhout 1988–9), 171–82 (letter 5), esp. pp. 73–5. For subsequent evidence of devotion to St Maurice at Tours, see Dupont Lachenal, 'À Saint-Maurice au XIIIe siècle', 420–3.

blood after his death, effecting a miraculous cure to a local man who kissed the saint's bleeding feet.[51] Thomas of Monmouth reports that wax pledged to the candle-loving martyr, St William of Norwich (d.1144), exuded blood when cut with a knife. There are also hints in Thomas' life of St William that the saint's blood may have been specially collected and preserved.[52] Following the execution of the London troublemaker William fitz Osbern in the 1190s, various of his followers are said to have carried away earth impregnated with blood from the place of his execution, claiming that William was a martyr whose relics could effect miraculous healing.[53] Various of these cults may well reflect the success of the blood cult of a much more famous English martyr, St Thomas of Canterbury. Thomas' blood had become the subject of extraordinary religious devotion almost from the moment of his death in 1170, supposedly endowed with miraculous powers including the ability to cure the sick when swallowed or brought into contact with the skin. One of the earliest accounts of these miracles draws a deliberate and intriguing comparison between Thomas' blood and the eucharistic blood of the sacrament. In death as in life Thomas so imitated Christ that, just as the blood of Christ mixed with water leads to the nourishment of the soul, to drink the blood of Christ's servant Thomas, mixed with water, leads to the health of the body. This, so it was claimed, was a unique privilege conferred on Thomas by God 'since it is recorded that only the blood of the lamb of Bethlehem and that of the lamb of Canterbury can be so consumed in all the world'.[54] Once again, there is a clear association here between blood relics, albeit the blood of the saints, and a heightened

[51] Reginald of Durham, *Libellus de vita et miraculis S. Godrici, heremitae de Finchale*, ed. J. Stevenson, Surtees Society XX (1847), 327–30 no. 170, as noticed by Ward, *Miracles and the Medieval Mind*, 80.

[52] *The Life and Miracles of St William of Norwich by Thomas of Monmouth*, ed. A. Jessopp and M. R. James (Cambridge 1896), 267–8, and for fresh blood exuded from the saint's mutilated body, a year after his death, see *ibid.*, 52. So fond was St William (born on Candlemas) of candles that on one occasion he is said to have brought death upon a monk who refused him lights for his shrine: *ibid.*, 136–45.

[53] William of Newburgh, 'Historia rerum anglicarum' 5.21, in *Chronicles of the Reigns of Stephen, Henry II and Richard I*, ed. R. Howlett, 4 vols., Rolls Series (London 1885–9), II 472.

[54] Benedict of Canterbury, 'Miracula S. Thomae', 1.12, in *Materials for the History of Thomas Becket*, ed. J. C. Robertson and J. B. Sheppard, 7 vols., Rolls Series (London 1875–85), II 43: *Christi sanguis cum aqua transit ad vegetationem animarum, ita et servi sui sanguis cum aqua bibitus transeat in sanitatem corporum, nec credimus aliquem hactenus extitisse, cui Deus hanc similitudinis praerogativam concesserit, solius enim agni Bethleemitici sanguis et cruor agni Cantuariensis in universo mundo hauriri legitur*, and for examples of miracles involving Thomas' blood see *ibid.*, II 49–59, 65–6, IV 199. For its preservation amongst relic-collections, see for example Rogers, 'The Waltham Abbey Relic-List', 178, 181; Owen and Blakeway, *History of Shrewsbury*, II 43, from Cambridge, Fitzwilliam Museum MS 88 (1972) (Shrewsbury lectionary) fo. 1r: *de panno intincto cerebro et sanguine (sancti Thome)*.

devotion to the sacraments of the mass. As Herbert of Bosham was to put it, what more appropriate gift could there be in commemoration of the martyr than that made by Louis VII of France, of a golden chalice and of wine with which it might be filled?[55] Blood was an essential feature of the Becket cult. Pilgrims, including in 1174 King Henry II, were encouraged to carry away metal phials containing water mixed with blood, whilst on occasion the blood itself appears to have been offered, presumably in very small and coagulated particles, to be consumed undiluted as a cure for sickness. The monks of Canterbury were swift to appreciate the significance of Becket's blood: on the night following his murder, the blood and brains were carefully collected from the flagstones where they had been spattered, whilst the monks kept watch over the martyr's corpse to collect any more blood that might flow from it.[56]

There is one further point that we should bear in mind before turning to the relics of the Holy Blood themselves: the need to distinguish such relics, believed to be literal and historical survivals from the time of Christ's Passion, from various other manifestations of the blood of Christ, most notably those given off by images, statues and icons, and those that resulted from eucharistic miracles, where it was claimed that the wine of the eucharist had been transformed literally into the human blood of Christ. Although it is the literal, historical blood of the Passion that principally concerns us here, we should bear in mind that claims to its possession were a relatively late development, and that they followed, indeed may well have been inspired by, a more ancient tradition of collecting the miraculous blood produced by images and the blessed sacrament. From at least the sixth century it is recorded that icons or images of Christ and the saints gave forth a miraculous flow of blood upon being struck or pierced.[57] Perhaps the most significant such miracle occurred around the year 765 in Beirut, where it is reported that an icon of Christ gave forth blood upon being subjected to ritual humiliation by the Jews; an incident no doubt related to the unequivocal reassertion, made by the Council of Nicaea in 787, of the validity of icons and relics

[55] *Materials for Thomas Becket*, III 539, and see also Bosham's remarks on the 'transubstantiation' of Becket's body in martyrdom, and on the sacred quality of his blood, *sacer ille sanguis . . . fons sanguinis et pietatis: ibid.*, III 493 4, 498, 500.

[56] Ward, *Miracles and the Medieval Mind*, 101 4. For the phial of the water of St Thomas obtained by Henry II, see Gervase of Canterbury, *Historical Works*, ed. W. Stubbs, 2 vols., Roll Series (London 1879 80), I 249.

[57] In general, see E. Kitzinger, 'The Cult of Images before Iconoclasm', *Dumbarton Oaks Papers* 8 (1954), 100 9; G. P. Galvaris, 'The Mother of God, "Stabbed with a Knife"', *ibid.*, 13 (1959), 229 33. Perhaps the earliest such bleeding icon was that attacked by a Jew, recorded by Gregory of Tours, 'Liber in gloria martyrum' 1.21/2, in Migne, *PL*, LXXI col. 724; *MGH Scriptores Rerum Merovingicarum*, I 501.

as aids to Christian worship.[58] In 975 the icon of Beirut was carried off to Constantinople. Part of its miraculous effluvia figured amongst the Passion relics eventually sold to King Louis IX in the 1240s and housed in the Sainte-Chapelle at Paris.[59] The annals of Worcester claim that a portion of the miraculous blood of Beirut reached England in the year 932, and according to Gerald of Wales, writing *c.* 1197, the relic of Beirut was famed for its curative properties.[60] Gerald also records a similar miracle, in which an image of Christ in Majesty, placed over the doorway of the Lateran Palace in Rome, gave forth blood on being stoned by a Jew. The miraculous effluvia effected many cures, and according to Gerald, both the image and the blood relic were still to be seen in Rome in the 1190s.[61] Elsewhere, from at least the eleventh century, the church of Orviedo in Spain claimed to possess a crystal vase containing blood and water given off from an image of Christ that the Jews had pierced with a lance, presumably an echo of the Beirut miracle.[62] Pilgrims to Glastonbury in the twelfth century were shown a miraculous silver

---

[58] Sigebert of Gembloux in *MGH Scriptores*, VI 333, and see the letters of the pseudo-Athanasius in Migne, *PG*, XXVIII cols. 797–824; Mansi, *Concilia*, XIII 24–32. In general, for the celebration of the festival of the icon of Beirut, popular in France and Spain but introduced to England only in the later Middle Ages, see R. W. Pfaff, *New Liturgical Feasts in Later Medieval England* (Oxford 1970), 116–28.

[59] K. Gould, 'The Sequences "De sanctis reliquiis" as Sainte-Chapelle Inventories', *Mediaeval Studies* 43 (1981), 330–1, 336 no. 6; J. Ebersolt, *Sanctuaires de Byzance* (Paris 1921), 21–2, and see 6–7 for a similar miraculous crucifix kept at the church of Hagia Sophia. A portion of the effluvia from the Beirut cross is said, much later, to have found its way to Nouaillé near Poitiers: X. Barbier de Montault, *Œuvres complètes* (Poitiers 1889–1902), VII 533–4. The *sanguis sacratissimus tam miraculose effusus* preserved at Basel, first recorded in the sixteenth century, though supposedly acquired by bishop Ortlieb (1138–64), cannot with any certainty be attributed to the image of Beirut, despite the confident statement of L. Vautrey, *Histoire des évêques de Bâle*, 2 vols. (Einsiedeln 1884–6), I 164–6. Various stories relating to miraculous images of Christ, including that of the bleeding icon of Hagia Sophia, are copied into BL MS Egerton 2947 fos. 51v–3r, an English MS of the mid-twelfth century, and for further evidence that this story was known in England, see S. G. Mercati, 'Santuari e reliquie Costantinopolitane secondo il codice Ottoboniano Latino 169 prima della conquista Latina (1204)', *Rendiconti della Pontificia Accademia Romana di Archeologia* 12 (1936), 136–7, 143–4.

[60] *Annales monastici*, IV 370. Sigebert's account of the Beirut miracle is entered in the annals of Winchester/Waverley under the year 766; *ibid.*, II 156–7. Since the annals of Worcester, Winchester and Waverley appear all of them to be derived from a lost prototype from Winchester, it is possible that the miraculous blood relic referred to in 932 is that mentioned in a later inventory of Winchester cathedral as *duo philateria argentea, in uno quorum habetur lapis in quem stillavit sanguis domini*; Barbier de Montault, *Œuvres*, VII 537, below p. 69 n. 128. For Gerald's account, which he attributes to St Basil (d. 379), see *Giraldi Cambrensis opera*, ed. J. S. Brewer, 8 vols., Rolls Series (London 1861–91) II 102–3.

[61] *Giraldi Cambrensis opera*, ed. Brewer, II 103.

[62] D. de Bruyne, 'Le plus ancien catalogue des reliques d'Oviedo', *Analecta Bollandiana* 45 (1927), 94. As late as the sixteenth century, bleeding crosses continued a regular phenomenon in Spain; see W. A. Christian Jr, *Local Religion in Sixteenth-Century Spain* (Princeton 1981), 190–2, drawn to my attention by Peter Linehan.

figure of Christ that had exuded blood, having been pierced with an arrow during a skirmish between abbot Thurstan of Glastonbury and his monks in the 1080s,[63] whilst both Gerald of Wales and Vincent of Beauvais record that at Châteauroux in 1187, a mercenary employed by Richard I blasphemously attacked a statue of the Virgin and Child, knocking off the arm of the infant Jesus. The stone arm, which gave forth a miraculous flow of blood, is said to have been preserved with great devotion by Richard's brother, the future King John.[64]

According to John Flete, writing in the fifteenth century, Henry III's gifts to the monks of Westminster included not only the phial of the Holy Blood received in 1247, but 'a great portion of blood from a miracle'.[65] Assuming that Flete is correct to attribute this gift to King Henry, there are two possibilities here; either that the miraculous blood was a eucharistic relic, similar to those recorded elsewhere in Europe where the wine of the mass was believed to have been transformed literally into blood, in both substance and form; or else that it represents yet another echo of the Beirut miracle, being the effluvia from some crucifix or icon. In the fourteenth century, Margery Kempe was obliged to travel as far as Wilsnack in Brandenburg to view 'that precyows blod whech be myracle cam owt of the blisful sacrament of the awtre'.[66] Although her

---

[63] *The Early History of Glastonbury: An Edition, Translation and Study of William of Malmesbury's 'De Antiquitate Glastonie Ecclesie'*, ed. J. Scott (Woodbridge 1981), 81, 157-9, whence *The Chronicle of Glastonbury Abbey: An Edition, Translation and Study of John of Glastonbury's 'Chronica sive Antiquitates Glastoniensis Ecclesie'*, ed. J. P. Carley, trans. D. Townsend (Woodbridge 1985), 157-9, advertised to pilgrims in the Glastonbury 'Magna Tabula' (Oxford, Bodleian Library MS Lat. hist. a. 2 sheet 3), as printed by J. Krochalis, '"Magna Tabula": The Glastonbury Tablets', *Arthurian Literature* 15 (1997), 158 no. 23.

[64] *Giraldi Cambrensis opera*, ed. Brewer, II 104-5, VIII 323-4; Vincent of Beauvais, *Bibliotheca mundi seu speculi maioris*, 4 vols. (Douai 1624), IV 1199-200, and see *ibid.*, IV 1194 for Vincent's report of various bleeding hosts recorded earlier in the 1180s, said to have been viewed amongst others by King Philip Augustus. *Gervase of Canterbury*, I 369-70 claims that it was not the future King John but the viscount of Limoges who carried away the arm from Châteauroux.

[65] Flete, *History*, 69, and see above pp. 12-14.

[66] *The Book of Margery Kempe*, ed. S. B. Meech and H. E. Allen, Early English Text Society CCXII (1940), 234-5, quoted by Rubin, *Corpus Christi*, 314. For evidence of devotion to the Wilsnack relic in fifteenth-century England, see A. P. Stanley, *Historical Memorials of Canterbury*, 2nd edn (London 1855), 231-3, 235; C. M. Barron, 'The Parish Fraternities of Medieval London', *The Church in Pre-Reformation Society: Essays in Honour of F. R. H. Du Boulay*, ed. C. M. Barron and C. Harper-Bill (Woodbridge 1985), 17. One possibility is that the miraculous blood of Westminster, like the spine from the Crown of Thorns also recorded by Flete, had been given to Henry III by King Louis IX of France. Although no such gift is recorded, Louis is known to have obtained a portion of the miraculous blood of Beirut, and to have made regular diplomatic offerings from his great store of Passion relics, although admittedly none of them to secular princes. One chronicler reports a discussion between Louis and Henry, supposed to have occurred in 1259, in which the English King's devotion to the sacraments was made abundantly clear; above p. 36.

pilgrimage owed more to the particular vogue of Wilsnack than to the scarcity of such eucharistic blood in England, in the absence of further evidence it seems more likely that the miraculous blood of Westminster was an effluvial rather than a eucharistic relic, possibly even the same as that relic which Henry's father, King John, is said to have collected at Châteauroux in the 1180s.

Turning from effluvial to eucharistic blood relics, in general it should be noted that eucharistic miracles tended to involve the consecrated wine far less frequently than the host. Partly this may have been because wine, which might be transformed into human blood, or which might boil or seethe in the chalice, offered the faithful less opportunity for invention than the host which could assume so many different guises; appearing as raw flesh, as the Agnus Dei, as the body of a child, as clear as glass, as fire, as a mass of congealed blood, and in many other forms besides. Even the blood-miracle of Wilsnack, announced in 1383, involved the host rather than the chalice, centring upon the preservation of three consecrated wafers that had miraculously survived the burning of the parish church and which on examination proved to be spotted or impregnated with the literal blood of Christ.[67] Caesarius of Heisterbach, whose *Dialogus miraculorum* (c. 1223–4) represents one of the most prolific collections of such stories, devotes only ten chapters of his book on the sacraments to miracles involving the eucharistic wine, set against more than forty that concern the host.[68] Caesarius does, however, make plain the dire penalties faced by a priest who accidentally spilled consecrated wine or who dropped the chalice; not only would he be forced to engage in a troublesome mopping-up operation, but in certain cases he might face suspension from the right to celebrate mass in future.[69]

Elsewhere, the customal of Cluny deals at length with the procedure that had to be gone through when wine was spilled during mass, specifying that any cloth or material impregnated with consecrated wine was

[67] For Wilsnack in general see E. Breest, 'Das Wunderblut von Wilsnack (1383 1552)', *Märkische Forschungen 16* (Berlin 1881), 131 301, and below pp. 118 23.

[68] Caesarius of Heisterbach, 'Dialogue' Book 9, in *Caesarii Heisterbacensis monachi ordinis Cisterciensis dialogus miraculorum*, ed. J. Strange, 2 vols. (Cologne 1851), II 164 et seq., translated as *The Dialogue on Miracles*, trans. H. von E. Scott and C. C. Winton Bland, 2 vols. (London 1929), II 103 et seq., and in general, see the important study by P. Browe, *Die Eucharistischen Wunder des Mittelalters*, Breslauer Studien zur historischen Theologie, neue folge band IV (Breslau 1938).

[69] Caesarius, 'Dialogue' 9.22 3, in *Dialogus*, ed. Strange II 181 2; *Dialogue on Miracles*, II 125 6. For the decretal letter, supposedly of Pope Pius I (AD 140 55), which underlay these operations, see Gratian, 'Decretum' III.2.27, in *Corpus iuris canonici* I, ed. E. Friedberg (Leipzig 1879), col. 1323; Jaffé, *Regesta pontificum Romanorum*, 18 no. 52.

to be preserved with reverence amongst a church's relic collection.[70] Spillage must have been a common occurrence, so that many churches would have numbered wine-soaked cloth amongst their relics. Just as on occasion, eucharistic or effluvial relics came to be mistaken or deliberately misrepresented as portions of the literal, historical blood of Christ's Passion, it is possible that the preservation of wine-soaked cloth may have given rise to at least some of the enormous number of claims to possess fragments of Christ's garments or shroud supposedly impregnated with his blood.[71] Beyond this, the growing interest in Christ's relics, especially from the twelfth century onwards, was matched by a tendency for the elements of the mass to be regarded as relics in their own right, worthy of veneration. The host was paraded and displayed in the same way as the bones of the saints, and on occasion consecrated wafers were placed together with other relics in altars at the time of their dedication.[72] Some but not all of these eucharistic relics were preserved because they had undergone a miraculous transformation into literal flesh and

---

[70] E. Martène, *De antiquis ecclesiae ritibus*, 4 vols. (Antwerp 1736–8), IV 211. Wine that had become polluted, so that it could not be swallowed, was to be burned. Similar injunctions are found in constitution 75 of the Council of Paris (1197 × 1208), cited in *Les Statuts synodaux français du XIIIe siècle: tome. 1, Les statuts de Paris et le synodal de l'Ouest (XIIIe siècle)*, ed. O. Pontal, Collection des Documents inédits sur l'histoire de France, series in octavo IX (Paris 1971), 80–1, and in various other monastic customals including that of Fleury, and the Augustinian customal of Oigny, with the added requirement that parts of any vestment stained with consecrated wine were to be burned and the ashes disposed of in the *sacrarium*; *Le Coutumier de l'abbaye d'Oigny en Bourgogne au XIIe siècle*, ed. P. F. Lefèvre and A. H. Thomas, Spicilegium Sacrum Lovaniense études et documents XXXIX (1976), 83–4; *Consuetudines Floriacenses saeculi tertii decimi*, ed. A. Davril, Corpus Consuetudinum Monasticarum IX (Siegburg 1976), 307. At Bec it was decreed that the area where any wine had been spilled should be scraped and the particles placed in the *sacrarium*. If the wine was spilled on the corporal or the altar cloth, such cloth should be washed three times in the chalice. The water of the first washing was to be consumed by the monks, and that of the second two washings be disposed of in the *sacrarium*. As a deterrent, both at Cluny and at Bec, the erring priest would be scourged, and the entire convent forced to recite the seven penitential psalms, a punishment which had been enforced from a very early date in church history: Martène, *De antiquis ecclesiae ritibus*, IV 210–12; *The Monastic Constitutions of Lanfranc*, ed. D. Knowles (London 1951), 90–2, and for the origins of this punishment, see Jaffé, *Regesta pontificum Romanorum*, I 8 no. 52.

[71] For eucharistic and effluvial relics misrepresented as the historic blood of Christ, see most notably the case of Fécamp, below pp. 57–8. Note also the frequent use of wine to wash the relics of the saints at the time of their translation, thereafter distributed as a secondary relic: P.-A. Sigal, 'Le déroulement des translations de reliques principalement dans les régions entre Loire et Rhin aux XIe et XIIe siècles', *Les Reliques: objets, cultes, symboles. Actes du colloque international de l'Université du Littoral-Côte d'Opale (Boulogne-sur-Mer) 4–6 septembre 1997*, ed. E. Bozóky and A.-M. Helvétius (Turnhout 1999), 226–7.

[72] Herrmann-Mascard, *Les Reliques des saints*, 159–61. For the use of relics in the consecration of altars, from a very early date regarded as symbol both of the tomb and of the place of eucharistic sacrifice, see J. Michaud, 'Culte des reliques et épigraphie. L'exemple des dédicaces et des consécrations d'autels', *Les Reliques*, ed. Bozóky and Helvétius, 199–212.

blood. By no means all churchmen were impressed by such miracles. The biographer of St Hugh of Lincoln, for example, records that at Joi near Troyes in Champagne, Hugh was told of a portion of the host which had been transformed literally into flesh and blood and which had since been venerated as a relic, stored behind the altar of the parish church. St Hugh dismissed the story, arguing that it was better for the faithful to marvel at the body and blood of Christ recreated daily in the mass than for them to gape at some more tangible proof of Christ's sacrifice.[73] Ironically, precisely the same argument, so often deployed against the material relics of Christ – that faith was superior to any trust in material proof – appears to have been current at the court of Henry III. In 1244, when Henry III commissioned a new reliquary for the arm of St Thomas, the doubting apostle who had insisted upon touching Christ's wounds, he asked that a ring be placed on the finger of the reliquary at Westminster Abbey, inscribed with St John's sentence 'Blessed are they that have not seen and yet have believed' (John xx. 29).[74] Despite such reservations, however, the popularity of eucharistic relics continued to gather pace, in tandem with but as a phenomenon distinct from the supposed rediscovery of portions of Christ's earthly body.

And so we return from effluvial and eucharistic relics, to the literal blood of Christ. Here we should begin with those visitors to Jerusalem, who from a very early date reported seeing the stains of blood in the places where Christ was scourged and crucified – perhaps, in reality the red or pink streaks in the site's malachite stone – and the blood stains upon the Holy Cross itself.[75] From this it was a simple though controversial step to claim the survival not only of the stain of Christ's blood but of blood relics that were more than simple stains.[76] The earliest

[73] *Magna Vita Sancti Hugonis: The Life of St Hugh of Lincoln*, ed. D. L. Douie and D. H. Farmer, 2 vols. (Oxford 1985), II 92–5, where the story is dated to the year 1200.

[74] *Close Rolls 1242–7*, 270, the Gospel sentence following on from verses, apparently composed by the court poet Henry of Avranches: 'He should give blessing who acquired blessing from all', whence *The Shorter Latin Poems of Master Henry of Avranches relating to England*, ed. J. Cox Russell and J. P. Heironimus, Mediaeval Academy of America Studies and Documents no.1 (Cambridge, Mass., 1935), p. xxiii.

[75] *Itinera Hierosolymitana et descriptiones terrae sanctae bellis sacris anteriora*, ed. T. Tobler, A. Molinier and C. Kohler, 2 vols. (Geneva 1879–85), I 64, 102, 371; J. Wilkinson, *Jerusalem Pilgrims before the Crusades* (Warminster 1977), 83, 177, and see St Jerome, Letter 108, in Migne, *PL*, XXII 884; Wilkinson, *Jerusalem Pilgrims*, 49, for a stain of Christ's blood on the pillar of Christ's scourging at Jerusalem, shown to Jerome and to his companion on pilgrimage, the lady Paula, in AD 385. I am indebted to Colin Morris for his remarks on the geology of the site.

[76] The only remotely reliable accounts of blood relics which I have been able to find are those provided by J. Sumption, *Pilgrimage: An Image of Mediaeval Religion* (London 1975), 44–8; Barbier de Montault, *Œuvres*, VII 324–37; P. Saintyves, *Les Reliques et les images légendaires* (Paris 1912),

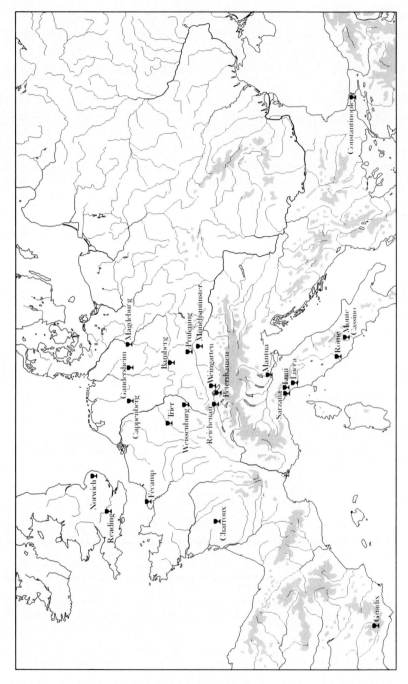

Map 1   The distribution of relics of the Holy Blood before 1204

recorded claim to possess such a relic may come from seventh-century Spain, where in the 640s bishop Braulio of Saragossa was questioned by a close associate, recently returned from Rome, on the authenticity of those relics of Christ's blood which, according to Braulio, were to be found in several cathedral churches, although not at Saragossa itself. Braulio's response prefigures to a remarkable extent the later debate on relics of the Holy Blood. Whilst admitting that portions of Christ's blood, and even his sweat, might have been preserved from the time of the Crucifixion, perhaps scraped from the pillar at Jerusalem where Christ had been scourged, Braulio was clearly concerned that such relics might invite mocking scepticism rather than veneration. He concludes, in a manner that we shall find reiterated from the twelfth century onwards, that whilst such relics are not an impossibility, they are in no way to be preferred to the true blood of Christ recreated daily in the sacrament of the mass.[77] Saragossa itself might boast no relic of the Holy Blood, but elsewhere in Visigothic Spain, from Guadix in Andalusia, we have independent testimony to the existence of a blood relic of the Passion, perhaps the first ever recorded, referred to in an inscription to be dated to much the same time as Braulio's letter, between 641 and 652.[78]

144–66; P. Boussel, *Des reliques et de leur bon usage* (Paris 1971), 125–34, and by N. Huyghebaert, 'Iperius et la translation de la relique du Saint-Sang à Bruges', *Annales de la Société d'émulation de Bruges* 100 (1964 for 1963), 110–87. Of these, the account by the sceptical Benedictine Huyghebaert is easily the best, used widely in what follows. Huyghebaert's footnotes are based to a large extent upon Frolow, *Vraie Croix*, again used extensively below. Saintyves and de Montault assemble lists of European churches which claimed to possess portions of the blood from the Middle Ages onwards, but their lists are incomplete and somewhat indiscriminate. A similar lack of discrimination is apparent in the devotional work of J. du Bocage, *Le Prix de notre salut: le très précieux sang de N. S. Jésus-Christ* (Paris 1970), 100ff, and in the travelogue of D. and E. Begg, *In Search of the Holy Grail and the Precious Blood* (London 1995). F. W. Faber, *The Precious Blood: Or, the Price of our Salvation* (London 1860), is almost entirely devotional in character, save for a brief historical digression at pp. 292–7. The account of Christ's relics provided by J. Bentley, *Restless Bones: The Story of Relics* (London 1985), ch. 5, is in many ways excellent, but is without references. In English and French libraries, I sought in vain for copies of either J. H. Rohling, *The Blood of Christ in Christian Literature before the Year 1000* (Washington 1932), or P. Natale da Terrinca, *La devozione al prez. Mo sangue di nostro signore Gesu Cristo* (Rome 1987). Very late in the day, I came across a reference to the studies of W. A. Volk, said to have assembled lists of more than 220 medieval relics of the blood, published in a periodical *Il Sangue della redenzione* (1973–5), which I have likewise been unable to obtain but which is noticed by Volk in his article 'La festa liturgica del preziosissimo sangue', *SA*, IV part 3 (1984), 1504.

77 Braulio of Saragossa, Letter 42, in Migne, *PL*, LXXX 687–90, and in translation by C. W. Barlow, *Iberian Fathers Volume 2: Braulio of Saragossa, Fructuosus of Braga*, Catholic University of America, The Fathers of the Church LXIII (Washington 1969), 88–95, referring specifically to Jerome's Letter 108 and his report of the blood stain at Jerusalem. For brief commentary, see C. H. Lynch, *Saint Braulio, Bishop of Saragossa (631–651), His Life and Writings* (Washington 1938), 95–105.

78 The inscription itself survives only in part, and refers merely to … *cruore domini: Inscriptiones Hispaniae Christianae*, ed. E. Hübner (Berlin 1871), 56–7 no. 175, whence Frolow, *Vraie Croix*, 194 no. 65; D. Mazzoleni, 'Il Sangue di Cristo nell'epigrafia cristiana greca e latina', *SA*, III

Thereafter, nothing more is heard for a century and a half, until, around the year 804, a further portion of the Holy Blood was discovered at Mantua in northern Italy. All that we know of this discovery is that it is said to have excited the interest of Charlemagne who requested an investigation by Pope Leo III.[79] However, a blood relic, supposedly the same as that unearthed in 804, was to be rediscovered in the 1040s, translated again in 1354 and remains even today amongst the most precious relics of the church of Mantua.[80] At a later stage it was to be claimed that the Mantuan relic formed part of the treasure of Longinus, the Roman soldier who had attended Christ's Passion. However, there is nothing in the earliest accounts of the discovery of 804 to substantiate this claim, which may, as we shall see, reflect a later phase of devotion to the cult of Longinus. More likely, the discovery at Mantua represents an echo of the miraculous blood of Beirut, publicized twenty years earlier. It may even be that the blood of Mantua was originally claimed as no more than an effluvial relic, that only later came to be advertised as the literal blood of Christ.

As at Mantua, the Emperor Charlemagne appears as a leading figure in the account devised towards the middle of the tenth century by the monks of Reichenau to explain their possession of a crucifix containing a portion of the Holy Blood. According to the monks, this crucifix had been one of several relics of the Passion sent to Charlemagne by 'Azan, prefect of the city of Jerusalem', including a portion of the Holy Blood in an onyx ampoule, the jewel encrusted crucifix *continens cruorem Christi per quatuor partes inclusum*, a fragment of the True Cross, one of the nails, a thorn from the Crown of Thorns and a portion of the Holy Sepulchre.[81] The crucifix is said to have been granted to the monks of Reichenau in 923,

part 3 (1983), 1493–1504, esp. 1502–3. The missing letters which preceded these words might have altered the entire meaning of the phrase, for example by suggesting that the blood was merely a stain upon some other object. Mazzoleni suggests that it may have referred merely to a eucharistic relic.

[79] *Annales regni francorum . . . qui dicuntur annales Laurissenses maiores et Einhardi*, ed. F. Kurze (Hannover 1895) 119, whence Ademar de Chabannes, *Chronique*, ed. J. Chavanon (Paris 1897), 94; *Recueil des historiens des Gaules et de la France*, ed. M. Bouquet and others, 24 vols. (Paris 1738–1904), V 365 (*sub anno* 803), 374, also noted in C. Baronius, *Annales ecclesiastici*, 12 vols. (Cologne 1601–8), IX cols. 634–5, and by the fifteenth-century Mantuan chronicle, 'Breve chronicon monasterii Mantuani sancti Andree di Antonio Nerli (AA. 800–1431)', in L. A. Muratori, *Rerum italicarum scriptores*, new edn ed. G. Carducci and V. Fiorini, vol. XXIV part 13 (Città di Castello 1908) 3–4, with a valuable footnote at p. 3.

[80] *Mantova: la storia*, ed. G. Coniglio, L. Mazzoldi, R. Giusti *et al.*, 3 vols. (Mantua 1959–63), II 16–18, with a valuable bibliography at 55–7 nn 50–6.

[81] 'Ex translatione sanguinis domini', ed. D. G. Waitz, *MGH Scriptores*, IV 444–9, from an eleventh-century MS, re-edited with illustrations and much incidental detail by W. Berschin and T. Klüppel, *Die Reichenauer Heiligblut-Reliquie*, Reichenauer Texte und Bilder I (Stuttgart 1999).

6   Reichenau, the reliquary cross, Byzantine, possibly tenth century
(Reichenau Abbey)

and was undoubtedly in their possession by 950, when it is referred to in a diploma of the Emperor Otto I as the *sanctam crucem in qua sanguis domini Iesu Christi continetur.*[82] The cross itself still survives and has been identified as the work of Byzantine craftsmen, suggesting that its accompanying relics may have originated not as the legend would have it in the Holy Land, but in Constantinople.[83] Again, it is tempting to suggest that the blood of Reichenau, like that of Mantua, was originally claimed as no more than an effluvial relic, related to the blood of Beirut. Only later did it come to be misrepresented as a historical survival from the time of the Crucifixion.

In due course the legend of Reichenau may have supplied the model for a similar wonder-working cross that makes its first appearance at Lucca around the middle of the eleventh century. This, the so-called *Volto Santo*, was destined to become one of the best-known images in Christendom, supposedly carved by Nicodemus, one of the attendants at Christ's deposition, and smuggled out of the Holy Land first to Luni on the western coast of Italy and then to Lucca, carried there by a ship that steered to Italy from the Holy Land of its own accord.[84] The cross of Lucca may well reflect a conscious desire to emulate, indeed to better, the relics at Reichenau. Whereas the Reichenau cross contained a quadripartite relic of the Holy Blood, the *Volto Santo* is said to have enclosed not only a portion of the blood, but a quarter part of the Crown of Thorns, a nail from the cross, the handkerchief (*sudarium*) that Christ had worn around his neck, and clippings from his hair and (finger) nails (*unguibus*) taken by the Virgin Mary and tied up in her

---

[82] 'Annales Augiensis', ed. G. H. Pertz, *MGH Scriptores*, I 68; 'Herimanni Augiensis Chronicon', ed. G. H. Pertz, *MGH Scriptores*, V 112. For Otto's diploma, see *Die Urkunden der Deutschen Könige und Kaiser*, ed. T. Sickel *et al.*, *MGH Diplomata*, I 198–9 no. 116, a reference which I owe to Henry Mayr-Harting.

[83] A. Manser and K. Beyerle, 'Aus dem liturgischen Leben der Reichenau', in *Die Kultur der Abtei Reichenau*, ed. K. Beyerle, 2 vols. (Munich 1925), I 361–78, with illustrations at 373 and II 1244. See also Frolow, *Vraie Croix*, 205–6 no. 75/3, where it is suggested that the surviving crucifix dates from as late as the twelfth or thirteenth century. Manser and Beyerle note that the legendary account of the relic's dispatch to Reichenau reflects a genuine diplomatic exchange recorded in Einhard's life of Charlemagne and the annals of Lorsch.

[84] For the various accounts of the relic's discovery and transmission to Lucca, see J.-C. Schmitt, 'Cendrillon crucifiée. A propos du "Volto Santo" de Lucques', *Miracles, prodiges et merveilles au Moyen Age: XXVe congrès de la Société de l'enseignement supérieur public* (Paris 1995), 241–69, citing an extensive literature in German and Italian, including the various essays assembled as *Lucca, Il Volto Santo e la Civiltà Medioevale: Atti convegno internazionale di Studi* (Lucca 1984), and the largely art-historical work of G. Schürer and J. M. Ritz, *Sankt Kümmernis und Volto Santo*, Forschungen zur Volkskunde XIII–XV (Dusseldorf 1934), 117ff, printing the legend at 127–33. For an account in English, see D. M. Webb, 'The Holy Face of Lucca', *Anglo-Norman Studies* 9 (1987), 227–37.

veil.[85] Given the general association between blood relics and devotion to the eucharist, it is interesting to note that by the late twelfth century pilgrims to Lucca were expected to show special devotion to the *Volto Santo* at the elevation of the host during mass.[86] The image appears to have enjoyed a particular vogue in Normandy – its first certain appearance comes in the famous oath of William Rufus 'By the Holy Face of Lucca' – which in turn may help to explain the appearance before 1120 of a portion of the Holy Blood at the Norman Abbey of Fécamp, again associated with a miraculous and unpiloted sea journey from the Holy Land.[87] The earliest version of the Fécamp legend, composed *c.* 1090, makes no reference to the true blood of Christ, but deals instead with a eucharistic miracle in which a Norman priest named Isaac discovered, after celebrating mass, that the bread and wine had been converted into real flesh and blood. These miraculous sacraments he deposited at Fécamp.[88] In origin, this particular eucharistic miracle may be related to

[85] D. Barsocchini, *Ragionamento sopra il Volto Santo di Lucca* (Lucca 1844), which at pp. 53–6 prints the legendary account of the relic's reception, of which there is a further copy in BL MS Additional 35112 fos. 18r–20r, a twelfth-century MS from St Martin Tournai. This MS contains various stories of bleeding images, including the Beirut icon, at fos. 20r–11r, 87r–90v. For further commentary, see A. Pedemonte, 'Richerche sulla primitiva forma iconografica del Volto Santo', *Atti della reale accademica Lucchese di scienze, lettere ed arti* new series 5 (1942), 117–44, esp. 138–9, where the list of the contents of the secret compartment is dated to the 1070s; F. Barlow, *William Rufus* (London 1983), 116–18. The legend claims that the relic arrived at Luni in the late eighth century and that one of the two ampoules of the Holy Blood, retained by the bishop of Luni, was translated to the church of Sarzana in 1204.

[86] See Gervase of Tilbury, 'Otia Imperialia', in *Scriptores rerum Brunsvicensium illustrationi inservientes*, ed. G. W. Leibnitz, 3 vols. (Hannover 1707–11), I 967–8, which preserves a series of prayers for the *Volto Santo*, including one to be used at the elevation of the host. In general, Gervase, who had close personal contacts with Italy, is one of the best-informed writers on the image's history and appearance, specifically referring to its inclusion of a relic of the Holy Blood, but claiming that it only left Jerusalem in the time of Pippin and Charlemagne, removed from the house of Seleucius at Jerusalem by a French bishop named Gilfredus, and thereafter shipped miraculously from Joppa. Gervase claims personally to have seen the ampoule of blood preserved in the castle at Sarzana, to which it had been temporarily removed by the bishop of Luni, in flight from his parishioners.

[87] There is an extensive literature on the Fécamp relic. See, most recently, R. Herval, 'En Marge de la légende du Précieux-Sang – Luques – Fécamp – Glastonbury', in *L'Abbaye Bénédictine de Fécamp, ouvrage scientifique du XIIIe centenaire 658–1958*, 4 vols. (Fécamp 1959–63), I 105–26, 359–61, and, although extremely speculatively, C. Beaune, 'Les Ducs, le roi et le Saint Sang', *Saint-Denis et la royauté: études offertes à Bernard Guenée*, ed. F. Autrand, C. Gauvard and J.-M. Moeglin (Paris 1999), 711–32. For the possibility that the image of Lucca also provided the model for the legend of the cross of Bermondsey, supposedly washed up on the banks of the river Thames in 1117, see R. Graham, 'The Priory of La Charité-sur-Loire and the Monastery of Bermondsey', *Journal of the British Archaeological Association* 2nd series 32 (1926), 174–7, which also notes the existence of a chapel in London dedicated to the image of Lucca by 1434, and see also *The Waltham Chronicle*, ed. L. Watkiss and M. Chibnall (Oxford 1994), p. xv, for further English connections.

[88] Migne, *PL*, CLI 717–18, with further early references cited by A. Legris, 'Le Précieux Sang de Fécamp', *Revue catholique de Normandie* 24 (1915), 278–82. As late as the 1180s, Robert de Torigni

a wider resistance to the teachings of Berengar of Tours and his denial
of the real presence at the mass: a resistance spearheaded in Normandy
from the 1040s onwards by abbot John of Fécamp and Maurilius archbishop of Rouen, a former monk of Fécamp.[89] Between 1090 and 1120,
however, the legend was rewritten, quite possibly to provide Fécamp
with a relic sufficiently prestigious to support the Abbey's claims to inde-
pendence from the authority of the archbishops of Rouen.[90] In this new
version Isaac is no longer described as a Christian priest, but becomes
instead the nephew of Nicodemus, the first-century Jew who is supposed
to have collected the blood of Christ after the Crucifixion. Various other
details found in the earlier legend, and in the legend of Lucca, were rear-
ranged to form an account in which the Holy Blood floated miraculously
from the Holy Land to Normandy, embedded in the trunk of a fig tree.[91]

Dating from much the same time as the relics at Lucca and Fécamp,
from *c.* 1100 the Abbey of Weingarten in Bavaria also laid claim to a
portion of Christ's blood. According to the Weingarten legend, this
relic sprang ultimately from the treasure of Mantua, first unearthed
around 804 and rediscovered in the time of Pope Leo IX (1048–54),
probably in 1048.[92] As we have seen, the circumstances of the original

refers to the eucharistic relic at Fécamp rather than to any historical portion of Christ's blood,
and a eucharistic relic was still on display as late as the seventeenth century, by then treated as
a relic independent of the Holy Blood: Torigni, 'Chronica', in *Chronicles of the Reigns of Stephen,
Henry II and Richard I*, ed. R. Howlett, 4 vols., Rolls Series (London 1885–9), IV 296–7; A.-P.
Leroux, *Une tapisserie du Précieux Sang de Fécamp* (Fécamp 1927), 64.

[89] For the Norman resistance to Berengar, see D. Bates, *Normandy before 1066* (London 1982),
203–4.

[90] J.-F. Lemarignier, *Etude sur les privilèges d'exemption et de juridiction ecclésiastique des abbayes Normandes
depuis les origines jusqu'en 1140*, Archives de la France monastique XLIV (1937), 198–200.

[91] Fécamp's claim to *custodia sanguinis domini Iesu humati a Nicodemo* is first recorded by Baldric of
Dol, writing *c.* 1120: A. du Monstier, *Neustria Pia* (Rouen 1663), 320, whereafter a plethora
of legends developed, for which see O. Kajava, 'Etudes sur deux poèmes français relatifs à
l'abbaye de Fécamp', *Annales academiae scientiarum fennicae* series B 21 (Helsinki 1928), 21–120; A.
Langfors, 'Histoire de l'abbaye de Fécamp', *Annales academiae scientiarum fennicae* series B 22 part 1
(Helsinki 1928); *Gallia Christiana in provincias ecclesiasticas distributa*, 16 vols. (Paris 1715–1865), XI
204; G. Le Hule, *Le Thresor ou abbrégé de l'histoire de l'abbaye de Fescamp*, ed. A. Alexandre (Fécamp
1893). Leroux de Lincy, *Essai historique et littéraire sur l'abbaye de Fécamp* (Rouen 1840), esp. 177–85,
186–7, preserves the liturgy of the Fécamp blood, together with a description of 1682 of its
pyramid-shaped reliquary. It is the Fécamp legends, rather than any genuine claim to possess
the Holy Blood, that underlie the satirical account by the sixteenth-century Huguenot, Henri
Estienne, *Apologie pour Herodote ou traité de la conformité des merveilles anciennes avec les modernes*, 3 vols.
(The Hague 1735), III 230–3, according to which the Abbey of Bec was named after the beak
of a bird via which Nicodemus dispatched a portion of Christ's blood from the Holy Land to
Normandy.

[92] For the date 1048, see the annals of Aosta, 'Annales Augustani a. 973–1104', ed. G. H. Pertz,
MGH Scriptores, III 126: *Sanguis domini, ut ferebant, Mantuae invenitur*. The later chronicle of S. Andrea
at Mantua dates the rediscovery to 1049: 'Breve Chronicon', in Muratori, *Rerum Italicarum
scriptores*, new edn, XXIV part 13 pp. 4–5.

discovery of 804 are shrouded in obscurity. It is the stories circulated by the monks of Weingarten, after 1100, that provide our earliest certain proof that the blood of Mantua was being advertised as part of the treasure of St Longinus, a figure who in legend had come to combine the persons of two men treated as distinct individuals in the synoptic Gospels: the centurion who had attended the Crucifixion, and the soldier whose lance had pierced Christ's side. The association of the relics of Mantua and Weingarten with Longinus may well reflect the peculiar reverence accorded in the Ottonian Reich to the Holy Lance, that most precious relic acquired by Henry I in the 920s and carried into battle by successive kings and emperors.[93] Liutprand of Cremona, our earliest witness, describes the Ottonian lance as being fashioned for the Emperor Constantine and decorated with nails from Christ's Cross.[94] In Germany it was known as the Lance of St Maurice, a Roman centurion supposedly martyred in Switzerland in the late third century. It may be that this represents a sensitivity to the claims of Byzantium, since it was the Byzantine emperors who claimed to possess the true lance of Longinus, one of the relics deposited in Constantinople by St Helena.[95] None the less, in popular tradition the Ottonian lance was identified with the lance carried by Longinus at the time of Christ's Passion, and hence could easily have become associated with the Mantuan cult of St Longinus. It is suggestive, for example, that in 933, shortly after his acquisition of the lance, Henry I fought his decisive battle against the Magyars at Riade on 15 March, the feast day of St Longinus.[96] According to the Weingarten legend, Longinus' treasure at Mantua included carefully separated portions of the blood and water that had flowed from Christ's side. Part of the blood was given to the Emperor Henry III, from whom it descended to Baldwin count of Flanders and via Baldwin's

---

[93] For the lance see W. Holtzmann, *König Heinrich I und die Hl. Lanze* (Bonn 1947); P. E. Schramm, *Herrschaftszeichen und Staatssymbolik*, Schriften der MGH XIII, 3 vols. (Stuttgart 1954–6), II 492–537. For the conflicting hagiographies of Longinus in the Latin and Greek churches, see *Acta SS: March*, II 376–90; *Bibliotheca sanctorum*, ed. F. Caraffa *et al.*, 12 vols. (Rome 1961–70), VIII 89–95. Further, apocryphal, details are recorded from the Mantuan tradition by I. Donesmondi, *Dell'Istoria ecclesiastica di Mantova*, 2 parts (Mantua 1612–16), I 1–21.

[94] Liutprand, 'Antapodosis' 4.23–4, in Migne, *PL*, CXXXVI 868–9.

[95] S. Runciman, 'The Holy Lance Found at Antioch', *Analecta Bollandiana* 68 (1950), 199–200, 203–4. Writing in the twelfth century, William of Malmesbury claims that the lance that had pierced Christ's side and the *vexillum* or standard of St Maurice had both belonged to Charlemagne, and that they were presented in the 920s by Hugh Capet to King Athelstan of England. The evidence for such a gift is reviewed by L. H. Loomis, 'The Holy Relics of Charlemagne and King Athelstan: The Lances of Longinus and St Maurice', *Speculum* 25 (1950), 437–56.

[96] H. M. Schaller, 'Der heilige Tag als Termin in mittelalterlicher Staatsakte', *Deutsches Archiv für Erforschung des Mittelalters* 30 (1974), 17, drawn to my attention by Henry Mayr-Harting.

step-daughter Judith to her husbands, Tostig earl of Northumbria, and Welf IV duke of Bavaria. Welf is said to have deposited the relic at Weingarten at the time of his departure for the Holy Land in 1101.[97]

Yet another blood relic is supposed to have arrived in Europe as a gift to Vilhilda, wife of duke Henry of Bavaria from Irene, wife of the Byzantine Emperor John Comnenus (1118–43). Once again, the relic is said to have formed part of a treasure enclosed in a crucifix, containing not only three rags soaked in the blood of Christ (*sanguis naturalis de corpore Christi effusus in tribus panniculis conglutinatus*), but relics of the hair and raiment of Christ and his mother, part of the True Cross, the tears that flowed *de corde Mariae matris Christi*, the flower that Mary had carried at the time of the Annunciation, relics of St Augustine and St Katherine, of the hair and beard of St John the Evangelist, and a further three rags soaked in the blood of St John the Baptist. This entire collection is said to have passed into the possession of Vilhilda's daughter Judith, the wife of duke Frederick II of Swabia (1105–47), who thereafter wore the Cross and relics around his neck in all his battles. Judith and Frederick eventually deposited their treasure at the Abbey of Cappenberg near Lippe in Westphalia, at some time after 1127, in exchange for the surrender of various castles by the Abbey's founders, St Godfrey and his brother count Otto.[98]

Of a later date, but claiming to record events of the ninth and tenth centuries, the chronicle of Eberhard of Gandersheim (*c.* 1216), reworked in the sixteenth century by Henry Bodo, claims that at the coronation of the Emperor Arnulph in 896, the Pope hung a cross around the Emperor's neck containing a portion of the Holy Blood, sent as a gift to Rome from the Byzantine Emperor Constantine, possibly to be identified as Constantine VI (780–97).[99] Bodo's story forms part of a more extended

[97] 'De inventione et translatione sanguinis domini', ed. G. Waitz, *MGH Scriptores*, XV part II 921–3, and see *Mantova: la storia*, ed. Coniglio, II 17; A. Haag, *Sanguis Christi in terra vindicatus seu discussio de sanctissimo sanguine . . . in imperiali monasterio Vinearum ultra sex saecula religiosissime adservato* (Ravensburg 1758), which is mostly taken up with a theological defence of relics of the Holy Blood, not merely the relic at Weingarten. For Judith, see M. Harrsen, 'The Countess Judith of Flanders and the Library of Weingarten Abbey', *Papers of the Bibliographical Society of America* 24 (1930), 1–13; E. van Houts, 'The Norman Conquest through European Eyes', *English Historical Review* 110 (1995), 838–9; D. Ó Riain-Raedel, 'Edith, Judith, Matilda: The Role of Royal Ladies in the Propagation of the Continental Cult', *Oswald: Northumbrian King to European Saint*, ed. C. Stancliffe and E. Cambridge (Stamford 1995), 216–22.

[98] 'Vita beati Godefridi' ch. 11, in *Acta SS: January*, I 844, whence the version printed as 'Vita Godefridi comitis Capenbergensis', ed. P. Jaffé, *MGH Scriptores*, XII 529–30.

[99] 'Eberhards Reimchronik von Gandersheim', ed. L. Weiland, *MGH Deutsche Chroniken*, II 407–8, 421; Henry Bodo, 'Syntagma', in *Rerum Germanicorum tomi III*, ed. H. Meibom, 3 vols. (Helmstadt 1688), II 486, 488, 492.

narrative in which Gandersheim is said to have received two relics of the Holy Blood, from Charlemagne's great-grandson, King Louis II (d. 875) and from the Emperor Arnulph. Part of this treasure is said to have been surrendered before 948 to Henry, the brother of the Emperor Otto I, but a relic of the Holy Blood continued to be venerated at Gandersheim throughout the Middle Ages, the Abbey's high altar being rededicated in its honour in 1350.[100]

The blood relics of Mantua, Reichenau, Lucca, Fécamp, Weingarten, Cappenberg and Gandersheim are by no means the only examples of their kind to be found in western Europe by the year 1200. They are unusual only in that they gave rise to detailed accounts of their reception and provenance at a fairly early date. In most cases these legends state that the portion preserved at a particular church represented only part of a more considerable store of Christ's blood, perhaps in the hope that this would explain to sceptical pilgrims the wider dispersal of such relics. The Weingarten blood, for example, is said to have been only one of the portions acquired from Mantua; the blood at Lucca is said to have represented one of two ampoules, the other being consigned to the Cathedral of Luni and later removed to Sarzana. Elsewhere, lists of the relics of St Peter's Bamberg (1012), Weissenburg on the lower Rhine (1072), Münchsmünster (1092) and St George's Prüfening (1119), the last two in the diocese of Ratisbon, all indicate the presence of portions of the Holy Blood, for the most part deposited in these churches at the time of their consecration.[101] A Magdeburg calendar claims that a relic of the blood was brought from Italy to Magdeburg by bishop Anno of Worms, at some time between 950 and 978.[102] Since Anno had previously held office as the first abbot of St Maurice's Magdeburg, where he was succeeded from 950 to 954 by abbot Othwin, formerly a

---

[100] The surrender of part of the blood to Henry is said to have been made in return for Henry's promise to enrol his daughter, Gerberga (d.1001), as a nun at Gandersheim. For Gerberga, see H. Goetting, *Das Bistum Hildesheim I: Das Reichsunmittelbare kanonissenstift Gandersheim*, Germania Sacra neue folge VII part 1 (Berlin and New York 1973), 293–5. For the Holy Blood, listed in an inventory of the late twelfth century, and the subject of collective episcopal indulgences, from 1296, the first being subscribed at Rome by the Englishman Thomas (Wouldham), bishop of Rochester, see *ibid.*, 29–30, 44–7; J. G. Leuckfeld, *Antiquitates Gandersheimenses* (Wolfenbüttel 1709), 58–9, 65–8.

[101] Frolow, *Vraie Croix*, nos. 191, 238, 251, 310; 'Notae Weissenburgenses', ed. G. Waitz, *MGH Scriptores*, XIII 47; 'Notae Sweigo-Monasterienses', ed. O. Holder-Egger, *MGH Scriptores*, XV part 2 1073; 'Notae Pruveningenses', ed. W. Wattenbach, *MGH Scriptores*, XVII 610; 'Annales et notae Babenbergenses', ed. P. Jaffé, *ibid.*, 635.

[102] 'Annales Magdeburgenses Brevissimi', ed. O. Holder-Egger, *MGH Scriptores*, XXX part II 750: *Preciosissimus thesaurus sanguinis domini per Annonem episcopum iubente domino Ottone augusto immo annuente domino Iesu Christo ab Italia Magdaburgum translatus est*, in the time of bishop Anno (950–78).

monk of Reichenau, it may be that Magdeburg's claim to the blood was made in direct imitation of that advanced by Reichenau.[103] In 1023 Pope Benedict VIII is said to have bestowed a portion of the blood formerly held in the Lateran at Rome upon the Abbey of Monte Cassino.[104] As early as the eleventh century, inventories of the Lateran relics refer to the existence of two flasks (*ampullae*) of the blood and water that had flowed from Christ's side, stored in the Lateran basilica where they continued to be displayed throughout the Middle Ages.[105] The Lateran relic may have originated at Mantua, from whose store of the Holy Blood Pope Leo IX is said to have demanded a portion in 1053, although according to Gerald of Wales, the blood of the Lateran was publicized in the 1190s, not as the true blood of Christ, but as the effluvia from a maltreated image.[106] In the 1070s the monks of Charroux near Poitiers claimed to have rediscovered a blood-smeared vase containing a relic of Christ's foreskin, supposedly granted to them by Charlemagne who had acquired it as a miraculous gift from heaven.[107] Part of the vase *in quo Longinus sanguinem domini suscepit*

---

[103] For Anno and Othwin, elected bishop of Hildesheim in 954, see Claude, *Geschichte des Erzbistums Magdeburg*, I 38–9, 41.

[104] 'Leonis Marsicani et Petri diaconi chronica monasterii Casinensis', ed. W. Wattenbach, *MGH Scriptores*, VII 720n.

[105] *Codice topografico della città di Roma*, ed. R. Valentini and G. Zucchetti, 4 vols., Fonti per la Storia d'Italia LXXXI, LXXXVIII, XC–XCI (Rome 1940–53), III 337, which also refers to a blood relic of John the Baptist, with commentary and details from an earlier recension of this list by H. E. J. Cowdrey, 'Pope Urban II and the Idea of the Crusade', *Studi Medievali* 3rd series 36 (1995), 732–3, 742 no. 54. For a later reference to the Lateran blood, see L. Wadding, *Annales minorum seu trium ordinum a S. Francisco institutorum*, new edition continued by J. M. Fonseca *et al.*, 25 vols. (Rome 1731–1933), VIII 60–1, and for blood relics preserved in others of the churches of Rome, possibly all derived from the Lateran relic which in turn was acquired from Mantua, see Barbier de Montault, *Œuvres*, VII 524–5. In exile at Avignon in the fourteenth century, the Popes appear to have possessed at least three reliquaries containing portions of Christ's blood: R. Lentsch, 'Dans le trésor des papes d'Avignon, la vaisselle liturgique contenant le sang du Christ', *Le Sang au Moyen Age*, ed. Faure, 451–2. Pfaff, *New Liturgical Feasts*, 118, 120, 122, 127, notes that the feasts of the dedication of the Lateran and the image of Beirut were both celebrated on the same day, suggesting that the Lateran blood relic, like so many others, including that of Mantua, may have begun as an effluvial relic, related to the miracle of Beirut, later misrepresented as the literal blood of Christ.

[106] *Mantova: la storia*, ed. Coniglio, II 17; *Giraldi Cambrensis opera*, ed. Brewer, II 103.

[107] For the particular relic at Charroux, see *Chartes et documents pour servir à l'histoire de l'abbaye de Charroux*, ed. D. P. de Monsabert, Archives historiques du Poitou XXXIX (1910), 29–41, 318–19; L.-A. Vigneras, 'L'abbaye de Charroux et la légende du pèlerinage de Charlemagne', *Romanic Review*, 32 (1941), 121–8; G. Chapeau, 'Les grandes reliques de l'abbaye de Charroux', *Bulletins de la Société des antiquaires de l'Ouest* 3rd series 8 (1931), 115–28; Bentley, *Restless Bones*, 138–40, and for a description of a reliquary which may once have housed the Abbey's treasure, see A. Brouillet, 'Description des reliquaires trouvés dans l'ancienne abbaye de Charroux (Vienne) le 9 août 1856', *Bulletins de la Société des antiquaires de l'Ouest* 8 (1859), 177 and plates 1–3. Yet another account of Charlemagne's legendary visit to Jerusalem mentions that the patriarch offered him a relic of the blood of St Stephen: *Itinéraires à Jérusalem et descriptions de la Terre Sainte aux XIe*,

is said to have been amongst the relics of Petershausen in the diocese of Constance in 1134, whilst in 1147, at the consecration of the church of St Paulinus at Trier, Pope Eugenius III is said to have disposed of yet another portion of Christ's blood.[108] Several early reliquaries, of uncertain provenance, bear inscriptions suggesting that at one time they contained blood relics.[109] Altogether, it is clear that by the year 1200 the churches of western Europe, and in particular those of Germany and the Rhineland, were very nearly awash with relics of Christ's blood.

We shall see in due course that the very idea of possessing portions of the Holy Blood was considered anathema by many theologians. Be that as it may, on a more practical level, such relics were claimed so widely and by so many different churches that it must have seemed improbable, even to the most sympathetic observer, that all of them could be genuine. The Middle Ages supply many examples of 'multiple relics' where a particular object, the head of St John the Baptist or the body of St Mary Magdalene, was claimed by more than one, sometimes by several churches. The apologists of such relics might argue that through God's omnipotence all things could be accomplished, so that a saint, if he so wished, could multiply his bodily remains to suit the needs of more than one earthly congregation.[110] None the less, in the Middle Ages as now, this was not a line of argument that commanded universal respect. With the Holy Blood, the quantities involved were not so large — most accounts, when they describe the appearance of the blood, speak merely of single drops, dried and coagulated. Like the Cross of Christ, the Holy Blood circulated in quantities that were not in themselves suspicious.

XIIe et XIIIe siècles, ed. H. Michelant and G. Raynaud (Geneva 1882), 5. I have been unable to consult A. V. Müller, *Die 'hochheilige Vorhaut Christi' im Kult und in der Theologie der Papstkirche* (Berlin 1907), which apparently supplies much of the information reviewed by Bentley. For a scurrilous but useful anti-clerical tract on this theme, noting several further examples, see A. S. Morin, *Le Culte du sacre prépuce de Jésus*, La documentation antireligieuse LXXIII (Herblay 1939).

[108] Frolow, *Vraie Croix*, nos. 323, 335; 'Notae dedicationis S. Paulini Treverensis', ed. H. V. Saverland, *MGH Scriptores*, XV part 2 1277; 'Casus monasterii Petrihusensis', ed. O. Abel and L. Weiland, *MGH Scriptores*, XX 670, and for Trier see also Heyen, *Das Erzbistum Trier I*, 339, 343–4, where by the fifteenth century the church was claiming only a piece of linen splashed with Christ's blood, not the blood itself. However, the Abbey of St Martin at Trier was by the same time laying claim to a portion of the True Cross *in qua adhuc apparent gutte coagulate palpabiles redemptoris nostri*, supported by archiepiscopal indulgences: *Pro abbatia beati Martini Treverensis ... de sanguine Christi corporali super terram relicto* (Cologne 1514), a tract of which there is a possibly unique copy in Paris, Bibliothèque nationale imprimés Res H-1 026(2).

[109] Frolow, *Vraie Croix*, nos. 166, 272–3, 331, 341; Barbier de Montault, *Œuvres*, VII 525–8.

[110] For examples of the multiplication of relics, see P. J. Geary, *Furta Sacra: Thefts of Relics in the Central Middle Ages* (Princeton 1978), 141; R. C. Finucane, *Miracles and Pilgrims: Popular Beliefs in Medieval England* (London 1977), 29–30.

Rather, with the blood as with the True Cross, it was the number and the wide distribution of such claims, not the individual quantities involved, that most excited scepticism. 'Scepticism' is itself a loaded term. In the present context, it should not imply the sort of rationalist mockery that flourished after the Reformation, and especially from the eighteenth-century Enlightenment. However, as we shall see, it is clear that there were many who doubted the authenticity of the relics of Christ's blood and whose doubts are recorded from a very early date. Even the very first of our references to the Holy Blood – that contained within the letter of bishop Braulio of Saragossa written in the 640s – carries with it the implication that such relics were likely to test the credulity of even the most pious of the Christian faithful.

The various legends employed to explain the miraculous survival of the Holy Blood share a number of common features. In particular, those of Mantua, Fécamp, Weingarten and Lucca draw in various ways upon the apocryphal *Acts of Pontius Pilate*, also known as the *Gospel of Nicodemus*. It is this apocryphal text, in circulation from at least the fourth century, that had first given a name to the centurion Longinus and had equated him with the soldier whose Lance pierced Christ's side; an important component of the legends of Mantua and Weingarten.[111] In addition, Nicodemus himself figures prominently in the legends of Fécamp and Lucca as the man responsible for abstracting a portion of the blood before Christ's burial. At Lucca, it was claimed that Nicodemus had carved an image of Christ after his deposition from the Cross; a motif that already occurs in the legend of the icon of Beirut, said to have been that same image carved by Nicodemus, that gave forth a miraculous flow of blood on being subjected to ritual humiliation by the Jews.[112] Once again we are brought up against the possibility that many of the supposed relics of the Holy Blood actually began their existence as portions or imitations of the effluvial blood of Beirut, and that only in the course of time did these effluvial relics become confused with, or deliberately misrepresented as the literal blood of the Passion. This may well have been the case at Mantua, Reichenau, Weingarten and for all those other relics, such as the blood in the Lateran, that were derived from them. The Lateran relic was advertised by Gerald of Wales merely as an effluvial relic. Elsewhere, a similar confusion arose between the literal, historic, blood of Christ and the remains of eucharistic miracles. At Fécamp, for

---

[111] *The Apocryphal New Testament*, trans. M. R. James, 2nd edn (Oxford 1953), 113, 155.
[112] For the introduction of the Nicodemus story into the fully fledged legend of Beirut, see Pfaff, *New Liturgical Feasts*, 117–18.

example, there seems little doubt that what had begun as a eucharistic relic was subsequently misrepresented as a portion of the Holy Blood, though here again, the monks of Fécamp turned to the legend of Beirut, and in particular to the figure of Nicodemus, to add verisimilitude to their account. The emphasis placed in most of the early legends upon Nicodemus, or on occasion upon Longinus, derives ultimately from the apocryphal *Acts of Pontius Pilate*. Although these latter have nothing direct to say either of Christ's blood or of the carving of any image, they none the less afford a far greater prominence to the immediate aftermath of Christ's burial than that allowed by the four evangelists. In particular they insert a long account of the tribulations suffered by Joseph of Arimathaea and Nicodemus, the two men who according to St John took responsibility for preparing Christ's body .[113] *The Acts* were widely known in the Middle Ages, and were translated into both Anglo-Saxon and Middle English.[114] As we shall see, they were to appear again in the legendary account devised to explain the origins of the Holy Blood at Westminster, although it is probably mere coincidence that the Westminster monks should themselves have been in possession of copies of the apocryphal *Acts* in both the Anglo-Saxon and the Middle English translations.[115]

By the end of the twelfth century at least twenty churches in western Europe claimed to possess portions of Christ's blood. Over the next two decades the number of such claims was to undergo an enormous increase, spurred on by the sack of Constantinople in 1204 and the wholesale export of Byzantine relics to the West. The precise date at which the Byzantine emperors first laid claim to a relic of Christ's blood remains uncertain. A Greek text, surviving from around the year 900, claims that a portion of the Holy Blood was collected at the Crucifixion by a man named James from whom it passed to a hermit, St Barypsaba. It is possible that it was Barypsaba's treasure to which the emperors of Byzantium were later to lay claim.[116] However, our evidence here is far from sure and depends all too heavily upon the dating of a single manuscript. From perhaps even earlier than the legend of Barypsaba, a commentary on the

---

[113] *Ibid.*, 105–15, 117.

[114] See R. Wülcker, *Das Evangelium Nicodemi in der abendländischen Literatur* (Paderborn 1872).

[115] *Medieval Libraries of Great Britain: A List of Surviving Books*, ed. N. R. Ker, 2nd edn (London 1964), 196, noting London, Sion College MS Arc. L. 40.2/E. 25 (s. xiv–xv). An unnumbered fragment of the Anglo-Saxon translation at Westminster Abbey Library has been drawn to my attention by Richard Mortimer.

[116] *Acta SS: September*, III 494–501, esp. 498–501 from a manuscript in the Vatican, Codex Graec. 1589, dated to the early tenth century by C. Giannelli, *Codices Vaticani graeci: codices 1485–1683* (Vatican 1950), 211–15. For Barypsaba, see also *Bibliotheca sanctorum*, II 785.

liturgy of the altar attributed to Germanos I patriarch of Constantinople (715–17) contains an account of the burial of Christ by Joseph and Nicodemus, followed by a metaphorical equation between the liturgical chalice and a cup which is said to have gathered up the blood shed from Christ's pierced side, from his hands and from his feet. There is no direct link here between Nicodemus, Joseph and the Holy Blood, although the conjunction of burial, blood and the image of the cup is undoubtedly remarkable.[117] Elsewhere, the *Book of Ceremonies*, compiled under the emperor Constantine VII (913–59), makes no mention of a blood relic whilst laying great stress upon other relics of the Passion, such as the Lance and the True Cross that had an integral role to play in the devotions of Easter week.[118] Nor is there any reference to the Holy Blood amongst the relics of the Passion described in a letter from the emperor Alexius Comnenus to count Robert of Flanders, supposedly written between 1088 and 1097.[119] Be that as it may, from at least the mid-tenth century the chapel of the Byzantine emperors advanced a claim to possess a relic of Christ's blood. Our earliest evidence for this claim is to be found in an oration, supposedly delivered by Constantine VII to his troops at some time between 913 and 959, referring to the instruments of the Passion, the Cross, the Lance, the *titulus* (the carved inscription placed above Christ's head upon the Cross), the reed 'and the life-giving blood which flowed from the reverend side (of Christ)'.[120] Writing *c.* 1110 at the request of the Emperor Alexius, to confound the teachings of the Bogomils and other heretics, the theologian Euthymios Zigabenos asserts that, contrary to certain teachings, the Christ who suffered upon the Cross must have been more than mere shadow, 'as the blood declares which flowed from his most holy body, which even today is preserved by the Christians, which has brought healing to the sick and which by the testimony of many miracles is proved to

[117] Germanos, 'Historia ecclesiastica', in Migne, *PG*, XCVIII 421–2, and for Germanos, see *The Oxford Dictionary of Byzantium*, 3 vols. (Oxford 1991), II 846–7, noting that the 'Historia' circulated in Europe in a Latin translation by Anastasius Bibliothecarius (d. *c.* 879).
[118] *Constantin VII Porphyrogénète: le livre des cérémonies*, ed. A. Vogt, 4 vols. (Paris 1935–40), I 149–50, 153–4, 167–8, and for commentary, see H. G. Thümmel, 'Kreuze, Reliquien und Bilder im Zeremonienbuch des Konstantinos Porphyrogennetos', *Byzantinische Forschungen* 18 (1992), 119–26. For a more general study of the imperial relics, see I. Kalavrezou, 'Helping Hands for the Empire: Imperial Ceremonies and the Cult of Relics at the Byzantine Court', *Byzantine Court Culture from 829 to 1204*, ed. H. Maguire (Harvard 1997), 53–79.
[119] *Die Kreuzzugsbriefe*, ed. Hagenmeyer, 134 (Letter I).
[120] R. Vári, 'Zum historischen Exzerptenwerke des Konstantinos Porphyrogennetos', *Byzantinische Zeitschrift* 17 (1908), 83 lines 22–9, drawn to my attention and translated for me by Jonathan Shepard.

be that of Christ'.[121] If it is indeed the blood of the Passion, rather than the blood sacrament of the eucharist to which Zigabenos refers here, this would provide us with our only certain proof that the blood relic of Byzantium was held to work miracles, including miracles of healing, prior to 1204. Thereafter, no mention of the relic has been traced until the mid-twelfth century, when it appears in two English manuscripts, preserving an anonymous list of the principal churches and relics of the Holy Land followed by an inventory of the relics housed in the emperor's chapel at Constantinople. Towards the end of this inventory its author notes that 'there is shown moreover a crystal phial containing, so they say, some of the blood of Our Lord'.[122] The qualifying phrase 'so they say' (*ut dicunt*) may well imply scepticism as to the relic's authenticity. At a slightly later date, *c.* 1190, a similar English list refers to relics of the Holy Blood in the church of the Blachernai Palace and at Hagia Sophia where it was closely associated with a blood relic of the decapitated martyr St Pantoleon (d. *c.* 305), supposedly mixed with milk, the milk and blood miraculously changing place with one another each year.[123] Although these are our only certain records of the Holy Blood at Constantinople prior to the Fourth Crusade, amongst earlier western relics, the blood at Reichenau, Gandersheim and Cappenberg may well have originated in Byzantium. Certainly, in 1203 Robert of Clari reports the existence of the blood relic at Blachernai.[124]

Thereafter, with the sack of Constantinople, portions of the blood were distributed far and wide. By the 1240s the Holy Blood was to be found at Venice, Soissons, the Abbey of Pairis in Alsace, Halberstadt, Clairvaux, St Martin's at Tournai, St Alban's at Namur, Liessies, Sélincourt, St Remi

---

[121] Euthymios Zigabenos, 'Panoplia Dogmatika', tit. 28.6, in Migne, *PG*, CXXX cols. 1339 40.

[122] BL MS Cotton Claudius A iv fo. 192r (188r); Cambridge University Library MS Mm.v.29 fo. 157r: *Hec sunt reliquie que apud Constantinopolim in capella imperatoris monstrantur . . . monstratur etiam cristallina fiala in qua, ut dicunt, de sanguine domini habetur.* The same list notes a portion of the blood of St Pantoleon mixed with milk. Both copies are to be dated to some time after 1150 and both are noticed in Riant, *Exuviae*, II 211 12, which preserves further evidence, from Anthony of Novgorod (*c.* 1200) and Robert of Clari (1203), of the Blachernai relic at pp. 223, 231. One might note that the Armenian church, possibly as early as the ninth century, and the Russian church from at least the mid-twelfth century, appear to have laid claim to relics of the Holy Blood: Frolow, *Vraie Croix*, nos. 81, 341.

[123] Mercati, 'Santuari e reliquie Costantinopolitane', 136 7, 140 1, 154n. The legend of St Pantoleon states that at the time of his martyrdom, milk rather than blood gushed out from the saint's neck; *The Oxford Dictionary of Byzantium*, ed. A. P. Kazhdan et al., 3 vols. (Oxford 1991), III 1572 3. For the dispatch of a relic of Pantoleon to Henry III in the 1230s, see above p. 23.

[124] Riant, *Exuviae*, II 231: *en une fiole de cristal, grant partie de Sen Sanc.*

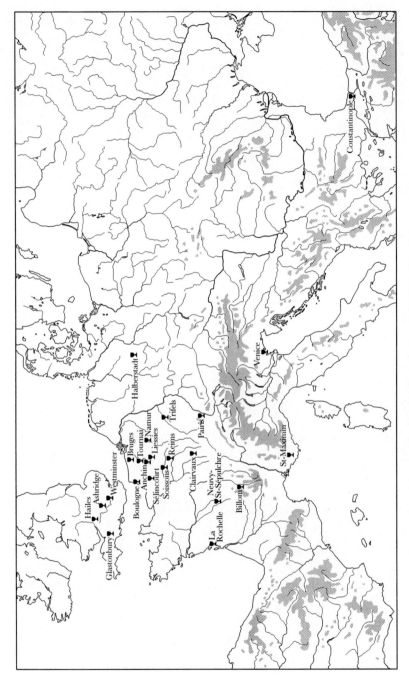

Map 2   The distribution of relics of the Holy Blood after 1204

at Rheims, the Abbey of Anchin, the chapel of the counts of Flanders and the church of St Basil at Bruges, the distribution of these relics reflecting the origins of the leaders of the Fourth Crusade.[125] In addition, the Latin Emperors of Constantinople claimed to have kept back a share of the Constantinople blood relic for themselves, only part of which was included amongst the relics of the Passion sold to Louis IX in the 1240s and deposited in the Sainte-Chapelle at Paris.[126]

From all of this it should be apparent that the portion of the Holy Blood delivered to Westminster in 1247 was by no means unique. On the contrary, it was merely one of a large number of such relics venerated in churches across Europe from the ninth century onwards. The blood of Westminster cannot even be claimed as the first such relic to have arrived in the British Isles. As early as the 1060s the Holy Blood later venerated at Weingarten is said to have belonged to Judith, wife of Tostig earl of Northumbria, whilst a list of the relics at Reading Abbey, compiled in the 1190s, before the sack of Constantinople, refers to a relic of the blood and water that flowed from Christ's side, and of the the earth where it was spilled (*Item sanguis et aqua de latere domini et de terra ubi ablutus fuit*).[127] A similar relic from a stone upon which the blood of Christ had been spilled is to be found in an inventory of treasures bequeathed to St Swithun's Winchester by bishop Henry of Blois (d. 1171).[128] Yet another portion of the blood is said to have reached Norwich Cathedral, from Fécamp, at some time in the 1170s. According to the Fécamp legend, the Holy Blood there had been deliberately hidden at the time of the Abbey's rebuilding in the eleventh century. It was rediscovered in July 1171, six months after the martyrdom of St Thomas Becket, and translated to a new shrine, a

---

[125] Huyghebaert, 'Iperius et la translation de la relique du Saint-Sang à Bruges', 147–56, provides the best account of the distribution of the blood from Constantinople, relying upon Frolow, *Vraie Croix*, nos. 459, 464, 470, 578.

[126] Gould, 'The Sequences "De sanctis reliquiis"', 326–7, 336–7 nos. 3, 6. A blood relic was still being exhibited in Constantinople as late as the fifteenth century: Ebersolt, *Sanctuaire de Byzance*, 115, 117–18. In his account of the Crucifixion, written between 1317 and 1335, Nikephorus Kallistos Xanthopoulos claims that Mary and St John collected a portion of the blood and water which flowed from Christ's side on the Cross: 'Ecclesiastical History', 1.30, in Migne, *PG*, CXLV 723–4.

[127] For the Weingarten relic, see above pp. 58–60. For Reading, see BL MS Egerton 3031 (Reading cartulary) fo. 6v; D. Bethell, 'The Making of a Twelfth-Century Relic Collection', *Popular Belief and Practice; Studies in Church History*, 8 (1972), 61–72. Besides the blood relic proper, the Reading list refers to two other, related relics: *de loco ubi factus est sudor domini sicut gutte sanguinis*, and *lapis de monte Calvarie super quem cecidit sanguis de latere domini*. I am grateful to Brian Kemp for his help with this list, of which he intends to publish an edition.

[128] E. Bishop, 'Gifts of Bishop Henry of Blois, Abbat of Glastonbury, to Winchester Cathedral', *Downside Review* (1884), reprinted in Bishop, *Liturgica Historica* (Oxford 1918), 400 no. 34: *duo philateria argentea in uno quorum habetur lapis in quem stillavit sanguis Domini*.

portion of it being carried off in a silver vase by Clement the precentor of Norwich.[129] Fécamp's fortuitous rediscovery, said to have been made by a workman who unwittingly swallowed part of the blood relic before being made aware of what he had found, suggests an attempt to distract pilgrims from the rival shrine of Canterbury, where from 1171 onwards the blood of St Thomas was being collected and consumed by numerous pilgrims.[130] Furthermore, the claim that Norwich had acquired a portion of the blood of Fécamp helps to explain why in 1247 it should have been the bishop of Norwich, master Walter of Suffield, who was chosen to deliver the sermon commemorating the delivery of the Holy Blood to Westminster. Walter's interest in the Holy Blood is confirmed by an account of the Norwich relic, according to which Walter himself gave a great silver cup to his cathedral, in which to place the crystal vase containing the Holy Blood brought from Fécamp. When Norwich

[129] Kajava, 'Études', 24, 35. This account of the translation at Fécamp occurs in at least three surviving English manuscripts: BL MS Harley 1801 fos. 4v 9v (c. 1250); Cambridge, Gonville and Caius MS 61/155 fos. 254v 66v (c. 1300), and Oxford, Magdalen College MS 53 pp. 212ff (c. 1300). Both the Harleian version (printed by Kajava) and the Oxford legend (printed below appendix 4) refer to Clement of Norwich, the Oxford MS adding significant later details. The Cambridge version, with no mention of Clement, is printed by H. Omont, 'Invention du précieux sang dans l'église de l'abbaye de Fécamp au XIIe siècle', *Bulletins de la Société de l'histoire de Normandie* 12 (1913 18), 52 66. There was undoubtedly a monk of Norwich named Clement active in the 1150s and 60s, whilst a connection between Norwich and Fécamp is provided by Herbert Losinga, prior of Fécamp before his election as bishop of Norwich (1091 1119); *English Episcopal Acta VI: Norwich 1070 1214*, ed. C. Harper-Bill (Oxford 1990), p. xxviii, nos. 102, 117. In the 1150s or 60s, the prior of Norwich wrote to the abbot of Fécamp, asking news of several Norwich monks, including Thomas the precentor, who had fled from Norwich and who, in light of the longstanding connections between Norwich and Fécamp, were suspected of taking refuge in Normandy: 'Epistulae Fiscannenses. Lettres d' amitié, de gouvernement et d' affaires (XI XIIe siècles)', ed. J. Laporte, *Revue Mabillon* 43 (1953), 27 8. For a list of others of the Norwich Cathedral relics, borrowed in the 1230s by King Henry III for his own private chapel, see *Calendar of Patent Rolls 1232 47*, 39. Prior to the translation of St William in the 1150s, the Cathedral is said to have lacked any major relic collection. A major fire in the 1170s may have provided the incentive to the Norwich monks to acquire relics from overseas. The majority of those subsequently collected were looted following a second, far more serious, fire in 1272, whereafter a new collection was installed in a special reliquary arch, built in 1278 in the north aisle of the Cathedral presbytery: Torigni, 'Chronica', in *Chronicles of the Reigns of Stephen, Henry II and Richard I*, ed. Howlett, IV 250; Thomas of Monmouth, *Life and Miracles of St William*, 117; J. R. Shines, 'The Veneration of Saints at Norwich Cathedral in the Fourteenth Century', *Norfolk Archaeology* 40 (1989), 133 44, esp. 138 40.

[130] For the invention of 1171, see Kajava, 'Études', 35, 75 7, below appendix 4. I can find nothing to substantiate the claim, repeated by several recent commentators (for example by Beaune, 'Les Ducs, le roi et le Saint Sang', 728), that in 1172 King Henry II attended the translation of the Fécamp blood relic. Elsewhere, the invention of the Holy Blood, generally dated to 1171, has been confused with Henry II's attendance at the translation of the bodies of the early dukes of Normandy at Fécamp, which undoubtedly occurred in March 1162: Langfors, 'Histoire de l'abbaye de Fécamp', 55 7, and more recently S. E. Jones, 'The Twelfth-Century Reliefs from Fécamp: New Evidence for their Dating and Original Purpose', *Journal of the British Archaeological Association* 138 (1985), 79 88.

Cathedral was destroyed by fire, in August 1272, and despite attempts by one of the monks to carry the Holy Blood to safety in the sacristy, the crystal vase was cracked and parts of the reliquary consumed by the flames. The cup, however, survived intact. The blood was removed from the cracked vase inside the cup, and rehoused in a newly made vessel, the monks noting that, as they saw it miraculously, the greater part of the blood was founded suspended of its own accord in the upper part of the old vase.[131]

Already it must be apparent that the Westminster relic laboured under several handicaps likely to affect its acceptance as a genuine relic of the Holy Blood. In particular, it was merely one amongst many such relics scattered across western Europe, few if any of which could claim to command universal acceptance as portions of the blood of Christ's Passion. Added to this, the Westminster blood came from a source, the treasury of the Holy Sepulchre in Jerusalem, that seems never before to have laid claim to such a relic. Admittedly, as we have seen, the memory of Christ's Crucifixion and the shedding of his blood played an important role in the imagery used by the church of Jerusalem in its dealings with the West. Various of the Holy Places within the church were said to be marked with the stain of Christ's blood, whilst it was from Jerusalem and Calvary that every blood relic claimed ultimately to be derived. However, at no time between the First Crusade and 1247, and indeed at no time after the dispatch of the Holy Blood to Henry III, do we have any firm evidence that the Latin church of Jerusalem laid claim to a store of Christ's blood. This in itself is hardly surprising, since in point of fact the church of Jerusalem had undergone such upheavals by the eleventh century that it was most unlikely that any holy objects could have survived there intact from the time of Christ to the arrival of the first crusaders. Both in the Catholic and the Orthodox traditions, it was accepted that the most precious of the Christological relics of Jerusalem, including

---

[131] Oxford, Magdalen College MS 53 pp. 219–20, an apparently unique account of the Norwich relic written in a hand of *c.* 1300, printed below appendix 4. The manuscript itself is a composite affair, but almost certainly of Norwich provenance. It includes a gathering, comprising the Latin Gospel of Nicodemus (pp. 169–89), and a series of brief Norwich annals (pp. 189–95), formerly part of the monastic library at Norwich: *Medieval Libraries of Great Britain*, ed. Ker, 139. The account of the Norwich blood relic follows from pp. 212–20 (as printed by Kajava, 'Etudes', 25–34, opening *Defuncto Willelmo*), as part of a new gathering (pp. 199–200), written in the same hand as a commentary by Methodius on Genesis (pp. 207–11). A second MS, formerly BL MS Cotton Vitellius D iii art. 1, may well have included a similar legend of the blood of Norwich, being listed in Thomas Smith's *Catalogue of the Manuscripts in the Cottonian Library 1696*, ed. C. G. C. Tite (London 1984) as *De fundacione abbatiae de Fiscamps . . . et de portione eiusdem sanguinis per episcopum Norwicensem advecta*, this section having been lost in the Cotton fire of 1731.

perhaps portions of the Holy Blood, had long ago been evacuated from Jerusalem itself, either to the Lateran Palace in Rome or to the city of Constantinople.[132] Of the blood relics of western Europe, all claimed to be derived from one of three basic sources: from the treasure brought by Longinus to Mantua; from the emperors of Byzantium; or, in the case of the relics of Reichenau, Lucca and Fécamp, from Jerusalem itself, but from Jerusalem long before the crusades. At Lucca and Fécamp miraculous sea crossings were used to explain the relic's journey from Jerusalem to the West. At Reichenau the blood was said to have been sent to Europe in the time of the Emperor Charlemagne, as a gift from Jerusalem's Muslim rulers; an account later echoed at Hailes, where the blood was assumed to have descended to Charlemagne from the Roman emperors of antiquity.[133] All of these accounts take it for granted that the blood had left the Holy Land long before the First Crusade.

After 1100, when Jerusalem was restored to Christian rule, there is no mention of a blood relic amongst the objects venerated in the city, or of any such relic being viewed by the many pilgrims who journeyed to the East. It was not the Holy Blood that was adopted by the crusader church as its emblem, but the Cross of Christ.[134] Likewise, in the century that followed, whenever the bishops of the Holy Land carried their relics into battle, it was not the blood of Christ that the chroniclers record, but the True Cross, the Lance of Antioch and a phial of the Virgin's milk.[135] With one exception, there is nothing to suggest that portions of the blood were dispatched from Jerusalem in the twelfth century as diplomatic gifts in the way, for example, that successive kings and patriarchs of Jerusalem

---

[132] For the Lateran relics, perhaps influential in Urban II's preaching of the First Crusade, see Cowdrey, 'Pope Urban II and the Idea of the Crusade', 733 9. For Heraclius and the supposed recovery of the True Cross, carried off to Constantinople in the seventh century, see C. Mango, 'Héraclius, Sahrvaraz et la Vraie Croix', *Travaux et mémoires* 9 (1985), 105 18. A much later tradition, reported in the 1850s by J. Mislin, *Les Saints Lieux, pèlerinage à Jérusalem*, 3 vols. (Paris 1858), II 396, reports that in 1099 the first crusaders took possession of a great gold vase weighing more than 200 marks, previously suspended from the centre of the dome of the mosque of Omar, and 'said' to contain 'ou de la manne ou du sang de Jésus-Christ'. This, however, seems to be nothing more than a nineteenth-century traveller's tale, retold by a pious pilgrim who himself (*Les Saints Lieux*, II 236, 267 8) had no problem in crediting any number of the other, better-known legends of the Holy Blood.

[133] For Hailes, see below pp. 137 51.

[134] See, for example, the many grants to the church of the Holy Sepulchre which refer directly to the Cross or to the tomb of Christ; *Cartulaire du Saint-Sépulcre*, ed. Bresc-Bautier, nos. 2, 7, 17 18, 20, 23, 42, 45, 68, 74, 76 7, 136, 139, 146, 150 1, 167, 170, 177, 180, and for the use of the Cross as the emblem of the Crusader Church, see J. S. C. Riley-Smith, 'Peace Never Established: The Case of the Kingdom of Jerusalem', *Transactions of the Royal Historical Society* 5th series 28 (1978), 89 94; C. J. Tyerman, 'Were There Any Crusades in the Twelfth Century?', *English Historical Review* 110 (1995), 574 5.

[135] Above p. 41 n. 39.

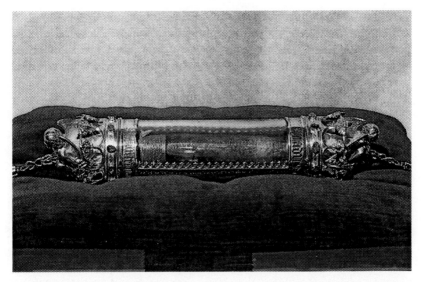

7 Bruges, the Holy Blood relic. Rock crystal phial, probably Byzantine, eleventh
or twelfth century, encased in a glass and gold reliquary 1388 (Bruges,
Confraternity of the Holy Blood)

dispatched portions of the Cross.[136] The one exception, the blood relic
later venerated at Bruges, is said to have reached Europe in 1148 as the
result of a gift from Baldwin III, King of Jerusalem, to his brother-in-
law, count Thierry of Alsace. In fact, there is no evidence for the relic's
presence in Bruges before the 1250s, whilst the legend of its acquisition,
itself full of inconsistencies, does not appear to have been written down
until the late fourteenth century. In all likelihood the blood of Bruges,
like so many other relics in the Low Countries, originated in the sack of
Constantinople, after 1204.[137] Far from the Holy Blood being brought

[136] For gifts of portions of the Cross, see Frolow, *Vraie Croix*, *passim*; Huyghebaert, 'Iperius et le Saint-
Sang', 140–2; 'Monachi Scaphusensis de reliquiis sanctissime crucis', in *Recueil des historiens des
croisades: historiens occidentaux*, 5 vols. (Paris 1844–95), V 335–9; G. Bautier, 'L'Envoi de la relique de
la Vraie Croix à Notre-Dame de Paris en 1120', *Bibliothèque de l'Ecole des Chartes* 129 (1971), 387–
97. For other relics, including portions of St John the Baptist and the Old Testament prophet
Elijah supposedly recovered from the church of Sebaste and dispatched to Nemours together
with indulgences from the patriarch of Jerusalem and the bishop of Sebaste in the late 1160s, see
G. Estournet, 'Les Origines historiques de Nemours et sa charte de franchises (1170)', *Annales de
la Société historique et archéologique du Gâtinais* 39 (1930), 240–8; N. Kenaan-Kedar, 'The Cathedral
of Sebaste', *The Horns of Hattin*, ed. B. Z. Kedar (Jerusalem 1992), 101–3; Riley-Smith, 'Peace
Never Established', 90.
[137] 'Chronica monasterii sancti Bertini auctore Iohanne Longo de Ipra', ed. O. Holder-Egger,
MGH Scriptores, XXV 802–3, and see 'Genealogiae comitum Flandriae', ed. L. C. Bethmann,

from Jerusalem to the West in the twelfth century, a vernacular poem celebrating the blood relic of Fécamp suggests that for the blood to reach Jerusalem it had first to be returned there from one of its more recent resting places in Europe. According to this poem, around the year 1200 a runaway monk of Fécamp stole a portion of the Abbey's blood relic and carried it off with him on pilgrimage to the Holy Land. There it was brought to the very place of Christ's Crucifixion before being recovered and restored to Fécamp where it was placed in a special reliquary over the Abbey's high altar, close by the chief portion of the Fécamp blood that had been rediscovered and translated to a new shrine in 1171.[138]

Besides the blood of Westminster, it is true that at least two other blood relics claimed to have originated as gifts from the church of Jerusalem after 1247. Even if these claims were true, as one of them may be, it would make little difference to our argument, since it is the absence of such claims prior to 1247, not afterwards, that casts doubt upon the account of the relic sent to Henry III. The first of these two relics, venerated at Neuvy-Saint-Sépulcre near Bourges, is said to have been obtained in 1257 from the French cardinal, Eudes de Châteauroux, who had accompanied Louis IX on crusade.[139] Eudes, who in May 1248 had been the chief ecclesiastical dignitary to preside at the consecration of the Sainte-Chapelle in Paris, undoubtedly acquired various relics in the Holy Land, including portions of the Holy Sepulchre.[140] Moreover, the church

---

MGH Scriptores, IX 326. For commentary see Huyghebaert, 'Iperius et le Saint-Sang', 110–87, which at 138 notes the forgery, in the seventeenth century, of a similar tradition whereby the blood relic venerated at Boulogne was said to have been sent from the Holy Land between 1100 and 1102 as a gift from Godfrey de Bouillon and his brother Baldwin. For a devotional study of this relic, which accepts its historical *bona fides*, see D. Haigneré, *Notre-Dame de Saint Sang* (Paris 1862). The reliquary which housed the blood of Boulogne is, however, medieval in origin: J. Biguet, *La Relique du Saint-Sang de Boulogne-sur-Mer* (St-Omer 1914), 19, 21.

[138] Kajava, 'Etudes', 77–81, 114–20; Langfors, 'Histoire de l'abbaye de Fécamp', 59–64, and for the special reliquary, a crystal vase, in which the misappropriated portion of the blood was restored to Fécamp, attached by a gilded chain to one of the angels who supported the principal, pyramid-shaped reliquary, see the inventory of 1682 in Paris, Bibliothèque nationale MS Français 14566 pp. 145–6, whence Lincy, *Essai historique*, 186–7.

[139] L'Abbé Caillaud, *Notice sur le Précieux Sang de Neuvy-Saint-Sépulcre* (Bourges 1865).

[140] For letters of Eudes dated at Viterbo, 8 November 1257, describing his acquisition of *quasdam particulas dominici sepulcri et etiam reliquias sanctorum litteris annotatas*, received as a gift from the prince of Antioch and other trustworthy persons, passed on to master Hugh, chancellor of Tours, Eudes' brother, see Paris, Archives Nationales LL 46 (Cartulary of St-Maur-des-Fosés) fo. 141r, whence Paris, Bibliothèque nationale MS Baluze 74 fo. 144r, printed by F. Duchesne, *Histoire de tous les cardinaux français*, 2 vols. (Paris 1660), II 183–4, together with an indulgence of one year and forty days remission of enjoined penance, issued by Eudes in May 1248 to those who visited the Sainte-Chapelle on the anniversary, or within the octave of the anniversary of its consecration. For the kinship between Eudes and Hugh, the chancellor of Tours, see *Cartulaire de l'église de Notre-Dame de Paris*, ed. M. Guérard, 4 vols. (Paris 1850), II 126. Intriguingly, the

of Neuvy, to which he is said to have granted a portion of the Holy Blood, had itself been built late in the eleventh century in emulation of the Holy Sepulchre, sited close to one of the principal routes to Compostela and serving as a pilgrimage centre, convenient for those who wished to make a figurative visit to Jerusalem as part of their journey to Santiago.[141] However, the letter in which Eudes describes his gift of the Holy Blood to Neuvy states merely that the blood relic of Neuvy had been acquired, together with a portion of the Holy Sepulchre, at great expense in the Holy Land, with no specific reference to the patriarch or the church of Jerusalem.[142] The second relic, claimed by the church of Billom in the Auvergne, goes unrecorded before the seventeenth century and can probably be dismissed as a post-medieval fraud.[143] On a slightly different note, we should also refute the suggestion, made by at least one recent commentator, that the Holy Blood venerated at Hailes in Gloucestershire

letters of 1257 request the veneration of such relics of places 'moistened by the blood of Christ', suggesting that the relic given to Neuvy may originally have comprised a portion of the Holy Sepulchre from which blood could later be extracted.

[141] For the church, see J. Hubert, 'Le Saint-Sépulcre de Neuvy et les pèlerinages de Terre-Sainte au XIe siècle', *Bulletin Monumental* 90 (1931), 91–100; F. Deshoulières, 'Communication', *Bulletin de la Société nationale des antiquaires de France* (1916), 190–229. A similar 'figurative' Holy Sepulchre on the Compostela route, almost certainly of the twelfth century, is to be found in the subterranean cave church at Aubeterre-sur-Dronne (Charente), for a tour of which I am indebted to Mrs Deirdre Webber. For a description, see M. de Fayolle, 'Les Eglises monolithes d'Aubeterre, de Gurat et de Saint-Emilion', *Congrès archéologique de France, 79eme session tenue à Angoulême en 1912*, 2 vols. (Paris and Caen 1913), II 365–97, with a wider discussion of the links between such cave churches and the Holy Sepulchre by M. Gervers, 'The Iconography of the Cave in Christian and Mithraic Tradition', *Mysteria Mithrae: Atti del Seminario Internazionale su la specificità storico-religiosa dei Misteri di Mithra*, ed. U. Bianchi (Leiden 1979), 579–96; M. Gervers, 'L'Eglise rupestre de Gurat près d'Angoulême', *Archéologia*, 148 (1980), 42–53, references which I owe to the kindness of the author.

[142] For the relic, see Boussel, *Des reliques*, 127–8, and Caillaud, *Notice sur le Précieux Sang de Neuvy-Saint-Sépulcre*, 90–2, 265–6, printing apparently authentic evidences, now Châteauroux, Archives départementales de l'Indre G166, G173, esp. G166, letters of July 1257 preserved in an inspeximus of 1380: *mittimus vobis de lapide sepulcri domini gloriosi ut veritas ymagini societur et, quod omnibus reliquiis pretiosius est, mittimus vobis de pretio[si]ssimo sanguine salvatoris nostri, quo redempti sumus a peccatis nostris*. Writing in the 1630s, the abbé Marolles suggests that the relic of Neuvy might have begun life as a eucharistic or effluvial relic, reporting that he himself failed to observe the miraculous liquefaction which was claimed for it by Neuvy's canons: *Les Mémoires de Michel de Marolles* (Paris 1656), 122–4.

[143] Caillaud, *Notice sur le Précieux Sang de Neuvy-Saint-Sépulcre*, 142; Boussel, *Des reliques*, 131–2; Saintyves, *Les Reliques*, 10, 160, citing the Jesuit writer, Raymond de St-Martin, *La Divine Relique du Sang Adorable de Jésus-Christ dans la ville de Billom en Auvergne* (Lyons 1645), of which there is a copy in Paris, Bibliothèque nationale imprimés 8-Lk7-1007. St-Martin claims (pp. 35ff) that the relic was brought from the Holy Land by Durand *d'Abanelly*, canon of Billom, together with a fragment of the True Cross, and that it attracted letters from Pope Clement V or VI, requesting a portion of the relic (the various papal letters being printed in garbled French translation at pp. 117–20). However, he is also forced to admit that the precise details of the relic's discovery are entirely lost.

8 Neuvy-St-Sépulchre, the basilica. Modelled upon the church of the Holy
Sepulchre in Jerusalem, *c.* 1080 (London, Conway Library)

had been obtained in the 1260s from the patriarch of Jerusalem.[144] We shall have cause to consider the relic of Hailes in much greater detail below. For the moment, we need merely note that the monks of Hailes stated consistently that their relic had been acquired in Germany. It is true that at a much later date they claimed that the blood had been authenticated in letters from Urban IV who, before his election as Pope, had served as patriarch of Jerusalem. But the reference to Urban's letters makes it plain that these letters were intended to support the legend of the relic's acquisition in Germany, that they were issued by Urban as Pope, not as patriarch, and that in any case they were almost certainly a fourteenth-century forgery.[145] In this way, there is no firm evidence that the patriarchs of Jerusalem claimed to possess a portion of Christ's blood, at any time either before or after 1247. Of course, it is conceivable that a blood relic had been preserved at the Holy Sepulchre, unnoticed by the surviving sources. It might even have been obtained at a later date, for example by washing part of the stain from the Cross, the nails, the pillar of scourging, or any of the other places where Christ's blood had been shed. But this is surely to make too great an allowance for the sources.

In general, the church of the Holy Sepulchre in Jerusalem differed from many of the shrines of western Europe in its failure to exploit the links, accepted elsewhere, between pilgrimage and the search for miraculous cures. In the twelfth century, the relics of the Holy Sepulchre appear to have been remarkably divorced from any miracles of healing, so that at least one visitor to Jerusalem was struck by the absence of *ex voto* offerings, noting the lack of such memorials of healing in the churches of

---

[144] Bentley, *Restless Bones*, 132, and independently in J. G. Coad, *Hailes Abbey Gloucestershire*, English Heritage Handbook (London 1985), 5, which provides a highly misleading account of the relic's pedigree.

[145] BL MS Harley 3725 (Hailes Chronicle to 1364) fos. 13v–14r: *Eodem tempore Edmundus comes Cornubie ibidem illum nobilem portionem sanguinis Ihesu Cristi perquisivit quam apud Hayles postea anno domini millesimo ducentesimo septuagesimo die exultationis sancte Crucis cum propria historia a beato papa Urbano quarto edita et confirmata deportavit*, also in Dugdale, *Monasticon*, v 686n. There is no mention of the Pope's letters in either of the earlier versions of the annals of Hailes in BL MS Cotton Cleopatra D iii. The metrical version of the Hailes legend, BL MS Royal 17 C xvii fo.147, printed in *Altenglische Legenden neue Folge*, ed. C. Horstmann (Heilbronn 1881) 275–81, esp. 276 lines 28–45, 278 lines 181–2, claims to set out the history of the relic as told by Pope Urban, although in fact this history is derived entirely from secular legends of the Holy Grail and seems most unlikely to have been supported by any Pope (see below pp. 140–1). Assuming Urban's letters to have been genuine, not merely a figment of the monks' imagination, it may be significant that Urban had served as archdeacon of Campines in the diocese of Liège (1243–8) and as bishop of Verdun (1252–5), locations close to various of the blood relics of Germany and the Low Countries.

the Holy Land set against their abundance in the shrine of the Virgin
Mary at Rocamadour in south-west France.[146] This insight comes to us
from a writer keen to laud the virtues of Rocamadour, and therefore
inclined to play down the healing properties of other shrines. It is none
the less intriguing, since it may help to explain why the Holy Blood of
Westminster subsequently failed to find acceptance as a thaumaturge,
capable of effecting miraculous cures. In addition, the blood of Westminster was acquired only a few years after doubts had been cast upon
one of the most popular miracles of the Holy Sepulchre, that of the 'New
Fire'. Each year on Easter Eve, when all lights in the church had been
extinguished, it was claimed that a lamp was miraculously rekindled by
a spark sent from heaven. This miracle of the New Fire was of great
antiquity, and had been widely publicized in western Europe by Popes
and scholars alike, from at least the time of the First Crusade. However,
in 1238 Pope Gregory IX intervened to pour scorn upon the event, describing it as fraudulent and forbidding any who believed in the miracle
from making the pilgrimage to Jerusalem to witness it.[147] Gregory's letters may not have circulated very widely, and may have been inspired by
political considerations rather than by zeal for religious truth. None the
less, it is worth remarking that shortly after the miracle of the New Fire
was called into question, similar scepticism was to be expressed about
the credentials of the Holy Blood sent from the patriarch to King Henry
III. The patriarch and the canons of Jerusalem may already by 1247
have enjoyed a somewhat tarnished reputation for truthfulness.

At the very least, the lack of previous evidence for a blood relic associated with the church of the Holy Sepulchre may have made it all
the more difficult for contemporaries to credit the account of the blood
sent to England. By the same token, there was nothing in the previous
history of Westminster Abbey, the relic's destination, to encourage easy
assimilation for the Holy Blood as an object of pilgrimage and devotion. By contrast to Mantua, which claimed a legendary association with

---

[146] *Les Miracles de Notre-Dame de Rocamadour au XIIe siècle*, ed. A. Albe (Paris 1907), 288–9, cited with
commentary by Ward, *Miracles and the Medieval Mind*, 122–3, 255 n. 96.

[147] Ward, *Miracles and the Medieval Mind*, 120–2, citing letters of Gregory IX dated 9 March 1238,
to be found in *Registres de Grégoire IX* no. 4151. For an even more ancient wonder, in which it was
claimed that whenever the True Cross was exhibited in the church of Jerusalem, a star would
appear in the sky, causing oil intended as pilgrimage souvenirs to bubble over in the flasks in
which it had been placed, see the account of the Piacenza pilgrim, c. AD 570, in Wilkinson,
Jerusalem Pilgrims before the Crusades, 83, with important material on the antiquity of the miracle
of the New Fire, placing it at least as early as the eighth century, at pp. 142–4 and n. 16. For a
modern, and less than reverential side-light on the ceremony itself, see S. Runciman, *A Traveller's
Alphabet: Partial Memoirs* (London 1991), 204–6, as drawn to my attention by Colin Morris.

St Longinus, or the Sainte-Chapelle in Paris, purpose-built for the reception of the Passion relics collected by Louis IX, Westminster before 1247 appears to have possessed no special interest in the story of Christ's Passion or in the legends of the Holy Blood. Had Henry III deposited his relic at an abbey that lacked any pre-existing cult, as Edmund of Cornwall was later to do at the Abbey of Hailes, the Holy Blood dispatched in 1247 might have developed into a focal point for pilgrimages. But Westminster already possessed a saint of its own, Edward the Confessor, whose relics, although the object of only limited popular devotion, were undoubtedly linked to the Abbey by historical and local associations far stronger than those that attended the gift of Christ's blood.

All things considered, it is easy to understand why the relic of the Holy Blood at Westminster should have failed to establish itself as an object of widespread devotion. Not only was it a late arrival, delivered some years after the wholesale broadcast of such relics from Constantinople, but it was acquired from a source that had never before laid claim to a relic of Christ's blood. Furthermore, it may have appeared to contemporaries just a little too much of a coincidence that the relic should have been bestowed upon Westminster at a moment so convenient both for Henry III and for the church of Jerusalem, a church which may already have been suspected of publicizing spurious miracles and wonders. Matthew Paris makes plain that from the very beginning the relic's authenticity was brought into question. 'When the affair was discussed', Paris writes, 'some slow to believe still doubted' (Luke xxiv. 25). In his letters, the patriarch of Jerusalem had gone out of his way to stress that the relic was a genuine one, extracted from the treasures of the church of Jerusalem where it had been kept since ancient times, 'and you should know for certain, and without doubt that . . . truly it is the same blood which flowed from the side of our lord Jesus Christ (on Calvary)'. According to Paris, the bishop of Norwich in his sermon did his best to dispel any further doubts: the relic, he suggested, had passed to England by divine dispensation, 'so that England might have no less joy and glory in the possession of this great treasure as France had in acquiring the Holy Cross'. The blood would be more venerated in England than in Syria, which was now left desolate. England by contrast was famed for its piety.[148] Unconvincing as such arguments might sound to modern ears,

---

[148] *CM*, iv. 642-3. For the bishop of Norwich, master Walter of Suffield, a doctor of canon law at the University of Paris, himself later venerated as a saint at Norwich, see A. B. Emden, *A Biographical Register of the University of Oxford to A.D. 1500*, 3 vols. (Oxford 1957-9), iii. 1813-14; Shines, 'The Veneration of Saints at Norwich Cathedral', 135, 137.

they were clearly calculated to appeal to the pride of the bishop's English audience. They also followed a well-established tradition, whereby relics could be acquired, translated or even taken by force from one location to another should God or a particular saint so wish it. The Holy Blood would not be venerated in Syria. How much better then, in God's plan, that it be brought to England where it would be both honoured and secure?[149]

Powerful as the bishop's sermon may have been, it was clearly insufficient to calm all doubt. According to Paris, a second and then a third line of argument had to be attempted. To begin with, the prior of the Hospitallers rose to ask what personal advantage those who had brought the relic might be thought to have asked in return. Did they ask for gold or silver from King Henry? 'Certainly not', Henry interjected. Why, the prior continued, should they have put their souls in peril by testifying to the relic's authenticity if they knew it to be false? The mention of gold and silver here may well represent a calculated side-swipe against Louis IX and the French, just as elsewhere the bishop of Norwich is said to have applied the title *princeps Christianissimus* to Henry III, a title which was becoming the peculiar prerogative of the kings of France.[150] As had been widely reported, Louis had purchased his own collection of Passion relics from the Emperor of Constantinople for an enormous sum, perhaps in excess of £25,000.[151] The Lateran Council of 1215 had forbidden the display of relics for financial profit. It had not entirely prohibited their sale from one party to another, although such transactions were clearly considered less than respectable.[152] Strictly speaking, it was true that Henry III's acquisition of the Holy Blood, unlike Louis IX's purchases from Constantinople, was untainted by any suggestion of commercial *quid pro quo*. The patriarch in his letters had been equally keen to stress that the blood was a gift freely given. And yet it must have been apparent to contemporaries that such claims were more than a little disingenuous.

---

[149] For justifications of the theft or forced removal of relics, see Geary, *Furta Sacra*, 132–42, 152–4.

[150] Above pp. 21–2.

[151] *CM*, III 518, IV 75, 90, reports the various sales made to Louis by the Emperor Baldwin, of the Crown of Thorns and the other Passion relics, and of the Cross rescued from Damietta. It is this latter to which Paris assigns a purchase price of £25,000. Baldwin himself refers only vaguely to 'a great quantity of money': Riant, *Exuviae*, II 134–5 no. 79. For an attempt to estimate the precise cost, see Herrmann-Mascard, *Les Reliques des saints*, 351–2.

[152] Lat IV clause 62: *statuimus ut antiquae reliquiae amodo extra capsum non ostendatur nec exponatur venales*, and for commentary, see Herrmann-Mascard, *Les Reliques des saints*, 339–63; J. W. Baldwin, *Masters, Princes and Merchants: The Social Views of Peter the Chanter and his Circle*, 2 vols. (Princeton 1970), I 109, where the restriction is assumed to apply to the sale or display of relics outside their reliquary.

Clearly the relic had been sent in the hope of obtaining considerable benefits in return: support for the exiled church of Jerusalem and for the forthcoming crusade. The blood of Christ was directly linked, as both symbol and reality, to the Holy Land and the crusade. Without this association, its bestowal upon Henry III would have made very little sense.

Beyond all of these difficulties, there was a yet stronger objection that played a part in damping enthusiasm for the blood of Westminster. So far, the arguments we have considered in favour of the Westminster relic have been entirely practical, intended to establish its provenance and the *bona fides* of those who sent it. Yet, opposed to such claims there was ranged a powerful theological polemic that threatened to dismiss all of the bodily relics of Christ as rank impossibilities. The Church proclaimed as a central tenet of faith that Christ had ascended into heaven in both body and spirit. It was this bodily Ascension that explains the absence of claims to possess relics of Christ's flesh and blood for the first eight hundred years after the Resurrection. When, from around the year 800, churches began to lay claim to such relics, they were brought up against a question fundamental to Christian theology: if Christ had risen to heaven in glory, perfect in every part, how was it that he had left behind remnants of his body on earth? Precisely this question was raised at Westminster in 1247 and according to Matthew Paris an answer to it was forthcoming from Robert Grosseteste, bishop of Lincoln.[153] Grosseteste's answer, set out in a short tract, was copied by Paris into the *additamenta* to his *Chronica majora*.[154] To appreciate its subtleties we must re-examine the history of blood relics, looking at them not as specific objects collected in the churches of western Europe, but as phenomena argued about in the schools and discussed in the writings of theologians.

---

[153] *CM*, IV 643–4.
[154] *CM*, VI 138–44, where it is signposted from Paris' account of the relic's reception in *CM*, IV 644, by a drawing of a chalice covered with a cloth.

CHAPTER 5

The scholastic debate

We have seen that at Lucca, Cappenberg and elsewhere, relics of the Holy Blood were accompanied by other human remains of Christ: clippings from his nails, or strands of his hair. At the Abbey of the Holy Trinity at Vendôme, for example, from at least the 1180s onwards, pilgrims were invited to venerate one of the tears supposedly shed by Christ over the tomb of Lazarus.[1] Perhaps the most bizarre such bodily remnant was a milk-tooth of Christ claimed by the Abbey of St Médard at Soissons. In all probability, the monks of Soissons first advanced their claim around the year 1049, in deliberate imitation of the church of St Arnulph at Metz which for many years had attracted visitors to a tooth relic, said to be that of St John the Evangelist.[2] Be that as it may, the claims made at Soissons were to excite violent opposition from Guibert of Nogent, who set out to ridicule the Soissons tooth relic in his treatise *De sanctis et eorum pigneribus* (1114 × 1126).[3]

Guibert has on occasion been championed as a rationalist, in advance of his time in his scepticism towards certain aspects of the cult of relics. More recently a reaction has set in, and it has been suggested that his hostility towards the claims of Soissons was inspired not so much by

---

[1] The most measured account of the Holy Tear of Vendôme is to be found in a pamphlet by the Abbé de Préville, *Note historique et critique sur la Sainte-Larme de l'abbaye de Vendôme* (Blois 1875). See also the account written in 1656 by Germain Millet, *Histoire de la Sainte-Larme de Vendôme* (Avignon 1891), which lists various other tear relics of Christ claimed by the churches of Picardy and the Touraine. For the fierce debate on the authenticity of the Vendôme relic, see J.-B. Thiers, *Dissertation sur la Sainte Larme de Vendôme* (Paris 1699); Jean Mabillon, *Lettre d'un Bénédictin à monsiegneur l'évêque de Blois, touchant le discernement des anciennes reliques* (Paris 1700), and Thiers' reply, *Réponse à la lettre du père Mabillon touchant la prétendue Sainte-Larme de Vendôme* (Cologne 1700). For other such relics, including that of Sélincourt in Picardy which supposedly survived the Revolution of 1789, see Boussel, *Des reliques*, 113 25; Abbé Pilon de Thury, *Histoire et thèse sur l'insigne relique du Précieux Sang dite de la Sainte Larme* (Paris 1858).

[2] See the important materials assembled in *Guibert de Nogent . . . de sanctis et eorum pigneribus*, ed. R. B. C. Huygens, CCCM CXXVII (Turnhout 1993), appendices 1 2, pp. 37 8, 179 88.

[3] For the tract see the edition by Huygens, Guibert, *De pigneribus*, 79 175, with a note on dating at pp. 32 6. This supersedes the inaccurate edition reprinted in Migne, *PL*, CLVI 607 80.

rational scepticism as by a desire to champion the rival treasures of Laon Cathedral, with its portions of the milk and hair of the Virgin Mary.[4] But this is to go too far. In reality, Guibert is just as scornful of the claims of Laon as he is of those of Soissons. Indeed he impicitly challenges the plausibility of the Laon hair relic. Whilst undoubtedly accepting the miracle-working properties of some bodily relics, such as those of St Edmund at Bury, or St Arnoul at Clermont, he elsewhere shows a near pathological distaste for other such corporeal remains.[5] Guibert's scepticism, although far removed from that of the post-Reformation or the post-Enlightenment mind, is powerful and posited upon his particular understanding of the incarnation of Christ. In short, it is a scepticism founded upon supernatural as much as upon rationalist premises. Just as elsewhere in Europe Guibert's contemporaries chose to employ the distinctly supernatural agency of the ordeal by fire to test the quality of relics whose authenticity was in doubt, Guibert employs one set of supernatural propositions to challenge another that he regards as fraudulent.[6] Throughout, his intention is to distinguish, not so much the rational from the irrational, as between those relics that are 'true' memorials of the saints, and those which are 'false'.[7] His objections to the supposed relics of Christ extend beyond the tooth of Soissons to cover all the supposed material relics of the Incarnation. Why, Guibert asks sarcastically, stop at such particles as teeth, or hair? Why not claim to possess Christ's

---

[4] For commentary see K. Guth, *Guibert von Nogent und die hochmittelalterliche Kritik an der Reliquienverehrung*, Studien und Mitteilungen zur Geschichte des Benediktiner-Ordens und seiner Zweige XXI (Augsburg 1970), 72–110; M.-D. Mireux, 'Guibert de Nogent et la critique du culte des reliques', *La Piété populaire au Moyen Age*, Actes du 99e congrès national des Sociétés savantes, Besançon 1974, Section de philologie et d'histoire jusqu'à 1610 vol. 1 (Paris 1977), 293–301; R. I. Moore, 'Guibert of Nogent and his World', *Studies in Medieval History Presented to R. H. C. Davis*, ed. H. Mayr-Harting and R. I. Moore (London 1985), 107–17, esp. 107, and works there cited. In attempting to dispose of the myth of Guibert as rationalist, Moore provides a potentially misleading paraphrase of Guibert's tract, concentrating upon its opening, more general, section, without dealing at any length with the arguments deployed against the tooth of Soissons. For Edmund, Arnoul and a balanced commentary on Guibert's attitude, see J. F. Benton, *Self and Society in Medieval France: The Memoirs of Abbot Guibert of Nogent*, revised edn (Toronto 1984), 28–30, 225–7.

[5] Guibert, *De pigneribus*, 149–50 lines 407ff, and for the hair, see Guibert's remarks in Benton, *Self and Society*, 191.

[6] T. Head, 'Saints, Heretics and Fire: Finding Meaning through the Ordeal', *Monks and Nuns, Saints and Outcasts: Religion in Medieval Society. Essays in Honor of Lester K. Little*, ed. S. Farmer and B. H. Rosenwein (Ithaca 2000), 220–38, esp. 236–7 nos. 2, 3, 16, for secondary relics of Christ (cloth and portions of the True Cross) subjected to the ordeal by fire to test their authenticity, although, as Head points out, the means employed for such 'tests' were themselves posited upon a belief in the divine judgement of the ordeal.

[7] A point well made by H. Platelle, 'Guibert de Nogent et le "De pignoribus sanctorum". Richesses et limites d'une critique médiévale des reliques', *Les Reliques*, ed. Bozóky and Helvétius, 109–21.

very flesh and bones?[8] In his youth Christ lived in obscurity. Who then would have collected the relics of his birth and childhood? Certainly not the Jews who, as Guibert points out, expressed a morbid abhorrence for bodily remains.[9] In any event, what need has the church for such relics, when the body and blood of Christ are translated daily into the mystic elements of the sacraments? Had God wished such relics to be preserved, why did he allow for the corporeal Ascension of his son? Material remains represent a hindrance not an encouragement to faith.[10] If Christ glorified in the mass is to be distinguished from Christ who died upon the Cross, surely this is to argue that Christ possessed more than one body?[11] Likewise, if it be suggested that Christ bequeathed material relics for the edification of mankind, intending to resume them at the last judgement, surely this is to argue that Christ is to undergo not one but two resurrections?[12] As to the blood and water that flowed from Christ's side, surely they were not absorbed by earth and stones to face corruption? Such decay would have represented a breach of the promises vouchsafed to mankind through Christ, since as St Luke says: 'Not a hair of your head shall perish' (Luke xxi. 18). On the contrary, Christ abandoned none of his physical parts, but rose entire in glory, just as in future he will gather together the dispersed fragments of individual men, that the saved may reside in heaven.[13]

In all of this Guibert demonstrates his awareness of a number of recent and bitter theological controversies; on the nature of the Trinity, on the Incarnation, and on the real presence of the body and blood of Christ in the eucharist.[14] His entire argument is directed towards demonstrating that a claim to possess portions of Christ's body runs contrary to orthodox belief. His tract is unusual, not so much for its opinions as for the vehemence with which those opinions are expressed. Contemporaries were undoubtedly aware of the difficulties associated with Christ's supposed bodily remains. In particular they were concerned

[8] Guibert, *De pigneribus*, 141 lines 130–4.
[9] *Ibid.*, 149 lines 393ff.
[10] *Ibid.*, 135–7, 147–8.
[11] *Ibid.*, 136–7.
[12] *Ibid.*, 145–6, 151–3, esp. lines 512–13.
[13] *Ibid.*, 139, 145, 148–9, esp. lines 373–8.
[14] Beyond the scholastic controversies over the Trinity and the mass, too well known to require sign-posting here, the twelfth century witnessed a heated debate as to whether Christ the Logos assumed a definite human substance at the Incarnation or merely put on an outer habit of flesh as if it were a garment. This latter, *habitus*, theory was to be be decisively rejected by the Lateran Council of 1215. See in general H. Tillmann, *Pope Innocent III*, trans. W. Sax (Amsterdam 1980), 3–4 and works there cited.

by the fact that the incarnate Christ was said to have risen to heaven perfect in every part. How if Christ had risen in perfection could he have left behind parts of his body and blood, or even such minor relics as hair and nail-clippings, to be viewed by the faithful? As early as the seventh century, Bishop Braulio of Saragossa had sought to address such problems. Prefiguring some if not all of the opinions later expressed by Guibert, Braulio had concluded that the blood of Christ in the mass was to be preferred to any supposed bodily remains.[15] Precisely the same problem was raised by Ralph, a monk of Villers, who in 1178/9 wrote to Guibert of Gembloux, asking that he solicit the opinion of the great Hildegard of Bingen.[16] Hildegard's reply is unrecorded, but Ralph would have found at least one response in the *Summa de arte praedicandi* of the Paris-trained master Thomas of Chobham, written around the year 1210. In his *Summa*, Chobham sets out to instruct preachers in the best way of contradicting various of the more vulgar errors that they were likely to encounter amongst their audiences – a sort of hammer for hecklers. In this way he tackles a question, clearly the subject of much controversy:

Certain people object [Chobham writes] that if Christ was resurrected in glory and his whole body was glorified, how is it that the Church claims that Christ's foreskin, cut off at the time of his circumcision, still remains on earth? There is an easy response to this, since just as by a miracle the body of Our Lord can be at one and the same time in several places, so that same body can exist in several forms. The Lord gave his body to his disciples in immaterial form (*inpassible*), although that same body took material form when he sat and ate. Had anyone kept the bread that the Lord gave to his disciples and stored it in a pyx until the time of his Passion, although blood flowed from Christ's body at the Passion, it would not have flowed in the pyx. In the same way, Christ's foreskin, glorified as part of his integral body, may exist in another place unglorified. It is not to be said that Christ's foreskin is glorified or not glorified, merely that in one place it is glorified and in another not.[17]

We would do well to note the important role played in Chobham's argument by eucharistic theology. Whereas to Guibert of Nogent the mystery of the eucharist seemed to invalidate any claim to mere physical relics of Christ's flesh and blood, to Thomas of Chobham quite the opposite held

[15] See above p. 53.
[16] *Guiberti Gemblacensis epistolae*, ed. A. Derolez, CCCM LXVI (Turnhout 1988-9), II 268, noticed by Huygens in his edition of Guibert, *De pigneribus*, 16.
[17] *Thomas de Chobham summa de arte praedicandi*, ed. F. Morenzoni, CCCM LXXXII (Turnhout 1988), 110 lines 698-715.

good. Guibert regarded claims to possess bodily relics of Christ as tantamount to heresy: an attempt to intrude a fourth person into the Trinity.
Chobham, by contrast, saw no such difficulty. In Chobham's argument
it is precisely the miraculous nature of Christ's bodily presence in the eucharist that justifies the miraculous co-existence of Christ glorified, and
Christ the begetter of material relics. As we have already suggested, the
claim to possess Christ's human remains seems to march hand in hand
with an exalted sense of the transformation wrought during the mass in
the elements of bread and wine.

Perhaps the most telling demonstration of this occurs in the treatise
De missarum mysteriis, ascribed to Pope Innocent III. The treatise itself
represents an attempt to explain the symbolism of the Christian liturgy,
and in particular of the eucharist, showing, for example, how the blood
of Christ can be said to represent the New Testament, how in the eucharist the two elements of wine and water mixed can be translated into
the single element of Christ's blood, and how the sacraments can be
regarded as both real and figurative. Like Thomas of Chobham, Pope
Innocent agrees that the body of Christ can be present simultaneously
in several places, both in heaven and on earth.[18] However, he is far more
circumspect than Thomas in his approach to the supposed bodily relics
of Christ:

When Christ rose from the dead [he asks] did he resume that blood that he had
shed upon the Cross? For if 'not a hair from your head shall perish' [Luke xxi.18],
how much more imperishable is that blood which is of the very truth of nature
(*de veritate nature*)? And what is to be said of the circumcision of Christ's foreskin, or
the cutting off of his umbilicus? Were they restored to Christ at his Resurrection
as part of his human substance? It is believed that they are preserved in the
sanctuary of the Lateran basilica, and some say that the foreskin of Christ was
borne by an angel to Jerusalem, to Charlemagne who carried it off to Aachen
(*Aquisgrani*), and that later it was placed by Charles the Bald in the church of
St Sauveur at Charroux (*Carosium*). Rather than attempt rash answers to such
questions, it is better that they be left entirely to God.[19]

---

[18] Migne, *PL*, CCXVII 875. The date and authorship of the tract are discussed by Tillmann, *Innocent III*, 7–8, 18–19 n. 92, and with particular reference to Innocent's treatment of the blood of Christ by A. Cuva, 'Il Sangue di Cristo nel "De Missarum Mysteriis" di Papa Innocenzo III', *SA*, VII part 1 (1991), 649–65.

[19] Migne, *PL*, CCXVII 876–7: *melius est tamen Deo totum committere quam alius temere diffinire.* For the relic of Charroux, see above p. 62. Innocent's discussion is founded upon the account of these relics by Peter Comestor, 'Historia scholastica: in evangelia', ch. 6, in Migne, *PL*, CXCVIII 1541 additio 2, noting a rival relic of the foreskin venerated at Antwerp. Comestor's account is further used by Aubrey of Trois Fontaines, writing in the mid-thirteenth century: 'Chronica Albrici monachi Trium Fontium', ed. P. Scheffer-Boichorst, *MGH Scriptores*, XXIII 721. Although Christ's foreskin

In this way Innocent avoids any firm definition, leaving everything to God's omniscience. None the less, it is obvious from all this that by the time that the Holy Blood was delivered to Westminster in 1247, there were grave doubts in the minds of many theologians as to whether it was possible for such relics to be regarded as the true blood of Christ. The opinions of Braulio of Saragossa, Guibert of Nogent, Thomas of Chobham and Innocent III must be seen as but the tip of an iceberg: a few chance reminders of what was clearly a lively and vexed debate in the schools.[20] Leave alone the fact that the sheer number of blood relics circulating in western Europe was bound to excite scepticism, the various theories concerning Christ's bodily resurrection, slowly crystallizing under the scrutiny of schoolsmen into fixed points of doctrine, tended to cast a lengthening shadow of doubt over any sort of relic, be it of blood or flesh, salvaged from the time of Christ's earthly ministry.

It was against this background that Robert Grosseteste composed his short tract in support of the Westminster blood relic, copied by Matthew Paris amongst the *additamenta* to his *Chronica majora*. Although only one manuscript of this tract is known to survive, its arguments were familiar to Aquinas and to writers of the later Middle Ages, at least one of whom, writing in the early sixteenth century, refers to Grosseteste's opinions

remains a favourite subject on which to ridicule the medieval church, claims to its possession are relatively rare. One is tempted to suggest that commentators have often misread the word *presepium* (Christ's crib, portions of which were claimed by a large number of churches) for the far more exceptional *preputium*. For the foreskin and the umbilicus housed at the Lateran by the 1080s, translated to a new shrine in 1279, see John the Deacon in *Codice di Roma*, ed. Valentini and Zucchetti, III 356; Gervase of Tilbury, 'Otia imperialia', in *Scriptores rerum Brunsvicensium*, ed. Leibnitz, I 967, noting its annual anointing with balsam. A further portion of the foreskin or umbilicus was claimed by Reading Abbey before 1200: BL MS Egerton 3031 (Reading cartulary) fo. 6v: *Preputium domini vel illud quod ab umbilico pueri Ihesu precisum est creditur esse cum cruce de ligno domini in textu quem imperator Constantin' misit Henrico regi Anglorum primo.* For other stories, including the remarkable legend of the Holy Camel said to have brought a relic of the foreskin, or more likely a miraculous cross, to the nuns of Niedermünster in Alsace, see Begg, *In Search of the Holy Grail*, 32–5, 136–7, with sources, none earlier than the picture of a camel displayed on the seal of abbess Susanna (after 1421), assembled in F. Wolff, *Die Klosterkirche St Maria zu Niedermünster im Unter-Elsass* (Strasbourg 1904), 28–38. For the foreskin of Coulombs later associated with Henry V and VI of England, see below p. 170 n. 44.

[20] Besides the treatises dealt with in detail here, see, for example, the continuing debate about the authenticity of relics of Christ's foreskin or teeth, rehearsed in the writings of the late twelfth- and early thirteenth-century Paris masters Simon of Tournai and Guy de Orchellis: *Les 'Disputationes' de Simon de Tournai*, ed. J. Warichez, Spicilegium sacrum Lovaniense études et documents XII (1932), 82–3 (disputatio 26); *Guidonis de Orchellis tractatus de sacramentis ex eius summa de sacramentis et officiis ecclesiae*, ed. P. Damiani and O. van den Eynde, Franciscan Institute Publications text series IV (New York and Louvain 1953), 230–2 ('De resurrectione', ch. 10 art. 1 pars 272–3).

on the Holy Blood long before Paris' *additamenta* were published.[21] As a result it seems reasonably safe to accept the attribution of the tract to Grosseteste, and to suggest that its arguments circulated after 1247 far beyond Westminster or St Albans. The tract itself is likely to have been written soon after October 1247, perhaps at the King's request, as a means of publicizing the Westminster relic. It is too polished a piece to have been preached *extempore* at the time of the delivery of the Holy Blood, although it is conceivable that the gist of it was announced before the tract itself was put into writing.[22]

What arguments does Grosseteste advance? To begin with he follows the traditional line which we have seen adopted at Fécamp, Lucca and elsewhere, resorting to the apocryphal *Acts of Pilate* to explain the collection of the blood after Christ's Passion. However, Grosseteste goes much further than previous writers in his account of the process by which Joseph of Arimathaea, without any assistance from Nicodemus, first attempted to wash the stain of blood from the Cross and nails, then from the various wounds in Christ's body and the sweat, that as St Luke reports (Luke xxii. 44) had fallen like great drops of blood. In all he distinguishes four sorts of blood, of which the most precious was that pure blood which flowed from Christ's heart and right side. This, Joseph is said to have placed reverently in a noble vase. Of the lesser kinds, mixed with the water from washing, he gave some as medicine to his friends. Throughout, it is intriguing that Grosseteste stresses the central role played by Joseph of Arimathaea in the collection of Christ's blood, relegating Nicodemus to a secondary role as Joseph's assistant. At the same time Grosseteste seeks to emphasize the plausibility of the apocryphal narrative by reference to details given by the Gospel of St John, of the way, for

---

[21] S. H. Thomson, *The Writings of Robert Grosseteste Bishop of Lincoln 1235–1253* (Cambridge 1940), 137–8 no. 102, notes no other MS. The *additamenta* were not published by Matthew Parker in his edition of the *Chronica majora* (1571). Grosseteste's tract appears to have been printed for the first time in the edition of Paris by William Wats, *Matthaei Paris . . . Historia maior* (London 1640), *additamenta* pp. 161–3, whence it was reproduced by William Prynne, *The Second Tome of an Exact Chronological Vindication and Historical Demonstration of our . . . Supream Ecclesiastical Jurisdiction* (London 1665), 712–14, with a brief, and extremely scornful notice of blood relics at 715. Silvestro Mazolini da Prierio, *Aurea Rosa, id est preclarissima expositio super evangeliis totius anni* (Paris 1516), fo. 251r v, conveniently reprinted in an edition by D. Zambelli (Venice 1599) fo. 308v, refers explicitly to the opinions of *Lincolniensis* on the Holy Blood, although the precise nature of those opinions is not made plain. For Aquinas, who rehearses the line of argument advanced by Grosseteste, but without attribution, see below.

[22] Grosseteste is not amongst the bishops known to have issued indulgences in favour of the blood of Westminster. His itinerary is very sparsely recorded but does not rule out the possibility that he attended the ceremony on 13 October 1247: *Rotuli Roberti Grosseteste episcopi Lincolniensis A. D. MCCXXXV–MCCLIII*, ed. F. N. Davis, Canterbury and York Society x (London 1913), p. xii.

example, that Nicodemus had brought myrrh and aloes in secret for the embalming of Christ 'about an hundred pound weight' (John xix. 39). He then goes on to explain that the liquids collected from Christ's body were passed down from father to son, Joseph, Nicodemus and their descendants being amongst the leading noblemen in Judea. Eventually the blood came into the possession of the patriarch of Jerusalem. Thereafter, echoing the debate recorded by Matthew Paris, Grosseteste recounts the relic's dispatch from Jerusalem in 1247; the fact that it was a free gift, safer in England than in the Holy Land, supported by unimpeachable testimony. Again, he repeats that the blood represents a more precious treasure than the Passion relics acquired by Louis IX, since it was merely through their association with the Holy Blood that those other relics had been sanctified: an argument which both Grossteste and the bishop of Norwich, Walter of Suffield, could have acquired from the *De fide orthodoxa* of the seventh-century John of Damascus.[23]

Thus far, Grosseteste's performance might be accounted a pretty indifferent one. Save for the detail with which he describes the washing of Christ's wounds and the various mixtures of blood, sweat and water, there is nothing here that is particularly original. Above all, his claims as to the relic's descent from father to son entirely fail to take into account the disruptions that had occurred in Judea since the time of the Passion, a problem solved at Mantua, Fécamp and elsewhere by allowing that the blood had been smuggled out of the Holy Land, either to Europe or to Constantinople, at a very early date. Yet however lack-lustre Grosseteste's performance appears on the surface, there may be more here than at first meets the eye. Whereas the legends of Lucca and Fécamp had stressed the part played in the collection of the Holy Blood by Nicodemus, with no mention of Joseph of Arimathaea; in Grosseteste's account Joseph replaces Nicodemus as the real hero of the story. Without any doubt the early thirteenth century had witnessed an upsurge of interest in Joseph, not least because in secular romance he had come to occupy a leading role within the legends of the Holy Grail. According to the French *Estoire de Saint Graal*, written down in the 1220s or 30s, Joseph is credited with collecting portions of Christ's blood in the vessel or Grail used at the Last Supper. Condemned by the Jews, he is said to have undergone a forty-two-year imprisonment from which he was rescued by the Emperor Vespasian at the time of Jerusalem's destruction by Rome. Thereafter,

---

[23] *CM*, VI 138–43; John of Damascus, 'De fide orthodoxa' 4.11, in Migne, *PG*, XCIV 1129–34, writing of the sanctification of the Cross, the nails and the lance through their contact with Christ's body and blood.

the *Estoire* records how, following many tribulations, it was Joseph who was responsible for converting Britain to Christianity. Earlier versions of the legend, from the late twelfth century onwards, had agreed in describing Joseph as Britain's first Christian missionary, although, unlike the *Estoire*, they had failed to draw an association between Joseph, the Holy Blood and the Grail.[24]

We have no direct evidence that Grosseteste had read the *Estoire de Saint Graal* or any of the other secular romances in which Joseph features. None the less, he does seem to have enjoyed an acquaintance with the romance *genre*. One of his most popular works, the *Château d'amour*, was composed in rhyming French couplets, probably to be declaimed with musical backing to an audience of laymen.[25] Assuming for the moment that Grosseteste was familiar with the secular legends, however vaguely, it would be easy to understand why Joseph of Arimathaea should occupy such a prominent position in his tract on the Holy Blood. Joseph, after all, was being canvassed in the Grail romances as England's first Christian saint, a saint who afforded England a Christian past even more ancient than that bestowed upon France by the legends of St Denis.[26] By stressing

---

[24] In general, see the important studies by V. M. Lagorio, 'The Evolving Legend of St Joseph of Glastonbury', *Speculum* 46 (1971), esp. 212–17; V. M. Lagorio 'The "Joseph of Arimathie"': English Hagiography in Transition', *Medievalia et Humanistica* 6 (1975), 91–101, and for the development of the theme of the Holy Blood in the Joseph legend, see also R. S. Loomis, *The Grail: From Celtic Myth to Christian Symbolism* (Cardiff 1963), 224–30, 260–1.

[25] R. W. Southern, *Robert Grosseteste: The Growth of an English Mind in Medieval Europe*, 2nd edn (Oxford 1992), 225–30.

[26] For St Denis, see G. M. Spiegel, 'The Cult of St Denis and Capetian Kingship', in *Saints and their Cults: Studies in Religious Sociology, Folklore and History*, ed. S. Wood (Cambridge 1983), 141–68. The more extreme version of the French Christian legend was asserting, from at least the time of abbot Suger in the twelfth century, that the Abbey had been consecrated in 636 by Christ himself in the company of SS Peter and Paul: J. Liebman, 'La consécration légendaire de la basilique de St Denis', *Le Moyen Age*, 3rd series 6 (1935), 252–64; *Abbot Suger on the Abbey Church of St Denis*, ed. E. Panowsky (Princeton 1946), 42–5, 50–2. When *c.* 1247 the monks of Glastonbury came to insert Joseph of Arimathaea into their history, they claimed that his conversion of Britain had occurred in the year AD 63. In doing so they deliberately ignored the passage in the *Estoire de Saint Graal* which stated that Joseph had been imprisoned for forty-two years after the Crucifixion. Their reason for departing from the *Estoire* in this way may well have been a desire to provide England and their own Abbey with a Christian past more venerable than that of France. Certainly the supposed primacy afforded by Joseph was to play an important part in Anglo-French rivalry after 1400. In general see Lagorio, 'The Evolving Legend', 215–17, 220–4; below pp. 151–3, and specifically for the rivalry between Glastonbury and St Denis, apparent as early as the early twelfth century, see William of Malmesbury, *De Antiquitate Glastonie Ecclesie*, ed. Scott, 51, whence *John of Glastonbury's 'Chronica'*, ed. Carley, 10–11. Guibert of Nogent is our sole authority for the equally remarkable legend of King Quilius, which would have granted England a Christian history even more ancient than that conferred by association with Joseph of Arimathaea. According to Guibert, Quilius, supposedly a King of Britain, visited Jerusalem shortly after the Crucifixion, where he collected various non-corporeal relics of Christ and the Passion, dying on his return journey at Nogent, where he was later venerated as a saint: Benton, *Self and Society*, 28, 119–25.

the connections between Joseph and the Holy Blood, Grosseteste could hope to emphasize the relic's patriotic English credentials. Since it was Joseph who had collected the Holy Blood, the relic might be seen as belonging by rights to the English Church which Joseph had been the first to establish. Indeed, with its delivery to Henry III in 1247 the relic might be viewed as returning at last to its rightful English owners. Patriotism, or at least Anglo-French rivalry, undoubtedly played a part, both in the sermon preached in October 1247 by the bishop of Norwich, and in Grosseteste's comparison between the Holy Blood and the Passion relics acquired by Louis IX. Our evidence here is far from certain, but it is at least a possibility that Grosseteste's account of Joseph of Arimathaea represents yet another attempt, albeit a tentative one, to play up the patriotic significance of the Holy Blood of Westminster to an English audience. At much the same time that Grosseteste was at work on his tract, the monks of Glastonbury Abbey were quietly appropriating the legends of Joseph of Arimathaea to add to their already rich stock of myth.[27] Before the 1240s there had been no association whatsoever between Glastonbury and Joseph. Following his first appearance in a Glastonbury source – an appearance that can be dated precisely to the late 1240s, perhaps to the very year in which the Holy Blood was delivered to Westminster and Grosseteste composed his treatise – Joseph was to become as important to the monks of Glastonbury as the equally mythical figure of King Arthur, already appropriated by the monks in the late twelfth century.[28] As we shall see, by the 1360s the Grail legends and the figure of Joseph were also to play a part in the popularization of the cult of the Holy Blood at Hailes. In this way, Grosseteste's account of the Westminster relic, which to a modern audience might appear both naive and implausible, may to contemporaries have exercised a very considerable appeal.

Be that is it may, it was for its hard scientific and theological content that Grosseteste's tract was to be remembered, not for any reference it might contain, real or imaginary, to the English legends of St Joseph. These scientific arguments are to be found in the second part of the

[27] Lagorio, 'The Evolving Legend', 215 17, 219, where it is suggested, very tentatively, that Grosseteste's account may have encouraged the Glastonbury monks in their forgery. Lagorio's suggestion chimes very well with the fact that Scott in his edition of William of Malmesbury, *De Antiquitate Glastonie Ecclesie*, ed. Scott, 34 9, is able to date the first surviving reference to Joseph at Glastonbury to c. 1247, since the MS in which it appears (Cambridge, Trinity College MS R. 5.33 (724) fos. 1 18v) is written in the same hand as a Glastonbury library list precisely dated to 1247, corrected in 1248.
[28] For the monks' appropriation of Arthur, see Lagorio, 'The Evolving Legend', 209 12; A. Gransden, 'The Growth of the Glastonbury Traditions and Legends in the Twelfth Century', *Journal of Ecclesiastical History* 27 (1976), 337 58, reprinted in Gransden, *Legends, Tradition and History*, 153 74.

tract, following on from Grosseteste's account of the relic's collection and preservation. Since they were to prove of considerable influence in the schools, they deserve to be quoted here at length:

But because the slow and the sceptical are accustomed to object [Grosseteste writes] that since Christ rose again on the third day with his body intact and not drained of blood, how can it be that he left his blood behind him on earth? To this there is an answer as follows: there are two bloods, or species (*genera*) of blood. The one sort of blood is produced by nutrition (*ex nutrimentis*) and on occasion there is too much of this, as when it bursts forth spontaneously from the nostrils or finds some other outlet, there being so much of it that it needs must be diminished. And it is this sort of Christ's blood that we have on earth, save that really it was not blood-like (*licet sane non fuisset sanguinolentus*), God so wishing that there should be a later memorial of the Lord's Passion. But there is another blood that is essential to the animate body, of which it is said that consumption (*tysis*) is the consumption of essential moisture, that is of the necessary blood of life; which blood is known by the physicians as 'the friend of nature' (*amicus naturae*), of which Moses said that 'the seat of the soul is in the blood' [cf. Lev. xvii. 11]. This blood is stored in the innermost chamber of the heart (*in triclinio cordis*) and without it no man can live. Of this sort of Christ's blood we perhaps have none on earth, although I say 'perhaps' because the Lord 'hath done whatsoever he hath pleased' [Ps. cxv. 3]. The Lord has risen, and with him fully whatever was of the substance and ornament of his body and of the truth of human nature; that is the blood that is consubstantial to him. The other sort, that he distilled, remains here yet.[29]

This is not quite the end of the matter. Grosseteste goes on to compare the Resurrection of Christ to the Resurrection of man, without any bodily mutilation or deformity. Christ, by contrast, chose to retain the outward signs of the wounds that he had received upon the Cross, to serve as visible proofs of his Resurrection for those who might otherwise lack faith. The carping of all sceptics should cease, since Christ is omnipotent, the lord of nature whose body is not subject to the customary, natural uses.

Parts of this argument are familiar. Even Guibert of Nogent had appreciated the significance of Christ's wounds, retained despite his perfect Resurrection, whilst the supernatural omnipotence of God had been employed before, by both Innocent III and Thomas of Chobham, as a trump card to silence opposition. Only in his attempt to distinguish two species or varieties of blood, that produced by nutrition and that stored in the innermost cavities of the heart, does Grosseteste advance a line of argument that was in any way original. Here he raises a question that was to trouble theologians for several centuries to come. The question

[29] *CM*, VI 143.

itself is derived in part from Peter the Lombard and in part from the natural sciences, in particular from the science of medicine. From a very early date, the nature of the resurrection body and, by extension, the degree to which its various constituent parts such as the humours, or the nails and hair, were necessary to resurrection, had formed a regular topic of scholastic debate.[30] The questions raised here had been discussed by Augustine and by many of the early church fathers, and had not surprisingly been taken up by Braulio of Saragossa in the very first commentary on relics of the Holy Blood, written as early as the mid-seventh century. Following Augustine, Braulio had attempted to distinguish between those elements of the human body, and by extension the body of Christ, which were essential, and those which might decently be discarded in the process of resurrection. In this way, as early as 650, Braulio had already distinguished between blood necessary for the human body, and the great quantity of blood that might be shed during the course of a human life, much of which – such as the blood of menstruation, or the blood of miscarried babies – could be regarded as polluted or positively harmful. As Braulio was aware, medical science argued that the body could produce a harmful superfluity of blood that had to be relieved through bleeding, either naturally, as in a nose-bleed, or through the common medical practice of phlebotomy. Not all of this superfluous blood, Braulio had suggested, would be necessary for the Resurrection, just as Augustine had argued that the resurrected body would not require the complete restoration of every superfluous hair and nailclipping that had been shed from it in life.[31] Even earlier, in the commentary on relics by Victricius of Rouen, composed in the year 396, Victricius had maintained that blood could remain on earth from the bodies of the saints who resided in heaven, sealed into the immutable particles of bone and flesh of the saints preserved as relics.[32] In all of this, as Caroline Walker Bynum has recently and most brilliantly shown, there was a wide diversity of opinion within Christianity, between those authorities such as Augustine, who tended to see the Resurrection in predominantly physical terms, as a reassembling of physical, bodily parts, and those such as Origen, who proposed a more subtle, less purely physical resurrection of mankind, supplied with distinct identity, but without the literal gathering together

---

[30] For a recent and comprehensive treatment of this debate, see C. Walker Bynum, *The Resurrection of the Body in Western Christianity, 200–1336* (New York 1995).

[31] Braulio of Saragossa, Letter 42, in Migne, *PL*, LXXX 687–90, cf. above p. 53 n. 77.

[32] Victricius of Rouen, *De laude sanctorum*, ed. J. Mulders, Corpus Christianorum Series Latina LXIV (Turnhout 1985), 83–4, as quoted by Bynum, *The Resurrection*, 107.

of bones, hairs and fluids that so exercised the mind of Augustine and his successors.

This debate had passed fully fledged into the twelfth century, where it finds a prominent place in the *Sentences* of Peter the Lombard, and thereafter in innumerable later sentence commentaries. The Lombard himself had started from the premise that only those parts of the body that pertained to the truth of human nature would undergo resurrection. The truth of human nature he defined as that part of the body inherited at birth from the parents and hence ultimately from the flesh of Adam. All of the flesh and blood acquired later, from nutrition, would be relinquished as superfluous when the body was resurrected.[33] Although this definition was rejected by later commentators, who allowed for the resurrection not only of the 'parental', inherited material of man, but also of a part of the nutrimental, added material that was necessary to complete the outward decoration or form of the resurrected body, it remained debatable as to precisely how much of this nutrimental matter would be required to make up the body at the time of resurrection.[34] We shall return to this question in due course, when we come to consider some of the later commentaries on the Holy Blood. For the moment, it is sufficient to note that the long-standing debate on the nature of the resurrection body serves merely as a starting point for Grosseteste's defence of the Holy Blood of Westminster. In his short tract *De dotibus*, in circulation from around 1230, Grosseteste had already exhibited a keen interest in the nature of the resurrection body, an interest which may well have helped qualify him as an apologist for the blood of Westminster a decade or so later.[35] However, whereas the *De dotibus* had represented a fairly straightforward contribution to the

[33] 'Sentences' 2.30.14–15, in *Magistri Petri Lombardi sententiae in IV libris distinctae*, ed. I. Brady, 3rd edn, 2 vols., Spicilegium Bonaventurianum IV, V (Grottaferrata 1971–81), I 503–5, and see also the passages in Peter's 'Sentences' 4.44 (ed. Brady, II 516–22) devoted to the same theme. Both of these passages inspired later commentaries on the resurrection of Christ's blood. A full exposition of the ideas of Lombard and his contemporaries on the resurrection body is provided by Bynum, *The Resurrection*, ch. 3, 117–55, and for 'the truth of human nature' debate, of great antiquity, see Bynum 128n, 133, 231–2, 238, 245.

[34] For an extensive discussion of this question, including references to the more important commentaries, see John Duns Scotus, 'Oxford Commentaries' 4.44 q.1, in *Johannis Duns Scoti doctoris subtilis, ordinis minorum, Opera omnia*, ed. L. Wadding, new edn, 26 vols. (Paris 1891–5), XX 161–208, and see *ibid.*, XXIV 530–40. See also Albert the Great, 'De resurrectione' I q.6.9–10, ed. W. Kübel in Albert, *Opera omnia*, ed. B. Geyer et al., XXVI (Cologne 1958), 254–6, and Alexander of Hales, *Summa theologica* 4.3.1.2 ch. 7, ed. Klumper et al., II 684–5. Once again, for commentary on all of these authors, see Bynum, *The Resurrection*, with indications of continuing debate in the Oxford schools of the late thirteenth century in Boureau, *Théologie, science et censure*, 215–16.

[35] J. Goering, 'The "De Dotibus" of Robert Grosseteste', *Mediaeval Studies* 44 (1982), 83–109, esp. 97–100.

debate on the qualities that Christ had bequeathed to the resurrected body and soul of man, the tract on the Holy Blood carried Grosseteste into far more controversial territory. Here, his originality lies in including Christ's blood amongst those nutrimental elements that would be relinquished from his body after Resurrection, an argument that owes far more to medical science than it does to the standard theological commentaries.

In his early years Grosseteste may well have practised as a physician. As Sir Richard Southern points out, he was in many ways a solitary thinker, self-taught, 'remote from the traditions and assured methods of the great schools but strong in his sense of the presence of physical nature and the scientific tradition'.[36] Certainly it is medical science, a science still dominated by the teachings of the Greek writer Galen, that informs Grosseteste's opinion upon the Holy Blood. To Galen, as to Grosseteste, it was blood that transmitted the very essence of life to the body. Without blood there could be no human life. The seed of man's generation was merely man's blood refined to its purest state, just as in women the blood of menstruation was transformed during pregnancy into the milk of lactation. Blood itself consisted of a mixture of various elements, spiritual as well as physical. Depending upon the relative proportions of this mixture it was possible to distinguish between various species of blood, a distinction that almost certainly originated in the observed difference between the colours of arterial and venous blood. To an age unaware that blood circulated through the body, pumped by the muscular contractions of the heart, the veins and the arteries were seen as two distinct systems, endowed with two distinct species of blood. To begin with, according to Galen, or at least according to the medieval interpretation of Galen, the blood flowing through the veins originated in food and water, transformed by the stomach into a fluid known as *chyle* and transmitted thence to the liver, where this *chyle* became charged with an imaginary essence or *pneuma*, known as natural spirits. It was these natural spirits that gave life to the inanimate *chyle* and transformed it into blood. At a later stage, a small quantity of venous blood entered the left ventricle of the heart where it became endowed with a second type of *pneuma*, known as the vital spirits. Only blood endowed with both natural and vital spirits was fit to enter the arteries. Thence a small quantity would eventually reach the brain, to be charged with yet another *pneuma*, the animal spirits. Blood mixed with animal

[36] Southern, *Robert Grosseteste*, 78–9, 230–1.

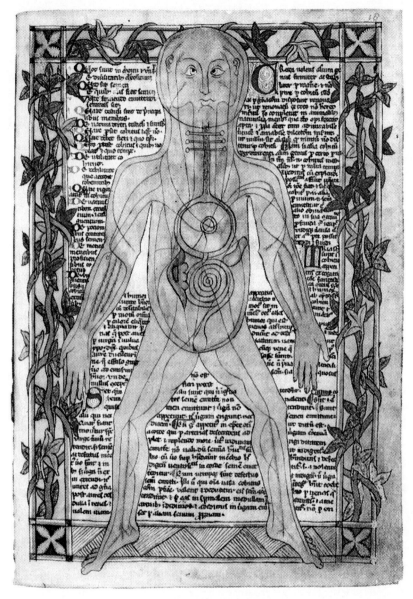

9   Medical diagram of the veins, English, *c.* 1280 (Oxford, Bodleian Library
MS Ashmole 399 fo. 18r)

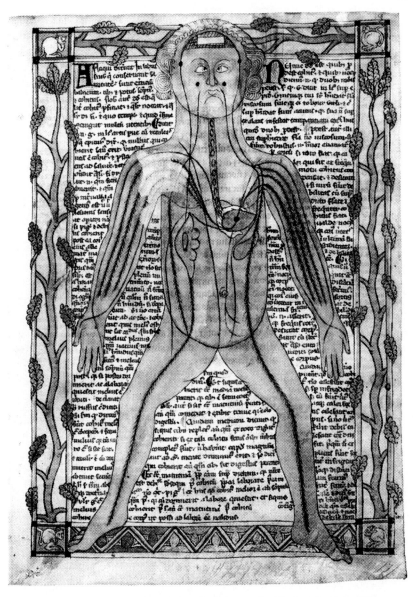

10   Medical diagram of the arteries, English, *c.* 1280 (Oxford, Bodleian Library
MS Ashmole 399 fo. 19r)

spirits passed through the nerves, conceived of as hollow tubes, to initiate motion.[37]

In this way, following Galen, blood could be divided into four species of fluid: the more or less inanimate *chyle* produced in the stomach, venous blood generated by the liver, arterial blood generated by the heart, and a final species produced in the brain and used to endow motion and the outward signs of life. This four-fold system is reminiscent of Grosseteste's description of the four varying mixtures of fluid collected from Christ's body by Joseph of Arimathaea. However, whilst it is Galen's distinction between venous and arterial blood that supplies Grosseteste with his basic framework, Grosseteste appears to adopt a less complicated view of the process overall. Here he follows not Galen but the treatise *De motu cordis* of the Englishman, master Alfred of Shareshill. Whereas Galen had allowed for a multiplicity of *pneumas* governing the various species of blood, Shareshill, heavily influenced by Aristotle, taught that after blood had been formed in the liver it underwent only one transformation, when it entered the heart and became charged with the essence of life, the *spiritus vitae*. It was the heart alone that regulated the production of life-blood, through the action of one, not several different spirits.[38] Grosseteste, following Shareshill, appears to have regarded the nutrimental blood

---

37 The simplest exposition of these theories is provided by C. Singer and E. A. Underwood, *A Short History of Medicine*, 2nd edn (Oxford 1962), 62–5, with useful incidental detail in M.-C. Pouchelle, 'Le sang et ses pouvoirs au Moyen-Age', *Affaires de Sang*, ed. A. Farge (Paris 1988), 17–41. For the evolution of Galen's ideas, see the introduction to *Galen on Respiration and the Arteries*, ed. D. J. Furley and J. S. Wilkie (Princeton 1984). For the distinction between Galen's own theories of the *pneuma* and the fully fledged system as elaborated by his followers, see O. Temkin, 'On Galen's Pneumatology', *Gesnerus* 8 (1951), 180–9; A. R. Hall, 'Studies in the History of the Cardiovascular System', *Bulletin of the History of Medicine* 34 (1960), 391–413, esp. 405.

38 'Des Alfred von Sareshel (Alfredus Anglicus) Schrift De Motu Cordis', ed. C. Baeumker, *Beiträge zur Geschichte der Philosophie des Mittelalters* 23 parts 1–2 (Münster 1923), esp. 14–17 for the heart's transformation of blood brought from the liver. Shareshill, whilst admitting (40–2, esp. 42 line 24) that there are two spirits, animal and vital, specifically denies (42) that blood is already infused with spirit in the liver, or (43–55) that it undergoes a further infusion of spirit once it has left the heart. In general his treatise represents a marriage between the ideas of Galen, on the function of the liver, veins and arteries, and the earlier, more primitive, system propounded by Aristotle in which there was only one *pneuma* and in which the heart played the principal role in the concoction of blood. Aristotle, however, had assumed that it was the heart, not the liver, which transformed digested food into blood, and had taught that pure spirits, not blood, travelled throught the arteries; *Galen on Respiration*, ed. Furley and Wilkie, 18–21; *Aristotle 'De partibus animalium I' and 'De generatione animalium I'*, trans. D. M. Balme, 2nd edn (Oxford 1985), 161–4. Aristotle's views could possibly have been known to Grosseteste who had assisted in the translation into Latin of others of Aristotle's works. However, the peculiar combination of Aristotle and Galen surely came to him from Shareshill. For a slightly different view of the process overall, allowing that blood could be generated both from the humours and from *chyle*, see Albert the Great, 'Quaestiones de Animalibus' 13 q.7, ed. E. Filthaut, in Albert, *Opera omnia*, ed. Geyer, XII (Cologne 1955), 241–2. For an overview of Shareshill's career, assigning his treatise to c. 1200, see J. K. Otte, 'The Life and Writings of Alfredus Anglicus', *Viator* 3 (1972), 275–91.

produced by the liver as an inanimate fluid, half way between *chyle* and the true blood of life and to this extent not really blood-like in the absolute sense of the word (*licet sane non fuisset sanguinolentus*). Being merely incidental to life, this species of blood or fluid could well have been left behind after Christ's Resurrection. Indeed, so abundant was it that on occasion it found spontaneous discharge from the body: a tacit reference to the practice of blood-letting, believed essential in releasing the harmful superfluity of nutrimental blood.[39] By contrast, it would have required some very special dispensation for any drop of Christ's heart-blood, charged with the very essence of life, to have survived his Resurrection and bodily Ascension into heaven.[40] The rejection of Galen here in favour of Alfred of Shareshill is most intriguing, and bears out the suggestion made by Sir Richard Southern that it was from precisely such writers of the English scientific school that Grosseteste drew much of his inspiration.[41]

Grosseteste, as has been said, was an idiosyncratic thinker. However, as the most renowned lecturer at the schools of Oxford, his views were to become broadcast throughout Europe. In this way his opinion on the Holy Blood was to be added to the long-standing controversy over the nature of Christ's bodily Resurrection, supplying the supporters of blood relics with one of their more significant lines of defence. Of course, Grosseteste's opinion was not without difficulties of its own. To begin with, it posited a view of the various species of blood different in many ways from the accepted orthodoxy propounded by Galen, and hence potentially confusing to later commentators. In addition, earlier on in his tract Grosseteste had claimed that Joseph of Arimathaea had collected not only the blood that flowed from Christ's skin, hands, head and feet, but a mixture of that water and heart-blood that had flowed

---

[39] For blood-letting in general, see P. Brain, *Galen on Bloodletting* (Cambridge 1986), ch. 7, and for its implementation by the monks of Westminster, see B. Harvey, *Living and Dying in England 1100–1540: The Monastic Experience* (Oxford 1993), 96–9. Grosseteste's contemporary, John Blund, had cited the capacity of blood to be produced in so great a quantity that it tended towards the destruction of the living creature, in countering the argument that the soul resided in the blood: Blund, *Tractatus de anima*, ed. Callus and Hunt, 7–8.

[40] Alexander of Hales in his discussion of the resurrection of the humours, *Summa theologica* 4.3.1.2 ch. 7, ed. Klumper *et al.*, II 684–5, esp. 684 column 1, takes it for granted that Christ was resurrected together with his blood. Like Grosseteste he describes blood as the friend of nature (*amicus naturae*) (*Summa* 4.3.1.2 ch. 5, ed. Klumper *et al.*, II 680, column 2). Although the precise origin of this phrase remains untraced, it is also to be found in the anonymous 'De medicina animae' ch. 4, in Migne, *PL*, CLXXVI 1187, and in Albert the Great, 'Quaestiones de animalibus' 10 q.2, ed. E. Filthaut in Albert, *Opera omnia*, XII 215 line 50, suggesting that it may possibly be derived from Aristotle. For the wider debate on the resurrection of the humours, see below pp. 103–4.

[41] For other links between Grosseteste and Shareshill, see Southern, *Robert Grosseteste*, 90–2, 149.

from the open wound in his side – *ipsum sanguinem cum aqua quem censuit praecordialem a latere dextro feliciter eliquatum et expressum*.[42] Admittedly, he had sought almost immediately to qualify his claim, referring to this, the fourth and most precious species of Christ's blood, as *cruor precordialis qui ex ipso corde Christi vel saltem latere constat effluxisse*, but the implication was clearly that a portion of the heart-blood had been preserved after Christ's death, and this despite Grosseteste's assertion that such a thing could have happened only through divine dispensation, contrary to the expected workings of nature. Be that as it may, the distinction that Grosseteste seeks to draw between nutrimental blood and the true blood of life was to prove extremely influential in later, scholastic debate. An important indication of this is to be found in the writings of Thomas Aquinas.

On at least two occasions in his vast theological output Aquinas was to consider the authenticity of relics of the Holy Blood. His final judgement is to be found in the third part of his *Summa theologiae* (pre-December 1273), amongst a wider discussion of the bodily Resurrection of Christ. Here Thomas asks whether Christ can have risen entire in perfection when relics of his blood are claimed by various churches on earth. To this his response is unequivocal: 'All the blood that flowed from Christ's body, belonging as it does to the truth of human nature, rose again in his body . . . The blood relics to be seen in certain churches did not flow from Christ's side but, it might be said, miraculously, from some maltreated image of Christ.'[43] In the same discussion, Thomas tackles a question that had been raised both by Guibert of Nogent and by Grosseteste. If none of Christ's flesh or blood can be said to have survived his Resurrection, how is it that he ascended into heaven still bearing the wounds of his Passion? Some might argue that the wounds represent a diminution of Christ's human body, and hence a means by which portions of his flesh and blood could have become detached to be left behind as relics. But to Aquinas the wounds represent not a reduction but an addition to Christ's body: the added tokens of his triumph over death, preserved so that his glory may be the more fully displayed.[44]

---

[42] *CM*, VI 140.

[43] Aquinas, *Summa theologiae* 3a q54 a3 ad3, in *S. Thomae Aquinatis opera omnia*, ed. R. Busa *et al.*, 7 vols. (Milan 1980), II 854 column 1, conveniently translated in *The 'Summa Theologica' of St Thomas Aquinas Literally Translated by Fathers of the English Dominican Province*, 22 vols. (London 1911–25) XVI 394–6.

[44] *Summa theologiae* 3a q54 a4 ad4, in Aquinas, *Opera omnia*, ed. Busa, II 854 columns 1–2. For Guibert's arguments on the wounds, see Guibert, *De pigneribus*, 146, 151–2. For the wounds of the martyrs, retained in the Resurrection, see Bynum, *The Resurrection*, 29, 43–5, 77, 98, 128, 333–4, 341 n.

On mature reflection, Aquinas appears to have adopted what we might describe as the hard-line attitude: that bodily relics of Christ's Passion were a theological impossibility. However, and much to the subsequent confusion of his followers, Aquinas' judgement in the *Summa* is at odds with a discussion of the Holy Blood that he had inserted, some time earlier, as one of the theological puzzles to which he devoted a *Quodlibet* question in 1271.[45] Here, Aquinas had begun by rehearsing the argument of his *Summa*, that none of Christ's blood could have survived the Resurrection separated from Christ's body. However, against this he admits that there was an objection. This objection is so close to the idiosyncratic line of argument advanced by Grosseteste that we must suspect that Aquinas had learned of Grosseteste's opinion, even though Grosseteste is not referred to by name in Aquinas' discussion.

Following one opinion [Aquinas writes] not all of the nutrimental blood (*sanguis nutrimentalis*), that is the blood generated from feeding, pertains to the truth of human nature. Since Christ ate and drank before the Passion, there was nothing to prevent the presence in him of such nutrimental blood, that would not pertain to the truth of human nature that should have been restored to his body at the Resurrection. However, since the question deals specifically with the blood shed at the Passion for the redemption of humankind, it appears better to say that everything returned at the Resurrection to the body of Christ, for three reasons.

These reasons can be summarized as follows. In the first place, at the time of his Passion, Christ had achieved that perfect age at which those things that most pertain to the truth of human nature were most to be found in his body. The exact meaning of this is unclear, but it may be that Aquinas seeks to assert both that Christ was in perfect health at the time of his Crucifixion, so that his body would not have produced superfluous nutrimental blood, and also that nutrimental blood was just as essential to Christ's human perfection as the blood to be found in his heart, an obvious riposte to Grosseteste's argument.[46] Certainly, in glossing this passage, later commentators were to assert that nutrimental blood was as essential to the form and ornament of Christ's body as life-blood was to its innate humanity.[47] Secondly Aquinas seeks to compare the Resurrection

---

[45] *Questiones quodlibetales* 5 q3 a1, in Aquinas, *Opera omnia* (1980), III 466 columns 1–2.

[46] For the related argument that in human history only the first man, Adam, and the most perfect, Christ, had achieved a perfect balance of blood and humours, see Pouchelle, 'Le sang et ses pouvoirs', 23.

[47] Domenico de Domenichi, *De sanguine Christi tractatus* (Venice 1557), fos. 16r–17v; Angelus Rocca, *Opera omnia*, 2 vols. (Rome 1719), I 244, and for this and the suggestion that Christ's age and temperance made it unlikely that his body would have produced a harmful superfluity of blood, see Pius II, 'Commentaries' Bk 11, in *Pii II Commentarii*, ed. A. van Heck, 2 vols., Studi e testi

of Christ to the coming Resurrection of mankind. St Augustine claims
that those parts of the body by which the Christian martyrs sustained
death are to enjoy a privileged brightness (*privilegiatum fulgorem*) at the time
of their Resurrection.[48] How much more, Aquinas comments, must this
apply to the blood of Christ and Christ's own Resurrection. Finally, if, as
John of Damascus states, the humanity of Christ possessed a more saving
grace by virtue of its unity with the Logos, it is clear that the blood shed
at the Passion, being united to Christ's divinity, must have been rejoined
to his other human parts at the Resurrection. Aquinas concludes from
all this that the blood of Christ displayed in certain churches cannot have
been shed at the Passion but must have flowed miraculously from some
maltreated image of Christ (*quadam imagine Christi percussa*) or at some
other time (*alias*) from Christ's body.

In its way Aquinas' answer is just as remarkable as the line of argument advanced by Grosseteste. Certainly, no better example could be
found to point up the contrasted methods of the two authors: Grosseteste
who used his observations of the natural world to challenge the theo-
retical logic-chopping of the schools, set against Aquinas who sought to
reconcile theology to natural science by a display of linguistic and logical
pyrotechnics. Both writers, of course, illustrate the point that scholastic theologians were striving to establish the truth both in natural and
in divine science, and that the debate over the Incarnation of Christ
had scientific and philosophical implications that extended far beyond
the realm of abstract theology.[49] In this particular instance, and despite
the fact that it depended upon a wholly fallacious account of the generation of human blood, it is Grosseteste's argument that emerges as
easily the more appealing. Aquinas, by contrast, does little more than
assert that Grosseteste's argument must be wrong because it runs contrary to accepted theological orthodoxy. He makes no attempt to challenge Grosseteste's distinction between the two species of blood and in
his *Quodlibet*, if not in his *Summa*, is forced to qualify his chief assertion.
Instead of denying that any of Christ's blood could have been preserved

CCCXII XIII (Vatican 1984), II 664–6; *The Commentaries of Pius II Books X–XIII*, ed. F. A. Gragg
and L. C. Gabel, Smith College Studies in History XLIII (Northampton, Mass., 1957), 721–3,
725. For Christ's eating after the Resurrection, see Bynum, *The Resurrection*, 148–9.

[48] The argument that the resurrected body of man would shine with some inner lustre is derived
from such passages in scripture as the Wisdom of Solomon iii. 7: *Fulgebunt iusti et tanquam scintille
in arundineto discurrent*, and Matthew xiii. 43: *Tunc iusti fulgebunt sicut sol in regno patris eorum*. For
the commentary of Augustine to which Aquinas refers, see Augustine, *De civitate Dei* 22.19, ed.
Dombart and Kalb, 837–9 esp. 839 lines 66–80.

[49] A point that is rightly and repeatedly stressed by Boureau, *Théologie, science et censure*, esp.
chs. 3, 9.

on earth, in his *Quodlibet* Aquinas argues merely that if such blood survived it cannot have been shed at the time of the Passion. It may, however, have flowed from Christ's body at some other time.

Aquinas' sentences were to be subjected to a barrage of arguments, for and against, throughout the later Middle Ages.[50] His pronouncement, made in the *Summa*, upon the impossibility of possessing relics of the blood shed at Christ's Passion was to be attacked in due course by Franciscan theologians, leading to a series of public controversies, in which Dominicans and Franciscans were ranged on opposing sides, and in which Aquinas' earlier *Quodlibet* discussion was dredged from retirement to trouble even his own Dominican disciples.[51] Ironically, although Aquinas himself had been one of the most trenchant opponents of veneration of the Holy Blood, a relic of his own blood is said to have been preserved after his death, subsequently displayed in the church of Fossanuova.[52] Aware that Aquinas had at least admitted a doubt as to the resurrection of all of Christ's blood, and bolstered by the christological teachings of the greatest of their own theologians, St Bonaventure, certain Franciscans, in the 1350s and again after 1461, were to argue passionately in favour of the authenticity of relics of the Holy Blood. Bonaventure, in fact, had reached no certain conclusion on the matter, stating merely that relics of Christ's foreskin and blood were claimed to exist, and that, through divine dispensation, it was possible that God had permitted them to survive the Resurrection – much the same argument that had been deployed by Innocent III as a potential explanation for the survival of Christ's foreskin.[53] To this debate, Bonaventure does, however, contribute a further argument, similar in some respects to that of Grosseteste. Following the medical science of Avicenna, he suggests

---

[50] Before the outbreak of full-scale public controversy in the 1350s, at least three early *quodlibetales* concerning the survival of Christ's blood are listed by P. Glorieux, *La Littérature Quodlibétique*, 2 vols., Bibliothèque Thomiste v, xxi (Paris 1925 35) II 171 2 (John of Naples OP, *Quodlibet* 13.5 6, before 1336), 246 (Raymond Rigauld OFM, *Quodlibet* 5.21, 1280 × 1295), 268 (Roger Marston OFM, *Quodlibet* 4.14, 1285/6). For the last of these, see below p. 63. I am grateful to Peter Biller for alerting me to the existence of these questions.

[51] For a general summary, see Wadding, *Annales minorum*, VIII 58 62, XIII 206 16, 264 5, with a synopsis of the debate of the 1460s in H. C. Lea, *A History of the Inquisition of the Middle Ages*, 3 vols. (New York 1888), II 170 4.

[52] Boussel, *Des reliques*, 271, and see 269 for the blood of St Francis preserved at Padua and elsewhere.

[53] Bonaventure, 'On the Sentences' 4.12 p. 1 dub.2, in Bonaventure, *Opera omnia*, ed. B. a Portu Romatino *et al.*, 10 vols. (Quaracchi 1882 1902), IV 287: *Quod ergo obiciit de preputio, dicendum, quod vel non fuit de carne secundum speciem sed divina dispensatione parum de carne secundum materiam ibi fuit ut daretur nobis in devotionem sicut reliquiae, et sic dicendum est de sanguine, vel aliquid fuit de veritate, et illud resurrexit cum Christo et est in caelo, et residuum mansit.*

that certain bodily fluids of man, defined as 'humidities' rather than humours, flowing outside rather than within the body's veins, might be shed in the Resurrection.[54] In this way, the Franciscan Richard of Middleton was to argue *c.* 1300 that such fluids as urine, sweat and milk might not be essential to the resurrection of mankind.[55] Neither Bonaventure nor Middleton sought to include blood, even nutrimental blood, amongst such inessential 'humidities'. However, in due course, the argument was to be taken up and modified by other Franciscan theologians, most notably by the Provençal friar Francis de Meyronnes (d. *c.* 1325).

In his sentence commentary, composed *c.* 1320, Meyronnes deals with the Holy Blood only in passing.[56] Entirely ignoring the earlier debate that had focused upon medical and scientific understanding of the necessity of blood to the resurrected body of Christ, Meyronnes instead poses one simple question: 'What is Resurrection', a question to which he claims no previous authority had supplied a definitive reply.[57] To define Resurrection, he suggests, it is necessary to define death. Death, in accordance with the *De ecclesiastica hierarchia* of the pseudo-Dionysius – a text which Meyronnes had analysed at great length and which was falsely held in the Middle Ages to emanate from the circle of St Paul – can be defined as 'the separation of those things which are joined, rather than as their consumption. Hence, by opposition, Resurrection is the joining together of various separated things.'[58] Following the teachings of the Oxford and

---

[54] Bonaventure, 'On the Sentences' 4.44 p. 1 art.1 q.1, in Bonaventure, *Opera omnia*, IV 907–8. For Bonaventure's general devotion to the blood of Christ, seen as the chief source of man's redemption, and for his dependence here upon the devotion shown by St Francis, his order's founder, to the passion and wounds of Christ, see E. Gilson, 'Saint Bonaventure et l'iconographie de la passion', *Revue d'histoire franciscaine* 1 (1924), 405–24; E. Caggiano, 'Il Sangue di Cristo in S. Bonaventura', *SA*, VI part 2 (1989), 1165–84.

[55] Middleton, 'On the Sentences' 4.44 art.1 q.2, in *Clarissimi theologi magistri Ricardi de Mediavilla . . . super quatuor libros sententiarum Petri Lombardi quaestiones subtilissimae*, 4 vols. (Brescia 1591) (henceforth Middleton, *Questiones*) IV 574–5.

[56] For Meyronnes, see B. Roth, *Franz von Mayronis OFM*, Franziskanische Forschungen III (Werl 1936); H. Rossmann, *Die Hierarchie der Welt: Gesalt und System des Franz von Meyronnes OFM mit besonderer Berücksichtigung seiner Schöpfungslehre*, Franziskanische Forschungen XXIII (Werl 1972), and the articles by C. Langlois, *Histoire littéraire de la France* 36 (1927), 305–42; E. d'Alençon, *Dictionnaire de théologie Catholique*, ed. A. Vacant and others, vol. X part 2 (Paris 1929), cols. 1634–45.

[57] Francis de Meyronnes, 'On the Sentences', 4.43 q.1, *Preclarissima ac multum subtilia egregiaque scripta illuminati doctoris fratris Francisci de Mayronis Ordinis Minorum in quatuor libros sententiarum* (Venice 1520), fo. 216v, and for the somewhat confused transmission of Meyronne's commentary, in particular to Book 1 of the Sentences, see V. Doucet, 'Commentaires sur les sentences. Supplément au répertoire de M. Frédéric Stegmueller', *Archivum Franciscanum historicum* 47 (1954), 114–16.

[58] Meyronnes, fo. 216v: *Quod est mors potest diffiniri secundum Dionysi 'De Ecclesiastica hierarchia': mors est coniunctorum separatio, non alicuius rei consumptio. Ergo per oppositionem resurrectio est aliquorum separatorum coniunctio.* For Meyronnes' still unpublished digests and commentaries on the pseudo-Dionysius,

Paris master John Duns Scotus (d. 1307), Meyronnes then suggests that in the death of Christ and in the three days that his body passed in the tomb (the *triduum mortis*) various aspects of his being became separated one from another. He lists four such separations, following Scotus in his assumption that soul and body, divinity and humanity became separated in the tomb, and again following Scotus in his assumption that a plurality of forms ensured that, although in the tomb Christ's body became separated from his soul, both body and soul remained united, individually, to the Logos.[59] As the fourth such separation, however, Meyronnes proposes the separation of Christ's blood from his body, after Christ's death, when the centurion opened his side with a lance.[60] Here, Meyronnes echoes a papal pronouncement made at the Council of Vienne in 1311–12 that Christ was already dead when the centurion caused blood and water to flow from his side – a pronouncement that at the time had been intended to buttress the near-mystical claim that the Church was formed from the blood and water flowing from Christ's side, and which in turn had been been intended to rebut the teachings of various Franciscan theologians, most notably Pietro Olivi, that Christ's side-wound had been inflicted before rather than after death, that the Church as a body was subject to decay and rebirth, and that Christ's soul was not the 'form' of his incarnate body.[61]

This last is an extremely complicated issue, recently analysed in detail by Alain Boureau. In a wide-ranging study, Boureau has traced the immediate origins of the debate on substance and form, supposedly concluded at Vienne, back to the 1270s and 80s, when the idea of plurality of forms, so essential in the christology of such writers as Scotus

see Langlois in *Histoire littéraire de la France*, XXXVI 325–6; Roth, *Franz von Mayronis*, 167–71. I can find nothing relevant in the brief synopsis of Meyronnes on the pseudo-Dionysius in Paris, Bibliothèque nationale MS Latin 16536 fos. 6or–2v.

[59] For Scotus' exposition here, and for commentary, see 'Oxford Commentaries' 3.21, in Scotus, *Opera omnia*, XIV 740–50; R. Cross, *Duns Scotus* (Oxford 1999), 73–7; A. Michel, 'Forme du corps humain', *Dictionnaire de théologie catholique*, ed. A. Vacant *et al.*, vol. VI (Paris 1924), cols. 546–88, esp. 574–5; Roth, *Franz von Mayronis*, 418ff.

[60] Meyronnes, fo. 216v: *Quarta separatio fuit sanguinis a corpore post mortem Christi quando unus militum latus eius aperuit.*

[61] For the pronouncement of May 1312, see *Enchiridion symbolorum definitionum et declarationum de rebus fidei et morum*, ed. H. Denziger and C. Bannwart, new edn (Fribourg 1922), 208–10: *emisso iam spiritu perforari lancea sustinuit latus suum, ut exinde profluentibus undis aque et sanguinis formaretur unica et immaculata ac virgo sancta mater Ecclesia, coniux Christi . . . Sacro approbante concilio, declaramus predictum apostolum et euangelistam Ioannem rectum in premissis facte rei ordinem tenuisse, narrando quod Christo, iam mortuo, unus militum lancea latus eius aperuit.* For commentary on various of the teachings against which this pronouncement was directed, see the article by Martin, *Dictionnaire de théologie catholique*, VI cols. 546–50; D. Burr, *The Persecution of Peter Olivi*, Transactions of the American Philosophical Society n.s. LXVI part 5 (Philadelphia 1976), esp. pp. 73–80.

and Meyronnes, had itself emerged from discussions in the schools of Paris and Oxford between the followers of Aquinas and Franciscan theologians, most notably John Pecham. During this debate, marked by an attempt made by Pecham in 1286 to proscribe Aquinas' teachings as tantamount to heresy, questions on the composition and nature of Christ's body *in triduum mortis* had been much discussed, since to the Francisans they appeared to challenge Aquinas' teaching that the soul was the substantial form of man. We need not pursue this earlier debate in any detail here, save to notice that the nature of the entombed body of Christ, and in particular the possibility that the bodies of the dead might still give off blood, had both been subjected to intense discussion in the decades immediately prior to 1300: a discussion which, at least on the Franciscan side, had depended much upon the influence, over Pecham and others, of ideas transmitted from the Oxford of Robert Grosseteste.[62] Amongst the Oxford masters who contributed to the debate of the 1280s, both Roger of Marston and Nicholas of Ockham had treated of the Holy Blood, questioning whether Christ's divinity had been truly united to the blood shed in the Crucifixion. After some fairly jejune discussion, both Marston and Ockham had retreated to the Thomist line: that the surviving relics of Christ's blood came not from the Crucifixion but from later miracles, such as the bleeding icon of Beirut.[63] Ranging far beyond this debate, Meyronnes' originality lies in his suggestion that Resurrection can be defined as the reunification of Christ's soul with his body, of his humanity with his divinity, of his blood with his body, and of Christ's divinity with his blood, 'since in the tomb Christ's divinity was not united to his blood as it was to his body and soul . . . It would be wrong to say that God was on the Cross because the blood of Christ was there, or that God lay scattered on the earth even though the blood of Christ lay there scattered.'[64]

---

[62] Boureau, *Théologie, science et censure*, especially chs. 1–3, 8–9. For Pecham's intellectual development in a field still dominated by the thought of Grosseteste, see chs. 4–7. It is worth noting that, like Meyronnes, Pecham was much interested in the thought of the pseudo-Dionysius, producing a brief Anglo-Norman synopsis of the 'Celestial Hierarchy' which he dedicated to Edward I's queen, Eleanor of Castile: *ibid.*, p. 190; A. Rosin, 'Die "Hierarchie" des John Peckham, historisch interpretiert', *Zeitschrift für Romanische Philologie* 52 (1932), 583–614.

[63] Roger Marston, 'Quodlibet' 4.14 (1285/6), printed as *Fr. Roger Marston O.F.M. quodlibeta quatuor*, ed. G. F. Etzkorn and I. C. Brady, Bibliotheca Franciscana scholastica medii aevi XXVI (Florence 1968), 393–4; Nicholas of Ockham, 'Questio' 5.8, in *Quaestiones disputatae de traductione humanae naturae a primo parente*, ed. C. Saco Alarcón (Grottaferrata 1993), 213. For other questions raised by Marston, on the bloody sweat of the Crucifixion, and on the power by which bodies might bleed in the presence of their assassins, directly inspired by the debate of the 1280s, see Boureau, *Théologie, science et censure*, 241–4.

[64] Meyronnes, fo. 216v: *Quarta unio fuit divinitas cum sanguine, nam in triduo divinitas non fuit unita cum sanguine sicut cum corpore et anima . . . In triduo verum fuit dicere Deus est sepultus quia corpus, cui divinitas*

This teaching is further expounded in Meyronnes' sermons 'In festo Pasche'[65] (where he reiterates the principal arguments of his sentence commentary on the separation of Christ's blood from his body and from that portion of his divinity that remained united with his body), 'In Parasceve'[66] (where he emphasizes the sacrificial nature of Christ's blood-shedding, essential to the redemption of mankind, and where he suggests that the blood shed in the Passion, like Christ's flesh, was preserved from corruption by divine grace, to be resumed into Christ's resurrected body),[67] and most significantly in the sermon 'De Sacramento in cena Domini'. Here Meyronnes poses a question that had long exercised theologians: what would have happened had the very first mass been celebrated not after but during Christ's three days in the tomb? In answering this, he suggests that the bread and wine of such a mass would have remained mere bread and wine, just as in Christ's death, God was placed in the tomb and did not remain on the Cross, even though Christ's blood remained there: 'because the body, not the blood, is the principal part of a man'.[68] From this he goes on to pose a further question, for the first and only time directly addressing the issue of blood relics. 'Should any blood relic of Christ be venerated save for the eucharist?', he asks. Although many allege that Christ resumed all of his blood, Meyronnes replies that it is not inconceivable that some portion of it remains on earth, 'since of this sort of blood, the glorified body would have no lack'. Quite what is meant by this is unclear, but it is more likely that Meyronnes seeks to disparage such relics because of his belief in the separation of Christ's blood from his soul and divinity, rather than that he is here echoing the much older debate on the various types of blood and the degree to which they were essential to resurrection. In any event, he continues, such blood relics, if they do indeed survive, would not merit veneration to the same extent as the blood of the eucharist.

---

erat unita, erat sepultum, et similiter erat verum dicere Deus descendit ad inferos quia anima Christi cui erat divinitas unita illuc descenderat, et tamen non fuit verum dicere Deus est in Cruce cum ibi esset sanguis Christi nec Deus iacet effusus super terram, cum tamen sanguis Christi effusus iaceret super terram.

[65] Meyronnes, 'In festo Pasche', in *Quadragesimale seu sermones de tempore F. de Mayronis* (Brussels 1484), here quoting from the copy in Paris BN livres D-2064, sermon 86, unfoliated, where there are minor differences from the scheme of the sentence commentary.

[66] Meyronnes, 'In Parasceve II', in *ibid.* sermon 85, incidentally repeating the much older theme that Christ's blood was formed from that of the Virgin Mary.

[67] *Ibid.* sermon 85: *Dicitur quod virtute divina fuit recollectus et a corruptione servatus sicut caro et corpori infusus. Intelligendum tamen quod quatuor fuerunt reunita, scilicet corpus et anima, sanguis et divinitas, licet enim divinitas fuerit cum corpore et anima, tamen in triduo non putatur unita cum effuso sanguine immediate.*

[68] Meyronnes, 'De Sacramento in cena Domini', in *ibid.* sermon 80: *propter sepulturam corporis dicimus Deum fuisse sepultum, non in cruce remansisse sicut ibi remansit sanguis, et istius ratio est quia corpus est principalis hominis pars et non sanguis.*

No historical relic of Christ's blood could be united to his divinity, just as it was not united to that divinity during the three days in the tomb. In the tomb, Christ's blood was no more united to his divinity than the wine of a mass celebrated during the three days of his death. The blood of the eucharist, being fully joined to Christ's divinity, is far more worthy of veneration than any supposed portion of the historic blood of Christ.[69]

Here Meyronnes skates close to, without actually formulating, a very startling proposition. If, as he suggests, Christ's blood and body, and his divinity and blood, had indeed become separated in the tomb, then it was possible to argue that the blood of the Passion was unworthy of veneration in the same way that Christ's body was venerated: an argument that, as we shall see, was to be taken up by later commentators and which was to pose a threat to some of the fundamental tenets of Christian orthodoxy. According to Meyronnes, it would be as ridiculous to assert that the blood shed by Christ in the tomb was united to his divinity as it would be to claim that a chalice placed in Christ's tomb could have become united to his divinity: an intriguing but almost certainly unconscious denial, this, of the sort of claims that were being made in contemporary romances for the mystical significance of the Holy Grail.[70] The issues touched upon by Meyronnes were so important and yet so complicated that by no means all his fellow Franciscans, let alone members of other orders, could accept them unchallenged. Pietro dell'Aquila, for example, known as 'Scotellus' for his adherence to the teachings of Duns Scotus, was to argue in his sentence commentary of the 1330s that Christ did indeed remain a man, materially (*materialiter*) if not in form (*formaliter*), during the three days in the tomb.[71] Later still, probably in the 1440s, another Franciscan, St Giovanni da Capestrano (1386–1456), was to compose a full-scale polemic against Meyronnes' position on the Holy Blood, restating the assertion of Aquinas that whatever blood relics were in existence could not be physical remnants of the Passion, but must

[69] *Ibid.: Remanet hic dubitatio: si sanguis Cristi est venerandus qui est in aliquibus reliquiis preter eukaristiam? Dicunt multi quod non, quia Cristus totum sanguinem resumpsit. Tamen non videtur inconveniens si aliqua portio remansit, cum non indiget tanto sanguine corpus glorificatum, et ideo venerari potest. Secundus dubitatio: si talis sanguis sit venerandus sicut in eukaristia? Dicitur quod non, quia non est unitus divinitati sicut nec in triduo mortis Cristi. Unde sicut in triduo nullus debuisset adorare calicem secundum latriam eo quod non erat divinitate unita, ita nec sanguinem istum qui est separatus a corpore cum sanguis in eukaristia est sibi coniunctus.*

[70] *Ibid.: nullus debuisset adorare calicem secundum latriam eo quod non erat divinitate unita.*

[71] Pietro dell'Aquila, 'On the Sentences', 3.21 2 q.2, in *Petri de Aquila questiones in quatuor libros* (Speyer 1480), unfoliated, referring to Scotus' opinion that *Christus in triduo non fuit homo formaliter*. For Pietro (d. 1361) see the article by A. Teetaert, *Dictionnaire de théologie catholique*, ed. A. Vacant *et al.*, vol. XIV (Paris 1941), cols. 1730–3.

have emerged subsequently from maltreated images or from eucharistic miracles.[72] Capestrano is one of the few such commentators to refer to specific historical relics of the blood, mentioning a relic that he himself had handled at Piscaria on the Adriatic, brought forth from a maltreated image; another said to have flowed from a series of hosts hidden from the Saracens of Aragon, and finally the bleeding hosts displayed at Brussels, said to have been pierced by the Jews in 1370, indulgenced by Pope Eugenius IV in 1436 and which Capestrano himself may have viewed in his role as Franciscan visitor-general to Brussels in 1443.[73]

Meanwhile, and no doubt inspired by a reading of Meyronnes, various Franciscan theologians began to develop a more radical line of argument in respect to the Holy Blood. There were to be two principal peaks to the ensuing controversy. In 1351, the Franciscan, Francis Bajulus of Barcelona, pronounced publicly that the blood of the Passion had become separated from Christ's divinity. This claim – nowhere attributed to a reading of Meyronnes, but, as we have seen, already present in Meyronnes' teaching – was referred to the local Dominican inquisitor and condemned, almost certainly with the approval of Pope Clement VI.[74] Clement VI may well have possessed a personal interest in the suppression of teachings associated with Francis de Meyronnes. In 1320–1, in his youth as the Paris theologian Pierre-Roger, he had engaged in public debate with Meyronnes precisely over the nature of Christ's Incarnation, in this instance accusing Meyronnes of attributing more qualities to God the Father than he allowed to God the

---

[72] N. Cocci, 'Il sangue di Cristo in San Giovanni da Capestrano. Problema Storico-Teologico', *SA*, VII part 3 (1991), 1287–1387, editing a treatise that survives in at least five Italian MSS, with specific reference to Meyronnes at pp. 1343–5, 1374. Capestrano cites Meyronne's teachings from a sermon 'De resurrectione domini' (the Easter sermon, no. 86 in the collection published in 1484) and from Meyronnes' still unpublished commentary on the 'De ecclesiastica hierarchia' of the pseudo-Dionysius. Capestrano (p. 1364) also cites Pietro dell'Aquila's assertion that Christ remained a man in death.

[73] Cocci, 'Il sangue di Cristo in San Giovanni', 1352, 1379–84. For Capestrano's visit to Brussels, see H. Lippens, 'S. Jean de Capistran en mission aux états bourguignons, 1442–1443', *Archivum Franciscanum historicum* 35 (1942), 113–32, 254–95, esp. 271–3, and for the Brussels miracle, see P. Lefèvre, 'La Valeur historique d'une enquête épiscopale sur le miracle eucharistique de Bruxelles en 1370', *Revue d'histoire ecclésiastique* 28 (1932), 329–46, and the same author's 'A propos d'une bulle d'indulgence d'Eugène IV en faveur du culte eucharistique à Bruxelles', *Hommage à dom. Ursmer Berlière* (Brussels 1931), 163–8.

[74] Wadding, *Annales minorum*, VIII 58–62, reported in the fourteenth-century inquisition manual of Nicholas Eymericus, *Directorium inquisitorum* 2.10, ed. F. Pegna (Venice 1607), 262–3. According to Nicholas, the Franciscan teaching was specifically condemned in letters of Pope Clement VI. In fact, the Pope's condemnation is known only through letters of the Dominican cardinal, John de Molendinis, who on 20 July 1351 wrote to the inquisitor, Nicholas Rosellus, asking that the Franciscan teaching be suppressed; *Bullarium ordinis ff. praedicatorum*, ed. T. Ripoll and A. Bremond, 8 vols. (Rome 1729–40), II 235–6 no. 22.

Son.[75] Although no papal letter survives relating to the Barcelona controversy of 1351, the Pope had already made his own position apparent in the jubilee bull *Unigenitus*, issued in 1343, asserting amongst other things that a single drop of Christ's blood, being united to the Logos, would be sufficient for the redemption of the whole of mankind.[76]

Following the Barcelona controversy, a century was to pass until the dispute was once again brought to papal attention.[77] Central to this second wave of controversy was the status of a relic of the Holy Blood venerated and displayed by the Franciscans of La Rochelle. In 1448, this relic had been referred to a committee of theologians from the University of Paris, presumably because it was even then exciting disapproval. Without lending any endorsement to the specific authenticity, as opposed to the general theological justifications for the relic of La Rochelle, the Paris masters declared that in itself 'it is not repugnant to the piety of the faithful to believe that some of the blood shed by Christ at the time of the Passion remains on earth'.[78] A year later, the matter was brought before the Pope, Nicholas V. Although, or perhaps precisely because, he was himself a native of Sarzana, home to one of the relics of the Holy Blood of Lucca, and despite the fact that as Pope he was himself the possessor of several relics of the Holy Blood, Nicholas declared that no relic of the blood of the Passion could be admitted to have survived the Resurrection, upholding Aquinas' judgement in both the *Quodlibetales* and the *Summa*. The La Rochelle blood should be accounted, at best, an effluvial relic from some such miraculous image as the icon of Beirut.[79] At La Rochelle, however, the Franciscans continued to advertise their relic as if it were the true blood of Christ, apparently claiming that it had been collected at the time of the Crucifixion in the glove of Nicodemus.[80]

---

[75] *François de Meyronnes, Pierre Roger, disputatio (1320–1321)*, ed. J. Barbet, Textes philosophiques du Moyen Age x (Paris 1961).

[76] *Enchiridion Symbolorum*, ed. Denzinger and Bannwart, 220–1, quoted amongst others by Giovanni da Capestrano in his refutation of Meyronnes (ed. Cocci, 1366), and in a much later discussion of blood relics by the Jesuit Gabriel Vazquez, *Opera omnia*, 7 vols. (Antwerp 1621), V 309.

[77] For the debate of the 1460s the best introduction is that by N. Cocci, 'Le Dispute teologiche del "triduum mortis" nei secoli xiv–xv: aspetto storico e dommatico', *SA*, VI part 2 (1989), 1185–1233, which none the less fails to take account of various of the evidences cited below.

[78] *Chartularium universitatis parisiensis*, ed. H. Denifle and A. Chatelain, 4 vols. (Paris 1889–97), IV 682–3 no. 2634: *non repugnat pietati fidelium credere quod aliquid de sanguine Christi effuso tempore Passionis remanserit in terris.*

[79] *Ibid.*, IV 683–4 no. 2635, for the bull *Exhibita nobis nuper*, 19 August 1449, taken from the papal registers.

[80] The association between Nicodemus and the blood of La Rochelle is reported by Jean Calvin, *Traité des reliques*, ed. A. Autin (Paris 1921), 102–3, as part of Calvin's wider discussion and dismissal of all blood relics as historically implausible imposters.

In July 1461, they obtained letters from pope Pius II, reiterating the Paris judgement of 1448 that it was in no way repugnant to true faith to teach that Christ might have relinquished some of his blood after the Passion, commanding the local church authorities to ensure that the relic was properly venerated and displayed.[81] Pope Pius himself had recently spent several months at the congress of Mantua (1459–60), where he had ample opportunity to view the Holy Blood supposedly brought to the city by Longinus, and during which he was to proclaim a new crusade against the Turks: yet a further reminder of the strong links between blood relics and the crusade.[82] His declaration in favour of the relic of La Rochelle followed in the train of a lively debate over the authenticity of all such relics of the Passion, initiated by enquiries into the eucharistic relic of Wilsnack in the early 1450s.[83] This debate over the Wilsnack relic had involved, amongst many other theologians, that same Franciscan, Giovanni da Capestrano, whom we have considered elsewhere for his denunciation of the teachings of Francis de Meyronnes. It is not inconceivable that it was via Capestrano's denunciation that an interest was rekindled during the 1450s in Meyronnes' opinion on the blood, albeit with results that Capestrano would have considered entirely perverse. Be that as it may, at Brescia, on Easter Sunday 1462, an attempt was made

---

[81] Pius II's bull *Illius qui se*, 18 July 1461, addressed to the precentor and two abbots of Saintes, appears to have escaped previous notice. It is known to me only through its appearance in a tract in favour of the blood relic of Trier, of which there is a single, possibly unique, copy in Paris, Bibliothèque nationale imprimés Res H-1026 (2): *Pro abbatia beati Martini Treverensis... de sanguine Christi corporali super terram relicto* (Cologne 1514), fos. 2v–3r, the bull declaring that *veritati fidei nullatenus repugnat affirmare redemptorem nostrum de sanguine prefato ob ipsius passionis memoriam aliquam partem in terris reliquisse*. According to the account that reached Trier, the Franciscans claimed that their relic had been at La Rochelle since the time of the town's foundation, presumably since the mid-twelfth century.

[82] *Mantova: la storia*, ed. Coniglio, II 13–16, esp. 16, states that Pius recovered from illness at the congress following prayers and veneration of the Holy Blood. The source for this story is untraced, but is possibly one of the unpublished treatises, still at Mantua, referred to in *ibid.*, p. 55 n. 50. In recounting the pope's arrival at Mantua in 1459, the *Commentaries* of Pius II (Book 2) do, however, refer unambiguously to the Holy Blood as one of the city's treasures, said to have been discovered miraculously in the time of Charlemagne and Leo III: *Commentarii*, ed. van Heck, I 168; *The Commentaries of Pius II, Books II and III*, trans. F. A. Gragg and L. C. Gabel, Smith College Studies in History XXV nos. 1–4 (Northampton, Mass., 1942), 185.

[83] For the debate over the Wilsnack relic, see *Das Gutachten der Theologischen Fakultät Erfurt 1452 über 'Das heilige Blut von Wilsnak'*, ed. R. Damerau (Marburg 1976), esp. 14–15 for conflicting opinions on historic, as opposed to eucharistic, relics of Christ's blood. For the involvement of Giovanni da Capestrano, see Cocci, 'Le Dispute', I 203–4; Breest, 'Das Wunderblut von Wilsnack', *Märkische Forschungen* 16 (1881), 255–74, citing letters in the archives of Capestrano, Göttingen, Dessau and Wolfenbüttel, none of which have I been able to consult. For questions on Christ's blood and Incarnation in the thought of Nicholas of Cusa, perhaps occasioned by the Wilsnack dispute and answered by Cusa in vindication of Aquinas, see R. Haubst, *Die Christologie des Nikolaus von Kues* (Freiburg 1956), 7–8, 313–28.

by the distinguished Franciscan preacher, Giacomo della Marca (1394–1476), to revive the condemned teaching of the 1350s that the blood of the Passion had become separated from Christ's divinity.[84] Marca, who had corresponded with Capestrano only a few years earlier on the common interests of their order, immediately became the object of public outcry.[85] The Dominicans sought the suppression of Marca's claims, leading to a public debate before Pius II and the production of several treatises from the opposing camps in December 1462, in which the Franciscans referred specifically to the earlier teachings of Bonaventure, Middleton and Meyronnes.[86] The debate itself proved inconclusive, and in 1464, Pope Pius intervened once more, declaring via the bull *Ineffabilis summi providentia* that the issues were uncertain and should be withheld from future public controversy pending a more definite papal pronouncement, meanwhile forbidding either side from raising a charge of heresy against those who taught that the blood of Christ was or was not separated from Christ's divinity in the tomb.[87]

---

[84] Cocci, 'Le Dispute', 1194–1205; M. Horster, 'Mantuae Sanguis Preciosus', *Walraf-Richartz-Jahrbuch* 25 (1963), 163–4, and for Giacomo, see T. Somigli, 'Vita di S. Giacomo della Marca scitta da Fra Venanzio da Fabriano', *Archivum Franciscanum historicum* 17 (1924), 378–414, esp. 393, 407–8; *Bibliotheca sanctorum*, VI 388–401, esp. col. 393. Giacomo's own arguments, or those of his Franciscan advocate, are preserved in Paris, Bibliothèque nationale MS Latin 12390 fos. 42r–5v, referring specifically to the historical blood relics of the Lateran, Venice, Mantua and La Rochelle at fo. 43r. Marca, or his advocate, makes the point that these relics have not been condemned: *Quidque in Laterano et Venetiis et Mantue et in Galliis apud Ruppellam et aliis in locis Cristi sanguis ostenditur, et is esse affirmatur qui de corpore suo fluxit in passione. Concurrunt populi et sanguinem Ihesu preciosum tollunt. Tolerat hec Romana ecclesia et non dampnat, non adversitur, non contradixit.* For the Dominican reply, referring to these same relics, see Pius II, 'Commentaries' Bk 11, in *Commentarii*, ed. van Heck, II 669; *Commentaries XI*, trans. Gragg, 725.

[85] For the one example of their correspondence, dated 14 December 1455, suggesting generally friendly relations, today preserved in the Archivio Communale at Monteprandone, see *Lettera autografia di San Giacomo della Marca (1393–1476) a San Giovanni da Capestrano (1386–1456)*, ed. U. Picciafuoco (Monteprandone 1976), also printed by N. Dal Gal in *Archivum Franciscanum historicum* 1 (1908), 94–7.

[86] For the theological arguments deployed, see the detailed analysis by Cocci, 'Le Dispute', 1205–16.

[87] For the principal evidences on this dispute, first announced in papal letters of 31 May 1462, and ended by the bull *Ineffabilis* of 1 August 1464, see Pius II, 'Commentaries' Bk 11, in *Commentarii*, ed. van Heck, ii 645–73; *Commentaries XI*, trans. Gragg, 703–29; *Bullarium ordinis ff. praedicatorum*, III 421 no. 56, 434 no. 69; *Bullarium privilegiorum ac diplomatum Romanorum pontificum amplissima collectio*, ed. C. Cocquelines, 14 vols. in 17 (Rome 1739–44), III part iii 116; A. Crivellucci, *I Codici della libreria raccolta da S. Giacomo della Marca* (Leghorn 1889), 78–9. The debate is referred to by various later commentators including Rocca, *Opera omnia*, 1241, and is summarized by Lea, *Inquisition*, II 170–4, and by M. D. Chenu, 'Sang du Christ', *Dictionnaire de théologie Catholique*, ed. A. Vacant et al., XIV part 1 (Paris 1939), cols. 1094–7, including a brief analysis of Paris, Bibliothèque nationale MS Latin 12390. This manuscript, also briefly analysed by P. O. Kristeller, *Iter Italicum III* (London and Leiden 1983), 253, assembles important and in large part unpublished sources gathered by the Dominicans in the aftermath of the dispute of 1462–4, together with materials

None the less, and in the absence of any final papal pronouncement, treatises continued to be written and in some cases published. At least four of them, by the Franciscan cardinal Francesco della Rovere, the future Pope Sixtus IV (d. 1484);[88] by the Dominicans Bartolomeo Lapacci bishop of Corone (d. 1466);[89] Gabriele de Barcelona, Giacomo de Brescia and Vercellino de Vercelli,[90] and Domenico de Domenichi, bishop of Brescia (1462–78),[91] were directly inspired by the debate of 1462–4. Others, for example by Leonardo Matteo de Udine OP (c. 1480),[92] Silvestro Mazolini (c. 1516),[93] Cardinal Cajetan (c. 1527),[94] Angelus Rocca bishop of Thagaste (d. 1620),[95] and at enormous length by Francesco Collius (c. 1617),[96] take the form of commentaries upon

on the contemporary scholastic dispute on future contingents, for which see L. Baudry, *La Querelle des futurs contingents* (Paris 1950). For a political analysis of the 1462 dispute, stressing the Pope's desire to ensure peace between the two great orders of friars and hence joint support for his own pontificate and plans for a crusade, see C. M. Ady, *Pius II* (London 1913), 253–4.

[88] Sixtus IV, *Tractatus de sanguine christi* (Rome 1472; reprinted Nuremburg 1473), BL references IB. 7586 and IB. 17385; Paris, Bibliothèque nationale imprimés D-295(1). A manuscript copy of this tract was made for the monks of Hailes (BL MS Royal 8 D xvii), and a further copy was inserted into the tract in favour of the blood of St Martin's Trier (Paris, Bibliothèque nationale imprimés Res H-1026(2) fos. 9v *et seq.*). For Cardinal Francesco's supposed dealings with Giacomo della Marca, see Somigli, 'Vita di S. Giacomo', 407–8.

[89] Paris, Bibliothèque nationale MS Latin 12390 fos. 58v–78v, noted by T. Kaeppeli, *Scriptores ordinis praedicatorum medii aevi*, I (Rome 1970), 156 no. 431, with a further MS copy at Florence and brief commentary by Kaeppeli, 'Bartolomeo Lapacci de' Rimbertini (1402–1466), vescovo, legato pontificio, scrittore', *Archivum fratrum praedicatorum* 9 (1939), 86–127, esp. 106–7.

[90] Paris, Bibliothèque nationale MS Latin 12390 fos. 72r–8v, noticed by T. Kaeppeli, *Scriptores ordinis praedicatorum medii aevi* II (Rome 1975), 3 no. 1170, with a further MS copy in Rome.

[91] Domenico de Domenichi, *De sanguine christi* (Venice 1557), and for commentary, see H. Jedin, *Studien über Domenico de Domenichi (1416–1478)* (Mainz 1957), 96–101. A copy of Domenico's treatise is included in Paris, Bibliothèque nationale MS Latin 12390 fos. 1–30v.

[92] Leonardo Matteo d'Udine, *Tractatus mirabilis de sanguine Christi in triduo mortis eius effuso* (Venice 1617).

[93] Silvestro Mazolini, *Aurea Rosa* (Paris 1516), fos. 251r–8v, 'questiones' 30–4, and more conveniently in the edition of the same by D. Zambelli (Venice 1599), fos. 308r–18r, 'quaestiones' 30–4 (misnumbered).

[94] *Commentaria luculentissima ac plane divina reverendissimi domini Thomae de Vio Caietani . . . in tertiam partem divi Thomae Aquinatis* (Rome 1527), fos. 319r–21r (misnumbered 309r–21r), reprinted in *Sancti Thomae Aquinatis doctoris angelici opera omnia iussu impensaque Leonis XIII P. M. edita*, 48 vols. (Rome 1882–1971), XI, 512–3.

[95] Rocca, *Opera omnia*, I 240–6. Rocca's tract is followed by a similar discussion of Christ's foreskin.

[96] F. Collius, *De sanguine Christi libri quinque* (Milan 1617), running to more than 900 pages, with a brief conspectus of the history of blood relics at 853–8. Horster, 'Mantuae sanguis preciosus', 163, and *Mantova: la storia*, ed. Coniglio, II 55 n. 50, also refer to treatises by the Carmelite Pietro de Nuvolaria, 'Opusculum de sanguine Iesu Christi qui est Mantuae', dedicated to the Mantuan cardinal Sigismondo Gonzaga (1469–1525), and by B. Spagnoli, 'Tractatus de sanguine Christi', of which possibly unique manuscripts are said to survive in Mantua, Biblioteca Comunale A.I.6; G.II.18. See also the involvement of cardinal Nicholas de Cusa: R. Haubst, *Die Christologie des Nikolaus von Kues* (Freiburg 1956), 299–304. All of these commentaries would repay a more detailed study than is possible here.

the earlier debate, concentrating in particular upon the differing opinions on the matter expressed by Aquinas in his *Summa* and his *Questiones quodlibetales*. For the most part the arguments advanced here are abstruse and theological, and tell us little of the history of the physical relics of Christ's blood.[97] Only two of the medieval commentaries, by John Hus and the Westminster monk William of Sudbury, merit a more detailed discussion, reserved for the following chapter.

In the meantime, we should note that there was far more at stake in these disputes than a simple question of relics and their veneration. Both in the 1350s and again between 1462 and 1464, it was not merely the authenticity of particular blood relics that had come under attack, but the veneration of Christ's blood in the mass, the Franciscans arguing that the blood shed by Christ at the Passion had become separated from his divinity in the three days during which he lay in the tomb, and that therefore it was unworthy of veneration in the way that Christ's body was venerated.[98] In essence this line of argument can be traced back to Francis de Meyronnes, and via him to the ideas on the formal separation of Christ's body from his soul, and of his humanity from his divinity, expounded by Duns Scotus and first debated at Oxford and Paris in the 1270s and 80s. Far from seeking to denigrate the sacrament of the mass, Meyronnes had in fact argued that the blood of the eucharist was far more worthy of veneration than any historical relic of Christ's Passion. As for the blood of the Passion, Meyronnes had specifically asserted that its shedding had been essential to Christ's sacrifice and hence to the redemption of mankind; that its reunification with the body and divinity of Christ was a necessary feature of Christ's Resurrection, and that for its saving grace, the blood so resumed had truly been glorified in Christ.[99] By allowing, however, that some portion of the blood of the Passion might have remained on earth, and by asserting that in the Passion Christ's blood became separated from his divinity, Meyronnes articulated ideas which sailed close to the furthest extreme of orthodoxy, posing troubling questions over the nature of the hypostatic union, the orthodox explanation of the means by which Christ the Logos was united to his incarnate form. In debate during the 1460s, both Franciscans and Dominicans were forced to refer to the historical relics of the Holy

---

[97] Again, for the theological positions, see Cocci, 'Le Dispute', 1216–33.

[98] See in particular Pius II, *Commentarii*, ed. van Heck, II 647–55; *Commentaries XI*, trans. Gragg, 706–12.

[99] For his emphasis on the redemptive qualities of Christ's blood, see Meyronnes, 'In Parasceve II', in *Quadragesimale seu sermones de tempore F. de Mayronis* (Brussels 1484) sermon 85, unfoliated, especially the seventh and final section: *Qualiter iste sanguis fuit glorificatus.*

Blood, since, as Aquinas himself had recognized, if the authenticity of such relics were to be accepted, they posed a considerable challenge to the argument that Christ's blood was fully and inseparably united to his divinity. In 1462, for example, the Franciscans were to argue that the fact that the blood relics of Mantua, Venice and the Lateran survived only in a dried and corrupted state suggested that Christ's blood could undergo corruption; something that would have been impossible had it been truly united to his incorruptible body.[100] As Dominique Rigaux has recently suggested, the debate of the 1460s may also have had repercussions within the world of Renaissance painting. After 1462, artists who sought to depict the deposition from the Cross could choose to colour the slab upon which Christ's dead body was laid either red (thereby declaring their adherence to Franciscan ideas upon the separability of Christ's blood and divinity), or grey, in adherence to the Dominicans.[101]

For the most part, the battle lines between Franciscan and Dominican opinion on the Holy Blood had been drawn as early as the time of Bonaventure and Aquinas in the thirteenth century, and were to remain in place well into the seventeenth century and beyond. There are, however, some minor but none the less intriguing exceptions to this rule. As we have seen, the Franciscan Giovanni da Capestrano had, in the 1440s, circulated a treatise arguing against the opinion of Francis de Meyronnes and in favour of that of the Dominican Aquinas. Much later, we might expect the Portuguese Dominican Vincent Pons to have been an opponent of all relics of the blood. In fact, in his tract on the controversy published in 1609, Pons seeks, albeit tentatively, to distance himself from Aquinas, inclining much more towards the line of argument advanced by Franciscan theologians. His motive here is worth remarking. As a member of the community of St Maximin in Provence, Pons found himself attached to a house, which, although under the Dominican rule, had inherited from its previous Benedictine inhabitants a substantial collection of the relics of St Mary Magdalene, supposedly rediscovered in 1279, including a sacred ampoule said to contain earth mixed with blood, collected by the Magdalene from beneath Christ's Cross. As a result, the Dominicans, established at St Maximin after 1295, found themselves in

[100] Pius II, *Commentarii*, ed. van Heck, II 657; *Commentaries* XI, trans. Gragg, 714, summarizing the Franciscan arguments presented in Paris, Bibliothèque nationale MS Latin 12390 fos. 42r v.
[101] D. Rigaux, 'Autour de la dispute "De sanguine christi". Une relecture de quelques peintures italiennes de la seconde moitié du XVe siècle', *Le Sang au Moyen-Age*, ed. Faure, 393 403. The argument is not entirely convincing, not least because red and grey are used as the colour in alternative paintings of the deposition, both attributed to Giovanni Bellini.

11   St-Maximin, retable showing the Crucifixion (attributed to Antonio Ronzen,
c. 1520), with the Magdalene at the foot of the Cross and angels catching the
blood from the wound in Christ's right side (James King)

the peculiar position of acting as guardians to a blood relic which the greatest theologians of their order taught could not in fact exist.[102]

As late as the 1740s, in writing of the canonization of Giacomo della Marca, Pope Benedict XIV (1740–58) was forced to review the controversy over blood relics. In his treatise on the saints, *De servorum dei beatificatione*, although declaring against the division of the blood of Christ's Passion from his divinity, Benedict rehearses the long and controversial history of the Holy Blood without reaching any firm conclusion as to whether, for example, the blood of Mantua was truly to be accounted a portion of Christ's blood rescued by Longinus or, as Aquinas would have it, merely the effluvia from some such source as the miraculous icon of Beirut.[103] In this way, and despite several hundred years of sophisticated polemic on either side, the Church was no nearer settling the issue under Benedict XIV than it had been in the time of Innocent III. Since then, no definitive ruling has been issued, either for or against the authenticity of relics of Christ's blood.[104] Although, in theory, all of the blood shed in the Passion is believed to remain united to Christ's resurrected divinity, at no point has the Church specifically condemned the veneration of relics of the blood of the Passion, and this despite the fact that in abstract terms such relics might appear to be a theological impossibility.

[102] Vincent Pons, *La Saincte Ampoulle de Sainct Maximin* (Aix-en-Provence 1609) (copy in Paris, Bibliothèque nationale imprimés Res P-D-125), with a theological enquiry at pp. 33–51, 59–61, and, at 53–8, a hopelessly misinformed account of the discovery and translation of Mary Magdalene's relics in 1279/80. Pons concludes (50–1) that 'une petite quantité de ce sang' might have survived the Resurrection, being separated *in triduum mortis* from its union with the Logos, perhaps as an extraneous humour: a thoroughly Franciscan line of argument. For accounts of the St Maximin relics, noting the coincidence between Charles of Salerno's 'invention' of the relics of St Maximin in 1279 and the translation of the rival remains of the Magdalene at Vézelay in the 1260s, see J. H. Albanès, *Le Couvent royal de Saint-Maximin en Provence* (Marseilles 1880), 39–44, with further notice of Pons and the blood cult at 405–6, 417–19. For further investigation, somewhat overliteral, see V. Saxer, 'Les Ossements dits de sainte Marie-Madeleine conservés à Saint-Maximin-la-Sainte-Baume', *Provence historique* 27 (1977), 257–311.

[103] Benedict XIV, 'De servorum Dei beatificatione' 2.30 and 4 part 2.10, and 'De festis domini nostri Iesu Christi' 1.8, in Benedict, *Opera omnia*, new edn, 15 parts (Venice 1767), II 131–3, IV 230–1, IX 100. At much the same time the Bollandists took up the argument, in *Acta SS: September*, III 495–8, inclining more towards the authenticity of relics of the blood. Benedict's sentence, declaring against the line of argument adopted by the Franciscans in the 1460s, relies heavily upon the commentaries of the Jesuit writers Gabriel Vazquez, *Opera omnia*, V 308–17, and Theophilus Raynaud, 'Christus Deus homo' 2.3.3, in Raynaud, *Opera omnia*, 20 vols. (Lyons 1665–9), I 135–9.

[104] For a review of the most recent theological opinions here, see Cocci, 'Le Dispute', 1221–33.

CHAPTER 6

Two commentaries: John Hus and William Sudbury

For the most part the later scholastic commentaries on the Holy Blood pursue abstruse theological questions and touch only briefly upon the history of the physical relics of the blood. However, there are two treatises that because of their historical content merit a more detailed consideration here: the *De sanguine Christi* of John Hus, written around the year 1405, and the treatise on the blood of Westminster composed in the 1380s or 90s by William Sudbury and dedicated to King Richard II. Hus' work can be dealt with fairly briefly. In essence it represents an attack upon eucharistic blood relics, above all the relic displayed at Wilsnack in Brandenburg, that Hus had investigated as one of the commissioners appointed by archbishop Zbynek of Prague.[1] To this extent Hus' work stands apart from the main stream of such treatises which were concerned principally with the literal blood of the Passion and which for the most part are taken up with commentary upon the opinions of Thomas Aquinas. Hus, by contrast, entirely disregards Aquinas, whose opinions are never once cited. Instead, he produces a line of argument that is far closer to that advanced by Guibert of Nogent in the twelfth century, dismissing all the supposed bodily relics of Christ, not merely the relics of the blood, as rank impostors. Like Guibert, Hus turns to scripture and the church fathers to supply his evidence, rather than approaching the problem indirectly, via the scholastic commentaries. Again like Guibert, he poses a series of practical questions designed to pour scorn upon such objects as the supposed foreskin of Christ or the milk of the Virgin Mary. Which of her contemporaries would have troubled to collect the Virgin's milk? To teach that Christ's foreskin survives is just as foolish as to teach that Christ's head survives, cut off from his body. Some might argue that the preservation of Christ's blood was intended by God as a

---

[1] John Hus, 'De sanguine christi', printed in Hus, *Opera omnia*, ed. W. Flajshans, vol. i fasc. 3 (Prague 1904). For the historical background and for a related commentary written by Hus in Czech, see M. Spinka, *John Hus a Biography* (Princeton 1968), 67–9.

means by which the faithful might be strengthened in their faith, just as St Thomas was persuaded to believe in the risen Christ, having touched his wounds. But, as the Gospels themselves make plain, 'Blessed are they that have not seen, and yet have believed' (John. xx. 29). Faith acquires merit precisely because it is faith, not mere physical observation.[2] Hus, like Guibert of Nogent, suggests that Christ, though omnipotent, was subject to God's promises made to mankind, that he would not suffer his holy one to see corruption (Ps. xvi. 10). Claims that parts of Christ's body, even such parts as the blood shed at his circumcision, could become separated from his resurrected glory are tantamount to heresy, not only because they suggest that God broke his covenant with man, but because they challenge the Church's teaching on the Resurrection, suggesting, like the dualist heretics, that the body and soul are two separate entities. As for the miracles that are claimed for portions of Christ's blood, only infidels would seek such signs. Christians should believe without demanding miracles. Belief should flourish in the spirit, not the flesh. Miracles distract attention away from Christ and focus men's minds instead upon the characters in the miracle stories.[3]

Having dismissed the supposed bodily remains of Christ, Hus then passes on to consider eucharistic relics, in which the wine of the sacrament was believed to have been transformed literally into the blood of Christ. Here he charges the proponents of such relics with outright fraud. Either the blood produced in the chalice is the work of the Devil, or else it is invented by depraved and mendacious priests. The miracles associated with such relics should in themselves excite suspicion since, as Hus observes, many of them involve the escape from imprisonment of convicted murderers and thieves – a point that finds an echo in England, where one of the four miracles recorded for the Holy Blood of Hailes involves the escape of a group of prisoners.[4] Many such relics, Hus claims, have been exposed as fraudulent and their inventors punished, such as the priest of Bohemia who, according to Hus, confessed his crimes and died a penitent, locked up in an iron cage at the city gates, like

---

[2] Hus, 'De sanguine', 10–12.
[3] *Ibid.*, 12–28.
[4] *Ibid.*, 26–7, 29–30. For Hailes, see J. C. T. Oates, 'Richard Pynson and the Holy Blood of Hayles', *The Library* 5th series 13 (1958), 269–77. For miracles involving escape from prison, see in general P.-A. Sigal, *L'Homme et le miracle dans la France médiévale (XIe–XIIe siècle)* (Paris 1985), 268–70. The release of prisoners from their chains was the special preserve of the Limousin saint, St Leonard of Noblat, whose basilica was hung everywhere with the chains of escaped captives; W. Melczer, *The Pilgrim's Guide to Santiago de Compostela* (New York 1993), 105–7, 255–7 and notes.

a bird.[5] In the diocese of Litomysl, a priest had smeared the host with
blood from his finger so that his parishioners might be deluded into
believing that a miracle had taken place. At Cracow, the effluvia from
an image of the Crucifixion, and the glow given off by a piece of metal
housed in a crystal thurible were for many years adored as if they were
the true blood of Christ – again, a point that reflects more widely upon
the history of blood relics, where we have seen that eucharistic or effluvial relics often came to be misrepresented as the historic blood of
the Passion.[6] As for the miraculous blood of Wilsnack, Hus had already
dismissed this as a ruse by the local priest, intended to raise money for
the rebuilding of his church.[7] In his treatise, he goes on to suggest that
the miracles worked at Wilsnack were equally fraudulent. For example,
a pilgrim from Prague left a silver model of a hand at the shrine, hoping
thereby to obtain a cure for his own withered hand. Although, after three
days, he was no better, he heard the priest proclaim from the pulpit that
a miracle had occurred and that the silver model was a sign that some
fortunate pilgrim had been healed. Not surprisingly the pilgrim held up
his withered member and denounced the priest as a liar.[8]

Towards the end of his treatise Hus makes plain quite why his opposition to eucharistic blood relics was so severe. In all he advances fifteen
reasons why such relics threatened evil. For example, the faithful were
deceived into placing more faith in outward signs than in God, trusting
more to what was created than to the creator himself – a similar point to
that made by St Hugh of Lincoln who more than two centuries before
had dismissed the eucharistic relic of Joi near Troyes as a mere physical sign of a more important spiritual reality, of interest only to those
whose faith was too weak to survive without tangible proofs of Christ's
sacrifice.[9] Eucharistic relics, according to Hus, encouraged ignorance
and false doctrine. Men might be persuaded to prize such 'relics', the
product of the Devil or of mendacity, above the sacraments of the altar.
Priests, seeing the profits that could be made, might be led to propagate

[5] Hus, 'De sanguine', 28–9, here preferring the alternative reading *Bohemia* to *Bononia* (i.e. Bologna).
[6] *Ibid.*, 28–9, 34: *rubigo in manubrio cristallino derelicta a lamella*. The precise meaning of the word
     lamella is unclear.
[7] Spinka, *John Hus*, 67–8, and in general, for the controversy over the Wilsnack relic, see
     H. Boockmann, 'Der Streit um das Wilsnacker Blut, zur Situation des deutschen Klerus
     in der Mitte des 15. Jahrhunderts', *Zeitschrift für Historische Forschung* 9 (1982), 385–408; *Das
     Gutachten . . . über 'Das heilige Blut von Wilsnak'*, ed. Damerau; Breest, 'Das Wunderblut von
     Wilsnack', esp. 296–301 for Latin articles against the relic. For evidence of devotion to Wilsnack
     in England, see above p. 48 n. 66.
[8] Hus, 'De sanguine', 32–3.
[9] *Magna vita sancti Hugonis*, ed. Douie and Farmer, II 95.

further lies, in effect teaching pilgrims to believe that the benefits conferred by the sacraments could be bought with votive offerings. As at Wilsnack, pilgrims were encouraged to adore something that they did not properly understand, not realizing that the consecrated sacrament of the bread and wine was a better and a truer path to salvation.[10] It was for this reason that, as Hus reports, the archbishop of Prague had in 1405 issued a decree, banning any inhabitant of his diocese from making the pilgrimage to Wilsnack.[11]

Eucharistic relics had been publicized for several hundred years as a means by which complex scholastic teachings on the mass and the doctrine of transubstantiation could be brought home to simple believers. Yet Hus, and St Hugh of Lincoln before him, argued that miracles of this sort caused more confusion than understanding. In reality they encouraged disrespect rather than respect for the sacraments. They suggested that only a few, special portions of bread and wine had been marked out through their miraculous transformation into the literal body and blood of Christ. Since such miraculous relics were confined to a select few churches, pilgrims would be encouraged to scorn the true mysteries, recreated daily by their own parish priest. Hus' arguments here can be related to two further developments. The first, for which Hus himself was to be branded a heretic and burned at the Council of Constance in 1415, was Utraquism – the demand that the sacrament be administered to the faithful in both kinds, as opposed to the practice sanctioned by the Church whereby the consecrated wine was reserved for the priest's communion, with the laity being offered no more than the consecrated host. Although, as it emerged in Bohemia after 1414, the Utraquist revolt extended far beyond Hus' teaching to encompass a wide range of theological and political causes, Utraquism can none the less be seen as a development related to the ideas presented in Hus' *De sanguine Christi*.[12] Hus had taught that the sacrament of the chalice was brought into disrespect by claims that one communion, where a eucharistic miracle occurred, was better than another, where no such visible or physical transformation took place. In the same way the Utraquists declared that it was wrong to place special emphasis upon the chalice by reserving it for the priest, when both the wine and the bread were of equal standing and therefore of equal, indivisible merit in the reception of communion.

[10] Hus, 'De sanguine', 36–7.
[11] *Ibid.*, 33–6.
[12] For the Utraquists in general, see H. Kaminsky, *A History of the Hussite Revolution* (Berkeley, Calif., 1967), 97–140, esp. 98–108.

Utraquism was to remain a subject of violent disagreement between Hus' followers and the Roman church. However, in at least one respect, Hus' teaching was to find favour with the local church authorities, if not with the papacy. As we have seen, doubts over the relic of Wilsnack persuaded the archbishop of Prague to place a ban upon pilgrimages to the shrine. In the same way, the arguments deployed by Hus were to be reflected in a series of fifteenth-century diocesan and provincial decrees, seeking to prohibit the display or veneration of eucharistic relics. At the provincial Council of Cologne in 1452, for example, it was decreed that whenever the sacrament was transformed literally into flesh or blood, no publicity was to be given to the supposed relics, nor were they to be displayed or held up for public veneration.[13] Similar prohibitions are to be found elsewhere in Germany, at Magdeburg for example, where veneration of the Wilsnack relic was to be branded as tantamount to idolatry.[14] Theologians such as Nicholas of Cusa and Heinrich Tocke were to argue that the sacrament had been given to mankind to be consumed, not to be preserved as relics. Practices such as the procession of the host at the feast of Corpus Christi, or the veneration of eucharistic relics, were criticized at least in part because they appeared to ignore a fundamental distinction between the cult of relics and the cult of the eucharist.[15] In practice, eucharistic miracles such as those of Wilsnack, Walldurn and Andechs continued to attract considerable devotion and were supported by extensive papal indulgences. As late as the 1440s, Pope Eugenius IV is said to have been responsible for dispatching a Holy Host, stabbed by a fanatic and thereafter marked by spots of blood and a miraculous image of Christ seated in majesty, as a gift to duke Philip of Burgundy.[16] None the less, the fifteenth-century provincial and diocesan decrees bring us full-circle from the situation that had obtained in the early Middle Ages. Then, miracles involving the consecrated wine, the restriction of such wine to the clergy and the growing emphasis placed

---

[13] Mansi, *Concilia*, XXXII 149.

[14] In general, see Boockmann, 'Der Streit um das Wilsnacker Blut', 385–408, esp. 391–2; C. Zika, 'Hosts, Processions and Pilgrimages: Controlling the Sacred in Fifteenth-Century Germany', *Past and Present* 118 (1988), 48–59, drawn to my attention by Miri Rubin.

[15] Zika, 'Hosts, Processions and Pilgrimages', 56, with a similar line of argument deployed by Hus, 'De sanguine', 35–6.

[16] For the Holy Host of Dijon, see the commentary and illustration in J. d'Arbaumont, 'Essai historique sur la Sainte-Chapelle de Dijon', *Compte Rendu des travaux de la commission départementale des antiquités de la Côte-d'Or* 6 (1864), 129–31 and plate V at p. 184. Support for the attribution to Pope Eugenius is provided by the Pope's contemporary issue of an indulgence for the Holy Host of Brussels, said to have bled on being stabbed by the Jews: above p. 109; P. Lefèvre, 'A propos d'une bulle d'indulgence d'Eugène IV en faveur du culte eucharistique à Bruxelles', *Hommage à dom. Ursmer Berlière* (Brussels 1931), 163–8.

upon the transformation of bread and wine into the body and blood of Christ had played an important part in preparing the way for claims that the historic blood of Christ had survived the Passion and might be viewed by pilgrims. So successful was this movement, that in the fifteenth century the church authorities were forced to intervene, in an attempt to defend the standing of the eucharist against the threat posed by eucharistic, effluvial and the supposed historic relics of Christ's blood.

In this way Hus' treatise marks an important stage in the history of blood relics. However, its arguments were by no means universally accepted. Indeed, as Hus himself makes plain, blood relics continued to enjoy great prestige in fifteenth-century Europe. To hear an alternative view, in their defence, we can do no better than turn to the treatise of the Westminster monk, William Sudbury, writing perhaps twenty years before Hus. Sudbury's work is particularly relevant here, since it refocuses our attention upon England, and in particular upon the lacklustre performance of the Holy Blood of Westminster. Himself a monk of Westminster from 1373 to his death in 1415, bachelor of theology at Oxford, refectorer and joint-treasurer of Westminster, and warden of the manors of Queen Anne 1392–3, Sudbury was also an author and anthologist on a prolific scale.[17] The greatest of his enterprises, a vast alphabetical concordance to the works of Aquinas, was begun in Oxford in 1382 and was not completed until 1403.[18] In addition, he composed an alphabetical index, listing the chief themes expounded in James of Voragine's sermons on the saints, assisted in compiling an inventory to the contents of Westminster's vestry, and is credited with the authorship of various other works, including tracts on the coronation and the regalia, and yet another concordance, to the works of the theologian Nicholas of Lire.[19] His treatise on the Holy Blood survives in a single manuscript,

[17] For Sudbury, see *The Westminster Chronicle 1381–1394*, ed. L. C. Hector and B. F. Harvey (Oxford 1982), xxxvi–viii; Emden, *Biographical Register of Oxford*, III 1813; R. Sharpe, *A Handlist of Latin Writers of Great Britain and Ireland before 1540* (Turnhout 1997), 811; Harvey, *Living and Dying*, 75–6, which suggests that he was the son of a London skinner named Henry of Sudbury. Hector and Harvey (p. xxxviii) dismiss Sudbury's claim to be considered the author of the Westminster Chronicle.

[18] BL MS Royal 9.F.iv, described and the introduction printed in full by T. Käppeli, 'Die Tabula des Wilhelm Sudbery, O.S.B., zu den Werken des hl. Thomas von Aquino', *Theologische Quartalschrift* 115 (1934), 62–85. See also the *Westminster Chronicle*, ed. Hector and Harvey, p. xxxvii.

[19] The concordance to James of Voragine, similar in form and script to the index to Aquinas, is preserved in a single manuscript opening with James' sermons, of English, perhaps Westminster, provenence, now Bordeaux, Bibliothèque municipale MS 286 fos. 254v–86v: headed (fo. 254v) *Incipit tabula super Ianuensem in sermonibus de proprietatibus sanctorum facta per fratrem Willelmum Sudbury monachum Westmon'*, traced via Emden, *Biographical Register of Oxford*, III 1813. Leland's list of the manuscripts in Westminster Abbey library includes both William's *tabula* to Aquinas and another

bound up with a long treatise defending Westminster's privilege of sanctuary, that may also be Sudbury's work.[20] The fact that the sole surviving manuscript of his treatise on the blood dates from the 1460s or 70s suggests that it may have been copied out in the aftermath of the great debate on the Holy Blood that took place before Pope Pius II in 1462.[21] Although undated, the treatise is dedicated to King Richard II (1377–99) and must have been written after 1382 when Sudbury obtained his bachelor's degree, probably in the late 1380s or 90s when we know him to been active on the fringes of Richard's court.[22] Besides being our most significant indication that the blood of Westminster continued to inspire curiosity into the later Middle Ages, Sudbury's treatise is most unusual for the keen antiquarian interest it displays in the history of blood relics, not just in England but elsewhere in France and the Low Countries. It opens with a long and obsequious dedication to Richard II, lavishing praise upon the King and his ancestors, and in particular upon Henry III, 'who had built the new church of Westminster from its foundations, who had endowed it with earthly privileges and with goods, and who most copiously decorated it (*venustabat*) with the relics of various saints'. Amongst such relics the most important and singular (*pre omnibus specialem et pre ceteris singularem*) was that drop (*portiunculam*) of Christ's blood, shed from his side upon the Cross. Misled by the wiles of the Devil, various

---

volume described as his *tabula . . . super Lyram*, not now known to survive; M. R. James and J. A. Robinson, *The Manuscripts of Westminster Abbey* (Cambridge 1909), 23. A further index, to the pastoral treatise of John de Burgo, 'Pupilla Oculi', survives as Cambridge, University Library MS Ee.5.11 fos. 24v 55r.

[20] Longleat House, Marquess of Bath MS 38, briefly noticed in *Historical Manuscripts Commission 3rd Report* (London 1872), appendix p. 182. The treatise on sanctuary runs from fos. 9r to 256v, lacking the opening few folios and hence any dedication or the name of its author. The treatise on the Holy Blood is copied, running on from the other treatise, at fos. 256v 308r, headed merely *Hic sequitur tractatus de sanguine Christi precioso*. The MS, which bears the ownership signatures of Richard Wright and of the antiquary Henry Spelman, was purchased in 1710 by the 1st Viscount Weymouth together with other MSS from Spelman's library. Much of the treatise on sanctuary, but not that on the Holy Blood, is copied in the hand of William Ebesham, a scribe who worked extensively for the Paston family and for Westminster Abbey in the 1460s and 70s. For Ebesham, see A. I. Doyle, 'The Work of a Late Fifteenth-Century English Scribe, William Ebesham', *Bulletin of the John Rylands Library Manchester* 39 (1956 7), 298 325, esp. 320; G. A. Lester, *Sir John Paston's 'Grete Boke'* (Cambridge 1984), 36 43 (references courtesy of Roger Lovatt). For permission to quote from the Longleat MS I am indebted to the Marquess of Bath.

[21] The debate certainly appears to have been known about in England, since the Abbey of Hailes took the trouble to acquire a copy of the arguments presented by the future Pope Sixtus IV; BL MS Royal 8.D.xvii.

[22] Longleat MS 38 fo. 256v, opening with the address: *Excellentissimo domino et principi invictissimo Ricardo Dei gratia Cristianissimo regi Anglie et Francie et domino Hibernie, suorum subditorum minimus et legius suorum capellanorum orator assiduus et regie sedis sue ecclesie Westm' monachus pauperimus, frater Willelmus Sudbury sacr(e) theologie bachallarius regnum regere in misericordia et equitate orationum pro magestate regia effusarum fore participem.*

people have been tempted to doubt the authenticity of this relic which Sudbury is determined to justify, recalling the faithful to the path of truth.[23]

Sudbury's treatise thereafter is divided into three basic sections, theological, historical and a third section dealing with the indulgences bestowed upon visitors to the Westminster relic. As might be expected, given Sudbury's interest in Aquinas, the opening theological section is dominated by an attempt to reconcile Aquinas' opinions on the Holy Blood with the claims of the Westminster relic. Indeed, the margin to Sudbury's concordance to Aquinas, which lists both of the references to the blood from the *Summa* and the *Quodlibetales*, has been specially marked, next to Aquinas' opinion from the *Summa*: *Notum qualis sanguis Cristi manet in terris et qualis non.*[24] Sudbury begins by stating the objections to relics of the Holy Blood; for example that, since Christ rose bodily in glory, all his blood must now be in heaven; that, just as Christ is the cause of man's coming resurrection, when man will rise leaving no human trace on earth, so Christ must have risen entire and undiminished; that, even supposing that Christ left behind some of his blood on earth, such blood could never subsequently be rejoined to his body and must instead become subject to decay, a heretical proposition, since as the Psalmist states, God would not suffer his holy one to see corruption (Ps. xvi. 10). In answering these objections he employs a series of arguments adapted, without attribution, from such writers as Aquinas, Bonaventure and in particular Duns Scotus. There is no indication that he read the furthest development of Scotus' ideas in the writings of Francis de Meyronnes. In essence he suggests that relics of the Holy Blood represent no diminution of Christ's glory, since only those parts of the human body, and hence by extension the body of Christ, that are essential to human nature will undergo resurrection; that the saints bequeathed relics from their bodies, and that even the Virgin Mary, despite her Ascension into heaven, left

---

[23] Longleat MS 38 fos. 256v–8v.

[24] BL MS Royal 9.E.iv fo. 385v, indexed under X for *Cristus*, and for the sentence from the *Quolibetales*, indexed under R for *Resurgere* see fo. 292r. The same marginal hand appears elsewhere at fo. 40v, making an addition to the list of authorities cited in the text. Since the concordance does not appear to have been completed until 1403, the marginalia must postdate the composition of the treatise on the blood, written before 1399. Sudbury's concordance to the sermons of James of Voragine also includes a special entry under *Sanguis; etiam quas proprietates habet sanguis Cristi et non optime*, referring to James' sermons for the feast of the Exultation of the Holy Cross, to the seven-fold shedding of Christ's blood referred to by James in his sermon for the dedication of the altar, and to the effects and claims of the blood of Christ and the saints, listed in James' sermons on the dedication of the altar and the feast of St Peter: Bordeaux, Bibliothèque municipale MS 286 fo. 278r.

behind such relics as the strand of her hair that, Sudbury notes, was displayed at Westminster.[25] As to the argument that relics of the blood must necessarily face corruption, Sudbury suggests that God, being omnipotent, can halt the process of putrefaction, just as he did with the body of Christ when it was placed in the tomb.[26] At two points, however, he is forced to tread with especial caution.

To begin with, in admitting that relics of the blood can never again be rejoined to the resurrected body of Christ (a point made three hundred years earlier by Guibert of Nogent, who had suggested that this would involve Christ in not one but two separate resurrections), Sudbury is forced to concede the divisibility of Christ the Logos from his incarnate form, or at least from those parts of his body that Sudbury suggests were inessential or superfluous. Here he adapts two ideas found together in their most sophisticated form in the *Oxford Commentaries* of Duns Scotus. First, like Scotus and the other Franciscan commentators, he adopts the concept of the plurality of forms within the incarnate Christ, so that during the three days during which Christ lay in the tomb, his body became separated from his soul, although both body and soul remained united, individually, to the Logos.[27] Such separation, Sudbury argues, in no way reduces Christ's glory, since glory is an inherent quality of the soul of the resurrected Christ and cannot be reduced save by the relaxation of one or other of the principles by which that glory is caused.[28] Secondly, like Scotus and virtually every other commentator, Sudbury suggests that before resurrection, both man and Christ must be purged of those superfluous elements that are not united to the truth of human nature, just as pure wine is better than wine mixed with water.[29] In this

---

[25] Longleat MS 38 fo. 281r–v. Sudbury claims that the Virgin's hair was given to Westminster by King Stephen in 1142, *prout in istius monasterii antiquis codicibus reperitur et in eius annalibus cronicis continetur*. No such entry is to be found in the Westminster *Flores*, although the hair relic is mentioned by Flete, *History*, 69–70, as a gift of Edward the Confessor. It may in fact have formed part of the relic collection made shortly after the conquest by Ilger Bigod, for which see above p. 41.

[26] Longleat MS 38 fos. 265v–6r, citing the tag *omnem motum quem nunc incipit potest terminare saltem nisi impediatur*. A variation on this tag, derived from Aristotle, is cited by Duns Scotus in much the same context, in Scotus, *Opera omnia*, XIV 743.

[27] For Scotus' exposition of the theory, which is very close to that given by Sudbury, see 'Oxford Commentaries' 3.21, in Scotus, *Opera omnia*, XIV 740–50, and in general the article by A. Michel, 'Forme du corps humain', *Dictionnaire de théologie catholique*, ed. A. Vacant and others, VI (Paris 1924), cols. 546–88, esp. 574–5.

[28] Longleat MS 38 fo. 269r: *eo quod per mortem ipsius, gloria anime ipsius propter seperationem a corpore* [non] *fuisset in aliquo diminuta, cum illa gloria anime Cristi ut accidens sit inherens, hec eius minoratio non potest contingere nisi propter remissionem alicuius principii ex quo in anima Cristi gloria causabatur.*

[29] *Ibid.*, fo. 270v: *notari oportet quid sit veritas humane nature et quid pertinet ad veritatem humane nature, sciendum igitur est quod verum prout hic sumitur contra potest sumi primo modo prout dividitur contra permixtum unde*

way it is possible to argue that many drops of Christ's blood were destined for resurrection, but that many others were not.[30] Here Sudbury comes close to defending a position on the divisibility of Christ the Logos from the blood of his Passion, that had already been raised by Francis de Meyronnes and rejected as heretical in the 1350s.[31] However, his argument that the body consists of a mixture of elements, some of which must be excised to produce the body fit for resurrection, skirts around the heretical position and reflects the work of those earlier theologians, such as Grosseteste, who had sought to distinguish between the parts of the body that they considered more, as opposed to less, essential to the Resurrection. As we have seen, from the time of Peter the Lombard onwards, it had been accepted that the matter that went to make up the human body could be divided between that which was innate, inherited from man's parents and ultimately from Adam, and that which was added later through the processes of nutrition, eating and drinking. In the commentaries, there was great debate as to precisely how much of this nutrimental matter would be required to make up the body at the time of resurrection.[32] For example, Aquinas, in company with the Franciscans, Bonaventure and Richard of Middleton, had allowed that, whilst blood and the principal humours would rise with the resurrected body, certain bodily fluids or 'humidities', such as urine, sweat and milk, might not.[33] Since, in any case, the body was constantly in a state of ebb and flow, with parts, such as hair and nails, being lost and replaced, it was inconceivable that the resurrected body could resume all its parts that had been shed during life. Such ebb and flow, addition and subtraction, in no way altered the essential form of man.[34] Rather than produce a monstrosity by assembling every lost hair and nail clipping, God had

---

purum vinum dicitur vinum verum et vinum multum aquosum dicitur falsum vinum. For the same metaphor of wine and water, used by Duns Scotus in much the same context and attributed to Aristotle, see Scotus, 'Oxford Commentaries' 4.44 q.1, in Scotus, *Opera omnia*, XX 178. For Scotus' argument on the nature of the Resurrection, see *ibid.*, XX 161–208.

[30] Longleat MS 38 fos. 270r–1v, esp. fo. 271r: *igitur plures gutte sanguinis que fuerunt in Cristo fuerunt ordinate ad resurrectionem et plures non,* and see *ibid.*, fo. 278v: *possibile fuit Cristum plures guttas sanguinis habuisse et ipsas non fuisse ad sui compositionem et constitutionem specialiter et principaliter ordinatas.*

[31] Above pp. 104–8.

[32] Above pp. 94–5.

[33] Bonaventure, 'On the Sentences' 4.44 art.1 q.1, in Bonaventure, *Opera omnia*, IV 907–8, closely followed by Middleton, 'On the Sentences' 4.44 art.1 q.2, in Middleton, *Questiones*, IV 574–5, and see Aquinas, 'On the Sentences' 4.44.1.2c d ad 2c–d, in Aquinas, *Opera omnia*, ed. Busa, I 636–8.

[34] Middleton, 'On the Sentences' 4.44 art.1 q.4, in Middleton, *Questiones*, IV 576–8, including the statement (at 577): *nutritionem nihil accrevit essentiae formae carnis . . . formae dico educte de potentia materiae quae nunquam fuit in homine a principio suae repositionis in specie usque in finem vitae suae.*

ordained that the resurrected body would be endowed with its appropriate and seemly complement of flesh, hair and nails.[35] Sudbury, like Grosseteste, in applying this idea directly to the blood shed by Christ at the Passion, goes far beyond those earlier commentators who had allowed that some of the superfluous parts, humours or humidities might be relinquished by the resurrected body. In the process he is forced to engage with a key passage in Aquinas, a passage which we have already considered in some detail.

In his *Quodlibetales* Aquinas had drawn attention to the distinction, proposed by Grosseteste, between nutrimental blood and the pure heart blood of Christ. As we have seen, this was a distinction based upon the medical or scientific belief that only blood, or rather *chyle*, that had entered the heart underwent that infusion of spirits which qualified it to be described as truly blood-like. Sudbury, although aware of the passage in the *Quodlibetales*, seems to have been entirely ignorant of, or at least to have been forced to 're-invent', the opinion of Grosseteste upon which Aquinas' opinion is based. This in itself is most intriguing, since it suggests either that Grosseteste's tract on the Holy Blood was not to be found in the monastic library at Westminster, or that, even if Sudbury had read it, he found its arguments on the physiology of blood quite unintelligible, a point that we have already considered when noting the divergence between Grosseteste's views and the accepted medical orthodoxy propounded by the followers of Galen.[36] Not knowing, or perhaps misunderstanding Grosseteste's argument that blood was to be divided between heart-blood infused with the spirit of life and the inanimate blood that had yet to achieve this infusion, Sudbury returns to the earlier definition proposed by Peter the Lombard, presenting the distinction between the two varieties of blood, nutrimental or essential, as one between the blood produced by nutrition and the much smaller quantity of blood which every creature inherits from the body of its parents, and

---

[35] Middleton, 'On the Sentences' 4.44 art.1 q. 3, in Middleton, *Questiones*, IV 575. In the 1460s Giacomo della Marca, was to claim that his fellow Franciscans, Bonaventure, Middleton, Duns Scotus and Francis de Meyronnes, had all specifically denied the resurrection of the blood of the Passion. However, in their commentaries on the *Sentences*, none of these authors goes so far as della Marca suggests, although they all agree that Christ's body became separated from his soul, and that, to a greater or lesser extent, not all of the humours or humidities will undergo resurrection; Pius II, *Commentaries XI*, trans. Gragg, 724–5 and notes, and for Middleton, see E. Hocedez, *Richard de Middleton, sa vie, ses œuvres, sa doctrine*, Spicilegium sacrum Lovaniense études et documents VII (1925), 65–6, 131, 289, above pp. 103 ff.

[36] The medieval library at Westminster appears to have been well supplied with others of Grosseteste's writings; James and Robinson, *The Manuscripts of Westminster Abbey*, 32–5, 37–8, 44–5, 50–1.

which Christ received from the body of the Virgin Mary.[37] This latter
'parental' blood, that in Sudbury's argument constitutes the blood essential to human nature, could be traced back via the Virgin Mary to the
very creation of mankind in Adam.[38] As illustration, he cites the example
of the egg divided into the white, from which the chicken is generated,
and the yolk from which the chicken is nourished. The body, like the
egg, is made up of two sorts of matter, one of which remains with man
even from before his birth, the other being transient, intended merely to
maintain the outward form or vessel in which the inner, essential, part
of man resides. In a fire, no matter how many logs are consumed in
the process of burning, the fire itself remains essentially unchanged; the
extra logs are consumed merely to preserve the basic species of fire – a
metaphor that had been employed many times before, and which Sudbury could have found in writings as diverse as the sentences of Anselm
of Laon, or the *Summa theologica* of Aquinas.[39] Likewise in man, only those
purer parts, generated *a parentibus*, not those parts received *de alimentis*,
are essential for species and form. At the resurrection, these parts will
be divided, the essential from the transitory. Only the essential parts will
be resurrected, together with sufficient of the transitory elements to make
up the appropriate outward form and decoration of the body.[40]

Many aspects of this argument would have been familiar to Aquinas
or Bonaventure, and many more were to recur in the debate of the 1460s.
The transitory flux and reflux of elements within the body had already
been described by Aristotle, whilst the discussion of Christ's inheritance

---

[37] Longleat MS 38 fo. 263v: *sed est illud ultra quod sibi de nutrimento requiritur ad essendum, et sic sibi dumtaxat accidentaliter et ex congruo est inherens, sive sit pars, sive sit qualitas, sive quantitas sive quocumque alio nomine appelletur . . . In corpore humano est aliquid de corpore paterno et aliquid de alimento, et maior est pars in quantitate de alimento quam de corpore paterno, sicut in ovo est magis de citrino quam de albo.*

[38] *Ibid.* fo. 265r–v: *sicut patet de costa Ade que non resurget in ipso sed in Eva, patet etiam de guttis Marie virginis de quibus formabatur corpus Cristi, que in Cristo resurrexerunt et in virgine non resurgent, patet etiam de carnibus humanis.* The question of Adam's rib, and in whose body it would be resurrected, was a long-standing scholastic puzzle. See for example Aquinas, 'On the Sentences' 2.18 q.1, in Aquinas, *Opera omnia*, ed. Busa, I 175–6. For the argument that Christ was formed from the blood of Mary by virtue of the Holy Spirit, whose implications were under discussion from at least the time of John of Damascus, see for example John of Damascus, 'De fide orthodoxa' 3.2, in Migne, *PG*, XCIV 986; Bonaventure, 'On the Sentences' 4.44 p.1 art. 2 q.1, in Bonaventure, *Opera omnia*, IV 910–12; Middleton, 'On the Sentences' 3.3 art. 2 q.1, in Middleton, *Questiones*, III 29–30.

[39] Longleat MS 38 fo. 264r: *totum quicquid est in corpore potest duplic(em) considerari vel ex parte materie et sic non est permanens, et ponitur in exemplo: sicut in combustione lignorum videmus quod si ignis attenditur et continue ligna addantur, secundum quod alia consumuntur, forma tamen ignis semper manebit in lignis, sed tamen materia quelibet consumetur, alia sibi materia succedente in qua salvabitur species et forma ignis,* and for the fire metaphor, see Bynum, *The Resurrection*, 137, 239.

[40] Longleat MS 38 fos. 264v–5r.

of the blood of Mary had appeared in Aquinas and was to play a key part in the Franciscan polemic of the 1460s. None the less, although the elements of his argument are by no means original, Sudbury combines them in a novel and for the most part lucid form, different in several important respects from that which had been attempted in the thirteenth century by Robert Grosseteste. Unlike Meyronnes or the Franciscans of the 1350s or 1460s, he makes no attempt to argue that all of Christ's blood shed at the Passion was separated from his divinity. Some, perhaps the vast majority, of Christ's blood was destined for resurrection, although some was not. In his discussion of God's control over the process of corruption, Sudbury argues that even the blood that was bequeathed to mankind as relics might have remained united in some way to Christ's glory, or at least that it was preserved from absolute corruption or dissolution, yet another line of argument that he appears to have acquired from Duns Scotus.[41] The staunchest defenders of the proposition that Christ resumed all the blood of his Passion were forced to admit that other parts of his body, such unseemly parts as excrement or sweat, or even the blood discharged spontaneously during his lifetime from the nostrils, were denied Resurrection.[42] Like Grosseteste before him, though without the medical and scientific learning that informs Grosseteste's discussion, Sudbury suggests merely that part of Christ's blood was akin to sweat or the more unseemly fluids. Grosseteste had written of nutrimental blood or *chyle*, set against the heart-blood infused with spirit. Sudbury, by contrast, writes of the 'alimental' or 'non-parental' blood of Christ. Being inessential to glory or to the truth of human nature, such blood could have remained on earth in the form of relics.

As so often with medieval scholasticism, an apparently simple question, whether all of the blood shed at Christ's Passion was resumed into his resurrected body, carries us very rapidly into a labyrinth of hypotheses, technicalities and disputed philosophical terms. Within the brief span of his argument, Sudbury is forced to engage with a whole host of such problems. Unlike Grosseteste, who to some extent had been able to stand aloof from the fray, Sudbury merely fashions new bricks from old straw, inheriting a dead weight of past scholastic lore. As for the truth of his argument, given the artificial nature of the question itself and the fact that it remains unresolved even today, the issue of truth or falsehood barely arises. Suffice it to say that Sudbury's argument, by allowing that

---

[41] See Scotus, 'Oxford Commentaries' 3.21, in Scotus, *Opera omnia*, XIV 743 50.

[42] Pius II, *Commentaries XI*, trans. Gragg, 718 19, 724: 'But if he sweat, and blood flowed from his nostrils these things were superfluities and never had union at all.'

even a small part of the blood of Christ's Passion became separated from his resurrected body, would have been regarded as anathema by those, mostly Dominican, authorities, who held such a separation to be quite impossible. Had the relics which Sudbury set out to defend been claimed merely as Christ's blood, rather than specifically as the blood of his Passion, they would not, perhaps, have met with such concerted opposition, although even here the Dominicans, whilst admitting the possibility that the resurrected body excluded certain superfluous fluids, appear to have suggested that such fluids were utterly destroyed or obliterated, and that therefore they could never have been collected as relics. As it is, by defending the survival of blood from the Passion, Sudbury sets himself a far harder task; a task which, given the artificial confines of the debate, he accomplishes with a reasonable degree of success. However, even he appears to have realized that the debate could not be won on theological grounds alone. Hence it is that he turns from abstract theology to antiquarianism, and in the second part of his treatise passes on to consider the practical, historical, nature of the claims to possess relics of Christ's blood. It is for this, the earliest concerted attempt to assemble evidence of relics of the Holy Blood, that his treatise deserves chiefly to be remembered.

Amongst the various relics whose history Sudbury recounts in detail, he not surprisingly devotes particular attention to the blood of Bruges, supposedly acquired from Jerusalem in the 1140s, and hence the only other relic in Europe that lent support to Westminster's claim that the patriarchs of Jerusalem had been in possession of a portion of the Holy Blood prior to 1247. The details that Sudbury assembles here are taken mostly from the chronicle of John of Ypres (d. 1383), although he also recites a papal indulgence of 1310 in favour of visitors to the Bruges relic, suggesting that he had gone to considerable trouble to gather local evidence, presumably by corresponding with the keepers of the chapel of St Basil, where the relic of Bruges was housed.[43] From elsewhere in Europe, he refers briefly to the relic of Fécamp, again adapting an account found in the chronicle of John of Ypres.[44] He also recounts the

---

[43] Longleat MS 38 fos. 282r–5v, derived and in part copied word for word from John of Ypres as printed in *MGH Scriptores*, XXV 802. The bull of Clement V, recited in full by Sudbury, survives in the original, Bruges, Archives de la Ville charte no. 239, variously printed, for example by A. Miraeus, *Opera diplomatica et historica*, ed. J. F. Foppens, 2nd edn, 4 vols. (Louvain 1723–48), III 156–7 no. 179. Sudbury also refers to indulgences of forty days each, offered by Popes Innocent IV and Alexander IV to visitors to the chapel of St Basil on the feast of St Basil, the anniversary of the chapel's dedication, and on Good Friday.

[44] Longleat MS 38 fo. 284r, identical to the account in *MGH Scriptores*, XXV 802.

legend that Joseph of Arimathaea came to England some years after the Crucifixion, bringing with him a vase containing the Holy Blood 'through which many miracles were accomplished'. His source for this legend, which he cites as the *Chronica aurea* of William of St Denis, has not been identified, although it was presumably based upon one of the many versions of the *Estoire de Saint Graal*.[45] From Hailes Abbey in Gloucestershire Sudbury obtained an account of the blood relic shared between Hailes and the college of Ashridge.[46] In addition, earlier on, in the theological section of his treatise, he had referred at length to a series of effluvial and eucharistic blood relics, including the story of the image of Beirut, for which he recites an account of the Council of Nicaea in 787;[47] the legend of a similar image displayed in the church of Hagia Sophia at Constantinople;[48] and the legend of the Mass of St Gregory, a well-known eucharistic miracle, in which the bread of a mass celebrated by Pope Gregory the Great is said to have been transformed into a bleeding finger.[49] As Sudbury himself makes plain, his reason for quoting these stories at such length is to provide support for the relic of Westminster by demonstrating its kinship to a large number of similar relics elsewhere in Europe. If only the historic credentials of these other relics could be accepted, then the more speculative, theological, elements of Sudbury's treatise would be rendered superfluous.

As to the Westminster relic itself, it is intriguing that the only direct testimony to its authenticity that Sudbury is able to quote is supplied by the letters from the patriarch and chapter of Jerusalem, written at Acre in May 1247. Sudbury claims to have transcribed these letters from the original, whereas previously we have found no more than a later, cartulary, copy.[50] None the less, the version he supplies differs in no important respect from that given in the Westminster Domesday. In general we must conclude that by the 1380s there was nothing else at Westminster by way of testamentary letters for Sudbury to draw upon in his defence.

---

[45] Longleat MS 38 fos. 281v–2r.

[46] *Ibid.* fos. 286r–8r, and for the relationship between this version of the legend and those circulated elsewhere by the monks of Hailes, see below p. 141 n. 14.

[47] *Ibid.* fos. 260v–2v, 271v, adapted from the same basic source as Migne, *PG*, XXVIII cols. 811–20.

[48] Longleat MS 38 fo. 271v, and for the possible sources see above p. 47 n. 59.

[49] *Ibid.*, fos. 272v–3r, identical to the anonymous life of St Gregory printed in *Acta SS: March*, II 134, and in general see Rubin, *Corpus Christi*, 308–10.

[50] Longleat MS 38 fos. 290r–2r, printed as appendix 1 below. At fo. 292r–v Sudbury claims that his transcript *est vera copia que de verbo ad verbum de predicta bulla plenarie est transumpta, ex qua patet quod de vero sanguine Cristi relicto super terra hoc sufficiens testimonium est repertum, cum predicta bulla in nulla sui parte sit cancellata, abolita aut abrasa, sed sit sigillis predicti patriarche et sui capituli consignata, quod parati sumus ostendere cuilibet si oporteat et necessarium fuerit requirenti.*

The best that he is able to provide, beyond the Acre letters of 1247, is an extract from the *Polychronicon* of Ranulph Higden, which provides a bare mention of the relic's delivery to Westminster, misdated to 1249.[51] Having set out the basic facts, Sudbury then passes on to the numerous episcopal indulgences that had been issued in favour of pilgrims to the Westminster relic. The precise details of these indulgences will be considered in due course. For the moment, what is most interesting is that Sudbury can find nothing else in the way of local evidence. In particular, he at no point claims that the blood of Westminster had worked many miracles or that its merits and prestige had been recognized in the world at large. Instead, his treatise peters out in a general disquisition on the nature of indulgences, defending the established system against the charge that bishops could only relax, not remit, the penance imposed upon any individual believer.[52]

Even the list of indulgences which he supplies has been artificially augmented, since although it appears at first sight to contain the names of nearly seventy individual bishops, offering a total of nine years' remission of penance, it emerges on closer examination that many entries are repeated. Take these repetitions away and we find that Sudbury can name no more than thirty-six individual bishops, whose indulgences total just under four years. In addition, he claims that a further eighteen unnamed bishops each offered forty days' remission, presumably via one of those collective indulgences that became common under the Avignon papacy of the fourteenth century.[53] The vast majority of the indulgences that he cites are also copied into the cartulary known as the Westminster Domesday, from which it is apparent that most of them were issued in the first fifty years after the relic's arrival at Westminster. Furthermore, as we shall see, the mere fact that indulgences were issued should not lead us to assume that the relic of Westminster had achieved any great

---

[51] *Ibid.* fo. 292v, and for Higden see above p. 2 n. 7.

[52] *Ibid.* fos. 293r 308r, with a long list of indulgences at fos. 300v 5r. The only authority cited by name in Sudbury's discussion, *quidam doctor Valens Notyngham nomine, super evangelia* (fo. 307v) is presumably to be identified as the Franciscan follower of Duns Scotus, master William of Nottingham (d. *c.* 1336), author of postills on Clement of Llanthony's *Unum ex quatuor*, for whom see Emden, *Biographical Register of Oxford*, 1377 8; B. Smalley, 'Which William of Nottingham?', *Mediaeval and Renaissance Studies* 3 (1954), 200 38. William was also the author of commentaries on the *Sentences* of Peter the Lombard, now Cambridge, Gonville and Caius College MS 300, which at fos. 267v 9r follows Scotus in respect to the nature of the Resurrection.

[53] The multiple indulgence is cited in Longleat MS 38, fo. 302v. No such indulgence for the blood relic survives in the Westminster Domesday which none the less preserves several collective indulgences on behalf of others of the Abbey's relics.

popularity. Indulgences could often accompany inherently unpopular as opposed to much venerated relics.[54]

For all of these reasons, Sudbury's treatise, like the tract of Grosseteste before it, presents us with a paradox; a carefully crafted theological argument in defence of relics of the Holy Blood, deployed upon behalf of a specific relic, that of Westminster, which enjoyed very little popularity. Neither Grosseteste nor Sudbury is able to muster much in the way of historical, as opposed to theological or circumstantial evidence, in favour of the Westminster relic. Sudbury, for example, devotes almost twice as much space to the relics of Bruges and Hailes as he does to that of Westminster. His work does at least suggest that the Westminster relic remained a subject of curiosity into the late fourteenth century. It may even be that he wrote his treatise in the hope that it might revive the King's interest in the blood of Westminster, just as on other occasions King Richard II is known to have made oblations to Westminster's shrine of Edward the Confessor, or in January 1386 conducted the visiting King of Armenia on a candle-lit tour of the Abbey's relics and regalia.[55] None the less, there is considerable irony to the fact that the general line of argument deployed by Grosseteste and Sudbury, in favour of relics of the Holy Blood, was still being cited in the sixteenth century, long after the particular relic that had inspired those arguments, the blood of Westminster, had faded from public consciousness. Grosseteste and Sudbury supplied potentially valuable ammunition to the defenders of blood relics in general. However, their tracts appear to have done little to encourage devotion to the specific relic of Westminster. Why was this so?

Here we would do well to remember the words of Peter Brown, that the cult of relics was a plant that needed careful pruning; 'A relic that is not acclaimed is candidly, not a relic ... Faced with an *embarras de richesse* of apparently indistinguishable holy objects, the local group wielded a tacit right to withhold recognition.'[56] Brown is writing here of sixth-century Gaul, but his words can be applied with equal force to England in the 1240s. A relic such as the Holy Blood was not a static combination of

---

[54] Below pp. 156–65.

[55] *Westminster Chronicle*, ed. Hector and Harvey, 8–11, 178–9, 373–3, 450–1, 506–11, and for the visit by the King of Armenia, see *ibid.*, pp. lv, 154–6. For Richard's gifts to the Abbey in general, see Harvey, *Westminster Abbey*, 29–31, 33, 51, 337–9, 350, 352–3, 360, 397, 403, 410; N. Saul, 'Richard II and Westminster Abbey', *The Cloister and the World: Essays in Medieval History in Honour of Barbara Harvey*, ed. J. Blair and B. Golding (Oxford 1996), 196–218.

[56] P. R. L. Brown, *Relics and Social Status in the Age of Gregory of Tours*, Stenton Lecture (Reading 1977), 13–14.

chemical elements, but a potentially wonder-working bridge between the mundane and the divine, a means by which man could communicate with God. For its potential to be released, a relic had to be generally recognized for what it claimed to be. It had to be welcomed into the community with honour and ceremony. Its reputation had to be carefully nursed. Above all it had to be invested with reverence and a belief in its sanctity.[57] Only then could its miraculous nature shine forth. For reasons that we have already considered, the Westminster blood relic failed to achieve this leap of faith. Henry III did all in his power to welcome it into the community. The ceremonial reception of October 1247 could hardly have been bettered. But scepticism, or indifference, was just that little bit too great. Just a little too much special pleading had to be advanced on the relic's behalf for it to be transformed from a mere object, albeit an intriguing, even a wonderful object, into a channel of communication between God and man.

If we wish to appreciate the full extent of Westminster's failure, we should measure it against the undoubted success of similar relics else-where in Europe. The cult of blood relics in the later Middle Ages re-quires a book all to itself. Certainly it is too extensive a subject to treat here in any detail. None the less, the already long list of churches claiming relics of the Holy Blood prior to 1247 continued to grow throughout the next three hundred years.[58] In some instances these relics achieved only short-lived fame. Others developed into major centres of pilgrimage. Some underwent miraculous liquefaction: at Bruges the Holy Blood was believed to boil and liquefy every Friday, whilst similar miracles are re-ported at Billom, Neuvy, Pairis and for that portion of Christ's blood mixed with earth, supposedly gathered from beneath the Cross by Mary Magdalene and displayed in the Abbey of St Maximin in Provence.[59]

---

[57] For an important recent study of one means by which relics might be 'tested' in the Middle Ages, see Head, 'Saints, Heretics and Fire', 220–38.

[58] Amongst later cults, not noticed above, see L. Dolberg, 'Die Verehrungsstätte des hl. Blutes in der Cistercienser-Abtei Doberan', *Studien und Mittheilungen aus dem Benedictiner und dem Cistercienser-Orden* 12 (1891), 594–604; W. Brückner, *Die Verehrung des Heiligen Blutes in Walldürn*, Veröffentlichungen des Geschichts und Kunstvereins Aschaffenburg III (Aschaffenburg 1958); T. Stump and O. Gillen, 'Blut', in *Reallexikon zur deutschen Kunst-Geschichte*, ed. O. Schmitt, II (Stuttgart 1948), cols. 947–58, with a useful bibliography at col. 958. Most of these cults involved eucharistic relics rather than portions of the blood preserved since the time of Christ's Passion.

[59] L. Pfleger, 'Hostienwunder und Heiligblutkapellen in Elsass', *Archiv für Elsässische Kirchengeschichte* 8 (1933) 462; Saintyves, *Les Reliques*, 5–55, which deals with the Holy Blood together with the famous blood relic of St Januarius at Naples, for whose liquefaction Saintyves offers a scientific explanation. For the first record of the miracle of St Januarius' blood, not reported before 1389, see Fasola, 'Il Culto del sangue dei martiri', *SA*, III part 3 (1983), 1473–5, with extensive bibliography. For the Bruges relic, whose liquefaction is mentioned in a papal indulgence as early

The distribution of these cults defies any simple analysis, although they are most common in Germany, the Rhineland and northern Italy. Some, such as the blood of Bruges, were housed in churches that lacked any other substantial relic. Others, such as the blood of St Maximin, Venice or Rome, achieved fame despite the close proximity of relics of equal or greater distinction. In England, if we wish to set the relic of Westminster in context, our starting point must be the portion of the Holy Blood shared between the Abbey of Hailes and the college of Ashridge in Hertfordshire.

as 1310, see Huyghebaert, 'Iperius et la translation de la relique du Saint-Sang à Bruges', 122–3, 169–73. The relic and its miracle have spawned a vast devotional literature, for a guide to which see *Bibliografie van de Geschiedenis van Brugge*, ed. A. Vanhoutryve (Bruges 1972), nos. 5225–462. The liquefaction of the relic at St Maximin is first referred to by Silvestro Mazolini, *Aurea rosa*, ed. Zambelli (1599), fo. 313v, where the process is said to have occurred each year on Good Friday. Vincent Pons, *La Saincte Ampoulle de Sainct Maximin* (1608), 58, claims that the miracle, in which the blood reddened in its glass container, occurred precisely between the hours of midday and one. Thomas Fuller, *The Church-History of Britain* (London 1655), book 6 p. 333, claims that the blood of Hailes was manipulated in such a way 'that it strangely spirted or sprang up to the great amazement of common people', which suggests some sort of liquefaction. However, Fuller's evidence here is far from certain and may be based upon the account of a miracle, circulated in the printed pamphlet on Hailes by Matthew Pynson, in which a priest who cast doubt upon the relic of Hailes, found on celebrating mass that the wine boiled up to the brink of his chalice. See below p. 197.

CHAPTER 7

The rivals: Hailes, Ashridge, Glastonbury

Twenty years after the Holy Blood was sent from Acre to Westminster, Edmund of Cornwall, Henry III's nephew, was to return from Germany bearing a relic of Christ's blood that in the course of time was to become the focal point of two major cults, at Hailes in Gloucestershire, and at Ashridge north of London.[1] At Hailes the arrival of the Holy Blood coincided with a major fire as a result of which the east end of the monastic church had to be rebuilt. Since, in common with the vast majority of Cistercian houses, the Abbey lacked any saint of its own, the Holy Blood was afforded a prominence that it might otherwise have lacked, being placed in a special shrine behind the high altar.[2] As early as 1275 the monks of Hailes obtained licence from the Cistercian general chapter to hold an annual ceremony in the relic's honour with all the solemnities normally reserved for major church festivals.[3] In the

---

[1] All versions of the annals of Hailes agree that the acquisition of the Holy Blood coincided with Richard of Cornwall's last visit to Germany, to be dated August 1268 to August 1269; N. Denholm-Young, *Richard of Cornwall* (Oxford 1947), 139–41; BL MSS Cotton Cleopatra D iii fos. 46r, 73r; Harley 3725 fo. 13v (misdated 1267). For the annals themselves, see M. N. Blount, 'A Critical Edition of the Annals of Hailes (MS Cotton Cleopatra D iii, ff. 33–59v) with an Examination of their Sources', (MA thesis, Manchester 1974).

[2] See Dugdale, *Monasticon*, v 686–7, quoting from the later version of the annals of Hailes (after 1360), in BL MS Harley 3725 fos. 13v–15r. The fullest account of the relic's reception is to be found in BL MS Cotton Cleopatra D iii fos. 46r–7v, written c. 1300, printed below appendix 3. For the shrine in general see W. St Clair Baddeley, *A Cotteswold Shrine, Being a Contribution to the History of Hailes* (Gloucester 1908), 56–61; W. H. Blaauw, *The Barons' War*, 2nd edn (London 1871), 351–2n; Coad, *Hailes Abbey*, 12.

[3] *Statuta capitulorum generalium ordinis Cisterciensis* III, ed. J.-M. Canivez, Bibliothèque de la Revue d'histoire ecclésiastique fasc. XI (Louvain 1933–4), 149 article 69. The late version of the annals of Hailes claims that in 1295 Edmund donated yet another portion of the blood to Hailes, contained within a gold and enamel cross. However, in the earlier version, this cross is said to have contained not a portion of the Holy Blood, but a piece of the True Cross; compare BL MSS Cotton Cleopatra D iii fos. 50v–1r (48v–49r): *crucem auream cum pede de aumail apud Heiles de dono suo transmisit que nobilissimam portionem preciosissime crucis Cristi in se insertam continuit (c. 1300);* Harley 3725 fo. 19r: *crucem auream cum pede de aumail apud Hayles de domo suo transmisit que nobilissimam portionem sanguinis preciosissime crucis Cristi in se insertam continuit (c. 1360).* In this later version the word *sanguinis* has been erased and then rewritten in a hand of the sixteenth century. The original

following year, Pope John XXI is said to have licensed the Abbey to employ two priests to serve the shrine, offering confession and penance to pilgrims visiting the Holy Blood.[4] Thereafter, the blood relic was to establish Hailes as one of the principal pilgrimage centres in the West of England, supported by a stream of papal indulgences and commemorated by such writers as Chaucer and Margery Kempe.[5] By the late fifteenth century, pilgrims to the relic were being offered indulgences totalling nearly twenty-two years' remission of enjoined penance, with a further relaxation of seven years, two hundred and eighty days for all who visited Hailes on the feast of Corpus Christi each year.[6] Meanwhile, at Ashridge, founded by Edmund as a college of Bonhommes *c.* 1283, the cult of the Holy Blood was incorporated from the beginning into the college's statutes, with a major festival being celebrated in the relic's honour, probably on the feast of the Exultation of the Holy Cross, besides provision for special daily prayers and a service to be held throughout the period of Lent and Easter.[7] Many of Edmund's charters refer to the college as the church of St Mary founded *in honore preciosi sanguinis Ihesu Cristi*, and, as at Hailes, the Ashridge relic was placed in a special shrine, containing not only the Holy Blood but the hearts of Edmund

letters are clearly legible under ultra-violet light. The changes here suggest that we should be treat the later version of the Hailes chronicle with a certain degree of suspicion.

[4] John XXI's letters are mentioned in a bull of Pope Innocent VIII, April 1487, renewing the licence and allowing the abbot and convent to offer the sacrament to all visitors to the Abbey, and to bless the beads with which pilgrims touched the shrine of the blood; *Calendar of Entries in the Papal Registers Relating to Great Britain and Ireland*, ed. W. H. Bliss, C. Johnson and J. A. Twemlow, 14 vols. (London 1894–1961), XIV (1484–92) no. 66.

[5] For Chaucer and Margery Kempe, see Bentley, *Restless Bones*, 132–3. For an indulgence of Eugenius IV, August 1438, referring specifically to the blood described as *quedam portiuncula sive gutta . . . sanguinis*, see *Calendar of Papal Registers*, ed. Bliss, Johnson and Twemlow, IX (1431–47), 38. Pynson's pamphlet on the blood, published *c.* 1515, provides a brief abstract of the legend, and provides a lengthy abstract of the Abbey's indulgences; Oates, 'Richard Pynson and the Holy Blood of Hayles', 269–77. An independent fifteenth-century account in English, preserved in Oxford, Bodleian Library MS Rawlinson K 42 p. 96, inserted into the diary of Thomas Hearne for 1712–13, and printed thence in John Leland, *De rebus Brittanicis collectanea*, ed. T. Hearne, 2nd edn (London 1770), VI 283–4, whence Blaauw, *The Barons' War*, 351n, refers to further indulgences from Popes John XXIII, Calixtus III and from fifteen cardinals. However, although such indulgences were issued, they make no direct reference to the blood relic; *Calendar of Papal Registers*, VI (1404–15) 376, XI (1455–64) 190.

[6] BL MS Cotton Vespasian B xvi fo. 95v, described below n. 14.

[7] For the statutes, see H. J. Todd, *The History of the College of Bonhommes, at Ashridge, in the County of Buckingham* (London 1823), 11–12, including the provision that *rursum a Septuagesima usque ad octavas Pasche fiat servicium de sanguine Christi*. The festival of the Holy Blood appears to have fallen at some time between Trinity and All Saints. Elsewhere, the commemoration of blood relics was linked to the feasts of Holy Cross or to Passion Week, especially to Good Friday. It was on 14 September 1270, the feast of the Exultation of the Cross, that Edmund had delivered the Holy Blood to Hailes: Dugdale, *Monasticon*, V 686n; below appendix 3.

of Cornwall (d. 1300) and of St Thomas Cantilupe, bishop of Hereford (d. 1282).[8]

With hindsight it is all too easy to assume that the success of the Holy Blood of Ashridge and Hailes was assured from the moment of the relic's arrival in England. But this was far from being the case. To begin with, Hailes, as a Cistercian foundation, might be expected to have eschewed the more vulgar trappings of the cult of relics. Relics were not condemned by the Cistercian order. As early as the 1170s, King Henry II of England had been sent a finger-bone of St Bernard by the abbot of Clairvaux, albeit with a request that the relic be kept in its reliquary and preserved from frequent handling.[9] It is none the less unusual to find a Cistercian abbey serving as a major centre of pilgrimage.[10] On the whole, such abbeys were planted in out of the way places, set apart from the hubbub and disturbance caused by pilgrims. Yet, in its way the Holy Blood could hardly have been better suited to the White Monks, whose writers had long celebrated the humanity of Christ and the mystery of the blessed

[8] For Edmund's charters, see for example *Calendar of Charter Rolls 1257–1300*, 324; Dugdale, *Monasticon*, VI 514–15. For the shrine, see Dugdale, *Monasticon*, VI 517 no. 2, apparently taken from the binding (*ad calcem libri*) of the former Oxford, Bodleian Library MS Digby in 4° no. 11, now BL MS Cotton Cleopatra D vii, from which the original binding materials have been entirely lost. For the later history of the shrine see W. Kennett, *Parochial Antiquities Attempted in the History of Ambrosden, Burcester, and Other Adjacent Parts in the Counties of Oxford and Bucks.*, new edn, 2 vols. (Oxford 1818), 1 423–6. Kennett, like several other commentators, follows a report, already to be found in William Sudbury's tract of the 1380s or 90s, repeated by Holinshed, in stating that Edmund donated a third part of his store of the Holy Blood to Hailes, and the other two-thirds to Ashridge; Longleat MS 38 fo. 288r; R. Holinshed, *The Third Volume of Chronicles . . . Now Newly Recognised, Augmented and Continued . . . to the Yeare 1586* (London 1587), 275. There is some evidence of rivalry between the two shrines, for example in their claims to the body of earl Edmund. Edmund died at Ashridge on 1 October 1300. His heart and viscera were buried there on 12 January 1301, but his bones were carried secretly (*clam*) to Hailes on 17 January, where they were buried on 22 March; BL MS Cotton Cleopatra D iii (Annals of Hailes) fo. 53v (51v).

[9] S. J. Heathcote, 'The Letter Collection Attributed to Master Transmundus, Papal Notary and Monk of Clairvaux in the Twelfth Century', *Analecta Cisterciensia* 21 (1965), 219–20 no. 177. In the immediate aftermath of the death of St Bernard, the abbot of Cîteaux is said to have commanded the saint to cease performing miracles. Within twenty years, however, a magnificent shrine had been erected over his tomb, whilst Bernard himself is said to have been buried together with a relic of St Jude the apostle, brought from the Holy Land; Sigal, *L'Homme et le miracle*, 224; *St Bernard of Clairvaux, The Story of his Life as Recorded in the 'Vita Sancti Bernardi'*, trans. G. Webb and A. Walker (London 1960), 126. In his life of St Malachy, Bernard had stressed the great treasure bestowed upon Cîteaux by its possession of the saint's bodily remains; McGuire, *The Difficult Saint*, 96–8, and see *ibid.*, 125, 171–3 for Bernard's own relics. In general, for Bernard on relics, see Bynum, *The Resurrection*, 173–4. The facial hair of the Cistercian St Stephen of Obazine (d. 1159) was preserved as relics, even before St Stephen's death; *Vie de Saint Étienne d'Obazine*, ed. M. Aubrun, Publications de l'Institut d'Etudes du Massif Central VI (Clermont-Ferrand 1970), 198–9. I am grateful to Simon Lloyd for questioning the association between the Cistercians and the cult of relics.

[10] A significant exception here is the Cistercian Abbey of Pontigny, home to the shrine of the English St Edmund of Canterbury after 1247.

sacrament. Aelred of Rievaulx, for example, had written in ecstatic terms of the blood and water that flowed from Christ's side upon the Cross:

Make haste [Aelred writes] lest you be too late; taste the honeycomb and your honey, drink your wine and milk, the blood transformed into wine for you so that you may become drunk upon it, the water changed to milk that you may be nourished. It was for you that the streams were made upon the rock, the wounds upon his limbs and the cavities within the outer wall of his body, in which the image of the dove lies concealed, so that from the kisses of his blood your lips and your speech may be sweetly scarlet-banded.[11]

Both at Hailes and at Ashridge the cult of Christ's blood required careful nurturing. The origins and the authenticity of Edmund's relic would have been subjected to scrutiny in just the same way as those of the Holy Blood of Westminster. Yet whereas doubts still lingered about the Westminster relic, the blood of Hailes appears to have won widespread acceptance. Why should this have been so? According to the earliest account, set out in a version of the annals of Hailes written before 1295, Edmund had obtained his relic in 1268 from 'the lord of Doilaunde', identified by later commentators, wrongly as we shall see, as Florence V count of Holland.[12] When the monks of Hailes came to rewrite their chronicle *c.* 1300, they inserted a long passage on the relic's discovery, claiming that it had been obtained from the castle of 'Trivelensi', where Edmund had stayed with his childhood friend, Roderick, son of the castle's constable, Warin de Boylande. The castle is said to have housed a great collection of relics and vestments belonging to the Holy Roman Emperors, amongst which the boys had particularly noticed a large gold brooch on a golden chain. It was this brooch that housed the relic of the Holy Blood, said to have belonged to Charlemagne and to have been placed around the neck of successive emperors at the time of their

---

[11] Aelred, 'De institutione inclusarum' ch. 31, in *Aelredi Rievallensis opera omnia*, ed. A. Hoste and C. H. Talbot, CCCM I–IIa (Turnhout 1971), 671 lines 1188–94, and in general, for Cistercian devotion to the body and humanity of Christ, see R. and C. Brooke, *Popular Religion in the Middle Ages* (London 1984), 141–5; McGuire, *The Difficult Saint*, 227–49, esp. 241–3.

[12] BL MS Cotton Cleopatra D iii (Annals of Hailes), fo. 73r: *Edmundus filius regis Alem(annie) per instructionem quorumdam virorum de nobili viro et domino de Doilaunde adquisivit nobilem portionem sanguinis domini nostri Ihesu Cristi cum innumerabili quantitate reliquarum*, printed in *MGH Scriptores*, XVI 483 (reading *Dilaunde*), from the earliest section of the annals of Hailes, containing brief entries, of which the latest is for the year 1295. For the identification of *Doilaunde* with Holland see W. St Clair Baddeley, 'The Holy Blood of Hayles', *Transactions of the Bristol and Gloucestershire Archaeological Society* 23 (1900), 277. Denholm-Young (*Richard of Cornwall*, 174) seeks to identify *Dilaunde* (*sic*) with Zealand, apparently following Holinshed; see Blaauw, *The Barons' War*, 351 n. Coad, *Hailes Abbey*, 5, cites no evidence for his claim that the blood was purchased from the count of Flanders. Blount, 'The Annals of Hailes', xxxv–vi, suggests that the annals refer to the count of Flanders and the castle of Trier.

inauguration by the imperial electors.[13] A metrical version of this legend, claiming to be based upon an account supplied by Pope Urban IV, repeats the story of the relic's discovery at 'Trivelence', but adds that before this, the blood had belonged in turn to the Emperors Titus, Vespasian, Charlemagne and Frederick II, having been collected at the time of the Crucifixion by a Jew who had been imprisoned for forty-two years.[14] This part of the narrative is in fact lifted in its entirety from the *Estoire de Saint Graal*, the most famous of the thirteenth-century Grail romances. The *Estoire*, as we have seen, tells how Joseph of Arimathaea collected Christ's blood after the Crucifixion and how he was imprisoned by the Jews, being released by the Emperor Vespasian after a period of forty-two years. The only changes made to this account by the author of the metrical legend of Hailes are the omission of Joseph's name, the transformation of Vespasian into Titus, and the insertion of the later Emperors Charlemagne and Frederick.[15] It seems hardly credible that Pope Urban could have provided this account, so that the claim that the relic was supported by papal testimonials may well be a fourteenth-century invention.

Without a cartulary or any original letters to guide us, it is difficult to unravel the full story of the blood of Hailes. Our only sources are the various annals and chronicles of the Abbey, inflated in the metrical version with details culled from the Grail romances. What cannot be doubted is that the Holy Blood deposited at Hailes and at Ashridge achieved a fame and a status denied to the Holy Blood of Westminster. There are many reasons for this, not least the fact that for all its apocryphal accretions, the Hailes legend was founded upon a solid basis of truth, or at least

---

[13] BL MS Cotton Cleopatra D iii fo. 46r–v, printed below appendix 3, from a version of the annals written in a single hand to 1301 and thereafter with miscellaneous additions to 1314. A version of this legend reached Holinshed in the sixteenth century, save that here the relic is said to have been housed in a golden box, whose inscription first aroused Edmund's interest; Holinshed, *The Third Volume of Chronicles* (1587), 275. For further versions of the legend, circulating in the fourteenth and fifteenth centuries, see below n. 14.

[14] *Altenglische Legenden neue Folge*, ed. Horstmann, 275–81, from BL MS Royal 17 C xvii fo. 147, where Urban's account is said to form the basis of the narrative from the time of the Crucifixion until the reign of Frederick II when the blood came to rest at *Trivelence*. This poem was printed by Pynson in his pamphlet on Hailes; Oates, 'Richard Pynson and the Holy Blood of Hayles', 269–77. At a later stage, yet further details were added to the legend, including a claim that the Roman emperors stored the blood in the 'Temple' at Rome, together with Christ's foreskin. Charlemagne took possession of only a small portion of the blood which he carried back to *Trevelense*; BL MS Cotton Vespasian B xvi fo. 95v, the end-leaf of a famous manuscript of Langland's *Piers Plowman* (drawn to my attention by Nigel Ramsay), which accords fairly closely with the account of the blood of Hailes supplied by William Sudbury in Longleat MS 38 fos. 286r–8r.

[15] Lagorio, 'The Evolving Legend', 218, and 'The "Joseph of Arimathie"', 98, notes the correspondences between the Grail legends and the metrical legend of Hailes.

12   The castle of Trifels (Bildarchiv Foto Marburg)

upon legends more appealing than those brought into play at Westminster. All in all, the account circulated by the monks of Hailes combines a variety of elements, real and imaginary. To begin with, Richard of Cornwall as King of Germany was indeed served by a steward named Werner von Bolanden, and it seems probable that the surname Boylande or Bolanden explains the claim that the blood of Hailes had been acquired from the 'lord of Doilaunde'.[16] As for the castle, *Trivelensi* or

[16] Denholm-Young, *Richard of Cornwall*, 93; *Regesta Imperii V: 1198–1272*, ed. J. F. Böhmer, J. Ficker and E. Winkelmann, 3 vols. (Innsbruck 1881–1901), no. 5314; *Urkundenbuch der Stadt Worms*, ed. H. Boos, 2 vols. (Berlin 1886–90), I no. 289, a charter of Richard issued at Worms, 16 September 1260, referring to Werner *dapifer* and Philip *fratres de Bollanden . . . dilecti fideles nostri*; G. C. Gebauer, *Leben und denkwürdige Thaten Herrn Richards, erwählten römischen Kaysers, Grafens v. Cornwall und Poitou*

Trivelence, this is undoubtedly to be identified as Trifels (*Trifelensi*), the greatest of the imperial fortresses in the Pfälz, south of Mainz. As Corfe castle had been to King John, so Trifels was to the emperors of Germany: a combination of stronghold, dungeon and treasury. Since 1125 it had indeed been Trifels that served as the principal repository for the jewels and vestments associated with the imperial coronation, whilst it was to Trifels that the Emperors dispatched booty and their most important state prisoners.[17] Between 1246 and 1269 the castle was in the keeping of Philip von Falkenstein, brother of Werner von Bolanden, Richard of Cornwall's steward.[18] Contrary to the legend circulated by the monks of Hailes, Werner von Bolanden, the steward, is not known to have had a son named Roderick. In any event, Werner may well have been dead by 1266, in which year Philip von Falkenstein deputed custody of Trifels and three others of his castles to his sons, Werner's nephews, Philip and Werner von Bolanden the younger.[19] However, the Bolanden, including Werner's nephew and namesake, were undoubtedly in a position to grant Edmund access to the treasures of Trifels.

Turning to the brooch from which Edmund is said to have abstracted the Holy Blood, here too the Hailes legend can claim at least some grounding in reality. The only brooch definitely employed at the coronation was used as a clasp to fasten the emperor's mantle, not as a pendant hung around the neck.[20] However, there is a strong possibility that a

---

(Leipzig 1744), 387, a charter of 18 November 1262, witnessed by Werner *dapifer*, Philip von Falkenstein *camerarius* and Philip his son. The annals of Hailes refer to Werner as *senescallus de feodo totius imperii*; BL MS Cotton Cleopatra D iii fo. 46r.

[17] N. Grass, *Reichskleinodien–Studien aus rechtshistorischer Sicht*, Österreichische Akademie der Wissenschaften, Philisophisch-Historische Klasse Sitzungberichte CCXLVIII part 4 (1964), 20–4, a reference which I owe to Patrick Zutshi; K. Bosl, *Die Reichsministerialität der Salier und Staufer*, 2 vols., MGH Schriften X (Stuttgart 1950–1), 1219–30; A. Schulte, *Die Kaiser-und Königskrönungen zu Aachen 813–1531*, Reinische Neujahrsblätter (Bonn and Leipzig 1924), 29–32, and for booty and prisoners, see for example 'Chronici ab Ottone Frisingensi conscripti continuatio', ed. R. Wilmans, *MGH Scriptores*, XX 325–6; 'Cronica S. Petri Erfordensis moderna', ed. O. Holder-Egger, *ibid.*, XXX part I 379, whence 'Cronica Reinhardsbrunnensis', ed. O. Holder-Egger, *ibid.*, 569–70.

[18] For Philip as keeper of Trifels see *Historia diplomatica Friderici secundi*, ed. J. L. A. Huillard-Bréholles, 6 vols. in 11 (Paris 1852–61), VI part II 878–9; J. D. Schöpflin, *Alsatia Illustrata Germanica Gallica* (Colmar 1761), 188–9; Bosl, *Reichsministerialität*, I 225. For the Bolanden family and its lands see *ibid.*, I 261–74; E. Jacob, *Untersuchungen über Herkunft und Aufstieg des Reichsministerialengeschlechtes Bolanden* (Giessen 1936) (a reference which I owe to Björn Weiler); A. Eckhardt, 'Das älteste Bolander Lehnbuch', *Archiv für Diplomatik* 22 (1976), 317–44.

[19] Gebauer, *Leben und denkwürdige Thaten Herrn Richards*, 244

[20] For the shoulder-brooch, see J. Deér, *Der Kaiserornat Friedrichs II* (Bern 1952), 47–54 and plates XXIII–IV. It is clearly visible in the portrait of Richard shown on his seal as King of Germany, for which see W. de Gray Birch, *Catalogue of Seals in the Department of Manuscripts in the British Museum*, 6 vols. (London 1887–1900), VI no. 21158 and plate 2. For Richard of Cornwall's own account of his coronation at Aachen in 1257, mentioning the imperial crown and the sceptre, see *Annales monastici*, I (Burton) 394.

13   The 'Talisman' of Charlemagne (London, Conway Library)

pendant-brooch or locket, known today as the 'Talisman', may also have
played some part in imperial coronations. It is traditionally supposed to
have been buried with Charlemagne, and to have been recovered during
one of the re-openings of his tomb, in 926, 1000 or 1165. From at least the
1620s until 1804 it was kept at Aachen, but it was then offered as a gift to
the Empress Joséphine, whereafter it passed via the Bonaparte family to
Rheims Cathedral where it remains today. Measuring seven centimetres
in diameter, it has at its centre two large gems framing a hollow compartment. By 1620 this compartment contained one of the hairs of the Virgin
Mary, replaced, probably in the nineteenth century, with a piece of the
True Cross.[21] To this extent it bears a close resemblance to the object
described in the legend of Hailes; a combination of reliquary and brooch,
supposedly owned by Charlemagne. It is by no means impossible that the

---

[21] *Charlemagne: Œuvres, rayonnement et survivances*, ed. W. Braunfels, Dixième exposition sous les
auspices du Conseil de l'Europe (Aix-la-Chapelle 1965), 370–2 no. 557 and plate 109;
Schramm, *Herrschaftszeichen und Staatssymbolik*, I 309–12 and plate 25; M. Conway, 'The Amulet of
Charlemagne', *Antiquaries Journal* 2 (1922), 350–3. According to Thietmar of Merseburg, it was a
cross, not a circular brooch, that was removed from around the neck of Charlemagne by Otto III
in 1000. A similar pendant reliquary, in the form of a crucifix, was found around the neck of
St Edward the Confessor in his tomb at Westminster; L. E. Tanner, 'The Quest for the Cross of
St Edward the Confessor', *Journal of the British Archaeological Association* 3rd series 17 (1954), 1–10.

'Talisman' once housed a portion of the Holy Blood, particularly since blood relics tended to take the form of solidified granules rather than fluid. It is unmentioned amongst the imperial regalia stored at Trifels in 1246, and its role in medieval ceremonial is uncertain.[22] However, the Mainz *ordo* for Otto I's crown-wearing in the 960s does refer to the two bishops who flanked the emperor as having 'sacred relics hanging from their necks', which at least suggests that pendant reliquaries were employed by the clergy if not by the emperor.[23] By 1216, the chronicler Eberhard of Gandersheim was claiming that at the coronation of the emperor Arnulph in 896, the Pope hung a cross around the Emperor's neck containing a portion of the Holy Blood. Eberhard suggests that the relic had been sent to Rome as a gift from the Byzantine Emperor and that later it passed to Henry, the brother of the Emperor Otto I.[24]

Although it would be wrong to place much trust in this account, it is none the less intriguing that both Eberhard and his later redactor, Bodo, should refer to a pendant blood relic, quite independently of the legend in circulation at Hailes. A similar story is to be found associated with the blood relic of Cappenberg, said to have been worn around the neck of Frederick II of Swabia, father of the future Emperor Frederick Barbarossa, in all his battles.[25] By 1620 it was customary for the King of the Romans to swear an oath at the time of his inauguration upon one of the reliquaries of Aachen, believed to contain the blood of

---

[22] For the regalia at Trifels in 1246, see Huillard-Bréholles, *Historia Diplomatica*, VI part II 878–9. *Charlemagne*, ed. Braunfels, 370–1 no. 557, notes that the 'Talisman' is unrecorded before the 1520s, although an inventory of the relics of Aachen *c.* 1200 mentions the Virgin's hair. This was housed in the 'Talisman' by the time of P. á Beeck, *Aquisgranum sive historica narratio de regiae S. R. I. et coronationis regum Rom.* (Aachen 1620), plate at p. 168.

[23] P. E. Schramm, 'Die Krönung in Deutschland bis zum Beginn des Salischen Hauses (1028)', *Zeitschrift der Savigny-Stiftung für Rechtsgeschichte* 55, Kanonistische Abteilung XXIV (1935), 310: *habentes sanctorum reliquias collo pendentes*. For the use of pendant reliquaries see most famously the case of the relics of Bayeux, upon which Harold is said to have sworn his oath to duke William of Normandy, and which, according to William of Poitiers, were worn by William in a reliquary hung around his neck on his landing at Hastings in 1066: E. van Houts, 'The Memory of 1066 in Written and Oral Tradition', *Anglo-Norman Studies* 19 (1996), 167–8, and for the relics, see further 'The Brevis Relatio de Guillelmo nobilissimo comite Normannorum', ed. E. van Houts, *Camden Miscellany XXXIV*, Camden Society 5th series X (1997), 16, 28; Rollason, *Saints and Relics*, 140. A pendant gold reliquary containing a portion of the blood and blood-soaked clothing of St Thomas of Canterbury, commissioned by bishop Reginald of Bath for presentation to Margaret, dowager Queen of Sicily (d. 1183), survives in the Metropolitan Museum, New York: P. A. Newton, 'Some New Material for the Study of the Iconography of St Thomas Becket', *Thomas Becket: Actes du colloque international de Sédières 19–24 Août 1973*, ed. R. Foreville (Paris 1975), 260–2.

[24] Eberhard in *MGH Deutsche Chroniken*, II 407–8, 420–1, and see Henry Bodo's 'Syntagma', in *Rerum Germanicorum Tomi III*, ed. Meibom, II 486, 488, 492 (above pp. 60–1).

[25] *Acta SS. January*, II 844: *in omnibus bellis collo suo appendit propter victorias quas consecutus est per eam.*

St Stephen. This reliquary, the so-called 'Stefansburse', now housed at Vienna, is probably of Carolingian workmanship, although as with the 'Talisman' there is no record of its role in imperial ceremonial prior to the seventeenth century.[26] This in itself is not surprising, since although we possess numerous recensions of the imperial coronation rite, the rite itself lacks any precise description of the regalia, the service-books or the vestments used in the ceremony. Were it not for their physical survival and the historical traditions that surround them, even such famous objects as the crown of St Stephen or the Aachen gospel books would be impossible to identify from the written rite.[27] Moreover, both with the brooch as described in the annals of Hailes, and with the Stefansburse, we are dealing with items that claim merely to have been employed in the inauguration of kings of Germany by the imperial electors, not in the imperial coronation as described in the surviving rites.

For all of these reasons, although there is no mention of the Holy Blood itself, or of the 'Talisman', in any of the medieval inventories of relics and regalia, either at Aachen or in the imperial treasury, this in itself is no guarantee that either the relic or the reliquary was unavailable to Edmund of Cornwall in the 1260s.[28] Certainly, a pendant reliquary associated with Charlemagne, and a blood relic, albeit a relic of the blood of St Stephen, may well have played a part in the medieval coronation. Nor is it impossible that a portion of the Holy Blood was numbered amongst the imperial treasures, at either Aachen or the Trifels; relic lists for Aachen in the early thirteenth century undoubtedly refer to both a piece of Christ's shroud stained with his blood, and a stone from Calvary *super quem sanguis domini effusus est.*[29] We have seen already that Charlemagne figures prominently in the legends of the blood relics of Reichenau and Mantua. Indeed the Mantuan legend, in which, three years after crowning Charlemagne with the imperial regalia, Pope Leo III travelled

---

[26] *Charlemagne*, ed. Braunfels, 369–70 no. 556, first mentioned by Beeck, *Aquisgranum* (1620), plate at p. 168, where it is described as containing *sanguis s(ancti) Stephani prot(omartyris) super quo rex Roman(orum) dum inauguratur iurament(um) facit.*

[27] For the various recensions of the rite, see *Die Ordines für die Weihe und Krönung des Kaisers und die Kaiserin*, ed. R. Elze, Fontes Iuris Germanici Antiqui in usum scholarum IX (Hannover 1960).

[28] For the imperial relics listed in the 1350s, see Grass, *Reichskleinodien*, 74–8. For those at Aachen *c.* 1200 and 1238, see H. Schiffers, *Aachener Heiligtumsfahrt*, Veröffentlichungen des bischöflichen Diözesanarchivs Aachen V (Aachen 1937), 175–82, which lists a stone from Calvary *super quem sanguis domini effusus est*, and in 1238 relics of Christ's sweat and a 'blood stained cloth with which Our Lord was wiped upon the cross' (*velamen sanguinolentum quo dominus pretinctus erat in cruce*).

[29] R. Folz, *Le Souvenir et la légende de Charlemagne dans l'empire germanique médiévale*, Publications de l'Université de Dijon VII (Paris 1950), 179–81; Schiffers, *Aachener Heiligtumsfahrt*, 176; C. Quix, *Geschichte der Stadt Aachen mit einem Codex Diplomaticus Aquensis*, 2 parts in 1 (Aachen 1839–40), part II 28 no. 41.

to Aachen to bring Charlemagne news of the finding of the Holy Blood, might well have given rise to a tradition in which the blood itself had been brought to Aachen by the Pope. As Robert Folz has shown, by the thirteenth century many of the relics housed at Aachen were believed to have been inherited from Charlemagne, together with the imperial throne.[30] By 1350 this tradition had been extended to cover a large part of the imperial insignia: the crown, the orb, the sceptre and so on.[31] To this extent, the relic of Hailes could claim a more respectable ancestry than the blood of Westminster. Whereas the Westminster relic came from a source, the Latin church of Jerusalem, that had never before laid claim to possess any portion of Christ's blood, the blood of Hailes was associated with Charlemagne and hence with the legends that for the past four hundred years had linked Charlemagne and the Holy Roman Emperors to blood relics elsewhere in Europe. In addition, by claiming that their relic originated with the imperial treasures stored in the castle of Trifels, the monks of Hailes tapped into yet another vein of mystery and myth that may have boosted the relic's prestige in England.

Trifels and the imperial regalia had both played a part in English history prior to Edmund's acquisition of the Holy Blood. It was at Trifels that in 1193 King Richard I had undergone some of the most difficult weeks of his captivity, placed in solitary confinement in the state prison of the Emperor Henry VI.[32] The English chronicler Ralph of Diss remarks upon the awesome impregnability of the castle, from which no prisoner had previously escaped. Adapting a tag from Aristotle, repeated by several later chroniclers, he comments that 'In the Trifels it is good to sacrifice one's father'.

> These their kinsmen sacrifice; this the people, this the place.
> Time has vanquished with a lock every pity, every grace.[33]

---

[30] Folz, *Le Souvenir de Charlemagne*, esp. 178–81.

[31] *Ibid.*, 453–64.

[32] In general, see J. Gillingham, *Richard I* (New Haven 1999), 239. The imprisonement at Trifels in April–May 1193 is referred to in the King's letters in Roger of Howden, *Chronica*, III 208-10; by the anonymous chronicler in 'Hugonis et Honorii Chronicorum continuationes Weingartenses', ed. L. Weiland, *MGH Scriptores*, XXI 479 (*sub anno* 1192); indirectly by Coggeshall, *Chronicon*, 58, and by Diceto and Wendover/Paris, below n. 33.

[33] *Radulfi de Diceto decani Lundonensi Opera Historica*, ed. W. Stubbs, 2 vols., Rolls Series (London 1876), II 106–7, whence Wendover/Paris in *CM*, II 396: *Bonum est mactare patrem* (or *parentes*) *in Trivallis. Sunt loca sunt gentes quibus est mactare parentes. Vel mos vel pietas cum sera supervenit aetas.* The verses are adapted from those attributed by Gervase of Tilbury to master Ralph Niger, written at the court of the Young King Henry (d. 1183) as a gloss upon Aristotle's description of the *Triballi*, a savage people of India; Aristotle, 'Topics' 2.11, in Aristotle, *Topica, Translatio Boethii, Fragmentum recensionis alterius et translatio anonyma*, ed. L. Minio-Paluello and B. Dod, Aristoteles Latinus V 1–3 (Brussels

Even earlier, Richard's grandmother, Matilda, daughter of King Henry I of England, had enjoyed an association with the castle. In 1125 it had been Matilda's husband, the Emperor Henry V, who on his deathbed had first used the Trifels as a repository for the imperial regalia.[34] When the empire passed to the imperial claimant, Lothar III, Matilda made her way back to England. With her she carried a great quantity of precious things, including at least two golden crowns formerly worn by Henry V, a number of vestments and a relic, the hand of St James, abstracted from the imperial treasury. The larger of the imperial crowns may have been used at the coronation of both Henry II and Richard, and was possibly still amongst the English crown jewels in 1207.[35] The hand of St James, housed after 1133 at Reading Abbey, became the focal point of a major cult, sponsored by the royal family. Later it was to be the subject of uneasy negotiations between Matilda's son, King Henry II, and the Emperor Frederick Barbarossa, with Henry refusing Frederick's demand that it be returned to Germany.[36] To this extent, the treasure of the Trifels was already woven into the fabric of English history, and in particular into the associations between the kings of England and the Holy Roman Empire.

Just as in 1125 Matilda returned from Germany with various of the imperial treasures, including the hand of St James, one of the most precious relics venerated by the kings of England; so in the 1260s it seems that Edmund, son of a later king of Germany, followed Matilda's example by abstracting yet further relics from the imperial collection. But whereas in 1125 the empress had left Germany with no real prospect of a return, in 1269 Edmund and Richard appear to have been motivated by no such

and Paris 1969), 48 lines 21–2, 223 line 2; Gervase of Tilbury, 'Otia Imperialia', in *Scriptores rerum Brunsvicensium*, ed. Leibnitz, 1911.

[34] *Frutolfi et Ekkehardi chronica necnon anonymi chronica imperatorum*, ed. F.-J. Schmale and I. Schmale-Ott (Darmstadt 1972), 374, whence the chronicle printed as 'Gesta Archiepiscoporum Magdeburgensium', ed. W. Schum, *MGH Scriptores*, XIV 411–12. See also M. Chibnall, *The Empress Matilda* (Oxford 1991), 41–4, for the fact that Matilda left Germany in a reasonably leisurely fashion, a point drawn to my attention by Christopher Brooke.

[35] K. Leyser, 'Frederick Barbarossa, Henry II and the Hand of St James', *English Historical Review* 90 (1975), 490–1; *Rotuli litterarum patentium*, ed. T. D. Hardy (London 1835), 77b: *magnam coronam que venit de Alemannia*, and for what may well have been one of the imperial *pallia*, granted by Matilda to Grandmont and still preserved today, see J. Martin and L. E. M. Walker, 'At the Feet of Stephen Muret: Henry II and the Order of Grandmont "Redivivus"', *Journal of Medieval History* 16 (1990), 6–7. Natalie Fryde, 'King John and the Empire', *King John: New Interpretations*, ed. S. D. Church (Woodbridge 1999), 342, suggests that the crown referred to in 1207 was a more recent acquisition, perhaps pawned to John by the Welf claimant Otto IV, and in general, see D. A. Carpenter, 'The Burial of King Henry III, the Regalia and Royal Ideology', in D. A. Carpenter, *The Reign of Henry III* (London 1996), 444–56, esp. 445.

[36] Leyser, 'Frederick Barbarossa, Henry II and the Hand of St James', 481–506.

sense of urgency. The earliest account of Edmund's haul suggests that the Holy Blood was only one of a large number of relics acquired from the Bolanden family. Quite why the Bolanden should have been willing to part with such treasures remains unclear. Perhaps Edmund offered money.[37] Perhaps the relics were given to him for safe-keeping. Perhaps the legend is correct in stating that the Bolanden regarded Edmund with special personal affection. Whatever the case, it is difficult to believe that he would have been allowed to make off with any part of the imperial regalia considered essential to the coronation of future emperors. More likely, he was offered relics, including the Holy Blood, which, although they may have been stored at the Trifels, had never formed part of the crown jewels proper. This very point is dealt with by the annals of Hailes, which state that the blood, or a part of it, was removed from the brooch in which it had formerly been housed, thereby implying that Edmund was not allowed to take possession of the brooch itself.

Edmund's father, Richard of Cornwall, had been crowned at Aachen in 1257 with the Trifels regalia. However, in 1262 he presented the chapel of St Mary at Aachen with a crown, a sceptre, a golden apple and a set of vestments, replicas of the true regalia, suggesting that in the interval he had experienced difficulty in obtaining access to his own crown jewels, or at least that he was fearful that some such difficulty might arise in the future.[38] In April 1269, at a major assembly held at Worms, Philip von Falkenstein surrendered Trifels and the regalia into Richard's hands, but the castle and the jewels were soon reassigned to another local magnate, Reinhard von Hoheneck.[39] In June 1269 Richard sailed for England, leaving behind both the Trifels regalia, and the copies at Aachen that had been manufactured at his own expense. There seems to have been no last minute scramble, as there had been in 1125, to rescue whatever

---

[37] In 1265 Richard of Cornwall certainly owed money to Werner and Philip von Bolanden, the sons of Philip von Falkenstein: Denholm-Young, *Richard of Cornwall*, 130, misdated to 1270 in Gebauer, *Leben und denkwürdige Thaten Herrn Richards*, 410.

[38] Gebauer, *Leben und denkwürdige Thaten Herrn Richards*, 380–1, noted by Denholm-Young, *Richard of Cornwall*, 115n, and treated in detail by H. Schiffers, *Die deutsche Königskrönung und die Insignien des Richard von Cornwallis*, Veröffentlichungen des bischöflichen Diözesanarchivs Aachen II (Aachen 1936), esp. 85–112. In 1208 bishop Henry of Speyer is said to have abused his position as keeper of the regalia at Trifels to blackmail Philip of Swabia, claimant to the imperial throne: 'Burchardi et Cuonradi Urspergensium Chronicon', ed. O. Abel and L. Weiland, *MGH Scriptores*, XXIII 372. For Richard's attempts to gain possession of Trifels shortly after his coronation; see the letter of Urban IV printed in *MGH Leges IV: constitutiones et acta publica imperatorum et regum: II (1198–1272)*, ed. L. Weiland (Hannover 1896), 525 lines 36–7.

[39] Gebauer, *Leben und denkwürdige Thaten Herrn Richards*, 404; 'Annales Wormatienses', in *MGH Scriptores*, XVII 68; *Acta imperii inedita seculi xiii*, ed. E. Winkelmann, 2 vols. (Innsbruck 1880–5), I 592 no. 751.

treasures could be salvaged from the wreckage of Richard's time as King of Germany.

Only in retrospect did the Holy Blood of Hailes come to represent a link between England and the vanished glory of Richard's German kingdom. Just as the floor tiles of Hailes were decorated with the imperial eagle, and just as for the remainder of his life Edmund continued to style himself 'Edmund earl of Cornwall, son of Richard the King of Germany of renowned memory', so after 1270 the Holy Blood may have had a symbolic significance to Edmund, as a reminder of the throne and the kingdom that might have been his.[40] The annals of Hailes tell us that Edmund delayed for some years before deciding what to do with his relic.[41] His decision to give part of it to Hailes coincides with an important event in his own life, being his last recorded action before departing for crusade in the spring of 1271, a fact that once again points up the association between devotion to the Holy Blood and devotion to the crusade. In the event, Edmund was never to reach the Holy Land, but was recalled following news of the murder of his elder brother, Henry of Almain, in March 1271.[42] Henceforth he became sole heir to his father's vast estates in England, and a hereditary, albeit hopeless, claimant to the imperial title to which his father had aspired. The Holy Blood was delivered to Hailes in September 1270, and was joined there nine months later by the body of Henry of Almain, brought back from Viterbo.[43] When Richard died in 1272, Edmund succeeded him as earl of Cornwall. Although there was no real prospect of his pursuing a claim to Richard's German kingdom, already a kingdom more in name than reality, and although after 1269 he seems never once to have returned to Germany, Edmund had been brought up in the Rhineland, a king's son, witness to his father's coronation at Aachen, all too aware of the splendours that were denied him in later life.

There is a tendency when writing of thirteenth-century England to stress the sense of inferiority felt by the English towards all things

---

[40] For the tiles, see W. Bazeley, 'The Abbey of St Mary, Hayles', *Transactions of the Bristol and Gloucestershire Archaeological Society* 22 (1899), 269, and *ibid.* 4 (1879–80), 22. For Edmund's title, used in many of his charters, see for example *The Thame Cartulary*, ed. H. E. Salter, 2 vols., Oxfordshire Record Society XXV–VI (1947–8), 97; *The Registers of Walter Bronescombe (A.D. 1257–1280) and Peter Quivil (A.D. 1280–1291) Bishops of Exeter*, ed. F. C. Hingeston-Randolph (London 1889), 361; *Collectanea Topographica et Genealogia* 8 (1843), 123, and the charters in favour of Ashridge cited above n. 8.

[41] Below appendix 3.

[42] *Annales monastici*, IV (Wykes) 243–4.

[43] *Ibid.*, II 110, 377, IV 244; below appendix 3. Henry's heart was placed in the shrine of Edward the Confessor at Westminster.

French.[44] In the case of Henry III and his court, still far from reconciled to the loss of the Plantagenet lands, such a hankering after French culture is only to be expected. However, it should not be forgotten that for at least two members of Henry's family, his brother Richard, and his nephew Edmund, it was not France that represented the lost continental domain, but Germany. Just as in the twelfth century, the Empress Matilda and her son, Henry II, could turn to the crown of Henry V and the hand of St James as reminders of their family's imperial past, so after 1270 Edmund of Cornwall had a vested interest in fostering the cult of the Holy Blood, one of the few material objects to keep alive the memory of his father's links with the Holy Roman Empire and the throne of Charlemagne.

Both at Hailes and at Ashridge the cult of the Holy Blood was carefully nurtured. Neither foundation possessed much else in the way of relics, so that the blood acquired an inevitable prominence. Beyond this, it was derived from a source in the Rhineland, and apparently from a particular treasure, that of the Holy Roman Emperors at Trifels, which shared features in common with various of the most successful blood cults elsewhere in Europe: a claim to have arrived in Europe at some time in the Dark Ages and to have passed through the hands of the Emperor Charlemagne. Subsequently, by grafting on details from the Grail romances, the monks of Hailes introduced a further element to their legend, likely to prove attractive to prospective pilgrims. The Grail may have had a particular significance to Edmund, earl of Cornwall, lord of Tintagel and hence heir to the rich vein of Arthurian legend associated with Cornwall and the West Country. None of these resonances is to be found in the story of the Holy Blood of Westminster, or indeed in the case of the even more obscure blood relics of Reading and Norwich.

There is one other English relic that deserves consideration here. Hailes and Ashridge possessed the only relics of Christ's blood to achieve widespread popularity in England. Yet one of the most remarkable English manifestations of the Holy Blood was not even a relic but a mere prophecy of one. Around the year 1250, as we have seen, the monks of Glastonbury had surreptitiously inserted Joseph of Arimathaea into the list of their supposed founders and benefactors. For the next hundred years, the legend of Joseph lay dormant at Glastonbury. However, towards the end of the fourteenth century, when John of Glastonbury came to produce a revised history of his abbey, he adopted Joseph as

---

[44] For the best account of England's cultural dependence upon France, see R. W. Southern, 'England's First Entry into Europe', in Southern, *Medieval Humanism and Other Essays* (Oxford 1970), 135–57.

one of his principal heroes.[45] Once again borrowing details from the *Estoire de Saint Graal* and the other Grail romances, John repeats the story that Joseph had collected Christ's blood and sweat at the time of the Crucifixion. To this, however, John adds a particular detail all of his own, suggesting that Joseph brought his treasure to England housed in two flasks (*fassula*), one of white and one of silver. These were buried with Joseph's body at Glastonbury in a grave whose site had been forgotten or deliberately concealed. A Welsh seer named Melkin, a figure possibly invented by John as an older rival to Arthur's Merlin, had prophesied that whenever the tomb and the Holy Blood should be rediscovered, the island of Britain would never again know drought.[46]

As James Carley has shown, there was a sequel to this story.[47] At the Council of Constance, in 1417, the Joseph legend was called into question by French and Spanish churchmen anxious to refute England's claim to be considered the most ancient Christian nation in Europe.[48] Probably to provide themselves with irrefutable proof of the justice of their claim, in 1419 the monks of Glastonbury carried out an excavation as a result of which they unearthed a series of tombs. News of their discovery was communicated to King Henry V, who was as anxious as the monks that the legend be proved correct. Yet it was perhaps convenient for all concerned that the results were inconclusive. The monks certainly 'discovered' a tomb, which might have been that of Joseph of Arimathaea, 'and from the middle of the body towards the head there was a great abundance of liquid which to those present in that place seemed as fresh blood both by its colour and its appearance'. At the Council of Siena in 1424, English proctors were to refer to this discovery as if it truly were

---

[45] John's chronicle is to be dated either *c.* 1340 or *c.* 1400, depending upon whether one accepts the arguments of James P. Carley (*John of Glastonbury's 'Chronica'*, esp. xxv–xxx), or those of Antonia Gransden, 'The Date and Authorship of John of Glastonbury's "Chronica sive Antiquitates Glastoniensis Ecclesie" ', *English Historical Review* 95 (1980), 358–63, reprinted with additional material in Gransden, *Legends, Traditions and History*, 290–8.

[46] *John of Glastonbury's 'Chronica'*, ed. Carley, 28–30; Lagorio, 'The Evolving Legend', 218–19; Lagorio, 'The "Joseph of Arimathie" ', 99, and for Melkin see J. P. Carley, 'Melkin the Bard and the Esoteric Tradition at Glastonbury Abbey', *Downside Review* 99 (1981), 1–17, which argues that Melkin's prophecy, although a later invention, may have been in circulation for some years before John of Glastonbury came to write his chronicle.

[47] J. P. Carley, 'A Grave Event: Henry V, Glastonbury Abbey, and Joseph of Arimathea's Bones', *Culture and the King: Essays in Honor of Valerie M. Lagorio*, ed. M. B. Shichtman and J. P. Carley (Albany, N.Y. 1994), 129–48. I am grateful to James Carley for allowing me to read a preliminary draft of the above paper, as drawn to my attention by Simon Keynes.

[48] For the disputes at Constance, see L. R. Loomis, 'Nationality at the Council of Constance: An Anglo-French Dispute', *American Historical Review* 44 (1938–9), 508–27.

the grave of Joseph.[49] But thereafter all is silence. As Carley comments, prophecies are to be dreamed about not experienced.[50] To the Glastonbury monks a legend of the Holy Blood was a more attractive and a more plausible source of prestige than an actual relic, a point with which Henry III might reluctantly have come to agree. At Hailes, Ashridge and even at Glastonbury, the cult of the Holy Blood remained a living tradition, subject to embellishment and the creation of new legends right up to the time of the Reformation. At Glastonbury, for example, the image of Joseph of Arimathaea carrying his two flasks charged with the blood and sweat of Christ is to be found incorporated within the heraldic arms of Richard Bere, the penultimate abbot (1494–1524), and in the stained glass of Langport church, nine miles from the Abbey, commissioned in the late fifteenth or early sixteenth century.[51] At Westminster by contrast, the legend of the Holy Blood appears to have been stillborn. Within fifty years of the Westminster relic's arrival, it had faded from popular memory; a mere object, the subject of curiosity perhaps, adding to the overall splendour of the Abbey, but like the portions of blood recorded elsewhere, at Reading and at Norwich, merely one amongst many relics, little more than an entry in the Abbey's list of treasures. Henry III had good cause to feel disappointment with the indifference of this response. Indeed there is evidence that for some years after the ceremony of 1247, he did his best to stir up interest in the Westminster blood. It is to these attempts, the grant of indulgences and the artistic commissions that may have been associated with Henry's relic, that we should turn next.

[49] Carley, 'A Grave Event', 137, which provides a transcript of Vatican Library MS Reg. Lat. 623 fo. 47r: *et a medio predicti mortui versus capud magna habundancia humoris qui sanguis recens inibi presentibus tam per tincturam quam per visum apparebat.*

[50] Carley, 'A Grave Event', 135.

[51] For illustrations and commentary, see R. F. Treharne, *The Glastonbury Legends* (London 1967), plate facing 39, and 114–15.

CHAPTER 8

The indulgences and the reliquary

At Hailes, Ashridge and elsewhere in Europe, relics of the Holy Blood were housed in shrines, the focal point of pilgrimages. The merits of such shrines were declared through miracles, through the healing of the sick and through such phenomena as the liquefaction of the blood of Bruges, or the preservation of the faithful from death or disaster. It is this sort of evidence that is almost entirely lacking at Westminster, its absence suggesting that the Westminster blood relic failed to achieve the fame that had originally been hoped for. Not even William Sudbury can cite a single miracle involving the blood of Westminster, for all his desire to popularize the relic's reputation, and to date it has proved possible to discover only one miracle story involving the Westminster relic, considered in detail below. However, in stating this we should not be misled into supposing that the Westminster relic was entirely forgotten, or that its presence in the Abbey conferred no prestige. Relics that were not the subject of pilgrimage or miracles might, none the less, by their sheer number, enhance the reputation of whatever church possessed them. Writing in the early thirteenth century, Adam of Domerham remarks upon the extraordinary power that dwelt in the church of Glastonbury, making it a celestial sanctuary on earth. In addition to those saints whose bodies were singled out for particular devotion, every altar, every stone concealed relics, many of them unnamed or unknown, but none the less suffusing the entire building with their holy presence: 'Wherever a stone triangle or square is deliberately placed in the paving, carefully set and bonded with lead, there lies some hidden, holy relic . . . By night no one presumes to loiter in the church, and by day no one would dare spit – one shudders at such a disgusting thought.'[1] It is into this category of

---

[1] Gransden, 'The Growth of the Glastonbury Traditions', in Gransden, *Legends, Traditions and History*, 165, quoting from *Adami de Domerham historia de rebus gestis Glastoniensibus*, ed. T. Hearne, 2 vols. (Oxford 1727), I 27, itself quoting from William of Malmesbury, *De Antiquitate Glastonie ecclesie*, ed. Scott, 66 7.

relic that the Holy Blood of Westminster may well have fallen: a holy object, not itself the subject of pilgrimage or miracles, but none the less contributing to the sanctity and prestige of the church that housed it. At the same time, however, there is evidence to suggest that this was not at all the role which Henry III had originally hoped the relic might play. Our evidence that the King expected more of the Holy Blood is to be found first and foremost in the chronicle of Matthew Paris.

Besides his report of the delivery of the Holy Blood to Westminster and his preservation of the tract ascribed to bishop Grosseteste, Paris has two further pieces of information to add. To begin with, he states that in October 1248, on the anniversary of the delivery of the blood, Henry III proclaimed that a fair, originally granted to the monks of Westminster in 1245, was to be extended from three days to a fortnight each year, around the feast of St Edward, prohibiting the holding of any other market at this time, not only in London but throughout England. This, according to Paris, was done so that all trade might be drawn to Westminster, and so that the influx of people might ensure greater devotion to the Holy Blood and an increased attendance in the Abbey at the feast of St Edward's translation.[2] On 15 October 1248, at the request of the abbot of Westminster, the King granted that all merchants attending the fair were to be free from prises: the forced provision of goods to the royal court, often at less than their true market value, and in 1250, again at the request of the abbot and convent, the site of the fair was moved from Westminster itself to the monks' manor of Tothill, closer to London.[3] The establishment of the fair is said to have been the subject of bitter complaints from London's citizens.[4] Altogether, it appears that in 1248 Henry was keen to boost the revenues of Westminster Abbey, which in turn suggests that the Holy Blood had not as yet attracted the number of pilgrims that had originally been hoped for. On the contrary, the evidence from Westminster suggests that from the mid-1240s there was a steep fall-off in private gifts to the Abbey, coinciding with the King's decision to spend ever increasing sums on rebuilding.[5]

---

[2] *CM*, v 29. For the original grant of the fair and for a detailed commentary, see G. Rosser, *Medieval Westminster 1200–1540* (Oxford 1989), 97–115.

[3] *Calendar of Charter Rolls 1226–57*, 334; *Calendar of Patent Rolls 1247–58*, 76, and see *Close Rolls 1247–51*, 557.

[4] *CM*, v 49–50, 100–1, 127–8; Rosser, *Medieval Westminster*, 97–8. Paris claims (*CM*, v 29) that the grant to Westminster impinged upon the privileges of the fair of Ely, awarded by Henry I, which must originally have been held around the feast of St Etheldreda's translation, 17 October, not as has been supposed her feast on 23 June; *Regesta regum Anglo-Normannorum II: regesta Henrici primi 1100–1135*, ed. C. Johnson and H. A. Cronne (Oxford 1956), no. 1620; *VCH Cambridgeshire*, IV 50.

[5] Rosser, *Medieval Westminster*, 255–60.

Secondly, Paris tells us that as part of his sermon in October 1247, the bishop of Norwich announced that indulgences totalling six years and one hundred and sixteen days had been awarded to all who should visit Westminster in future to venerate the Holy Blood. At Westminster as elsewhere by the mid-thirteenth century, indulgences were a regular accompaniment to the cult of relics. To appreciate the particular significance of the indulgences offered on behalf of the Holy Blood, we need to understand something of the background to the system overall. Whereas in the past, pilgrimage, prayer and alms-giving had been considered sufficient in themselves to earn favour from the saints, from around the year 1100 it became increasingly common for the Church authorities to intervene in the relationship between saint and supplicant by remitting a specified number of days of enjoined penance to all who performed a specified pilgrimage, or who carried out particular prayers or acts of charity. The change is to be seen as part of a wider movement in Church history, brought about by the clarification of theories of penance and purgatory, and reflecting a desire by the bishops to regulate popular devotion through the exercise of their newly articulated powers to bind and loose. This same desire was to lead, in due course, to the reservation to the bishop, or in the ultimate extreme to the papacy, of cases of serious wrongdoing, where previously it had been the parish priest who had been expected to impose penance on the individual sinner.[6]

From the very beginning, the cult of relics, with its emphasis upon the communication that could be achieved between the individual believer and God through the mediation of the saints, had challenged such claims by the Church and its authorities to serve as man's sole route to salvation. Hence the anxiety shown by bishops from an early date that the shrines and relics of the saints be removed from private, family control and established instead in cathedrals and other churches under the supervision of the priesthood.[7] Hence, too, the growing insistence, established in canon law by the early thirteenth century, that the Pope alone had the power to license the cult of any new saint via an official process of canonization.

[6] J. Longère, 'Les évêques et l'administration du sacrement de pénitence au XIIIe siècle: les cas réservés', *Papauté, monachisme et théories politiques: études d'histoire médiévale offertes à Marcel Pacaut*, ed. P. Guichard *et al.*, 2 vols. (Lyons 1994), II 537–50, and for much of what follows, see the more detailed survey by N. Vincent, 'The Earliest English Indulgences: Some Pardoners' Tales', *Transactions of the Royal Historical Society* (forthcoming).
[7] In general see P. Brown, *The Cult of the Saints: Its Rise and Function in Latin Christianity*, Haskell Lectures on the History of Religions, new series II (Chicago 1981), esp. ch. 2.

In this context, the issue of papal and episcopal indulgences is to be seen not merely as a fiscal exercise, intended to solicit alms in return for spiritual benefits, but as yet another means by which the Church authorities sought to establish control over the potentially subversive power of the saints. Clause 62 of the Lateran Council of 1215 specifically linked legislation on indulgences to a demand that all newly discovered relics obtain papal licence before being publicly displayed. As to the indulgences themselves, issued in writing by individual Popes and bishops, these too became subject to official regulation.[8] Concerned that they offered remission from sin on an indiscriminate basis, without directing the faithful through the proper channels of confession, penance and absolution, bishops in the later twelfth century came to insist, via the wording of their indulgences, that remission of enjoined penance was available only to those who, in a standard formula, were 'truly penitent, contrite and confessed' – a formula which was itself derived from that employed by Pope Eugenius in his crusading indulgence, *Quantum predecessores*, issued for the Second Crusade in 1145.[9] To ensure that this condition was met, special confessors were appointed to minister to pilgrims at particular shrines. It was in this way, as we have seen, that in the 1270s the monks of Hailes obtained licence to retain two priests to hear the confessions of pilgrims to the Holy Blood.[10] Simultaneously, to assert

---

[8] The most comprehensive account of the development of indulgences in the twelfth and thirteenth centuries remains that by N. Paulus, *Geschichte des Ablasses im Mittelalter*, 3 vols. (Paderborn 1923), I. Despite the existence of an extensive literature in both French and German, there is as yet no comprehensive study in English. H. C. Lea, *A History of Auricular Confession and Indulgences in the Latin Church*, 3 vols. (London 1896), III, whilst still useful, is written from a vigorously Protestant standpoint and lays excessive stress upon the financial and, as Lea would argue, the more disreputable aspects of the system.

[9] The link with *Quantum predecessores* is noted by Henry Mayr-Harting, *The Acta of the Bishops of Chichester 1075–1207*, Canterbury and York Society LVI (1964), 31–2, and for further English examples of the restriction, before 1184, of indulgences to those who were *vere confessi et penitentibus*, see *English Episcopal Acta II: Canterbury 1162–1190*, ed. C. R. Cheney and B. E. A. Jones (Oxford 1986), nos. 72, 186, 223–4. This supersedes the earlier insistence that pilgrims merely trust to the merits of a particular saint and confer alms, for which see, for example, A. Saltman, *Theobald Archbishop of Canterbury* (London 1956), 337 no. 114, 498 no. 266; *English Episcopal Acta I: Lincoln 1067–1185*, ed. D. M. Smith (Oxford 1980), nos. 33, 258, although even here, before 1150, it is possible to find examples where the element of confession is cited as a prerequisite; *English Episcopal Acta VI: Norwich 1070–1214*, ed. C. Harper-Bill (Oxford 1990), no. 8; *English Episcopal Acta VII: Hereford 1079–1234*, ed. J. Barrow (Oxford 1993), no. 32. For early criticism of the system, see Lea, *Confession and Indulgences*, III 162–3; M. G. Cheney, *Roger, Bishop of Worcester 1164–1179* (Oxford 1980), 58–61.

[10] Above p. 138. At Norwich Cathedral, there are indications that the bishop may have deputed special powers to one of the Norwich monks to hear the confessions of those visiting the shrine of St William as early as the 1140s: Thomas of Monmouth, *Life and Miracles of St William of Norwich*, 30, 84.

further control over the system, and to prevent it from being brought into contempt through indiscriminate or excessive awards, the papacy intervened to restrict the number of days of remission from penance that any bishop could offer, and the number of the faithful who could expect to benefit from any particular indulgence. Pope Alexander III declared that bishops could remit the sins only of those under their direct spiritual jurisdiction, effectively outlawing the practice by which the indulgences of several bishops were lumped together to form a total, often of several years, offered to the faithful on a cumulative basis. Alexander's ruling was reiterated at the Lateran council of 1215, which at the same time sought to limit the average run of episcopal indulgences to a maximum of forty days.[11]

After 1215, in theory though not in practice, forty days' indulgence was the standard award that any pilgrim could expect, save under special circumstances or where the Pope himself had intervened to offer more. In reality, far greater indulgences were easily obtainable. Churches continued to proclaim their indulgences on a cumulative basis, lumping together all the various grants of twenty, thirty or forty days to produce a more impressive running total. Although frowned upon, this practice was near universal.[12] Archbishops continued to offer indulgences on a provincial rather than a diocesan basis, effectively doubling the standard forty days of remitted penance. Similarly, over time, the renewal of indulgences by successive incumbents of a see came to be regarded as cumulative in effect. Diocesans reserved the right to license the benefits proclaimed in the indulgences issued by bishops of other sees, whilst the financial and other inducements offered to suffragans and to bishops in exile continued to ensure that churches were bombarded with large numbers of indulgences from men who for the most part exercised no direct spiritual jurisdiction over the pilgrims to a particular

[11] Lea, *Confession and Indulgences*, 163–4, 171–6. Constitution 62 of the council of 1215 allowed that at the dedication of a church, bishops might issue an indulgence of 100 days, with 40 days for the anniversary, but without any cumulation of indulgences by several bishops.

[12] From England, see for example the running totals for Furness (5 years, 95 days) and Glastonbury (64 years, 197 days); *The Coucher Book of Furness Abbey*, ed. J. C. Atkinson, 3 vols., Chetham Society n. s. IX, XI, XIV (1886–8), III 621–3; Krochalis, 'Magna Tabula', *Arthurian Literature* 15 (1997) 180–3, 16 (1998) 66–82. These lists do at least distinguish the grants by individual bishops, which was not always the case; see for example the letters sent out from Great Bricett Priory, offering 380 days assorted and unspecfied indulgence to all who should contribute to the Priory's fabric; Cambridge, King's College muniments MS GBR 278, an interesting collection of documents, considered by R. N. Swanson, 'Fund Raising for a Medieval Monastery: Indulgences and Great Bricett Priory', *Suffolk Archaeology* (forthcoming). For France, see the totals of more than 43 years of indulgence offered, mostly by the papacy, for the Abbey of Mont-St-Michel; Avranches, Bibliothèque municipale MSS 212 fos. 54r–9r; 213 fos. 247v–50r.

shrine. In England, for example, it was common for Irish, Welsh and Scottish bishops, for papal legates and for visiting bishops from the crusader church, to offer the standard indulgence of forty days, under a clause providing for ratification by the diocesan bishop of any particular pilgrim.[13]

It is in this context that we should regard the offer of six years and one hundred and sixteen days' indulgence, said to have been announced by the bishop of Norwich in October 1247. Assuming the maximum individual indulgence to have been forty days, the figure quoted by Paris suggests that at least fifty-seven bishops participated in the award. It is tempting to suggest that Paris was exaggerating, since even had all the bishops in the British Isles and a large number of eastern bishops contributed, it is unlikely that Westminster could have mustered as many as fifty-seven individual grants of forty days. More likely, the figure quoted by Paris represents the total that had been awarded to all visitors to Westminster Abbey from the twelfth century onwards, topped up with the more recent awards made specifically for the Holy Blood. Even so it is an impressive figure, and one that over the next few years was to undergo even further augmentation. The cartulary known as the Westminster Domesday preserves twenty-eight episcopal indulgences referring entirely or in part to the relic of the Holy Blood, issued between 1247 and 1305, awarding just under three years' remission of penance. William Sudbury's treatise on the blood, written in the 1380s or 90s, lists at least a further seven indulgences in addition to those preserved in the Westminster Domesday, whilst by the time that John Flete wrote, in the mid-fifteenth century, pilgrims to the blood were being offered a grand total of nineteen years one hundred and ninety days' indulgence together with participation in the spiritual benefits of nineteen other cathedrals and churches, suggesting that between 1247 and the 1440s, a further one hundred and twenty bishops had each offered indulgences of

[13] See, for example, the indulgence issued in 1247 by Goffredo bishop-elect of Bethlehem to visitors to the Holy Blood, addressed to all of Christ's faithful, offering forty days' remission of enjoined penance to *omnibus quorum diocesani hanc nostram ratam habuerint . . . si vere confessi fuerint et contriti*; Westminster Abbey MS Domesday fo. 395r, whence Vincent, 'Goffredo di Prefetti', 235. Similar phrases, allowing for the extension of the spiritual benefits on offer to 'all whose diocesans ratify this present writing' are to be found in the vast majority of indulgences from suffragan and 'foreign' bishops, as well as amongst the average run of indulgences by English diocesans. See, for example, *Llandaff Episcopal Acta 1140–1287*, ed. D. Crouch, South Wales Record Society v (1988) nos. 92, 97, 104, 106; *The Cartulary of the Augustinian Friars of Clare*, ed. C. Harper-Bill, Suffolk Records Society Suffolk Charters XI (1991), nos. 62, 158–9, 161–4, 167–73, amongst which nos. 62 and 172–3 specifically ratify the indulgences issued for the same purpose by all other bishops.

forty days.[14] According to the figures provided by Flete, the Holy Blood was the most extensively indulgenced relic in the Abbey, well ahead of such objects as the stone upon which Christ had stood at the time of his Ascension (just over twelve years of indulgence) and the nail from the Cross (just over fourteen years). Visitors to the Holy Blood could expect to receive greater indulgences even than those who attended the Abbey on the feasts of St Edward's deposition and translation (nineteen years respectively), and far more than those who said prayers for the soul of King Henry III (a mere five years, two hundred and forty days).[15]

Quite how Flete's figures are calculated remains a mystery, though they presumably reflect the totals advertised to visitors to the Abbey, just as at Glastonbury the total number of days of indulgence was posted up on wooden boards, the so-called *Magna Tabula*, displayed prominently in the Abbey church.[16] As we have seen, the figures themselves represent a cumulative total, whereas in theory the individual pilgrim could claim no more than the indulgences awarded by his own diocesan, his archbishop, the Pope and, where appropriate, those issued by a papal legate. Moreover, we should not be misled into supposing that because it was the most heavily indulgenced relic, the Holy Blood was necessarily the most popular pilgrimage destination at Westminster. On the contrary, the greater the number of indulgences, the more anxious a church must have been to attract pilgrims to a particular relic or enterprise, and hence, we may assume, the less appeal such a relic or enterprise might have commanded on its own merits alone. To this extent, the more extensive indulgences often accompany innately unpopular, rather than innately popular, relics. It is remarkable, for instance, that during its most successful years the enormously prestigious shrine of St Thomas at Canterbury appears to have attracted only a handful of indulgences, virtually none of them episcopal, whereas there are large numbers for shrines, relics and churches

---

[14] Flete, *History*, 74. For Sudbury's list of the indulgences, see Longleat MS 38 fos. 300v 5r, described above p. 133. Amongst those mentioned by Sudbury but not preserved in the Westminster Domesday, note the awards of forty days each issued by John bishop of Winchester (1262 × 1268, or 1282 × 1333), John archbishop of Dublin (after 1279), Ralph bishop of Norwich (1293), Charles bishop of Elphin (1355 × 1357), Thomas bishop of Rochester (1283 × 1337 or 1365 × 1389), David bishop of *Recreens'* (unidentified) and eighteen unnamed bishops acting in concert.

[15] Flete, *History*, 73 5.

[16] Oxford, Bodleian Library MS Lat. hist. a. 2 sheet 6. For a photograph and description of these tables see J. A. Bennett, 'A Glastonbury Relic', *Proceedings of the Somerset Archaeological and Natural History Society*, 24 part 2 (1888), 117 22, with a complete edition by Krochalis, 'Magna Tabula', *Arthurian Literature*, 15 (1997), 93 183, 16 (1998), 41 82.

that commanded little of Canterbury's prestige.[17] Our evidence here is sketchy and should not be pressed too far, since indulgences were rarely copied into monastic cartularies, and were destroyed in huge numbers after the Reformation. None the less, it would be quite wrong to suppose that the indulgences for the Holy Blood were necessarily a sign of the relic's popularity.

If we look a little more closely at those preserved in the Westminster Domesday, it soon becomes apparent that they tell us far more of the attempts made to advertise the relic, in particular the efforts made on its behalf by King Henry III, than they do of any great upsurge of devotion by pilgrims. The twenty-eight letters in the Westminster Domesday can be no more than a selection of the total number issued.[18] Conspicuous by their absence are any awards by the bishop of Norwich, by Robert Grosseteste or by the patriarch of Jerusalem, all of whom are likely to have participated in the first spate of indulgences announced at the time of the relic's arrival in England, in October 1247. Eighteen of the twenty-eight letters in the Westminster Domesday can be dated between October 1247 and September 1250. Just as Henry III is said to have planned his fair at Westminster in 1248 in order to encourage devotion to the Holy Blood, so there appears to have been a deliberate campaign to persuade bishops to support the relic through the grant of indulgences. By comparing the dating clauses of the early indulgences with the King's itinerary, it emerges that eleven of the eighteen awards were made when the bishop in question was at court. On the very day of the relic's delivery in October 1247 Goffredo, bishop-elect of Bethlehem, contributed forty days' indulgence, being followed over the next two months by four English, one

[17] In 1220, at the time of Becket's translation, the Pope and numerous bishops are said to offered indulgences totalling 540 days; *The Historical Collections of Walter of Coventry*, ed. W. Stubbs, 2 vols., Rolls Series (London 1872–3), II 246; R. Foreville, *Le Jubilé de Saint Thomas Becket du XIIIe au XVe siècle (1220–1470)* (Paris 1958), 165–6. None of these episcopal letters survives amongst the Canterbury archives. However, as popular enthusiasm for the shrine went into decline during the fifteenth century, there do appear to have been attempts to boost this waning support by the offer of ever more impressive indulgences; C. E. Woodruff, 'The Financial Aspect of the Cult of St Thomas of Canterbury', *Archaeologia Cantiana* 44 (1932), 21–5.

[18] They are preserved in a section of Domesday devoted to the muniments of the Abbey's sacristry, together with the letters of the patriarch of Jerusalem printed as an appendix below, and a large number of other papal and episcopal indulgences relating to the Abbey's assorted relics; Westminster Abbey MS Domesday fos. 386r–405v, continued in a later hand to fo. 409v. Two of these indulgences, including one for the Holy Blood, are printed in *Llandaff Episcopal Acta*, ed. Crouch, nos. 92, 101. References to the printing of legatine indulgences are to be found in *Westminster Abbey Charters*, ed. Mason, nos. 187–93. For the keeping of the relics and the altar at Westminster, entrusted to one of the four obedientiary monks known as subsacrists, see *Customary of the Benedictine Monasteries of St Augustine Canterbury and Saint Peter, Westminster*, ed. E. Maunde Thompson, 2 vols., Henry Bradshaw Society XXIII, XXVIII (1902–4), II 52–3.

Welsh and two Irish bishops. On 12 May 1248 Walter Mauclerk, the former bishop of Carlisle who had resigned his see to join the Franciscans
at Oxford, issued an indulgence whilst the royal court was at Oxford.
A fortnight later, the newly consecrated bishop of Lismore followed
Mauclerk's example, on the day after his consecration at Woodstock,
itself the site of a royal chapel built in the form of a *rotunda*, in deliberate
emulation of the church of the Holy Sepulchre in Jerusalem.[19] It seems
almost as if the indulgence for the Holy Blood was a *quid pro quo*, issued
by the bishop in gratitude to the King for permitting his consecration. In
August 1249, Thomas bishop of St David's issued an indulgence of forty
days when the court was at St Neots in Huntingdonshire, whilst three
of the indulgences granted before 1250 were issued at Windsor, in the
presence of the court. Of the bishops whose letters are preserved, six
were Irish, including two separate awards in slightly different terms by
Reginald archbishop of Armagh; three were Welsh and one Scots.[20] For
the rest, the archbishops of York and Canterbury, the bishops of Hereford
and Bath and Wells, and the archbishop of Bordeaux, the metropolitan
of Plantagenet-controlled Gascony, each contributed forty days. Eight of
the eighteen awards adopt an identical text, beginning *De Dei misericordia*,
suggesting that a common form was made available for engrossment by
individual bishops; a practice that was by no means confined to Westminster, but is to be found elsewhere whenever a church was actively
soliciting indulgences.[21] Fifteen of the eighteen awards are of forty days;
the last three, issued in 1250, by the archbishop of Armagh and the bishops of Ossory and St Asaph, are for thirty days only, the archbishop's
indulgence referring to the Holy Blood in company with all the other
relics displayed at Westminster. Whether or not this suggests a decline

[19] Gervers, 'Rotundae Anglicanae', 374.
[20] The archbishop of Armagh and the bishops of Waterford, Llandaff, Lismore, Killaloe, Dunblane,
    St David's, Ossory and St Asaph. The first of the archbishop of Armagh's awards, dated
    28 October 1247, is the only one in the entire series to survive in the original; Westminster
    Abbey MS Domesday fo. 398r; muniments no. 6674. The archbishop's second award, dated 31
    May 1250, is for thirty rather than forty days and follows a different text, including not only the
    blood but all the other (unspecified) relics at Westminster; MS Domesday fo. 396v.
[21] At Westminster, for example, all fourteen indulgences for the piece of the True Cross adopt a
    common text beginning *Ut hostis antiqui malignis*; Westminster Abbey MS Domesday fos. 399v
    402v. For examples away from Westminster, see *Reading Abbey Cartularies*, ed. B. R. Kemp, 2 vols.,
    Camden Society 4th series XXXI, XXXIII (1986–7), I nos. 191, 194, 196; Salisbury Cathedral
    Library MS D. & C. Press IV Box Indulgences. Clause 62 of the Lateran Council of 1215
    had itself laid down a model for such letters, in a form beginning *Quoniam ut ait apostolus 'omnes
    stabimus ante tribunal Cristi'*, adopted by numerous later bishops, including Boniface archbishop of
    Canterbury in his indulgence for the Holy Blood, 28 September 1249; Westminster Abbey MS
    Domesday fos. 397v–8r, also given in full by William of Sudbury in Longleat MS 38 fos. 300v–1r.

in enthusiasm for the Holy Blood, it is certainly remarkable that after September 1250 there is no further indulgence recorded for the relic until 1267.

When the series resumes, after a silence of twenty years, the form of the indulgence undergoes a significant change. Of the eleven awards dated between 1267 and 1305, only two, including that issued by Wolfram bishop of Bethlehem in October 1305, are directed solely towards visitors to the Holy Blood. The rest refer to the blood as only one of several relics preserved at Westminster. For example, the three letters issued in 1287 by the bishops of Ely, Emly and St Andrews, following an identical text, offer forty days' remission of penance to all who visit Westminster to bestow alms, to pray at the tomb of King Henry III or to venerate any of the Abbey's relics, naming in particular those of St Edward, St Peter, the Holy Blood, the girdle of the Virgin Mary, the footstep of Christ and St Edward's ring. The resumption of the series, in October 1267, came shortly before the translation of the relics of St Edward to their new shrine on 13 October 1269, for which event Pope Clement IV in March 1268 had offered an indulgence of three years and one hundred and twenty days.[22] It may be that a revival of interest in the Holy Blood occurred in the late 1260s, coinciding with the excitement surrounding the new shrine of St Edward. Of the first three indulgences recorded for the Holy Blood after 1250, two, both apparently issued by foreign bishops, are directed jointly to visitors to the Holy Blood and to the relics of the Confessor.[23] The third, issued by Nicholas of Ely bishop of Worcester on 13 October 1267, exactly thirty years after the relic's first delivery, is specifically directed to pilgrims to the blood, but is none the less intriguing in its assertion that not only was the blood to be accounted a true relic, but that it was appropriate to draw pilgrims to its veneration.[24] This reference to the relic's authenticity and the appropriateness of pilgrimage (*dignum est non solum vocare verum etiam invitare et trahere*) can itself be read as an

[22] Westminster Abbey MS Domesday fo. 386r v. An earlier indulgence of Pope Clement, dated 22 June 1266, intended to encourage attendance at the feasts of St Edward's translation and deposition, had referred in its preamble to the price of man's redemption, *precio sanguinis fusi de precioso corpore redemptoris*, but the reference to the blood is probably purely accidental. Similar pious phrases involving Christ's blood are to be found in an indulgence of Innocent IV for Westminster, issued in July 1245, long before the Abbey had obtained possession of its relic; *ibid.* fo. 386r v. referring to Christ who redeemed mankind *sanguinis sui precio preciosi*.

[23] *Ibid.* fo. 397v, in common form by Reginald bishop of Cork (*Crokagens*') (February 1269/70), and brother Henry bishop of *Hasiliens*' (December 1277). I have been unable to identify brother Henry's see.

[24] *Ibid.* fo. 397r, printed in *English Episcopal Acta 13: Worcester 1218–1268*, ed. P. M. Hoskin (Oxford 1997), 144–5 no. 180.

indication that, even in the 1260s, doubts still lingered over the relic's credentials and over the merits of pilgrimage to an object that remained so controversial.

Overall, our analysis suggests that between 1247 and 1250 a concerted effort was made by the King to obtain support and publicity for his new relic, doubtless in the hope that this would increase the number of pilgrims and hence the number of benefactions to Westminster Abbey; but that thereafter the Holy Blood ceased to enjoy any great prominence amongst the Abbey's relic collection. Indulgences continued to be issued, but for the most part they were directed towards all of the Abbey's relics, not merely the Holy Blood.[25] The wording of these awards does, on occasion, throw a little new light on the way that the blood relic was presented to the public. For example, the letters issued in 1248 by Walter Mauclerk, former bishop of Carlisle, include pious references to man's redemption 'through the most precious blood of Jesus Christ, the immaculate and uncontaminated lamb', mercifully bequeathed to the world *in argumentum dilectionis et augmentum meritorium fidelium.*[26] Following a patriotic line of argument which we have already seen adopted, both by Robert Grosseteste and in the sermon preached by the bishop of Norwich, the bishop of Llandaff lauds the King of England, Henry III, 'exalted above the kings of all other nations', explaining that the Holy Blood is to be regarded as the greatest of the Passion relics, such objects as the Cross, the nails and the Crown of Thorns being sanctified only through their contact with Christ's body and blood.[27] However, the sheer number of indulgences issued on behalf of the relic is not to be interpreted as a sign that the Holy Blood enjoyed any great appeal to pilgrims; if anything, quite the reverse. Paris tells us of the efforts made to attract visitors to the relic in 1248, and of its veneration by those in attendance at the feast of St Edward's deposition in January 1249. In the following year, he includes the delivery of the blood to Westminster amongst his list of the most memorable events of the previous fifty years. But thereafter, the relic goes virtually unmentioned.[28] Sacrist's accounts from 1317,

---

[25] The only exception, the award made by the bishop of Bethlehem in 1305, might suggest, none the less, that the Holy Blood continued to enjoy a special place in the affections of visiting crusader bishops, who were no doubt reminded of the part played in its initial dispatch to England by the patriarch of Jerusalem and the bishop-elect of Bethlehem, Goffredo de Prefetti. Besides the indulgences issued in 1247 and 1305 by Goffredo and Wolfram, in March 1291/2 Hugh bishop of Bethlehem awarded a further forty days' remission of penance, referring to the blood and to various others of the Abbey's relics: *ibid.* fos. 395r, 399r-v.

[26] *Ibid.* fo. 396r.

[27] *Llandaff Episcopal Acta*, ed. Crouch, no. 92 (December 1247).

[28] *CM*, v 29, 47–8, 195.

although useful for their evidence of the Abbey's income from its relics, fail to distinguish any particular sums allotted to the Holy Blood. Overall they suggest a considerable fluctuation in the Abbey's income from pilgrims, reaching a high-point of £120 in 1372–3, but thereafter declining to less than £10 a year for much of the reign of Henry VI.[29] In general, it is possible that the fifteenth century witnessed a dramatic decline in the revenues obtained by the English cathedrals from their traditional shrines and relics. At Hailes, where we know that the Holy Blood continued to attract large numbers of visitors well into the sixteenth century, the proceeds of the shrine were assessed by Henry VIII's commissioners at only £10 a year.[30] At Canterbury, Hereford and Winchester, it has been assumed that offerings tailed off to virtual insignificance some years before the Reformation. None the less, the decline may not have been so drastic as was once supposed. Important offerings may have continued to be paid in kind, or in jewels and precious metals used to decorate the various shrines, rather than in cash. Furthermore, the surviving obedientiary accounts may include only a fraction of the total cash received.[31] However, even at their zenith the figures from Westminster were hardly spectacular and represent only a fraction of the income obtained at Canterbury from the shrine of Thomas Becket.[32] Ironically, it was the chapel of St Thomas Becket in Westminster Abbey that, to

---

[29] Harvey, *Westminster Abbey and its Estates*, 44–5.

[30] *Valor ecclesiasticus tempore Henrici VIII, autoritate regia institutus*, ed. J. Caley and J. Hunter, 6 vols. (London 1810–34), II 456, and for the continued popularity of Hailes, see below pp. 197–8.

[31] For Hereford, see P. E. Morgan, 'The Effect of the Pilgrim Cult of St Thomas Cantilupe on Hereford Cathedral', *St Thomas Cantilupe, Bishop of Hereford, Essays in his Honour*, ed. M. Jancey (Hereford 1982), 145–52, with important revisions suggested by R. N. Swanson, 'Devotional Offerings at Hereford Cathedral in the Later Middle Ages', *Analecta Bollandiana* 111 (1993), 93–102. For the evidence from Winchester, based upon the sole surviving sacrist's roll, for the year 1536–7, in which, perhaps not suprisingly, nothing whatsoever was received from any of the relics, see *Compotus Rolls of the Obedientiaries of St Swithun's Priory, Winchester*, ed. G. W. Kitchin, Hampshire Record Society VII (1892), 108–111. However, as recently as 1476 there had been a major translation of the relics of St Swithun to a new shrine at Winchester; J. Crook, 'St Swithun of Winchester', *Winchester Cathedral Nine Hundred Years 1093–1993*, ed. Crook (Chichester 1993), 64. For Canterbury, see below n. 32. Overall, the subject is one that richly deserves a more detailed study. For various preliminary suggestions, see Finucane, *Miracles and Pilgrims*, 192–216; Swanson, 'Devotional Offerings', 93–9, and in general, G. W. Bernard, 'Vitality and Vulnerability in the Late Medieval Church: Pilgrimage on the Eve of the Break with Rome', *The End of the Middle Ages: England in the Fifteenth and Sixteenth Centuries*, ed. J. L. Watts (Stroud 1998), 199–233.

[32] For the figures at Canterbury, see Woodruff, 'The Financial Aspect of the Cult of St Thomas', 13–32; *Valor Ecclesiasticus*, I 8, where from a highpoint of over £1,000 in the jubilee year 1220, the offerings at the shrine maintained a reasonably steady level, somewhere between £400 and £600 a year until the fifteenth century, when they underwent a dramatic decline, perhaps to as little as £10 a year. Here and elsewhere the figures may be misleading, since it is tempting to suggest that a portion of the monks' income, perhaps a considerable portion, was excluded from the surviving accounts.

judge by the number of burials there, proved the most popular of the Abbey's chapels in the later Middle Ages.[33]

The Westminster blood relic seems never to have developed into the focus of miracles or miraculous cures. However, it may be that in its earliest days, attempts were made to promote the relic as source of healing. Our one piece of evidence here is a brief note, apparently copied into a Westminster manuscript dealing with the coronation rite, transcribed in the seventeenth century by the antiquary, Elias Ashmole.[34] The story preserved by Ashmole can be dated only very loosely to the reign of Henry III, perhaps to the last decade of Henry's reign.[35] It records that in the month of August a two-year-old boy, named William son of Thomas le Brown, was discovered drowned in his father's pond at Hyde (now Hyde Park), a Westminster manor adjoining the Abbey precinct. However, when the boy was measured, that is to say when a wax taper of the same height as the boy was placed before the blood of Jesus Christ, he was restored to life. Not only this, but it was found that the boy, previously incapable of talking, had acquired the power of speech. In memory of this event, King Henry III led a procession from the bridge near Tothill (in the modern St James' Park) to Westminster Abbey where he ordered the Abbey's bells to be rung and promised the monks a gold cup decorated with precious stones, in commemoration. This, so far as can be established, is the one and only miracle story associated with the Westminster blood. Whilst significant as an indication of Henry III's continued interest in the relic, it is important to note that the story is unique, that it survives in a local Westminster source, and that it involves relatively humble tenants of Westminster, dwelling less than a mile from the Abbey itself. From this, we might conjecture that, although King Henry and the monks did their best to promote the curative properties of their new relic, the relic failed to take off as an object of pilgrimage and made only a modest impression outside the immediate vicinity of Westminster itself. A similar fate appears to have been met by the Holy Blood of Norwich, whose one recorded miracle, again recorded in a unique and local source, involved the relic's own

---

[33] Harvey, *Westminster Abbey and its Estates*, 366n.

[34] Oxford, Bodleian Library MS Ashmole 842 fo. 80v, printed below appendix 2. I am extremely grateful to Richard Sharpe for drawing my attention to this account.

[35] Of the monks of Westminster named as witnesses in the miracle story, John le Foundour, William de Hasele and William de Peryndon are recorded elsewhere as being active during the years of abbot Richard of Ware (1258–83); E. H. Pearce, *The Monks of Westminster* (Cambridge 1916), 52, 56. I can find no other reference to Thomas le Brown or his tenancy at Hyde.

miraculous preservation from the fire that swept through Norwich Cathedral in 1272.[36]

Elsewhere we receive further confirmation that the Holy Blood made relatively little impact either upon the finances or the religious life of Westminster Abbey. For example, a royal almoner's roll for the period January to June 1265 records special offerings at Westminster by Henry III to the girdle of the Virgin Mary, and on Good Friday more than £2 distributed in alms to pilgrims coming to Westminster for the adoration of the Cross. There were likewise numerous special masses said throughout the year in honour of St Edward the Confessor, besides special offerings to his shrine at Westminster and to the Abbey's high altar in Holy week.[37] However, there is nothing to suggest that the King continued to devote special attention to the relic of the Holy Blood.[38] In the same way, the blood relic finds no mention amongst the prayers and celebrations recorded in the fifteenth-century Westminster Missal, or in any other of the Abbey's service-books. In the later Middle Ages, when feasts such as those of the miraculous blood of Beirut, the wounds of Christ and the Crown of Thorns, came to be adopted by various English churches, there is nothing to suggest their observance at Westminster.[39] Although the collects in the Westminster Missal, for the Tuesday, Thursday and Friday following Easter, all refer to Christ's blood, in standard phrases, as the price of man's redemption, there appears to have been no special commemoration of the blood relic at any of the appropriate feasts; the feast of the Abbey's relics on 16 July each year, or those of the Holy Cross,

[36] Below appendix 4.
[37] PRO E101/349/30 m. 2, including 5 shillings spent on Good Friday at the adoration of the Cross and 49 shillings and 6 pence spent at the same time *in ob(lationibus) eiusdem peregrinatis per diversas ecclesias in civitate London' et in elem(osinis)*. Individual oblations, mostly of gold pieces, were made to the Virgin's girdle on 22 March, to the high altar on Palm Sunday and Easter Saturday, to the Cross on Good Friday, and to the shrine of St Edward on 25 January, Maundy Thursday and Easter Sunday.
[38] There is no mention of the Holy Blood in any of the almoners' accounts or associated records for the reign of Edward I, which none the less record gifts to a large number of shrines, most prominently that of St Thomas of Canterbury. See for example PRO E101/350/18 (household account of Henry, son of Edward I 1273–5) mm. 3, 6, which includes offerings at the tombs of St Edward and Henry III at Westminster; E101/350/23 (almoner's roll 1276–7) mm. 1–4; E101/351/15 (*ibid.* 1283–4) mm. 1–2; E101/363/30; E101/364/1 (lists of oblations to various shrines 1303). One might note that in the year 1301–2 the King's chapel recited the Mass of St Edward on only four occasions, as opposed to six recitals of the Mass of St Thomas; PRO E101/361/2 m. 2d.
[39] Pfaff, *New Liturgical Feasts*, chs. 5 and 6. Although at Weingarten there appears to have been a liturgy of the Holy Blood in use from an early date, with the exception of communion prayers *in illatione sanguinis Domini*, there is no indication of any general medieval feast of the Holy Blood: W. A. Volk, 'La Festa liturgica del preziosissimo sangue', *SA*, IV part 3 (1984), 1505–6.

14 The high altar of Westminster Abbey as shown in the mortuary roll of
abbot Islip *c.* 1532 (Westminster Abbey, Dean and Chapter)

which elsewhere, as at Hailes and Ashridge, seem to have been adopted as the occasion for a special festival of the Holy Blood.[40] By contrast, in the 1460s a list of the vestments and service-books delivered to the keeper of St Edward's shrine, refers to two quires, one of them containing collects and Gospel-readings for the Virgin's girdle, and the other for unspecified 'relyquys'. This same list also mentions a wooden staff covered with silver, used to carry the Cross upon Holy Rood day, suggesting that both objects, the girdle, regarded as a specific for child-birth, and the fragment of the True Cross, played a prominent part in the Abbey's ceremonial.[41] The sacrists' rolls from Westminster suggest that in 1317–18 oblations were still being made to the relic of Christ's footstep and to the ring of St Edward.[42] The footstep had been housed in a special silver reliquary, whilst the ring, or at least an image of it, appears to have been mounted on a pillar, placed besides the Confessor's shrine.[43] In 1338 two of the Abbey's monks spent more than twenty weeks overseas, guarding the Virgin's girdle that had been sent to accompany Queen Philippa during her pregnancy, and in 1354 the King and Queen paid a further £12 to have the girdle brought to Woodstock, shortly before the birth of the

---

[40] See *Missale ad usum ecclesie Westmonasteriensis*, ed. J. Wickham Legg, 3 vols., Henry Bradshaw Society I, V, XII (1891–7), II 591–2 for the collects after Easter; *ibid.*, I p. xi, and III 1362 for the feast of relics; II 643, 658–9, 946–9, 803–5 and III 1354–5 for the feasts of the Cross. The lack of a comprehensive index to this edition makes it very difficult to check for references to the Holy Blood, some of which I may have overlooked. For the other surviving service books, a breviary and a benedictional, see Oxford, Bodleian Library MSS Rawlinson C 425; Liturg. g. 10. For the indulgences at Hailes which appear to suggest particular devotion to the blood relic at the feasts of Corpus Christi, the Holy Cross and during Lent, see BL MS Cotton Vespasian B xvi fo. 95v; Leland, *Collectanea*, ed. Hearne (1770), VI 283–4.

[41] Westminster Abbey muniments 9477, 9478: *also ii bokys of cronyclis, oun callyd Polycronicon' and the oyer callyd Flores Historiarum, also a portos of Salysbury use, also ii quayers, oun with collects and gospell for our lady gyrdyll, anoyre of ye relyquys... a staff of tre and a part kuveryd with sylver to bere the holy cros upon holy rode day* (21 December 1467, repeated 9 October 1479), and see Westlake, *Westminster Abbey*, II 501, for a mention of the staff in 1520. The reference to the Westminster chronicles in the lists of 1467 and 1479 is not without an interest of its own. For the Virgin's girdle, which, as with similar relics elsewhere in England, appears to have been regarded as a cure for barren women, see E. Duffy, *The Stripping of the Altars: Traditional Religion in England c. 1400–c. 1580* (New Haven and London 1992), 384.

[42] Westminster Abbey muniments 19618–19, referring to oblations *ad anulum, passum et alias reliquias*.

[43] Tudor-Craig, *New Bell's Guides: Westminster Abbey*, 115–18; J. D. Tanner, 'Tombs of Royal Babies in Westminster Abbey', *Journal of the British Archaeological Association* 3rd series 16 (1953), 28 and plate VI; L. E. Tanner, 'Some Representations of St Edward the Confessor in Westminster Abbey and Elsewhere', *ibid.* 3rd series 15 (1952), 5–10. The suggestion that the footstep was incorporated into the tomb built for Henry's children who had died in childhood is contradicted by the evidence that it had been housed in silver in 1251, and that it was later stored together with the remainder of the Abbey's relics; above p. 12 n. 21. For Henry III's devotion to the legend of St Edward's ring, see also *King's Works*, ed. Colvin, 127–8; *Calendar of Liberate Rolls 1240–1245*, 14; *ibid. 1245–51*, 342; *ibid. 1251–60*, 268, 347, 350–1, 367.

future duke of Gloucester.[44] Much earlier, we know that in 1242 the Virgin's girdle had been sent to Henry III and his wife Queen Eleanor in Gascony, no doubt in preparation for the birth of their daughter Beatrice, born on 25 June that year.[45] Beyond the income from the Confessor's shrine, others of the sacrists' accounts record specific gifts to images of the crucified Christ and the Virgin Mary, oblations made at the chapel of the Virgin Mary in the Abbey's north entrance and to the altar of St Thomas. Likewise we find references to monks standing with relics at the altars of the Holy Trinity and St John on Good Friday and on the feast of St Peter, and of payments made to proclaim the Abbey's indulgences to the people of London three times a year.[46] However, nowhere do these accounts refer directly to the relic of the Holy Blood. Our one indication that the blood was still venerated at Westminster in the late thirteenth century, comes in a wardrobe book of Edward I, recording an offering of seven shillings made 'at Westminster at the Blood of Jesus Christ' on 29 June 1285, shortly before the King set out on pilgrimage to the shrine of St Thomas at Canterbury.[47] For the rest, all is silence.

Flete tells us that the indulgences for visitors to the blood were still available in the 1440s, so that the relic must have been displayed, but where remains a mystery. The most likely place would have been the

---

[44] Westminster Abbey muniments 19621: *de portionibus fratrum R. de Byby et I. de Asshwele exeuntium cum zona beate Marie in partibus transmarinis cum regina pregnante per xxiii septimanas*, from 4 July to 13 December. *Ibid.* 19623: *de dono regine apud Wodestok' pro zona beate Marie et de c(entum) solidos de dono regis ibidem*. The pregnancy of 1338 preceded the birth of Lionel, future duke of Clarence. A similar relic, of the girdle of St Mary Magdalene, much in demand by women in labour, is said to have been granted by the Empress Matilda to Monkton Farleigh Priory in Wiltshire: *Three Chapters of Letters relating to the Suppression of the Monasteries*, ed. T. Wright, Camden Society XXVIII (1843), 59 no. 24. In 1422, Henry V sent for a relic of Christ's foreskin, housed at the Abbey of Coulombs near Chartres, considered a cure for barren women, to attend the pregnancy of his Queen with the future Henry VI; *Gallia Christiana*, VIII instr. cols. 389–91, printing an instrument relating to the subsquent deposit of this relic in the Sainte-Chapelle and the Abbey of St-Magloire at Paris, of which there are copies in Paris, Bibliothèque nationale MSS Latin 5413 (St Magloire cartulary) fos. 200r–1r; Latin 5414 pp. 405–7; Baluze 83 p. 287; Chartres, Archives départementales de l'Eure-et-Loir H1261 (Coulombs inventory) p. 497. For a general account of the relic, said to have been sent to France at the time of the First Crusade, and for its rediscovery in 1860 inside an old wardrobe in the sacristy of the local parish church, see E. Lefèvre, *Documents historiques sur les communes du canton de Nogent-le-Roi, arrondissement de Dreux*, 2 vols. (Chartres 1864–6), I 347–57.

[45] *Customary of Westminster*, ed. Maunde Thompson, II pp. xviii, 73, misdated 1246.

[46] Westminster Abbey muniments 19621, 19623, 19626, 19628, 19630.

[47] PRO C47/4/2 m. 27d: *in oblatione regis apud Westm' ad sanguinem Ihesu Cristi vii. solidos*, as noticed by A. J. Taylor, 'Edward I and the Shrine of St Thomas of Canterbury', *Journal of the British Archaeological Association* 132 (1979), 22. It is worth noticing the conjunction between Edward's gift, the controversy in the schools of Oxford over the bleeding relics of St Thomas of Hereford (d. August 1282) and John Pecham's condemnation of teachings on the unity of form and the nature of Christ's body *in triduum mortis* (April 1186), so cleverly drawn together by Boureau, *Théologie, science et censure*, esp. ch. 7.

high altar, but this is no more than a calculated guess.[48] Certainly, there appears to have been nothing to compare to the shrines erected in honour of the Holy Blood at Hailes and Ashridge, or to the rededication of the high altar in honour of the blood relic that is known to have taken place at Gandersheim in the 1350s.[49] Beyond the treatise on the Westminster blood composed by William Sudbury in the late fourteenth century, which in itself provides little evidence that the relic enjoyed a popular following, the most significant references we have to the blood after 1300 occur in a series of relic lists, the earliest of them dated 1467. Since these are arranged according to an order found in many other European churches, placing the relics of Christ ahead of those of any other saint, we should not read too much into the fact that the Holy Blood is consistently placed at the head of the Westminster lists. None the less, their references to the blood are not without interest, since they describe it as *a cuppe of gold with stonys with ye blode of oure lord*.[50] When the relic was delivered to Westminster it had been housed, according to the patriarch of Jerusalem, not in a golden cup but in a pyx of crystal (*pixis cristallina*). This same 'most handsome crystal vase' (*vasum cristallinum venustissimum*) is referred to by Matthew Paris and illustrated in his drawing of the procession led by Henry III, where it appears as a translucent oval, encircled by two gold bands, with a gold top or stopper.[51] In his *Historia Anglorum*, a synopsis of the *Chronica majora*, produced between 1250 and 1255, Paris provides another, very different, illustration of the *vasculum sanguinis*, shown as a rectangular tower with a triangular top, a flattened base, two encircling bands and a series of nine rectangular shaded areas, perhaps representing jewels, set into its side.[52] This is presumably the same 'vessel to contain the Blood of Christ', for which the King purchased nearly £25 worth of gold and precious stones from a Venetian merchant in July 1248, and whose crafting was to cost a further £32 accounted in January 1250. But by no stretch of the imagination could this vessel, as drawn by Matthew Paris, be described as a golden cup.[53] From this it would appear that the blood was translated at least twice between 1247 and the 1460s, from

[48] The suggestion that the blood relic was displayed in the niche carved in the pillar behind the tomb of Henry III appears to be based on hearsay only; F. Bond, *Westminster Abbey* (Oxford 1909), 242; A. L. N. Russell, *Westminster Abbey* (London 1943), 132.

[49] Above pp. 61, 137–9.

[50] Westminster Abbey muniments 9477, 9478; Westlake, *Westminster Abbey*, II 499.

[51] Below appendix 1; *CM*, IV 641, and for the drawing see the references above p. 4 n. 9.

[52] *Matthaei Parisiensis, monachi sancti Albani, historia anglorum*, ed. F. Madden, 3 vols. Rolls Series (London 1866–9), III 29, from BL MS Royal 14. C. vii fo. 142r (fo. 131r, 134r, p. 262).

[53] *Calendar of Liberate Rolls 1245–51*, 193, 271.

15   Matthew Paris' drawing of the *vasculum sanguinis, c.* 1250 (London, British
Library MS Royal 14. C. vii fo. 142r)

its original vase into a tower-shaped reliquary at some time between
1247 and 1255, and later, before the 1460s, into a cup of gold. The
cuppe of gold with stonys referred to here might conceivably be the same *vas
aureum pretiosis lapidibus ornatum* which Henry III is said to have given to
Westminster in commemoration of the miraculous restoration to life of
William le Brown, perhaps in the late 1250s or 60s.[54]

   Elsewhere in Europe, blood relics seem for the most part to have been
stored in reliquaries of crystal or glass, such as that depicted on the seal
of Hailes Abbey, or the many that still survive in the abbeys of Germany
and France.[55] The blood brought from Fécamp to Norwich, for example,
although originally contained in a silver vessel (*vasculum argenteum*) was

---

[54] Below appendix 2.
[55] For the seal, see figure 16, depicting a monk holding in his right hand a round vase with a cross at
the top, and in his left hand what may perhaps be a sprinkler for holy water. For the blood reliquary
at Venice, a standing gold and crystal monstrance, depicted in the 1280s, see figure 18; D. Pincus,
'Christian Relics and the Body Politic; A Thirteenth-Century Relief Plaque in the Church of San
Marco', *Interpretazioni Veneziane: studi di storia dell'arte in onore di Michelangelo Muraro*, ed. D. Rosand
(Venice 1984), 41, and in general see J. Braun, *Die Reliquiare des christlichen Kultes und ihre Entwicklung*
(Freiburg 1940), 100–112, plates 59, 92; *Reallexikon zur deutschen Kunst-Geschichte*, ed. O. Schmitt,
vol. II (1948), cols. 949–50. At Fécamp the Holy Blood is said to have been kept in two tubes of
lead, covered in silver and housed in a metal pyramid: *Gallia Christiana*, XI 204. For the confused
history of the Fécamp relic, several times rehoused, see Leroux, *Une tapisserie*, 64ff.

16   The seal of the fraternity of Hailes Abbey, *c.* 1400 (London, British Library)

subsequently translated to a crystal vase, the better to be seen and honoured.[56] Why should the Westminster relic have been transferred to a cup? With nothing more than the brief description of the 1460s to go on, and with no certain idea of the date at which the transfer took place, it would be rash to make any but the most tentative of suggestions.

[56] Below appendix 4.

However, there is one possibility that springs immediately to mind. We have seen that at Hailes in the fourteenth century, the monks had recourse to the legends of the Holy Grail to fill in the missing years in the early history of their relic. Likewise, we have suggested that in his tract on the Westminster blood relic, Robert Grosseteste may deliberately have emphasized the role played by Joseph of Arimathaea in the preservation of the Holy Blood, in order that his account might strike a chord with the romances circulated together with the legends of the Holy Grail, linking Joseph to the history of the English Church. William Sudbury, likewise, refers to the story of Joseph of Arimathaea in his account of the preservation of the Holy Blood. In origin the Grail stories combine a number of disparate elements; stories of King Arthur culled from Celtic legend and more recently from the fantasies of Geoffrey of Monmouth; visions of the Grail as interpreted through the French chivalric tradition of the *Chansons de geste*, and finally various ideas borrowed and embellished from the New Testament, amongst them the figure of Joseph of Arimathaea and the idea that the Grail could be identified with the vessel or chalice used by Christ at the Last Supper. It was not until a relatively late date, after 1200, that all of these elements were welded together into the form in which they were to be transmitted throughout the later Middle Ages, and even then the Grail remained an object of mystery with no very certain imagery or iconography.[57] The Grail stories did, however, become overlaid with a heavy layer of eucharistic symbolism, linked to the mass and above all to the sacrament of the wine-blood of Christ.[58] In this context it is at least a possibility that the Holy Blood of Westminster was deliberately transferred from a crystal flask to a golden cup, in order that it might more closely resemble the popular image of the Holy Grail.[59] Once again there is an indication here that attempts were being made,

[57] Amongst the vast literature on the Grail legend, see in particular R. S. Loomis, *The Grail: From Celtic Myth to Christian Symbolism* (Cardiff 1963); D. D. R. Owen, *The Evolution of the Grail Legend* (Edinburgh 1968), esp. ch. 8.

[58] Rubin, *Corpus Christi*, 139–42. As might be expected the symbolism here has attracted more than its fair share of lunacy, none more notorious than that of M. Baigent, R. Leigh and H. Lincoln, *The Holy Blood and the Holy Grail* (London 1982), a work of fiction, more incredible in its way than any of the medieval legends associated with Christ's blood.

[59] For the great diversity of such images, some of them derived from the eucharistic chalice or monstrance, others from the bowls used in illustrations of the Old Testament to depict vessels for the collection of the blood of animal sacrifice, see Alison Stones, 'Seeing the Grail: Prolegomena to a Study of Grail Imagery in Arthurian Manuscripts', *The Grail: A Case Book*, ed. D. Mahoney (forthcoming). I am indebted to Professor Stones for allowing me to see a typescript of her article. Since the Grail legends were so closely bound up with the legends of King Arthur, it is worth noting that in the late fifteenth century Caxton claimed that the monks of Westminster possessed an impression of King Arthur's seal, set in beryl; Tudor-Craig, *New Bell's Guides: Westminster Abbey*, 117.

perhaps many years after 1247, to popularize the Westminster relic, or at least to draw attention to it, by translating it at least twice, from its original container. Something similar appears to have taken place at Norwich, where bishop Walter Suffield, the same man who had been chosen to preach on the reception of the blood of Westminster, gave the monks of Norwich a great and handsome silver cup in which to place their crystal reliquary, itself fashioned some years earlier as a more fitting container than the vessel in which the blood had originally been brought to Norwich from Fécamp.[60]

There is one final question concerning the Westminster blood that deserves consideration: a question closely related to the artistic presentation of relic and reliquary. Elsewhere in Europe, at Mantua for example, at Venice, and even as we have seen on the seal of the Abbey of Hailes, blood relics were advertised to potential pilgrims through painting and sculpture.[61] Images such as the figure of *ecclesia* holding a chalice to catch the blood from Christ's wounds, of Christ treading the wine press, or of the pelican, a beast supposed to nurture its young with the blood from its own breast, had a clear role to play in popularizing the Church's teachings on the mass and upon the redemptive power of the sacramental blood of Christ.[62] The image of *ecclesia* catching the wine-blood from Christ's side is at least as ancient as the time of Augustine, and was definitively enshrined in Christian doctrine by the Council of Vienne in 1312.[63] Such images were dispersed far and wide and became deeply embedded in the medieval subconscious. For example, one of the eucharistic miracles reported by Caesarius of Heisterbach in the 1220s involves a vision of Christ, with the blood pouring from his wounds into the chalice, supposedly experienced by a monk of the Cistercian Abbey of Himmerod, but surely originating in the traditional, artistic representation of the

---

[60] Below appendix 4.

[61] For Venice, see Pincus, 'Christian Relics and the Body Politic', 39–57. For Mantua, see Horster, 'Mantuae Sanguis Preciosus', 151–80.

[62] See in general G. Schiller, *Iconography of Christian Art*, 2 vols., trans. J. Seligman (London 1971–2), II esp. 106–8, 228–9; Bynum, 'The Body of Christ', 427–34; L. Kretzenbacher, *Bild-Gedanken der spätmittelalterlichen Hl. Blut-Mystik und ihr Fortleben in mittel- und südosteuropäischen Volksüberlieferungen*, Bayerische Akademie der Wissenschaften Philosophisch-Historische Klasse Abhandlungen n. f. CXIV (Munich 1997); *Le Pressoir mystique. Actes du colloque de Recloses*, ed. D. Alexandre-Bidon (Paris 1990). For the pelican, see Rubin, *Corpus Christi*, 310–12. For similar images and for devotion to the five wounds of Christ, which in England as elsewhere laid particular stress upon the side-wound through which it was believed that Christ had displayed his heart, the refuge of mankind, see Duffy, *The Stripping of the Altars*, 102–8, 238–48.

[63] Augustine, 'Sermons' 336.5, in Migne, *PL*, XXXVIII 1475: *de isto latere facta est Ecclesia que nos pariendo vivificaret*, and see B. Neunheuser, 'Il Sangue di Cristo, effuso alla Croce e nell'eucaristia, secondo le miniature di libri liturgici del primo medio evo', *SA*, IV part 3 (1984), 1419–33. For the Council of Vienne, see above p. 105.

Passion, with the chalice at the foot of the Cross catching Christ's blood.[64]
The legend of Hailes claimed that the blood had been collected in a cup
placed beneath the Cross down which Christ's blood had flowed, whilst
even Robert Grosseteste appears to have been influenced by such images. In his account of the preservation of the Holy Blood he writes of
the heart-blood that flowed from the wound in Christ's right side.[65] An
elementary knowledge of anatomy would have alerted him to the fact
that the heart is to found on the left, not the right hand side of the body.
The Gospels had made no attempt to define the position of Christ's
wound. However, iconographically, it was traditional to portray Christ
with the wound in his right-hand side, in accordance with the wording
of the Easter anthem in which Ezekiel's description of the Temple is
taken to prefigure the incarnate Christ: *Vidi aquam egredientem de templo
a latere dextro, Alleluia, Alleluia* (Ezekiel xlvii. 1).[66] In this respect at least,
Grosseteste appears to have allowed imagery to take precedence over
medical science.

Elsewhere, the later Middle Ages witnessed an outpouring of art in
which the blood from Christ's Passion spurts out in great streams, is projected into the chalice, envelops the Cross like rain, or in which Christ
himself stands on the altar, the bleeding sacrifice.[67] The seven blood-
sheddings of Christ became a recognized iconographic series, commemorated in painting, poetry and liturgical drama.[68] At the great Corpus
Christi day celebrations held at Viterbo in 1462, for example, the Pope
walked in procession before a series of tableaux which included a youth
painted so that he seemed to be exuding blood whilst another, dressed
as Christ, sweated blood and filled a cup as if it were from a healing
stream from the wound in his side.[69] So literally were such devotions

---

[64] Caesarius, 'Dialogue' 9.41, ed. Strange, II 197–8; *Dialogue on Miracles*, II 144–5.

[65] *CM*, VI 140: *ipsum sanguinem cum aqua quem censuit praecordialem a latere dextro.*

[66] See V. Gurewich, 'Observations on the Iconography of the Wound in Christ's Side, with Special
Reference to its Position', *Journal of the Warburg and Courtauld Institutes* 20 (1957), 358–62; A. A.
Barb, 'The Wound in Christ's Side', *ibid.* 34 (1971), 320–1.

[67] See for example Schiller, *Iconography*, figures 806, 808–10; Cambridge University Library MS
Add. 5944/11, a remarkable fifteenth-century printed indulgence from Flanders, offering
80,000 years (*sic*) of indulgence to all who should say the prayer to the sacred heart of Jesus,
reproduced by A. Arnould and J. M. Massing, *Splendours of Flanders* (Cambridge 1993), 160–1,
185 no. 53, which notes other, similar, images, and below figure 17.

[68] L. R. Muir, *The Biblical Drama of Medieval Europe* (Cambridge 1995), 247 n. 20; R. Woolf, *The
English Religious Lyric in the Middle Ages* (Oxford 1968), 222–7.

[69] *The Commentaries of Pius II Books VI–IX*, ed. F. A. Gragg and L. C. Gabel, Smith College Studies
in History XXXV (Northampton, Mass., 1951), 553, 556, and in general, for the uses to which
Christ's blood was put in liturgical drama, see Muir, *Biblical Drama*, 104, 130, 249 n. 27, 254
n. 59.

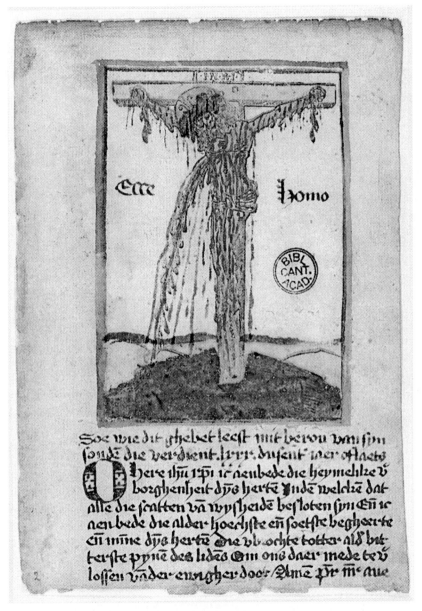

17 Image of the wounded Christ, Flemish *c.* 1450 (Cambridge University
Library MS Add. 5944/11)

18   Venice, bas-relief showing the relic of the Holy Blood held by two angels, amidst
others of the city's relics, thirteenth century (Osvaldo Böhm)

interpreted that in England, as elsewhere, calculations were made as to
the exact number of the scourges of the lash that Christ received – generally agreed to have been something approaching 5,500 – and the precise
number of the drops of blood shed in the Passion – estimated at anything
between 28,000 and 547,000 droplets.[70] At Weingarten in Bavaria, the
relic of the Holy Blood gave rise to a whole plethora of images: pilgrim
badges, medallions, a major cycle of fifteenth-century panel-paintings
now at Stuttgart, and still each year a great procession of the relic, known
as the *Blutritt*, attracting pilgrims in their thousands.[71] Into the eighteenth
century, the annual procession of the flagellant penitents of the Confraternity of the Most Precious Blood at Perpignan was a familiar sight,
revived in the 1950s with red-hooded robes and other accoutrements
more appropriate to a rally of the Klu Klux Klan.[72] At Bruges, Fécamp
and at Neuvy-St-Sépulcre, all of whose blood relics were supposedly rescued from the pillage of the 1790s, post-revolutionary Catholic reaction

---

[70] Hirsh, *The Boundaries of Faith*, 98–9.
[71] G. Spahr, *Kreuz und Blut Christi in der Kunst Weingartens, eine ikonographische Studie* (Constance 1962),
esp. pp. 82–119, with a study of the *Blutritt* at 116–20.
[72] See J.-G. Deloncle, *La Procession de la Sanch* (Portet 1985).

was to ensure that pilgrimage, and with it miraculous cures, continued well into the nineteenth century.[73]

Such outpourings of devotions to the Holy Blood were accompanied in the early years of the nineteenth century by the foundation, at first in Italy, but rapidly spreading thereafter to both France and England, of a Congregation of Missionaries of the Precious Blood, established with papal approval by the anti-Napoleonic priest Gaspare del Bufalo (d. 1837, canonized 1954), and numbering the future Pope Pius IX amongst its earlier recruits.[74] It is the influence of this Congregation which explains an upsurge of pious publications devoted to the Holy Blood, and to attempts to dedicate the months of June or July to the blood's particular veneration.[75] In 1849, amidst the turmoil of revolutions, Pius IX instituted the first Sunday in July as the feastday of the most precious blood. In 1914 the feast was transferred to 1 July. It was abolished in February 1969 by the Second Vatican Council, which none the less renamed the feast day of Corpus Christi 'The Feast of the Body and Blood of Christ'.[76] This same influence, focusing chiefly upon the blood of the sacrament, may lie behind the decision, made by the English Catholic hierarchy, to incorporate the Holy Blood within the dedication of the newly founded Roman Catholic Cathedral at Westminster in 1910.[77]

---

[73] For Fécamp and its nineteenth-century miracles, see Leroux, *Une tapisserie*, 89ff; A.-P. Biard, *La Relique de Fécamp. Messe, litanie et histoire du Précieux Sang de N. S. Jésus-Christ, suivies du récit de guérisons récentes opérées à l'ancienne fontaine où aborda la souche du figuier, dépositaire de cet inestimable trésor* (Paris 1866), several times reprinted. For Neuvy-St-Sépulcre, see A. Piétu, *Neuvy-St-Sépulcre: les gloires de son passé* (Bourges 1920), 155ff. Similar movements are to be found at Bruges, Boulogne and in Germany.

[74] For Gaspare del Bufalo, his Congregation (founded 1815 in succession to a slightly earlier confraternity of 1808), and its sister order of the Adoratrici del Preziosissimo Sangue, see *Bibliotheca sanctorum*, VI 40–3.

[75] See, for example, amongst an extensive literature, Vincenzo Strambi (alias G. Bonanni), *Mois de Juin consacré à honorer le précieux sang de N. S. Jésus-Christ* (Paris 1842; rep. Limoges 1843); Père Marin de Boylesve, *Le Mois du Précieux Sang de N. S. Jésus-Christ, suivi de pieux exercices auxquels sont attachées des indulgences* (Paris 1883). In 1854, it was under a dedication to the Holy Blood that the five congregations of Augustinian nuns in the diocese of Arras were united into one: *Notice sur la congrégation des religeuses Augustines du Précieux-Sang* (Arras 1928).

[76] W. A. Volk, 'La Festa liturgica del preziosissimo sangue', *SA*, IV part 3 (1984), 1503–45, esp. 1506–7.

[77] Note here the close attachment of the Oratorian Father Frederick Faber (1814–63) to the Congregation of the Precious Blood. Not only was Faber himself the author of a pietist work *The Precious Blood* (London 1860, immediately translated into French with several further French editions appearing between 1860 and 1881), but his bon-mots were later assembled as the *Maxims and Sayings of the Reverend F. W. Faber... Arranged for Every Day in the Year by a Religious of the Congregation of the Adorers of the Most Precious Blood* (London 1877, again with a French translation, introduced by the Chartiste Léon Gautier, Paris 1879). As an Anglican received into the Catholic faith in 1845 only a month after Newman, and as the first superior of the London (later the Brompton) Oratory,

19 Bruges, the reliquary of the Holy Blood, Jan Crabbe, 1617 (Bruges, Confraternity of the Holy Blood)

Certainly, the Cathedral's founders seem to have been unaware of, or uninterested in, the earlier association between Westminster and the relic acquired by Henry III. In France, such pious exercises carried political overtones, representing part of a wider upsurge of Catholic reaction against what was regarded as the godless Socialism of the Second and Third Republics.[78] At Fécamp, the blood relic was to be authenticated by successive archbishops of Rouen, most recently in 1888, and in its turn was to inspire one of the most remarkable works of art ever devoted to the Holy Blood: a needle-work, one hundred feet long, retelling the apocryphal legend of Fécamp in fake-Gothic style, executed by a local estate agent and his wife after 1909 in imitation of the tapestry of Bayeux.[79] In 1894, pilgrimage to the Blood Chapel at Bruges, though pointedly not to the Bruges blood relic, was made the subject of a plenary indulgence by Pope Leo XIII.[80] The chapel at Bruges was raised to the status of a basilica by Pope Pius XI in 1923, a year after the promotion of King Albert of the Belgians as honorary provost of the *Noble Confrérie du S. Sang*. Each year on Ascension Day, the Bruges relic is processed with much mock-medieval pageantry: a ceremony attended in 1973 by the present Pope John Paul II, then a cardinal.[81]

What evidence is there for the use of imagery or artistic advertisement in the propagation of the cult of the Holy Blood at Westminster? Here, we can turn to the investigations of M. E. Roberts, who suggests that the ceremonial north transept entrance to the Abbey, constructed *c.* 1245 × 1253, and the south portal of Lincoln Cathedral, built a decade or so later, and perhaps modelled on the work at Westminster, both originally included sculpted figures in which Christ was to be found pointing quite deliberately to the wound in his side. Roberts goes on to identify other

Faber was in close touch with many of the figures influential in the planning of Westminster Cathedral, first conceived in 1865 in light of the establishment of the archdiocese of Westminster in 1850; building begun 1895, dedicated 1910.

[78] See, for example, the tract by Henri Delaage, *Le Sang du Christ: Jésus ami du peuple . . . ésprit anti-socialiste de l'évangile. Influence malfaisante du socialisme sur l'élément révolutionnaire des faubourgs* (Paris 1849) (BN livres LB55 586), dedicated to Victor Hugo in the aftermath of the Revolution of 1848, and preaching a form of Christian Socialism, although with little direct interest in the cult of the Holy Blood.

[79] Leroux, *Une tapisserie*, with further illustrations in *La Broderie du Précieux-Sang de Fécamp*, Musée Municipal de Fécamp Exhibition Catalogue (Fécamp 1987), noting the attempt to reconstruct the scheme though not the style of a tapestry series commissioned for Fécamp in the sixteenth century, but subsequently destroyed.

[80] Bruges, Holy Blood Chapel, Museum, original MS, offering a plenary indulgence to *omnibus . . . utrinsque sexus . . . qui memoratum sacellum memorato die* (8 May) *devote visitaverint*, 17 April 1894. Leo XIII had earlier served as legate to Belgium, and in 1888 had presented the chapel with a splendid gilt chalice, also displayed in the museum.

[81] Bruges, Holy Blood Chapel, Museum, MS Livre d'Or.

20   Reichenau, the reliquary of the Holy Blood, Franz Wech, 1746
(Reichenau Abbey)

21   The Fécamp tapestry, *c.* 1910, embroidered in imitation of the tapestry of Bayeux, showing the deposition from the Cross (Fécamp, Musée des Arts et de l'Enfance)

22   Lincoln Cathedral, Christ displaying the wound in his right side
(London, Conway Library)

examples of English stone-carving and illumination that display the same
emphasis on Christ's wound, suggesting that the motif coincides with and
was directly influenced by the arrival of the Holy Blood in 1247.[82] Although much of this argument is conjectural, the sculptural programme
at Westminster having been obliterated since the seventeenth century, it
is at least a possibility that an image of Christ gesturing to his wounds
might have been fashioned in an attempt to alert the Abbey's visitors to
the relic of the Holy Blood displayed within. Certainly, it is intriguing
that the motif should occur at Lincoln, Robert Grosseteste's cathedral,
albeit some years after Grosseteste's death. Other images at Westminster, from around 1300, show Christ forcing St Thomas the apostle to
touch the wounds in his side, an image related perhaps to Westminster's
possession of an arm relic of St Thomas that had been refurbished by

[82] Roberts, 'The Holy Blood', 129–42, especially 135–7, with reservations expressed in the footnotes
at 142. Binski, *Westminster Abbey*, 71, is sceptical whether there was any copying from Westminster
in the Lincoln portals, suggesting that the Westminster portal may have housed an image of
St Peter rather than of Christ.

Henry III in 1244.[83] St Thomas' arm may have been considered all the more sacred because it had actually penetrated the wounds and hence had come into contact with Christ's very flesh and blood.[84] Combined with the evidence we have already assembled, on indulgences, on the work of William Sudbury, on the Westminster fair and on the reliquary itself, all of this would suggest that valiant efforts were made, most prominently by Henry III between 1247 and 1272, to stir up enthusiasm for the blood of Westminster. What is most remarkable about these efforts is that they should have met with what appears to have been almost complete popular indifference.

[83] Tudor-Craig, *New Bell's Guides: Westminster Abbey*, 112; *Close Rolls 1242–1247*, 270, 276, and see above p. 51 n. 74.

[84] See for example the finger of St Thomas preserved at Constantinople before 1204, *quem misit in latus domini*: Mercati, 'Santuari e reliquie Costantinopolitane', 140.

Epilogue

We began this study with the various hopes and expectations invested in the Holy Blood by Henry III and by the church of Jerusalem. To the King, the blood appeared a fit rival to the Passion relics acquired by Louis IX. It offered Henry the opportunity to enhance his reputation for piety, dented over the past few years by the magnificent endeavours of the French. By depositing the relic in Westminster Abbey he clearly hoped to attract pilgrims and money to his cherished, spiritual, home. Furthermore, by the manner of the relic's reception, it appeared possible to speed the assimilation of the King's half-brothers, the Lusignans, into the affections of the court. As for the patriarch and the church of Jerusalem, by sending the relic to England they hoped to recruit support for the forthcoming crusade and for their own financial plight in exile. These were extravagant hopes, yet it is remarkable that not one of them was to be realized.

The Westminster blood was never to rival the reputation of the Passion relics of France. This is perhaps hardly surprising, since even had it won universal acclaim, the Westminster blood was but a single memorial of the Passion. Louis IX had collected several dozen such memorials, including a portion of the Holy Blood formerly displayed in Constantinople. Grosseteste and the bishop of Norwich might boast that the Westminster relic was greater than those of France because the instruments of the Passion were sanctified only by their contact with Christ's blood. Yet Louis himself possessed just such a portion of the Holy Blood; a portion, moreover, acquired from the Emperor of Constantinople and hence from a more creditable source than that from which the blood of Westminster had been obtained. Over the next thirty years, Louis could afford to make numerous gifts from his great relic collection, dispatching splinters from the Cross, or thorns from the Crown of Thorns, as potent symbols of his piety and affection.[1] By contrast, Henry III's relic was but a single object, given to Westminster alone. Even at Westminster, it does not appear to have excited popular devotion in the way that had been hoped. There is no evidence that it brought pilgrims flocking to the Abbey. The Holy Blood, like the relics of St Edward the Confessor, was greeted with only luke-warm enthusiasm. The full cost of rebuilding the Abbey continued to fall upon the King's own purse.

As for the Lusignans, welcomed at court on the same day that Henry's blood relic was paraded to Westminster, whatever good may have been achieved by their ceremonial reception was soon to be dispelled. Over the next ten years, their greed and insensitivity were to earn them widespread hatred at court.[2] The hopes invested in the Holy Blood by those who had sent it, the patriarch and chapter of Jerusalem, were to bear equally little fruit. Not only was Henry III unable or unwilling to answer their appeal for help in recovering the English lands of the Holy Sepulchre, but it was not for another three years that he was to be induced to take vows as a crusader. In the meantime, by refusing Louis IX's request for a prolonged extension of the Anglo-French truce, and by soliciting papal letters that postponed the departure of English crusaders for a year after the sailing of the French, far from answering the patriarch's appeal, it can be argued that Henry did positive damage to the crusader cause. Even after he had taken the cross in 1250, albeit that his intentions may have been honourable, he was to prove more of a hindrance than a support to the defence of the Holy Land.[3]

For all of these reasons, the gift of the Holy Blood to Westminster must be accounted a failure. Above all, as Matthew Paris makes plain, it failed to win universal acceptance as a true relic of Christ's blood.

---

[1] For Louis' gifts, see W. C. Jordan, *Louis IX and the Challenge of the Crusade* (Princeton 1979), 107 9, 191 5.

[2] See especially H. W. Ridgeway, 'King Henry III and the "Aliens", 1236 1272', *Thirteenth Century England II*, ed. P. R. Coss and S. D. Lloyd (Woodbridge 1988), 81 92; D. A. Carpenter, 'What Happened in 1258?', in Carpenter, *The Reign of Henry III*, 106 19.

[3] In general, see R. C. Stacey, 'Crusades, Crusaders and the Baronial "Gravamina" of 1263 1264', *Thirteenth Century England III*, ed. P. R. Coss and S. D. Lloyd (Woodbridge 1991), 144 150. It is unnecessary to accept all of Stacey's arguments to appreciate that Henry was one of the least successful crusader kings in the history of Europe. As the result of the crusade of his son, the Lord Edward, Henry was none the less granted the benefits of the crusade indulgence, complete remission of sins for himself and participation in the indulgence for those who granted assistance to the Holy Land for his father and his mother, King John and Isabella of Angoulême: PRO E36/274 (Exchequer Liber A) fo. 250r (211r), letters of Bernard penitentiary of the church of Jerusalem dated at Acre, 20 September 1272.

This, it can be argued, led to the collapse of all those incidental benefits that might have accrued had the relic been accepted as genuine. There were many reasons for the relic's failure: the wide dispersal of such relics across Europe, the fact that it came from a source that lacked credibility, the long-standing scepticism of theologians towards all bodily relics of Christ. To these we might add yet another cause. As various theologians had objected as long ago as the twelfth century, what need had the church for relics of Christ, when his body and blood were renewed daily in the sacraments of the mass? Within twenty years of the arrival of the Holy Blood at Westminster, Europe was to be swept with enthusiasm for the cult of Corpus Christi, a cult which permitted an outpouring of devotion to the body and humanity of Christ without requiring the faithful to accept the credentials of any particular relic supposedly preserved for a thousand years or more from the time of Christ's Passion. The feast of Corpus Christi enjoyed the explicit support of the papacy. Its devotees were required simply to accept the orthodox teachings of the church in respect to the doctrine of transubstantiation. As a result they were spared the various niggling doubts, factual and doctrinal, that attended all the supposed historical relics of Christ's body and blood. Thomas Aquinas, although the leading scholastic opponent of relics of the Holy Blood, could respond to the cult of Corpus Christi with whole-hearted enthusiasm; it was almost certainly Aquinas who composed the liturgy for the new Corpus Christi feast.[4]

The success of Corpus Christi may help to explain the relative failure of such relics as the Holy Blood of Westminster; and yet this explanation is not a wholly satisfactory one. As we have seen, within a few years of the declaration of the new feast, Edmund of Cornwall was to return from Germany with a relic that at Hailes and Ashridge was to prove the focal point of pilgrimages to the Holy Blood. Elsewhere in Europe, blood relics, not just the eucharistic blood of shrines such as Wilsnack, but the supposed historical blood of Christ displayed at Bruges, Venice and Gandersheim, were to excite considerable popular devotion. Indeed it can be argued that by concentrating men's minds upon the sacraments and upon the transformation of the bread and wine into the body and blood of Christ, the newly instituted feast of Corpus Christi provided a boost, not a set-back to the veneration of the supposed historical relics of Christ's blood.

In the end we are thrown back upon one, rather pitiful, conclusion. Henry III appears to have made valiant efforts to stir up enthusiasm for

---

[4] Rubin, *Corpus Christi*, 185–9; J.-P. Torrell, *Saint Thomas Aquinas* (Washington 1996), 129–36.

the blood of Westminster, but those efforts failed, not merely because the relic lacked credibility, or because it was overshadowed by rival cults, but because the King himself lacked the ability to achieve anything other than failure. No one could have done more than Henry to advertise the merits of Westminster Abbey, to adorn it with relics and works of art, indeed to rebuild it more or less stone by stone from the foundations upwards. Yet popular enthusiasm for the Abbey appears to have faded almost in direct proportion to the amount of money that was spent upon it by the King. The general indifference to Westminster, to the shrine of St Edward and to such relics as the Holy Blood, reflects a more deep-rooted indifference towards the King himself, an indifference that bordered upon contempt. As crusader, financier, administrator and as would-be reconqueror of France, Henry fared just as dismally as he did as a patron of relics. The failure of the Holy Blood is to this extent symptomatic of the far wider failure of King Henry III.

Precisely this point has been taken up by Geoffrey Koziol, who in a wide-ranging study alludes to the scepticism expressed towards Henry's blood relic as if it were symptomatic of the Plantagenet family's more general failure to manipulate 'the holy' or to preserve the sacral authority of the throne. Developing a line of argument first advanced by Marc Bloch and thereafter pursued by Karl Leyser – that the Plantagenet kings of England sought an association with the saints and with Holy Men as a means of buttressing their own sacrality, gravely dented in the aftermath of the Investiture Contest – Koziol seeks to trace the roots of this dilemma, not so much to the Investiture Contest, as to a new ethos of royal authority espoused by the Plantagenets.[5] The Plantagenets, in Koziol's analysis, rather than seeking to preserve their sacral, mimetic, functions as vicars of Christ – a role which the Capetian kings of France are assumed to have maintained long into the thirteenth century and beyond – based their claim to rule upon a new knightly ethos. Chivalry, a claim to rule by conquest, and secular legends such as those of King Arthur, were deployed by the Plantagenets to justify the legitimacy of their rule over a newly secularized, bureaucratized, realm of England. In this respect, Koziol suggests, Plantagenet kingship diverged significantly from the more ancient, sacral, aspirations of the Capetian kings of France.[6] Marc Bloch

---

[5] K. Leyser, 'The Angevin Kings and the Holy Man', *St Hugh of Lincoln*, ed. H. Mayr-Harting (Oxford 1987), 49–73.

[6] G. Koziol, 'England, France, and the Problem of Sacrality in Twelfth-Century Ritual', *Cultures of Power: Lordship, Status and Process in Twelfth-Century Europe*, ed. T. N. Bisson (Philadelphia 1995), 124–48, noting the reception afforded the Holy Blood at 139. A similar line of argument is deployed by Colette Beaune, 'Les Ducs, le roi et le Saint Sang', arguing that the Holy Blood of Fécamp was originally intended to bolster the sacral authority of the dukes of Normandy,

had already laid out the bare bones of this argument as long ago as the 1920s. Commenting upon the disparity between the wealth of legends associated with Capetian sacrality – unction with the holy oil of Rheims, the fleurs-de-lys, the oriflamme – and what he perceived as the failure of such legends to take root in England, he questioned whether this was the result of mere chance, or 'a case of deep collective psychological differences between the two nations'.[7] Sacrality – if by sacrality we mean such phenomena as unction with holy oil, institutionalized religiosity, the abrogation of sacerdotal functions and the claim to thaumaturgic powers – appears to have lodged far more securely with the Capetians than with the Plantagenets.[8]

There is much to commend this line of argument, but, as I have suggested elsewhere, there is equally much with which to take issue. In particular, those modern commentators who stress the contrast between Plantagenet and Capetian sacrality are inclined to overlook the fact that French and English historians, who work from such very different sources, share a tendency to assume that it is the form, as opposed to the fabric of their national histories that is so radically different. English historians, blessed with the most abundant administrative records in medieval Europe, have concentrated upon administration at the expense of royal ideology. Even those who write on the Church have, in many cases, preferred to deal with bishops as administrators or politicians, rather than as purveyors of sacred truth. Power, ideology and the sacred are topics which English historians writing on the twelfth and thirteenth centuries have largely abandoned, bequeathing them instead to 'experts' in literature, social anthropology and the history of art. In France, by contrast, where administrative sources are far thinner on the ground,

---

with their palace at Fécamp, but (728–32) that by the time of the rediscovery of the relic in the 1170s, Henry II Plantagenet had effectively abandoned any pretension to sacrality. There are flaws in the detail here. Beaune may exaggerate the significance of the ducal palace at Fécamp, leaving Rouen out of the equation. She assumes that the legends of Fécamp were controlled by the dukes, which is unproved, and she accepts unchallenged the apparently mythical tradition that Henry II attended the translation of the rediscovered blood relic in 1171/2.

[7] Bloch, *The Royal Touch*, 140.

[8] The four-fold definition is that proposed by J. Le Goff, 'Aspects religieux et sacrés de la monarchie française du Xe au XIIIe siècle', *La royauté sacrée dans le monde chrétien (colloque de Royaumont, mars 1989)*, ed. A. Boureau and C. S. Ingerflom (Paris 1992), 19–28, at 20, defining a concept which, as has been pointed out by J. Nelson, 'Royal Saints and Early Medieval Kingship', *Studies in Church History* 10: *Sanctity and Secularity*, ed. D. Baker (1973), 39–44, is too often assumed to be identical with the indwelling tribal sacrality of early medieval kings. To Le Goff's list I would add descent from the royal blood line as an essential feature of both the Capetian and the Plantagenet claims. See here A. W. Lewis, *Royal Succession in Capetian France: Studies on Familial Order and the State* (Cambridge, Mass., 1981).

and in America, where it is as easy to gain access to French periodicals as it is to the resources of the Public Record Office, historians have made far more of the French kings' sacral pretensions as reflected in Capetian court chronicles. Here, in essence, lies one of the more significant points of divergence between the histories produced under the influence of Manchester or Paris – of Tout and Cheney, or Bloch and Le Goff.[9]

To suggest that the Plantagenet kings had recourse to secular legends, as with the legends of Joseph of Arimathaea deployed in favour of the Holy Blood, or that a large part of their authority was based upon their purely secular claim to rule as heirs to the Norman conquerors, should not obscure the fact that such claims were matched by a continuing desire to portray the Plantagenets as Christ's vicars on earth. Capetian ideology, let it be noted, was just as heavily indebted as that of the Plantagenets to secular legends, of Charlemagne and the Franks, without this inclining French historians to assume that the Capetians had abandoned their complementary claim to royal sacrality. The Plantagenet kings were no less keen than their Capetian rivals to stress their own special relationship to God. The piety and the religious observances of King Henry III; his commissioning of the singing of the *Laudes* in which he was ritually proclaimed as higher than the stars, decked with all the pomp of Solomon; his great collection of relics; his frequent pilgrimages and his offerings to the saints; his readiness, as reported by Matthew Paris, to reel off a list of nearly a dozen of the sainted kings of Anglo-Saxon England from whom he was directly descended, all follow in a tradition whereby the King laid claim to a wisdom and majesty that transcended the purely secular and human.[10] Even within Henry III's immediate family there were at least three of Henry's kinsmen – his uncle Henry the Young King, his half-brother Aymer de Lusignan and his cousin William Longespée – who were reputed to have effected cures or wonders from beyond the grave.[11]

9 Much of what follows is adapted and condensed from my article, 'The Pilgrimages of the Plantagenet Kings of England 1154–1272'. For recent comparative critiques of French and English writing on the late Middle Ages, see J.-P. Genet, 'Histoire politique anglaise, histoire politique française', *Saint-Denis et la royauté: études offertes à Bernard Guenée*, ed. F. Autrand *et al.* (Paris 1999), 621–36; N. Vincent, 'Conclusion', *Noblesses de l'espace Plantagenêt (1154–1224)*, ed. M. Aurell (Poitiers 2001), 207–14.
10 For Henry's naming of the Anglo-Saxon saints, see *CM*, v 617. For the *Laudes*, commissioned with great frequency by Henry III after 1234, see E. H. Kantorowicz, *Laudes Regiae: A Study in Liturgical Acclamations and Mediaeval Ruler Worship* (Berkeley 1946), 171–9. For Henry III's manipulation of the image of Solomon, see P. Binski, *The Painted Chamber at Westminster* (London 1986), 42–3; Binski, *Westminster Abbey and the Plantagenets*, 61–2, 138–9.
11 For Henry the Young King, see William of Newburgh in *Chronicles of the Reigns of Stephen, Henry II and Richard I*, ed. R. Howlett, 4 vols., Rolls Series (London 1885–9), I 234, expressing scepticism, by contrast to the semi-hagiographical report by Thomas Agnellus, 'Sermo de morte et sepultura

Such claims may never have achieved popular acceptance. For our knowledge of them we depend upon sources close to the Plantagenet court, just as the sacral legends of the Capetians are recorded with greatest approval in Capetian court sources. None the less, the Plantagenet claim to sacrality was clearly not abandoned under Henry III, for all that it may have become overlaid with other, more secular, traditions.

That there was uneasiness, even in the King's own mind, about certain aspects of the Plantagenet claim is not to be doubted. Shortly before the delivery of the Holy Blood to Westminster, for example, Henry III is known to have written to Robert Grosseteste, asking precisely what powers were conferred upon a king through his coronation and his unction with holy oil. Grosseteste replied that, although unction brought with it various gifts of the Holy Spirit, these gifts imposed particular responsibilities and in no way placed royal power on a level with the sacerdotal or transformed the King into a priest.[12] As David Carpenter has pointed out, it was precisely because he recognized that he was not a priest that Henry deliberately refused to hold a candle during an excommunication ceremony in 1253, preferring to participate merely as an onlooker, in much the same way that at the mass, as we are informed, he would hold the priest's hand at the moment of consecration, serving in the role of deacon, without any claim to priestly power.[13] Even here, however, the fact that Henry served at mass as both King and deacon should put us on our guard against assuming that Plantagenet kingship had become an entirely secularized phenomenon. Henry III made no claim to priestly orders, but then no more did the Capetian saint Louis IX. As Marc Bloch commented as long ago as the 1920s, Grosseteste 'would clearly not have taken such trouble to guard against what seemed to him such a scandalous confusion unless he had cause to believe that (such a confusion) was current with regard to the King he was intent

Henrici regis iunioris', in Coggeshall, *Chronicon*, 265–73. For Aymer de Lusignan and William Longespée, see H. W. Ridgeway, 'The Ecclesiastical Career of Aymer de Lusignan, Bishop Elect of Winchester, 1250–60', *The Cloister and the World: Essays in Medieval History in Honour of Barbara Harvey*, ed. J. Blair and B. Golding (Oxford 1996), 174–5; S. D. Lloyd, 'William Longespée II: The Making of an English Crusading Hero', *Nottingham Medieval Studies* 35 (1991), 65–6, with verses and a metrical 'mass' in honour of Longespée preserved in Oxford, Corpus Christi College MS 232 fos. 64v–6v. To these could be added the cases of Henry III's maternal kinsman, the Blessed John of Montmirail, for whom see Vincent, 'Isabella of Angoulême', 176, 212–13, and Henry's brother-in-law, Simon de Montfort, himself a decidedly anti-royal saint.

[12] *Roberti Grosseteste episcopi quondam Lincolniensis epistolae*, ed. H. R. Luard, Rolls Series (London 1861), 350–1.

[13] Carpenter, 'Burial of King Henry III', 437, citing *CM*, v 37. For Henry's reputed activities at the mass, see Rishanger, *Chronica*, 74–5.

upon instructing'.[14] Henry III, after all, was not once but twice blessed
by the Holy Spirit, having been crowned and anointed both at Gloucester in 1216, and again at Westminster in 1220. In parading the Holy
Blood from Whitehall to Westminster, barefoot and walking beneath a
pall, Henry was surely straying well beyond the role that we would expect of a wholly laicized king. Even Robert Grosseteste, who sought to
deflate the Christocentric pretensions of Henry III's coronation, could
respond with enthusiasm, not to say considerable ingenuousness, to the
claims of the King's most precious Christological relic.

In 1247, it was less than a century since Henry's grandfather, King
Henry II, had been presented with a family tree in which his ancestry
was traced back through the Anglo-Saxon kings of Wessex, to Woden
and via Woden to Noah.[15] As descendants of Noah, the Plantagenets
were in effect direct, if distant, kinsmen of Christ himself.[16] Indeed,
following this interpretation, the blood of Christ processed by Henry III
through the streets of Westminster in 1247 was, in some small portion,
the same blood that flowed through the King's own veins. Not even
the Capetians, for all their boasting of a descent from Charlemagne,
could lay claim to cousinhood with Christ. Plantagenets and Capetians
alike, whatever their claim to kinship with the almighty, were recognised
as royal dynasties. As such, even in medieval scientific opinion, they
were considered to be possessors of royal blood: a liquor judged by
many to be clearer, more transparent and uncommonly lustrous when
compared with the blood of ordinary mortals.[17] Henry III, it is true,
failed to stir up popular enthusiasm for his blood, for his sainted ancestor
Edward the Confessor, or for the Confessor's newly refurbished Abbey
at Westminster. Even in death, the one miracle attributed to Henry III's
royal remains at Westminster is said to have been dismissed as fraudulent,
not by a sceptic from outside the royal court, but by Henry's own son,
King Edward I.[18] This did not, however, prevent King Edward from
laying claim to the power to cure scrofula by the royal touch. Henry II
had been credited with such power in the twelfth century, and although it

---

[14] Bloch, *The Royal Touch*, 112, and see also 114.
[15] Diceto, *Opera*, 1 299, rehearsing a genealogy of Henry II first proposed by Aelred of Rievaulx.
[16] W. A. Chaney, *The Cult of Kingship in Anglo-Saxon England* (Manchester 1970), 41 2, citing F. P. Magoun, 'King Aethelwulf's Biblical Ancestors', *Modern Language Review* 46 (1951), 249 50. Chaney's work has been poorly received. It does, however, contain a significant germ of truth which historians ignore at their peril.
[17] Pouchelle, 'Le Sang et ses pouvoirs', 23, citing the discussion by C. Beaune, *Naissance de la nation France* (Paris 1985), 217, 223 5.
[18] Rishanger, *Chronica*, 98. For the circumstances of Henry III's burial, see Binski, *Westminster Abbey and the Plantagenets*, 101 2; Carpenter, 'Burial of Henry III', 427 59.

may have lain dormant under Henry III, it was to be claimed again from the 1270s onwards.[19] As few people prayed for cures before the tomb of Henry III as before the Holy Blood of Westminster, albeit that Henry's tomb was built in conscious imitation of the shrine tombs of the saints, supplied with indulgences to those who prayed there and with niches let into its sides, perhaps for the display of holy relics rather than for the reception of pilgrims.[20] None the less, in the royal palace nearby, men and women were to queue up in their hundreds before Henry's son to be touched for scrofula.[21] The sacral power of kings was neither disowned nor eradicated by Henry III. Under Henry III, however, and beyond the immediate circle of the King and his court, the royal claim to sacrality does seem to have met with widespread popular indifference. Whether or not this suggests some more long-standing or inevitable decline in the sacrality of England's kings, and whether or not the Capetians won a greater popular acceptance for their own sacral claims, are points that remain unclear. Alain Boureau, for one, has questioned the power even of Capetian ceremonial to establish the 'impossible sacrality' of the kings of France beyond a small circle of court ritualists and sycophants.[22]

Writing of France, rather than of Plantagenet England, Boureau notes 'the great indifference of the Church towards political sacrality: tolerated out of Pauline respect for legitimacy, accepted as a tribute rendered to the Church, but never admitted to the status of true belief'.[23] In a further development of this thesis, employing anthropological models of the 'self-denying king', Boureau reminds us of one aspect of sacrality that may have a direct bearing upon the case of Henry III. Although the role of the Church, as mediator between God and King, necessarily diluted the royal sacrality of Christian Europe, there were means by which the king could turn this ecclesiastical strait-jacket inside out. By abstention and self-denial, it was possible for kings greatly to magnify whatever indwelling sacral qualities they might be deemed to possess, focusing and accentuating their sacral image through deliberate asceticism. Boureau

---

[19] The survey by F. Barlow, 'The King's Evil', *English Historical Review* 95 (1980), 3–27, despite (19) quoting Peter of Blois' remarks on Henry II's supposed powers, overlooks one further proof of touching for scrofula by Henry II, noted by Koziol, 'The Problem of Sacrality', 128–9, 139–40, citing a miracle story in *Acta SS: October*, VIII 575–6.

[20] Binski, *Westminster Abbey*, 101–4.

[21] See the general account, including estimates of numbers, by M. Prestwich, 'The Piety of Edward I', *England in the Thirteenth Century: Proceedings of the 1984 Harlaxton Symposium*, ed. W. M. Ormrod (Stamford 1985), 120–8.

[22] A. Boureau, *Le Simple Corps du roi: l'impossible sacralité des souverains français XVe–XVIIIe siècles* (Paris 1988), 5–63, esp. 40–2.

[23] Boureau, *Le Simple Corps*, 9.

23　The tomb of Henry III, Westminster Abbey, with niches perhaps for the display of relics (Westminster Abbey, Dean and Chapter)

cites the case of Louis, son of Charles of Anjou, who abandoned his
royal inheritance, became a Franciscan and died in the aura of sanctity
in 1318.[24] No king of England or France went to quite such extremes, but
consider again Matthew Paris' description of the ceremony conducted
by Henry III in October 1247. After a night spent in fasting and prayer,
Henry led his procession dressed in a simple cloak, barefoot and carrying
the relic in his own naked hands. Only after the relic had been deposited
at Westminster did he resume his royal persona, putting on cloth of gold to
conduct the knighthood of his half-brother, and thereafter to preside at a
splendid feast. Henry's transformation of himself into a humbly dressed
penitent is typical of a fairly common phenomenon: the royal display
of humility that remains royal precisely because it is so ostentatiously
humble. Consider here an eyewitness report by the Italian chronicler
Salimbene de Adam, recording the arrival of King Louis IX of France
at Sens on his journey to crusade in 1248. To Salimbene it was the very
fact that Louis arrived at Sens dressed as a humble pilgrim, on foot
and with scrip and staff, that appeared so remarkable. Having arrived
dressed as a pilgrim, however, Louis did not depart from Sens until his
court had been served with a sumptuous banquet that included cherries,
crayfish and eels cooked in the finest sauce.[25] For all his crayfish and fine
sauces, Louis IX was destined for sainthood. Henry III, for all his fasting
and prayer, was not. However, is there really that great a difference
between their respective styles? In the end, the story of the Holy Blood
may tell us more of Henry III the man than it does of the Plantagenets
and their sacral ideology. The popular indifference towards Henry III,
amply illustrated in the case of the Holy Blood of Westminster, renders
his failure to establish the *bona fides* of either his blood relic or his own
claim to sacrality that much more poignant and more personal.

By the time that Chaucer came to write in the late fourteenth century,
it was not at Westminster that pilgrims expected to find the Holy Blood,
but at Hailes:

> By Goddes precious herte, and by his nailes,
> And by the Blood of Christ that is in Hailes.[26]

[24] A. Boureau, 'Un obstacle à la sacralité royale en occident: le principe hiérarchique', *La royauté
sacrée dans le monde chrétien (colloque de Royaumont, mars 1989)*, ed. A. Boureau and C. S. Ingerflom
(Paris 1992), 29–37, esp. 32–5.

[25] Salimbene de Adam, *Cronica*, ed. F. Bernini, 2 vols. (Bari 1942), I 316–21, whence L. Carolus-
Barré, *Le Procès de canonisation de Saint Louis (1272–1297): essai de reconstruction*, Collections de
l'Ecole française de Rome CXCV (1994), 294–5.

[26] Chaucer, 'The Pardoner's Tale', lines 651–2, in *Canterbury Tales*, ed. A. C. Cawley (Everyman,
2nd edn, London 1975), 353.

Even this is not a statement that should be taken entirely at face value. It occurs, after all, as one in a series of oaths uttered by Chaucer's Pardoner, a character hardly famed for his honesty, willing to hawk 'pigges bones' and bits of old cloth as if they were the relics of the saints. Scepticism towards relics of the Holy Blood was never far beneath the surface, whether at the court of King Henry, in the writings of the schoolsmen like Thomas Aquinas or amongst Chaucer's fictional pilgrims. When, around 1515, the printer Matthew Pynson, came to publish a series of miracle stories involving the blood of Hailes, it is worth noting that two of his four stories concern priests who denied the merits of the blood. The first, described as a Lollard from Shropshire, is said to have been punished, on celebrating mass, by finding the communion wine boil up to the very brim of the chalice. The second, from near Derby, attempted to dissuade his parishioners from joining the pilgrimage to Hailes, but at mass found that his service book had become spattered with blood. Even so, Pynson's ballad confirms that pilgrimage to Hailes retained its far-flung popularity well into the sixteenth century; one of his miracles involves a baker from 'Stone' (probably Stow-on-the-Wold), who was able to support his family by selling bread to pilgrims at Hailes between Whitsun and the feast of Corpus Christi, presumably the time of the year when the relic attracted most visitors, suggesting once again that the celebration of Corpus Christi could prove a positive incentive to veneration of the Holy Blood. At the very least, Pynson's ballad proves that the blood of Hailes was believed to work miracles. By contrast, as we have seen, only one such story is recorded for the blood of Westminster, involving a local Westminster family, a story preserved in a manuscript from the Abbey's own library, to be dated within a decade or so of the relic's arrival in 1247.[27]

In the 1530s, when the relic collections of England faced destruction, it was still the blood of Hailes that caught the popular imagination. Hugh Latimer, writing in 1533, remarks upon the flocks of pilgrims passing near his house, out of the West Country, 'to many images, but chiefly to the blood of Hailes'.[28] A century earlier, when the shrine was robbed of

---

[27] Oates, 'Richard Pynson and the Holy Blood of Hayles', 275–6, and see also Leland, *Collectanea*, ed. Hearne (1770), VI 283–4, referring to Hailes, 'where God daylie shewithe miracles throwe ye vertue of that precyous blode'. For the offer of special indulgences to pilgrims at the feast of Corpus Christi, see above p. 138.

[28] *Sermons and Remains of Hugh Latimer, Sometime Bishop of Worcester, Martyr 1555*, ed. G. E. Corrie, Parker Society XXII–III (1844–5), II 364, repeating the theological argument against all such relics, that Christ could not undergo two resurrections, and cf. *Letters and Papers, Foreign and Domestic, of the Reign of Henry VIII*, ed. J. S. Brewer, J. Gairdner and R. H. Brodie, 21 vols. in 35

as much as 1,000 marks, it is described as being one of the wealthiest in England, second only to that of St Thomas Becket at Canterbury.[29] As late as 1535, even the most conservative estimate of offerings to the blood assessed them at £10 a year.[30] But soon afterwards rumours began to circulate against the relic, spurred on no doubt by Hugh Latimer, recently elected bishop of Worcester. As Latimer himself was later to admit, the relic's detractors had to cope with considerable opposition, not least from King Henry VIII: 'What ado was there to bring this out of the King's head. This great abomination of the blood of Hailes could not be taken a great while out of his mind.'[31] In February 1538, in a sermon preached at St Paul's Cross in London, the bishop of Rochester, John Hilsey, is said to have denounced the blood of Hailes as a fraud. Far from being a survival from the time of Christ's Passion, Hilsey declared that it was topped up each week with the blood of a freshly slaughtered duck. This account he claimed to have received from a miller's wife who had been courted by the abbot of Hailes and to whom the abbot had admitted his fraud, hoping thereby to persuade her to accept a jewel that he had plundered from the shrine.[32]

Alarmed by Hilsey's accusations, and still goaded by Latimer, the abbot of Hailes removed the relic from public display, requesting Cromwell's permission to pull down the shrine, and asking that a commission be appointed to investigate the blood, 'lest I should condemn myself to be guilty in misusing of it, as charging and renewing it with

London 1864 1932), VI no. 247. For evidence of continued devotion to the shrine, see Finucane, *Miracles and Pilgrims*, 202. For pilgrims to the shrine from Bourne in Lincolnshire, *c.* 1440, see *Visitations of Religious Houses in the Diocese of Lincoln*, ed. A. H. Thompson, 3 vols., Lincolnshire Record Society VII, XIV, XXI (1914 29), II 37 8.

[29] *Historia vitae et regni Ricardi secundi*, ed. G. B. Stow (Philadelphia 1977), 175: *Hoc etiam anno* (1402) *17 Kalendas Ianuarii, despoliatum est scrinium de Hayles, in quo cruor Christi reconditus est, de multis diviciis, ad dampnum ut putatur 1000 marcarum. Quod quidem scrinium ditissimum regni tenebatur, excepto illo de Cantuaria* (reference courtesy of Nigel Ramsay). The same source refers to a robbery at Westminster *c.* 1402 in which many jewels and a *tabula aurea* were stolen.

[30] *Valor ecclesiasticus*, II 456.

[31] Latimer, *Sermons and Remains*, I 231 2, from a sermon preached before Edward VI in 1549.

[32] Charles Wriothesley, *A Chronicle of England during the Reigns of the Tudors*, ed. W. Douglas Hamilton, Camden new series XI, XX (1875 7), I 75 6. For rumours that the blood was that of a dog or a duck, apparently already in circulation as early as the 1460s, see A. Hudson, *The Premature Reformation: Wycliffite Texts and Lollard History* (Oxford 1988) 304n; J. A. F. Thomson, *The Later Lollards 1414 1520* (Oxford 1965), 70 1. For Hilsey's preaching and its effects, see P. Marshall, 'The Rood of Boxley, the Blood of Hailes and the Defence of the Henrican Church', *Journal of Ecclesiastical History* 46 (1995), 689 96; G. R. Elton, *Policy and Police: The Enforcement of the Reformation in the Age of Thomas Cromwell* (Cambridge 1972), 214 16. John Speed, *The Theatre of the Empire of Great Britaine* (London 1611), Buckinghamshire fo. 43r, claims that it was the blood relic of Ashridge that the bishop denounced in February 1538, confusing the relics of Hailes and Ashridge and conflating two separate sermons, preached in February and November.

drake's blood'.[33] The commission, which travelled to Gloucestershire in October 1538, took possession of the blood, 'inclosid within a rownde berall garnysshid and bownd on every syde with sylver'. Inside the glass, the relic had glistened red like blood, but once taken out it became yellow, 'lyke ambre or basse golde, and doth cleve to as gumme or byrdlyme'.[34] In the following month, it was displayed at St Paul's Cross by bishop Hilsey, who withdrew his earlier claim that it was the blood of a duck, declaring instead that it was nothing more than honey clarified and coloured with saffron.[35] Even graver charges were laid by William Thomas, former clerk to Edward VI, who in the late 1540s revived the slander that the relic was duck's blood, and claimed that it had been displayed by the monks in a curious glass vessel, clear on one side but opaque on the other. Since it was believed that those in mortal sin would be unable to view the Holy Blood, Thomas claimed, the opaque side was deliberately displayed to richer pilgrims in the hope that their sense of remorse might prompt hefty gifts.[36]

Holy Blood or the blood of a Gloucestershire duck, the relic of Hailes at least enjoyed a few last hours of fame. Not so the relic of Westminster, which vanishes after the 1530s without a single trace. Presumably it was swept away at the Dissolution, together with so many other reminders of the medieval past. Already, in 1535, Cromwell and his allies are said to have carried away various of Westminster's relics, including the girdle of the Virgin Mary.[37] In the following year the precious outer covering of the shrine of St Edward was broken up. By November 1538, when the monks were expelled from the Abbey, an inventory of their treasures refers to nothing in the way of relics save the marble base of St Edward's shrine.[38] Even in the 1550s, when Queen Mary briefly restored Westminster to monastic control, although the body of St Edward was rediscovered and replaced in its tomb — the sole surviving saint's body to have remained

[33] *Letters and Papers Henry VIII*, XIII part 1 no. 347. For continuing hostility from Latimer, and for a report that the relic had been suppressed as early as March 1538, see *ibid.*, XIII part 1 nos. 564, 580, XIII part 2 no. 186; Latimer, *Sermons and Remains*, II 400.
[34] See the letters to Thomas Cromwell, printed in *Benedictus abbas Petroburgensis de vita et gestis Henrici II et Ricardi I*, ed. T. Hearne, 2 vols. (Oxford 1735), II 751–3; *Letters and Papers Henry VIII*, XIII part 2 nos. 709–10; Latimer, *Sermons and Remains*, II 407–8.
[35] Wriothesley, *Chronicle*, I 90; Holinshed, *The Third Volume of Chronicles* (1587), 946.
[36] William Thomas, *The Pilgrim: A Dialogue of the Life and Actions of King Henry the Eighth*, ed. J. A. Froude (London 1861), 38–9, also found in Oxford, Bodleian Library MS Bodley 53 fo. 85r–v.
[37] Wriothesley, *Chronicle*, I 31, which refers also to a girdle of St Elizabeth, not otherwise recorded at Westminster.
[38] M. E. C. Walcott, 'The Inventories of Westminster Abbey at the Dissolution', *Transactions of the London and Middlesex Archaeological Society* 4 part 3 (1873), 313–64, noting the shrine base at 351.

in situ in England from the Middle Ages to the present day – nothing is heard of the recovery of any others of the Abbey's relics.[39] Most probably the Holy Blood of Westminster was destroyed, together with those other objects, dismissed in the vivid language of Nicholas Shaxton, bishop of Salisbury, as 'stinking bootes, mucke, combes, ragged rochettes, rotten girdles, pyl'd purses, great bullock horns, lockes of heer, filthy ragges and gobbetts of wodde'.[40]

Our search for the Holy Blood of Westminster has carried us far from our original starting point at the court of Henry III. In the process we have traversed a daunting sweep of events and ideas, from the very moment of Christ's Passion, via the legends of Joseph of Arimathaea, the court of Charlemagne, the treasures of the Holy Roman Empire, the collapse of the Latin kingdom of Jerusalem and the contortions of late medieval scholasticism, through to the Henrician Reformation of the 1530s. Even so, it is not entirely inappropriate that our story should end with the banalities of the rubbish heap, and the sweeping away of bullock horns and rotten rags. Most studies of the cult of relics have focused upon objects that, if only for a decade or so, enjoyed near universal acclaim. By contrast, with the Holy Blood of Westminster, we have from the very outset been dealing with a Cinderella amongst cults, a cult that never really was. To this extent, it is entirely fitting that, just as the story of the blood of Westminster has no proper beginning, being lost amongst legend, invention and wishful thinking, so it should have no clearly defined end. We know no more of the destruction of the Westminster relic than we do of its creation. Was it truly a portion of the blood preserved from the time of the Crucifixion? Or was it fabricated by mendacious and desparate churchmen in the 1240s, only to be destroyed by fanatics in the 1530s? I have no hesitation in leaving these questions unanswered. Yet for all the mystery in which our story is shrouded, one thing at least is clear. It is not merely those cults that achieved popular success, or those relics that worked miracles, that provide us with an insight into the assumptions and attitudes of medieval men and women. The Holy Blood of Westminster was very far from a success. After the 1270s, it appears to have worked

---

[39] For the monastic revival at Westminster 1556–9, see M. D. Knowles, *The Religious Orders in England*, 3 vols. (Cambridge 1948–59), III 424–38, esp. 433 for the restoration of the shrine of St Edward; C. S. Knighton, 'Collegiate Foundations, 1540 to 1570, with Special Reference to St Peter in Westminster' (PhD thesis, Cambridge 1975), 130–68, as drawn to my attention by Eamon Duffy.

[40] Shaxton's injunctions against idolatory (1538), quoted in *Ceremonies and Processions of Salisbury*, ed. Wordsworth, 40–1 n.

no miracles, effected no cures. Apparently it attracted few pilgrims. Even in secular, political terms, it failed to achieve any of the ends that had been set for it by its sponsors, King Henry III and the patriarch of Jerusalem. None the less, as a means of access to some of the darker corners of popular, scholastic and royal spirituality, it should indeed be accounted a most precious and a most wonderful resource.

Letters of Robert patriarch of Jerusalem and papal legate, and his chapter, to King Henry (III), asking that he provide assistance to the bearers, John and master Matthew, in their attempts to recover the rights of the church of Jerusalem with respect to certain churches and priories that were once subject to the church of Jerusalem but that have long failed to communicate with or to aid their mother church, ceasing to wear the badge of the Cross that they wore originally on their cloaks and caps as a symbol of their subjection. The patriarch is sending with the two messengers a true relic of Christ's blood so that the King may have our Lord's Passion always before his eyes. The Sultan of Cairo has recovered various castles in the vicinity of Damascus, held against him by Saracen noblemen. On the Saturday after Easter (4 May 1247) he entered the province of Jerusalem and on the Saturday after Ascension (11 May) set siege to the castle of Tiberias. Leaving behind various of his emirs to continue this siege, with the rest of his army he then set out for Ghaza and on the Saturday after Pentecost (25 May) lay siege to the castle of Ascalon, confident of taking this and other Christian fortresses. Unless King Henry and his fellow Christian rulers send help, the Sultan's power is much to be feared.

Acre, 31 May 1247

B = Westminster Abbey MS Domesday fos. 394v–5r. s.xiv in. Headed: *Littere testimoniales patriarche Ierosolimit' et eiusdem loci capituli de sanguine domini et de transmissione eiusdem sanguinis ad regem Henricum tercium qui contulit eundem sanguinem ecclesie Westm'.* C = Longleat, Marquess of Bath MS 38 (William of Sudbury's *De sanguine*) fos. 290r–2r. s.xv ex. Apparently copied from the original, sealed with the seals of the patriarch and the chapter of Jerusalem.

Excellenti et egregio viro domino Henrico Dei gratia illustri regi Angl(ie), Robertus eadem gratia sancte Ierosolimitane ecclesie patriarcha, apostolice sedis legatus, et eiusdem ecclesie capitulum salutem et felices ad vota successus. Antiquorum memoria recordatur et sic pro veritate tenemus quod progenitores vestri felicis memorie inter omnes alios mundi principes catholicos ad sanctam Ierosolim' ecclesiam precipuam

devocionem habentes, eam munificentiis et honorificentiis multipliciter
honorarunt, ob illius reverenciam et honorem qui propter redemptionem
humani generis in eadem ecclesia proprium sanguinem effundendo in
ara crucis holocaustum se optulit Deo patri, de vestra clementia sperantes
hoc inde quod predecessorum vestrorum imitando vestigia iamdictam
Ierosolim' ecclesiam, quam Dei filius suo precioso sanguine consecravit,
in suis iusticiis et iuribus vestra sublimitas habeat commendatam. Ad hoc
cum in regno vestro Angl(ie) sancta Ierosolim' ecclesia communis mater
quasdam ecclesias, prioratus et domos habuerit ab antiquo, priores, rec-
tores et fratres eorumdem locorum ad eandem sanctam Ierosolimitan'
ecclesiam nullam devotionem habentes, sicut per operis exhibicionem
ostendunt, eam quamvis in magnis necessitatibus constitutam et potentia Saracenorum oppressam, nec litteris nec nunciis a longis temporibus
visitare curarunt, immo, quod est deterius, quidam ex eis signum vivifice
crucis quod in palliis et cappis portare consueverunt in signum subiec-
tionis penitus abiecerunt, quasi non teneantur ecclesie sancte Ierosolim'
subiecti. Sane, quia de vestre clementia maiestatis indubitatam fidu-
ciam reportamus, quod vos, qui tanquam princeps catholicus et amator
iusticie in suis iuribus et libertatibus fovetis ecclesias universas, iamdictam Ierosolim' ecclesiam matrem vestram, quam Dei filius inter omnes
alias orbis ecclesias speciali et singulari privilegio decoravit exemplo,
alius per quam vivitis et regnatis, eandem ecclesiam honorabitis et in
suis iuribus et rationibus defendetis, ita quod vestro felici tempore, iura
et rationes suas integraliter rehabebit, vestra gratia et munificentia
faciente, et recuperabit ea que absque modo per negligentiam seu in-
curiam sunt obmissa, mittimus itaque ad pedes regie maiestatis dilectos
in Cristo filios dominum Iohannem canon(icum) Ierosolim' ecclesie et
magistrum Matheum fratrem eiusdem ecclesie, pro predictis bonis et
ecclesiis requirendis, cum omni devotionis genere, vestram clementiam
humiliter implorantes quod regia magnitudo, ob illius reverentiam et
honorem qui eandem ecclesiam sua corporali presentia honoravit, dignetur interponere partes suas ut loco predicta recuperet et filii subtractionis[a]
ad sinum matris sue revertantur, eius uberibus lactaturi qui satis
deplorare deberent, et compassionem habere super oppressionibus et
afflictionibus quibus incessanter affligitur, bonis omnibus temporalibus
in regno Ierosolimit' hostium fidei potentia destituta. Ceterum de pignoribus que Dei filius in thesauris ecclesie sancte Ierosolimit' reliquit[b]
personam vestram honorare volentes, vestre celsitudini mittimus per

---

[a] MS fo. 395r
[b] reliquid MS

predictos nuncios nostros, presentium portitores, in quadam pixide
cristallina parvo sigillo nostri patriarch(ii) signata, aliquam particulam
de preciosissimo sanguine domini Ihesu Cristi quem in loco Calvarie
sito intra Ierosolimit' ecclesiam, pendens in crucis patibulo, pro salute
et redemptione vestra et omnium Cristianorum habundanter effudit, ut
ipsum sanguinem nostre redemptionis preciosum[c] habentes pre oculis,
passionem eius semper in memoriam habeatis, gloriantes in cruce ipsius
in qua gloriari oportet, scituri certissime et sine dubitatione quacumque
quod nos eiusdem preciosi sanguinis quantitatem extraximus de thesauris ecclesie nostre ibidem ab antiquissimis temporibus conservatam
cum summa reverentia et honore, et veraciter est sanguis ille qui de
latere domini Ihesu Cristi in loco predicto manavit. Si vero de statu
Ierosolimit' provincie regiam maiestatem audire delectat, noveritis quod
Soldanus Babilonie cum tota potentia sua veniens ad partes Damascenas,
recuperatis[d] quibusdam castris adiacentibus civitati Damasci que contra
ipsum detinebant quidam nobiles Saraceni, introivit Ierosolimit' provin-
ciam post festum dominice resurrectionis et die sabbati post festum as-
cencionis dominice castrum Tyberiadis fecit obsidione vallari, et dimissis
ibi quibusdam admiratis et quadam parte exercitus sui ad obsidionem
ipsius castri, ipse Soldanus cum alio exercitu suo ivit ad partes Gazare et
die sabbati post festum Pentecost' obsedit castrum de Ascalona et per-
sonaliter in eadem obsidione moratur, confidens de viribus suis quod
tam ipsum castrum quam alias munitiones Cristianorum suo dominio
subiugabit, et multum timeri potest de ipsius potentia nisi virtus divine
clementie suis conatibus duxerit resistendum, et vos et alii catholici mundi
principes in militia et armatis succursum miseritis festinatum, ad quod
faciendum dominus Ihesu Cristus vestrum et eorum animos inclinare
dignetur. De ceteris autem que pertinent ad statum Terre Sancte, predicti
nuncii nostri presentium portitores, vestre caritati plenam certitudinem
enarrabunt. Dat' apud Acon anno domini m°cc°xlvii° mense Maii[e] die
penultima eiusdem mensis.

[c] precium MS preciosum *supplied*
[d] rucuperatis MS
[e] Madii MS

An account of the restoration to life of William, son of Thomas le Brown, drowned in his father's pond at Hyde in the month of August but revived having being measured (in wax) against the blood of Jesus Christ. Thereafter King Henry III led a special procession to Westminster, presenting the monks with a golden cup set with precious stones.

[1247 × 1272]

B = Oxford, Bodleian Library MS Ashmole 842 fo. 8ov. Copy by Elias Ashmole out of an 'old vellum MS which the duke of Yorke delivered to Sir Edward Walker 28 October 1660'. apparently a roll containing the order for the queen's coronation at Westminster. C = *ibid*. MS Ashmole 863 p. 436. Copy by Ashmole from B.

Memorandum quod tempore incliti regis Henrici tertii Willielmus le Brown filius Thome le Brown fuit submersus in vivario patris sui apud Hyde in quo iacuit in mense Augusti sic submersus per dimidium diem et quesitus apud Padyngton et Knytebruge et in confinio circumiacenti et tandem repertus mensuratus erat ad sanguinem Iesu Christi et a morte resuscitatus, et cum ante submersionem puer biennis loqui nesciret, statim resuscitatus a mortuis incepit loqui. Quo comperto per fidedignorum iuramentum rex Henricus discalciatus apud pontem versus Tothulle in magna comitiva cleri et populi accessit et facta solempni processione in ecclesia Westmonasteriensi magnas campanas et alias pulsari precepit et pro istius miraculi novitate vas aureum pretiosis lapidibus ornatum fabricari constituit. Testes istius miraculi fuerunt isti iurati: frater Bacinus tunc elemosinarius Westmonasteriensis, et frater Gilbertus Cademan, et fratres Willielmus de Hampton, Johannes le Foundour, Willielmus le Peryndon, et Willielmus de Hasele, Johannes de Padynton, Nicholaus Messor cum aliis clericis et laicis sufficienter examinatis pariter et iuratis.

APPENDIX 3

An account of the discovery of the Holy Blood made by Edmund, son of Richard King of Germany, amongst the imperial treasures stored in the castle of Trifels then under the care of Werner von Bolanden, and of the relic's delivery to Hailes Abbey on 14 September 1270.

[c. 1300]

BL MS Cotton Cleopatra D iii (Hailes annals) fo. 46r–v (44r–v), headed *Qualiter sanguis Cristi venit apud Heiles.*

Quoniam nonnullis in dubium vertitur quod nostris temporibus satis licuit manifeste et opinionibus erroneis inherentes palpitando conantur asserere quasi de antiquissimis temporibus et omnino modernis ignotis quo volveretur quod testibus fidedignis probis et honesti<ss>imis liquido poterit declarari, videlicet qualiter et quando et quo mediante Deus et dominus noster Ihesu Cristus Anglorum gentem venerabilissimis reliquiis sui sacratissimi sanguinis decoravit, ad decus et decorem totius Britannice insule et regni et ecclesie tutamentum, hinc est quod Cristianissimus et illustris dominus Edmundus comes Cornubie huius rei merito pre omnibus conscius testis verus superstes cum et ipso impetrante ad partes devenerint Anglicanas et aliquanto temporis intervallo in monasterio de Heiles per ipsum fuerint honorifice collocate ad omnem ambiguitatem tollendam rei seriem et exitum sic narravit et ad perpetuam rei memoriam scribi mandavit posteris relinquendum.

Cum illustrissimus rex Alemannie Ricardus ab Anglia in partes Theutonicas ultimo transitum faceret, filium suum Edmundum bone indolis puereum secum duxit, qui tum propter regis patris sui reverentiam tum propter bonitatem innatam in tam iuvenili corpore radiantem, quadam amoris prerogativa ab omnibus amabatur et maxime a quodam milite nobili et strenuo, Warennario de Boylande custode castri Trivelensi ubi vestimenta imperialia habebantur et senescallo de feodo totius imperii. Qui quidem miles ob amorem filii sui, Rodigeri nomine, cum quo prefatus puer Edmundus frequenter ludebat, talem gratiam eidem concessit ut per omnia loca illius castelli iret ac luderet pro sue libito voluntatis, et archana cuncta conspiceret et videret. Inter que, cum vestimenta et reliquias diversas existentes ibidem satagebat frequentius intueri, firmaculum aureum quoddam conspexit grande mirabiliter et decorum cum quaddam aurea magna cathena, in quo prefate reliquie preciosissimi sanguinis dulcissimi domini nostri Ihesu Cristi pro totius humani generis redemptione effusi quondam a Karolo Magno rege victoriosissimo et invictissimo, qui Romanum imperium ac totius orbis optinuit principatum, gloriosissime delate et illuc impetrate ad presens tempus honorabiliter sunt incluse, quod etiam ante portus circa collum principum per proceres electorum cum iniungerentur in imperatores pendere solebat. Rem vero tam sacram et insignem ibidem existere non levi animo preteriens, puer Edmundus, multiplicatis precibus et interpellante pro eo diligentissime predicto Rodigerio eiusdem consorte, quod petiit impetravit, et in quodam vasculo ab hoc per sepedictum Edmundum honorifice deputato supradictus miles et eiusdem filius Rodigerus eidem partem memorati sanguinis in karissimum donarium contulerunt. Predictus vero Edmundus tam venerandas reliquias, honore quo debuit et potuit, custodivit, et in Angliam secum tulit et in castro Walingfordie patris sui ad tempus veneranter deposuit, quousque plenius deliberaret quem locum aut quod monasterium re tam sacratissima insigniret. Processu vero temporis aliquando placuit prefato Edmundo ut illud, tam insigne et incomparabile, monasterio de Heiles Cister(ciensis) ordinis donaretur, cuius siquidem monasterii supradictus rex illustris Ricardus, pater Edmundi, gloriosus patronus exstitit et fundator, et tam ipse quam venerande memorie domina Schenchia eiusdem regina pro se ipsis ibidem necnon et pro filio suo prenominato Edmundo elegerant sepulturam. Cum vero ad predictum locum deferreretur, in abbatia de Winchecumbe non multum ab illo loco distante per unam noctem pausavit. Mane autem facto, eiusdem loci abbas, dominus I(ohannes), et conventus processione rite ac honorabiliter ordinata versus abbatiam de Heiles una cum predicto Edmundo baiulo predictis reliquiis concomitantes devotissime processerunt usque in pratum quod Rouleie vocabulo dicitur, ubi venerabilem patrem dominum Walterum abbatem de Heiles cum conventu ornatu simili obvium habuerunt et, rumore diffuso per patriam et turbis undique confluentibus et concurentibus, quieverunt quod ad tam grande spectaculum tota vicinia confluebat. Ubi predictus abbas de Heiles, sermonem ad populum faciens, gestum rei et ordinem exponebat, erectoque tentorio et altari constituto, ostensum publice sanguinem benedictum totus populus adorabat. Sermone vero finito, uterque abbas et conventus easdem reliquias ad monasterium de Heiles processionaliter cum hympnis et iubilo deducebant, ipso Edmundo illas semper propriis manibus defferente ad locum prefatum, ubi illum tam inestimabilem, tam preciosum, tam venerandum thesaurum ille idem Edmundus ad magnum altare reverenter obtulit et devote. Circumstantes autem abbas de Winchecumbe cum suo conventu ex una parte chori, et dicti loci abbas et conventus ex altera, laudes domino debitas unanimiter persolvebant, die exaltationis sancte Crucis, die dominico, anno domini m°cc°lxx°.

An account of the relic of the Holy Blood brought from Fécamp to Norwich after July 1171, and of its miraculous preservation from the fire in Norwich Cathedral in August 1272.

[c. 1300]

Oxford, Magdalen College MS 53 pp. 219–20, s.xiv in.
Printed (part only, here enclosed in square brackets) from an earlier, less elaborate, recension in BL MS Harley 1801 fo. 9v, by Kajava, 'Etudes sur l'abbaye de Fécamp', 35.

[Anno incarnati verbi mc°lxx°i, xiiii. kal' Aug(usti), regnante Lodowico nobilissimo Francorum rege, venerabili Thoma Cantuariensi archiepiscopo in ecclesia Cantuariensi martyrizato, inventum est mundi precium in ecclesia Fiscannensi in columpna rotunda materia undique cicumclusa diligentissime collocatum, pro quo precio idem venerabilis[a] et legatus sanguinis precium exsolvere non renuit, retribuens domino que sibi retribuerat. Pars autem purpurei sanguinis agni illius benignissimi, qui veteris piaculi cautionem pio cruore detersit, a Clemente tunc ecclesie Norwicensis precentore, qui sacre inventioni apud Fiscannum interfuit, sancte Norwicensi ecclesie in vasculo argenteo illata est]. Eadem autem postea pars sanguinis, ut melius videri et honorari possit, in vase cristallino est collocata. Lapsis aliquibus temporis circulis,[b] bone memorie Walterus quondam Norwycenc(is) episcopus <ecclesie> sancte Trinitatis eiusdem quandam cupam argenteam magnam et pulchram contulit, in qua vasculum cristalinum, preciosissimum sanguinem continens,[c] erat reponitum, et in eadem usque ad annum gratie m°cc°lxx°ii° cum omni veneratione illesum permansit. Quo an(n)o, iiii. Yd(us) Augusti, quidam monachus tunc reliquiarum habens custodiam, cum homines malivoli in ecclesiam prefatam et eiusdem ministros seviebant, eorumdem timens maliciam, cupam cum precio mundi ab hostium incursu proponens salvare, eandem in loco secretiori, videlicet in camera sacriste, occultavit. Contigit quod ignis per inimicos crucifixi appositus, ecclesiam monasteriumque totum destruens,

---

[a] Kajava *inserts* archiepiscopus, *the subject, however, is clearly Christ*
[b] circulus MS
[c] continet MS

cameram totam in qua cupa fuerat occultata conbussit, et licet ignis immensus in quantitate maxima ex omni parte cupe iacens et estuans, pedem et summitatem eiusdem consumpserit, dominus tamen noster Iesu Cristus flammas ignium excutiens, ciphum et in eodem sanguinem suum conservavit indempnem. Quod quidem monachus, die sequenti perpendens, cum videret quod ciphus ad manus predomini deveniret, caute vasculum cristallinum, licet ruptum, cum preciosissimo sanguine amovit et in loco secreto honeste deposuit. Postea vero per aliquod temporem, cum ad eiusdem sanguinis conservationem novum vas cristallinum fuerat confectum et coram quampluribus monachis de vase antiquo ad novum, cum omni veneratione debita, sanguis sine diminutione, ut omnes circumastantes et qui interfuerant credebant, fuerat translatus et utrumque vas in loco tuto positum, contigit quodam mirandum, videlicet quod q(uedam) maior pars sanguinis inventa est in summitate vasis antiqui per se sine sustentatione dependens miraculose, qui quidem cum altera parte in novum vas reclusum usque in hodiernum diem in ecclesia Norwyci remanet, [ut sit ibi mundi precium salus presentium, presidium futurorum, largiente summo pontifice qui per proprium sanguinem introivit semel in secula, cui cum patre et spiritu sancto laus et perpetua manet iubilatio per infinita seculorum secula, Amen].

Bibliography

MANUSCRIPT SOURCES CITED

Avranches
  Bibliothèque municipale MSS 212 and 213 (Extracts for Mont St Michel)
Bordeaux
  Bibliothèque municipale MS 286 (William of Sudbury's Concordance to James of Voragine)
Bruges
  Archives de la Ville MS Charte 239 (Indulgence of Clement V)
  Holy Blood Chapel, Museum, MSS
    Indulgence of Leo XIII
    Livre d'Or
Cambridge
  Fitzwilliam Museum MS 88 (1972) (Shrewsbury Lectionary)
  Gonville and Caius College MSS
    61/155 (Legends of Fécamp)
    300 (William of Nottingham's Sentence Commentary)
  King's College muniments GBR 278 (Indulgence for Great Bricett)
  Trinity College MS R.5.33 (724) (Glastonbury Histories)
  University Library MSS
    Ee.v.11 (William of Sudbury's Concordance to John de Burgo)
    Mm.v.29 (Tracts)
    Add. 5944/11 (Printed Indulgence)
Chartres
  Archives départementales de l'Eure-et-Loir MS H1261 (Coulombs Inventory)
Châteauroux
  Archives départementales de l'Indre MSS G166 and G173 (Evidences for the Holy Blood of Neuvy)
Durham
  University Library Special Collections MS D. & C. Durham Misc. Charter 5045 (Letters of Innocent IV)

London
  British Library MSS
    Additional 35112 (Tracts)
    Cotton Claudius A iv (Tracts)
      Cleopatra D iii (Annals of Hailes to *c.* 1300)
      Cleopatra D vii (Ashridge Miscellanea)
      Nero D vii (List of Benefactors of St Albans)
      Vespasian B xvi (Langland)
      Vespasian D x (Chronicle of Ralph of Coggeshall)
      Vitellius D iii (Legends of Fécamp, destroyed)
    Egerton 2947 (Tracts)
    Egerton 3031 (Reading Cartulary)
    Egerton Charter 455 (Certificate from the archbishop of Tyre)
    Harley 1801 (Legends of Fécamp)
    Harley 3725 (Hailes Chronicle to 1364)
    Royal 8 A. v (Hailes Sermons and Homilies)
    Royal 8 D. xvii (Sixtus IV on the Holy Blood)
    Royal 9.F.iv (William of Sudbury's Concordance to Aquinas)
    Royal 14.C.vii (Matthew Paris' 'Historia Anglorum')
    Royal 17 C. xvii (Verses on the Blood of Hailes)
  Public Record Office
    C47 (Chancery Miscellanea)
    E36/274 (Exchequer Liber A)
    E101 (Receipt and Issue Rolls)
    E326 (Exchequer Ancient Deeds)
    E372 (Pipe Rolls)
    SC7 (Papal Bulls)
  Sion College MS Arc.L.40.2/E25 (Gospel of Nicodemus)
  Westminster Abbey MS Domesday
    Muniments 6318A; 6674; 9477; 9478; 19618; 19619; 19621; 19623;
      19626; 19628; 19630
Longleat House
  Marquess of Bath MS 38 (William of Sudbury on the Holy Blood)
Oxford
  Bodleian Library MSS
    Ashmole 399 (Medical Treatise)
    Ashmole 842 (Miracle Story)
    Ashmole 863 (Miracle Story)
    Bodley 53 (William Thomas' 'The Pilgrim')
    Lat. hist. a2 (Glastonbury Magna Tabula)
    Liturg. g10 (Westminster Benedictional)
    Phillipps-Robinson e77 (Abstract of the Thelsford Cartulary)
    Rawlinson C 425 (Westminster Breviary)
    Rawlinson K 42 (Diary of Thomas Hearne)

Corpus Christi College MSS
    32 (Moral Exempla from Llanthony)
    232 ('Mass' of William Longespée etc.)
    Magdalen College MS 53 (Legends of Fécamp)
Paris
    Archives nationales MS LL46 (Cartulary of St-Maur-des-Fosés)
    Bibliothèque nationale MSS
        Latin 5413 (St Magloire Cartulary)
        Latin 5414 (St Magloire Cartulary)
        Latin 12390 (Tracts on the Holy Blood)
        Français 14566 (Legends of Fécamp)
        Baluze 74 (Miscellaneous Transcripts)
        Baluze 83 (Miscellaneous Transcripts)
Salisbury
    Cathedral Library D. & C. Press IV Box Indulgences
Vatican
    Library MSS
        Codex Graec. 1589 (Life of St Barypsaba)
        Reg.Lat. 623 (Account of the Relics of Glastonbury)

PRIMARY SOURCES

AACHEN, P. á Beeck, *Aquisgranum sive historica narratio de regiae S. R. I. et coronationis regum Rom.* (Aachen 1620)
    C. Quix, *Geschichte der Stadt Aachen mit einem Codex Diplomaticus Aquensis*, 2 parts in 1 (Aachen 1839–40)
Acta imperii inedita seculi xiii, ed. E. Winkelmann, 2 vols. (Innsbruck 1880–5)
ABINGDON, *Chronicon monasterii de Abingdon*, ed. J. Stevenson, 2 vols., Rolls Series (London 1858)
ALBERT the Great, *Opera omnia*, ed. B. Geyer *et al.*, vol. XXVI (Cologne 1958)
Altenglische Legenden neue Folge, ed. C. Horstmann (Heilbronn 1881)
Annales minorum seu trium ordinum a S. Francisco institutorum, ed. L. Wadding, new edn continued by J. M. Fonseca *et al.*, 25 vols. (Rome 1731–1933)
Annales monastici, ed. H. R. Luard, 5 vols., Rolls Series (London 1864–9)
Annales regni francorum . . . qui dicuntur annales Laurissenses maiores et Einhardi, ed. F. Kurze (Hanover 1895)
AOSTA, 'Annales Augustani a. 973–1104', ed. G. H. Pertz, *MGH Scriptores*, III (Hanover 1839), 123–36
AQUINAS, St Thomas, *Sancti Thomae Aquinatis doctoris angelici opera omnia iussu impensaque Leonis XIII P. M. edita*, 48 vols. (Rome 1882–1971)
    S. Thomae Aquinatis opera omnia, ed. R. Busa *et al.*, 7 vols. (Milan 1980)
ARISTOTLE, '*De partibus animalium I*' and '*De generatione animalium I*', trans. D. M. Balme, 2nd edn (Oxford 1985)

Topica, translatio Boethii, fragmentum recensionis alterius et translatio anonyma, ed. L. Minio-Paluello and B. Dod, Aristoteles Latinus V 1–3 (Brussels and Paris 1969)

ASHRIDGE, H. J. Todd, *The History of the College of Bonhommes, at Ashridge, in the County of Buckingham* (London 1823)

AUGUSTINE, St, *De civitate Dei*, ed. B. Dombart and A. Kalb, Corpus Christianorum series Latina XLVII–VIII, 2 vols. (Turnhout 1955)

AUGUSTINIANS, *Chapters of the Augustinian Canons*, ed. H. E. Salter, Canterbury and York Society XXIX (1922)

AVICENNA, *Avicenna Latinus: liber de anima seu sextus de naturalibus I–III*, ed. S. van Riet (Louvain 1972)

AVRANCHES, Henry of, *The Shorter Latin Poems of Master Henry of Avranches relating to England*, ed. J. Cox Russell and J. P. Heironimus, Mediaeval Academy of America Studies and Documents no. 1 (Cambridge, Mass., 1935)

BAMBERG, 'Annales et notae Babenbergenses', ed. P. Jaffé, *MGH Scriptores* XVII (Hanover 1861), 634–42

Baronius, C., *Annales ecclesiastici*, 12 vols. (Cologne 1601–8)

BASLE, L. Vautrey, *Histoire des évêques de Bale*, 2 vols. (Einsiedeln 1884–6)

BEAUVAIS, Vincent of, *Bibliotheca mundi seu speculi maioris Vincentii Burgundi*, 4 vols. (Douai 1624)

BECKET, St Thomas, *Materials for the History of Thomas Becket*, ed. J. C. Robertson and J. B. Sheppard, 7 vols., Rolls Series (London 1875–85)

Bede's Ecclesiastical History of the English People, ed. B. Colgrave and R. A. B. Mynors (Oxford 1969)

BENEDICT XIV, *Opera omnia*, new edn, 15 parts (Venice 1767)

BERNARD, St, *St Bernard of Clairvaux, the Story of His Life as Recorded in the 'Vita Sancti Bernardi'*, trans. G. Webb and A. Walker (London 1960)

BIBLE, *The Apocryphal New Testament*, trans. M. R. James, 2nd edn (Oxford 1953)

Bibliotheca sanctorum, ed. F. Caraffa *et al.*, 12 vols. (Rome 1961–70)

BLUND, John, *Iohannes Blund tractatus de anima*, ed. D. A. Callus and R. W. Hunt, Auctores Britannici medii aevi II (London 1970)

BONAVENTURE, St, *Opera omnia*, ed. B. a Portu Romatino *et al.*, 10 vols. (Quaracchi 1882–1902)

BOULOGNE, D. Haigneré, *Notre-Dame de Saint Sang* (Paris 1862)

BRINTON, Thomas, *The Sermons of Thomas Brinton, Bishop of Rochester, 1373–1389*, ed. M. A. Devlin, 2 vols., Camden Society 3rd series LXXXV–VI (1954)

BRUGES, *Bibliografie van de Geschiedenis van Brugge*, ed. A. Vanhoutryve (Bruges 1972)

Bullarium ordinis ff. praedicatorum, ed. T. Ripoll and A. Bremond, 8 vols. (Rome 1729–40)

Bullarum privilegiorum ac diplomatum Romanorum pontificum amplissima collectio, ed. C. Cocquelines, 14 vols. in 17 (Rome 1739–44)

Calendar of Charter Rolls, 6 vols. (London 1903–27)

Calendar of Close Rolls (London 1892–)

Calendar of Entries in the Papal Registers relating to Great Britain and Ireland, ed. W. H. Bliss, C. Johnson and J. A. Twemlow (London 1894–)

Calendar of Liberate Rolls, 6 vols. (London 1917–64)

Calendar of Patent Rolls (London 1891–)

CALVIN, Jean, *Traité des reliques*, ed. A. Autin (Paris 1921)

CANTERBURY, Gervase of, *Historical Works*, ed. W. Stubbs, 2 vols., Rolls Series (London 1879–80)

CANTERBURY, A. P. Stanley, *Historical Memorials of Canterbury*, 2nd edn (London 1855)

CAPESTRANO, Giovanni da, 'Il sangue di Cristo in San Giovanni da Capestrano. Problema Storico-Teologico', ed. N. Cocci, *Sangue e antropologia nella teologia medievala: atti della VII settimana, Roma 27 novembre–2 dicembre 1989*, ed. F. Vattioni, 3 vols. (Rome 1991), III 1287–1387

CHABANNES, Ademar of, *Chronique*, ed. J. Chavanon (Paris 1897)

Charlemagne: œuvres, rayonnement et survivances, ed. W. Braunfels, Dixième exposition sous les auspices du Conseil de l'Europe (Aix-la-Chapelle 1965)

CHARROUX, *Chartes et documents pour servir à l'histoire de l'abbaye de Charroux*, ed. D. P. de Monsabert, Archives historiques du Poitou XXXIX (1910)

CHOBHAM, Thomas of, *Thomas de Chobham summa de arte praedicandi*, ed. F. Morenzoni, CCCM LXXXII (Turnhout 1988)

Chronicles of the Reigns of Edward I and Edward II, ed. W. Stubbs, 2 vols., Rolls Series (London 1882–3)

Close Rolls 1227–72, 14 vols. (London 1902–38)

COGGESHALL, Ralph of, *Radulphi de Coggeshall chronicon Anglicanum*, ed. J. Stevenson, Rolls Series (London 1875)

Collius, F., *De sanguine Christi libri quinque* (Milan 1617)

CONSTANTINE VII, *Constantin VII Porphyrogénète: le livre des cérémonies*, ed. A. Vogt, 4 vols. (Paris 1935–40)

R. Vári, 'Zum historischen Exzerptenwerke des Konstantinos Porphyrogennetos', *Byzantinische Zeitschrift* 17 (1908), 75–85

CORNWALL, Richard of, G. C. Gebauer, *Leben und denkwürdige Thaten Herrn Richards, erwählten römischen Kaysers, Grafens v. Cornwall und Poitou* (Leipzig 1744)

Corpus iuris canonici I, ed. E. Friedberg (Leipzig 1879)

Councils and Synods with Other Documents relating to the English Church, vol. II: *1205–1313*, ed. F. M. Powicke and C. R. Cheney, 2 vols. (Oxford 1964)

COVENTRY, Walter of, *The Historical Collections of Walter of Coventry*, ed. W. Stubbs, 2 vols., Rolls Series (London 1872–3)

DICETO/DISS, Ralph of, *Radulfi de Diceto decani Lundonensi opera historica*, ed. W. Stubbs, 2 vols., Rolls Series (London 1876)

Die Kreuzzugsbriefe aus den Jahren 1088–1100, ed. H. Hagenmeyer (Innsbruck 1901)

Die Ordines für die Weihe und Krönung des Kaisers und die Kaiserin, ed. R. Elze, Fontes iuris Germanici antiqui in usum scholarum IX (Hanover 1960).

Diplomatic Documents Preserved in the Public Record Office Volume I: 1102–1272, ed. P. Chaplais (London 1964)

Domenico de Domenichi, *De sanguine Christi tractatus* (Venice 1557)

Duchesne, F., *Histoire de tous les cardinaux français*, 2 vols. (Paris 1660)

DURHAM, *Extracts from the Account Rolls of the Abbey of Durham*, ed. J. Fowler, 3 vols., Surtees Society XCIX, C, CIII (1898–1901)

Eadmeri historia novorum in Anglia, ed. M. Rule, Rolls Series (London 1884)

EDMUND, St, *The Life of St Edmund by Matthew Paris*, ed. C. H. Lawrence (Stroud 1996)

'La Vie de saint Edmond archevêque de Cantorbéry', ed. A. T. Baker, *Romania* 60 (1929) 332–81

EDWARD, St, *The Life of King Edward Who Rests at Westminster*, ed. F. Barlow, 2nd edn (Oxford 1992)

Lives of Edward the Confessor, ed. H. R. Luard, Rolls Series (London 1858)

Enchiridion symbolorum definitionum et declarationum de rebus fidei et morum, ed. H. Denzinger and C. Bannwart, new edn (Freiburg 1922)

English Episcopal Acta I: Lincoln 1067–1185, ed. D. M. Smith (Oxford 1980)

English Episcopal Acta II: Canterbury 1162–1190, ed. C. R. Cheney and B. E. A. Jones (Oxford 1986)

English Episcopal Acta VI: Norwich 1070–1214, ed. C. Harper-Bill (Oxford 1990)

English Episcopal Acta VII: Hereford 1079–1234, ed. J. Barrow (Oxford 1993)

English Episcopal Acta IX: Winchester 1205–1238, ed. N. Vincent (Oxford 1994)

Estienne, H., *Apologie pour Herodote, ou traité de la conformité des merveilles anciennes avec les modernes*, 3 vols. (The Hague 1735)

Exuviae sacrae Constantinopolitanae, ed. P. E. D. comte de Riant, 2 vols. (Geneva 1877–8)

EYMERICUS, Nicholas, *Directorium inquistorum*, ed. F. Pegna (Venice 1607)

Fasciculus Morum: A Fourteenth-Century Preacher's Handbook, ed. S. Wenzel (Philadelphia 1989)

FÉCAMP, 'Anciens inventaires du trésor de l'abbaye de Fécamp', ed. C. de Beaurepaire, *Bibliothèque de l'Ecole des Chartes* 20 (1859), 153–70

'Epistulae Fiscannenses. Lettres d'amitié, de gouvernement et d'affaires (XI–XIIe siècles)', ed. J. Laporte, *Revue Mabillon* 43 (1953), 5–31

O. Kajava, 'Etudes sur deux poèmes français relatifs à l'abbaye de Fécamp', *Annales academiae scientiarum Fennicae* series B 21 (Helsinki 1928), 1–154

A. Langfors, 'Histoire de l'abbaye de Fécamp', *Annales academiae scientiarum Fennicae* series B 22 part 1 (Helsinki 1928), 1–281

FINCHALE, Godric of, *Libellus de vita et miraculis S. Godrici, heremitae de Finchale*, ed. J. Stevenson, Surtees Society XX (1847)

FLANDERS, 'Genealogiae comitum Flandriae', ed. L. C. Bethmann, *MGH Scriptores* IX (Hanover 1851) 302–36

FLETE, John, *The History of Westminster Abbey by John Flete*, ed. J. A. Robinson (Cambridge 1909)

FLEURY, *Consuetudines Floriacenses saeculi tertii decimi*, ed. A. Davril, Corpus consuetudinum monasticarum IX (Siegburg 1976)

Flores historiarum, ed. H. R. Luard, 3 vols., Rolls Series (London 1890)

Foedera, ed. T. Rymer, new edn vol. I part I, ed. A. Clark and F. Holbrooke (London 1816)

FRANCE, *Recueil des historiens des Gaules et de la France*, ed. M. Bouquet et al., 24 vols. (Paris 1738–1904)

Les Statuts synodaux français du XIIIe siècle: Tome.1 , Les statuts de Paris et le synodal de l'Ouest (XIIIe siècle), ed. O. Pontal (Paris 1971)

FREDERICK II, *Historia diplomatica Friderici secundi*, ed. J. L. A. Huillard-Bréholles, 6 vols. in 11 (Paris 1852–61)

Frutolfi et Ekkehardi chronica necnon anonymi chronica imperatorum, ed. F. J. Schmale and I. Schmale-Ott (Darmstadt 1972)

Fuller, T., *The Church-History of Britain* (London 1655)

Galen on Respiration and the Arteries, ed. D. J. Furley and J. S. Wilkie (Princeton 1984)

Gallia Christiana in provincias ecclesiasticas distributa, 16 vols. (Paris 1715–1865)

GANDERSHEIM, Henry Bodo, 'Syntagma', in *Rerum Germanicorum tomi III*. ed. H. Meibom, 3 vols. (Helmstadt 1688), II

'Eberhards Reimchronik von Gandersheim', ed. L. Weiland, *MGH Deutsche Chroniken*, II (Hanover 1877) 385–429

J. G. Leuckfeld, *Antiquitates Gandersheimenses* (Wolfenbüttel 1709)

GEMBLOUX, Guibert of, *Guiberti Gemblacensis epistolae*, ed. A. Derolez, 2 vols., CCCM LXVI (Turnhout 1988–9)

GEMBLOUX, Sigebert of, 'Sigeberti Gemblacensis chronica cum continuationibus', ed. D. L. C. Bethmann, *MGH Scriptores*, VI (Hanover 1844), 268–474

GLASTONBURY, *Adami de Domerham historia de rebus gestis Glastoniensibus*, ed. T. Hearne, 2 vols. (Oxford 1727)

The Chronicle of Glastonbury Abbey: An Edition, Translation and Study of John of Glastonbury's 'Chronica sive antiquitates Glastoniensis ecclesie', ed. J. P. Carley, trans. D. Townsend (Woodbridge 1985)

The Early History of Glastonbury: An Edition, Translation and Study of William of Malmesbury's 'De Antiquitate Glastonie Ecclesie', ed. J. Scott (Woodbridge 1981)

GREGORY I, *Gregorii I papae registrum epistolarum*, ed. P. Ewald and L. M. Hartmann, 2 vols., *MGH Epistolarum*, I–II (Berlin 1891–9)

GREGORY IX, *Les Régistres de Grégoire IX*, ed. L. Auvray, 4 vols., Bibliothèque des Ecoles françaises d'Athènes et de Rome (Paris 1896–1955)

GROSSETESTE, Robert, J. Goering, 'The "De Dotibus" of Robert Grosseteste', *Mediaeval Studies* 44 (1982), 83–109

Roberti Grosseteste episcopi quondam Lincolniensis epistolae, ed. H. R. Luard, Rolls Series (London 1861)

Rotuli Roberti Grosseteste episcopi Lincolniensis, ed. F. N. Davis, Canterbury and York Society X (London 1913)

GUALA, *The Letters and Charters of Cardinal Guala Bicchieri, Papal Legate in England 1216–1218*, ed. N. Vincent, Canterbury and York Society LXXXIII (1996)

HAILES, M. N. Blount, 'A Critical Edition of the Annals of Hailes (MS. Cotton Cleopatra D iii, ff. 33–59v) with an Examination of their Sources', M A thesis (University of Manchester 1974)

J. G. Coad, *Hailes Abbey Gloucestershire*, English Heritage Handbook (London 1985)

HALES, Alexander of, *Summa theologica*, ed. B. Klumper, C. Koser *et al.*, 4 vols. (Quaracchi 1924–48)

HEISTERBACH, Caesarius of, *Caesarii Heisterbacensis monachi ordinis Cisterciensis dialogus miraculorum*, ed. J. Strange, 2 vols. (Cologne 1851)
The Dialogue on Miracles, trans. H. von E. Scott and C. C. Winton Bland, 2 vols. (London 1929)

HENRY III, 'Historiola de pietate regis Henrici III, A. D. 1259', ed. E. A. Bond, *Archaeological Journal* 17 (1860), 318–19

HIGDEN, Ranulph, *Polychronicon Ranulphi Higden, monachi Cestrensis*, ed. C. Babington and J. R. Lumby, 9 vols., Rolls Series (London 1865–86)

HILDERSHEIM, H. Goetting, *Das Bistum Hildersheim I: Das Reichsunmittelbare Kanonissenstift Gandersheim*, Germania Sacra neue folge VII part 1 (Berlin and New York 1973)

HOLINSHED, R., *The Third Volume of Chronicles ... Now Newly Recognised, Augmented and Continued ... to the Yeare 1586* (London 1587)

HOWDEN, Roger of, *Chronica magistri Rogeri de Hovedene*, ed. W. Stubbs, 4 vols., Rolls Series (London 1868–71)

HUS, John, 'De sanguine Christi', in Hus, *Opera omnia*, ed. W. Flajshans, vol. 1 fasc. 3 (Prague 1904)

INNOCENT IV, *Les Registres d'Innocent IV (1243–54)*, ed. E. Berger, 4 vols. (Ecole française de Rome 1884–1921)
P. Sambin, 'Problemi politici attraverso lettere inedite di Innocenzo IV', *Memorie del Instituto Veneto di scienze, lettere ed arti, classe di scienze, morali e lettere* XXXI fasc. 3 (Venice 1955), 1–71

Inscriptiones Hispaniae Christianae, ed. E. Hübner (Berlin 1871)

JERUSALEM, *Le Cartulaire du chapitre du Saint-Sépulcre de Jérusalem*, ed. G. Bresc-Bautier, Documents relatifs à l'histoire des croisades XV (Paris 1984)
Itinera Hierosolymitana et descriptiones terrae sanctae bellis sacris anteriora, ed. T. Tobler, A. Molinier and C. Kohler, 2 vols. (Geneva 1879–85)
Itinéraires à Jérusalem et descriptions de la Terre Sainte aux XIe, XIIe et XIIIe siècles, ed. H. Michelant and G. Raynaud (Geneva 1882)
Jerusalem Pilgrims before the Crusades, ed. J. Wilkinson (Warminster 1977)

JOINVILLE, *Œuvres de Jean sire de Joinville comprenant l'histoire de Saint Louis*, ed. N. de Wailly (Paris 1867)

KEMP, Margery, *The Book of Margery Kemp*, ed. S. B. Meech and H. E. Allen, Early English Text Society CCXII (1940)

KNIGHTON, Henry, *Chronicon Henrici Knighton vel Cnitthon, monachi Leycestrensis*, ed. J. R. Lumby, 2 vols., Rolls Series (London 1889–95)

LANFRANC, *The Monastic Constitutions of Lanfranc*, ed. D. Knowles (London 1951)

LATIMER, Hugh, *Sermons and Remains of Hugh Latimer, Sometime Bishop of Worcester, Martyr 1555*, ed. G. E. Corrie, Parker Society XXII–XXIII (1844–5)

Layettes du trésor des chartes, ed. A. Teulet *et al.*, 5 vols. (Paris 1863–1909)

LELAND, John, *De rebus brittanicis collectanea*, ed. T. Hearne, 2nd edn (London 1770)

Leonardo di Matteo d'Udine, *Tractatus mirabilis de sanguine Christi in triduo mortis eius effuso* (Venice 1617)

Letters and Papers, Foreign and Domestic, of the Reign of Henry VIII, ed. J. S. Brewer, J. Gairdner and R. H. Brodie, 21 vols. in 35 (London 1864–1932)

LINCOLN, St Hugh of, *Magna Vita Sancti Hugonis: The Life of St Hugh of Lincoln*, ed. D. L. Douie and D. H. Farmer, 2 vols. (Oxford 1985)

Llandaff Episcopal Acta 1140–1287, ed. D. Crouch, South Wales Record Society V (1988)

LOMBARD, Peter the, *Magistri Petri Lombardi Sententiae in IV libris distinctae*, ed. I. Brady, 3rd edn, 2 vols., Spicilegium Bonaventurianum IV, V (Grottaferrata 1971–81)

LONDON, *De antiquis legibus liber. Chronica maiorum et vicecomitum Londoniarum*, ed. T. Stapleton, Camden Society XXXIV (1846)

LUCCA, D. Barsocchini, *Lucca, il Volto Santo e la civiltà medioevale: atti convegno internazionale di studi* (Lucca 1984)

Ragionamento sopra il Volto Santo di Lucca (Lucca 1844)

MAGDEBURG, 'Annales Magdeburgenses brevissimi', ed. O. Holder-Egger, *MGH Scriptores*, XXX part II (Leipzig 1926), 748–9

D. Claude, *Geschichte des Erzbistums Magdeburg bis in das 12. Jahrhundert*, 2 vols. (Cologne 1972–5)

MALMESBURY, *Eulogium (historiarum sive temporis) . . . a monacho quodam Malmesburiensi exaratum*, ed. F. S. Haydon, 3 vols, Rolls Series (London 1858–63)

MANTUA, 'Breve chronicon monasterii Mantuani Sancti Andree di Antonio Nerli (AA. 800–1431)', in L. A. Muratori, *Rerum Italicarum scriptores*, new edn, ed. G. Carducci and V. Fiorini, XXIV part 13 (Città di Castello 1908)

I. Donesmondi, *Dell'Istoria ecclesiastica di Mantova*, 2 parts (Mantua 1612–16)

MAROLLES, Michel de, *Les Mémoires de Michel de Marolles* (Paris 1656)

MARSTON, Roger, *Fr. Roger Marston O.F.M. quodlibeta quatuor*, ed. G. F. Etzkorn and I. C. Brady, Bibliotheca Franciscana scholastica medii aevi XXVI (Florence 1968)

Martène, E., *De antiquis ecclesiae ritibus*, 4 vols. (Antwerp 1736–8)

Mazolini, Silvestro, da Prierio, *Aurea Rosa, id est preclarissima expositio super evangeliis totius anni* (Paris 1516), reprinted by D. Zambelli (Venice 1599)

Medieval Libraries of Great Britain: A List of Surviving Books, ed. N. R. Ker, 2nd edn (London 1964)

MEYRONNES, Francis de, *François de Meyronnes, Pierre Roger, Disputatio (1320–1321)*, ed. J. Barbet, Textes philosophiques du Moyen Age X (Paris 1961) *Preclarissima ac multum subtilia egregiaque scripta illuminati doctoris fratris Francisci de Mayronis ordinis minorum in quatuor libros sententiarum* (Venice 1520) *Quadragesimale seu sermones de tempore F. de Mayronis* (Brussels 1484)

MIDDLETON, Richard of, *Clarissimi theologi magistri Ricardi de Mediavilla . . . super quatuor libros sententiarum Petri Lombardi quaestiones subtilisimae*, 4 vols. (Brescia 1591)

Miraeus, A., *Opera diplomatica et historica*, ed. J. F. Foppens, 2nd edn, 4 vols. (Louvain 1723–48)

MONASTICON, Sir William Dugdale, *Monasticon Anglicanum*, ed. J. Caley, H. Ellis and B. Bandinel, 6 vols. (London 1846)

Monstier, A. du, *Neustria pia* (Rouen 1663)

MONTE CASSINO, 'Leonis Marsicani et Petri diaconi chronica monasterii Casinensis', ed. W. Wattenbach, *MGH Scriptores*, VII (Hanover 1846), 551–844

MÜNCHSMÜNSTER, 'Notae Sweigo-Monasterienses', ed. O. Holder-Egger, *MGH Scriptores*, XV (Hanover 1887), 1073–5

NEWBURGH, William of, 'Chronicle', in *Chronicles of the Reigns of Stephen, Henry II and Richard I*, ed. R. Howlett, 4 vols., Rolls Series (London 1885–9)

NOGENT, Guibert of, *Guibert de Nogent . . . de sanctis et eorum pigneribus*, ed. R. B. C. Huygens, CCCM CXXVII (Turnhout 1993) *Self and Society in Medieval France: The Memoirs of Abbot Guibert of Nogent*, ed. J. F. Benton, revised edn (Toronto 1984)

NORWICH, St William of, *The Life and Miracles of St William of Norwich by Thomas of Monmouth*, ed. A. Jessopp and M. R. James (Cambridge 1896)

OBAZINE, St Stephen of, *Vie de Saint Etienne d'Obazine*, ed. M. Aubrun, Publications de l'Institut d'Études du Massif Central VI (Clermont-Ferrand 1970)

OCKHAM, Nicholas of, *Quaestiones disputatae de traductione humanae naturae a primo parente*, ed. C. Saco Alarcón, Spicilegium Bonaventurianum (Grottaferrata 1993)

OIGNY, *Le Coutumier de l'abbaye d'Oigny en Bourgogne au XIIe siècle*, ed. P. F. Lefèvre and A. H. Thomas, Spicilegium Sacrum Lovaniense études et documents XXXIX (1976)

ORCHELLIS, Guy de, *Guidonis de Orchellis tractatus de sacramentis ex eius summa de sacramentis et officiis ecclesiae*, ed. P. Damiani and O. Van den Eynde, Franciscan Institute Publications text series IV (New York and Louvain 1953)

OTTO I, *Die Urkunden der Deutschen Könige und Kaiser*, ed. T. Sickel *et al.*, *MGH Diplomata*, I (Hanover 1879–84)

OVIEDO, D. de Bruyne, 'Le plus ancien catalogue des reliques d'Oviedo', *Analecta Bollandiana* 45 (1927), 93–6

OXENEDES, John, *Chronica Johannis de Oxenedes*, ed. H. Ellis, Rolls Series (London 1859)

PARIS, *Chartularium Universitatis Parisiensis*, ed. H. Denifle and A. Chatelain, 4 vols. (Paris 1889–97)

PARIS, Matthew, *Chronica majora*, ed. H. R. Luard, 7 vols., Rolls Series (London 1872–84)

'Gesta abbatum', in *Gesta abbatum monasterii sancti Albani a Thoma Walsingham . . . compilata*, ed. H. T. Riley, 3 vols., Rolls Series (London 1867)

Historia Anglorum, ed. F. Madden, 3 vols., Rolls Series (London 1866–9)

The Illustrated Chronicles of Matthew Paris: Observations of Thirteenth-Century Life, ed. R. Vaughan (Stroud 1993)

Matthaei Paris . . . historia maior, ed. W. Wats (London 1640)

PETERSHAUSEN, 'Casus monasterii Petrihusensis', ed. O. Abel and L. Weiland, *MGH Scriptores*, XX (Hanover 1868), 621–83

PIUS II, *The Commentaries of Pius II Books II and III*, ed. F. A. Gragg and L. C. Gabel, Smith College Studies in History XXIV (Northampton, Mass., 1942)

The Commentaries of Pius II Books VI–IX, ed. F. A. Gragg and L. C. Gabel, Smith College Studies in History XXXV (Northampton, Mass., 1951)

The Commentaries of Pius II Books X–XIII, ed. F. A. Gragg and L. C. Gabel, Smith College Studies in History XLIII (Northampton, Mass., 1957)

Pii II commentarii, ed. A. van Heck, 2 vols., Studi e Testi CCCXII–CCCXIII (Vatican 1984)

Pons, Vincent, *La Saincte Ampoulle de Sainct Maximin* (Aix-en-Provence 1609)

PRÜFENING, 'Notae Pruveningenses', ed. W. Wattenbach, *MGH Scriptores*, XVII (Hanover 1861), 610–12

Prynne, W., *The Second Tome of an Exact Chronological Vindication and Historical Demonstration of our . . . Supream Ecclesiastical Jurisdiction* (London 1665)

Quinti belli sacri scriptores minores, ed. R. Röhricht (Geneva 1879)

Raynaud, T., *Opera omnia*, 20 vols. (Lyon 1665–9)

Reading Abbey Cartularies, ed. B. R. Kemp, 2 vols., Camden Society 4th series XXXI, XXXIII (1986–7)

Recueil des historiens des croisades: historiens occidentaux, 5 vols. (Paris 1844–95)

Regesta imperii V: 1198–1272, ed. J. F. Böhmer, J. Ficker and E. Winkelmann, 3 vols. (Innsbruck 1881–1901)

Regesta pontificum Romanorum, ed. P. Jaffé, new edn by W. Wattenbach *et al.*, 2 vols. (Leipzig 1885–8)

REICHENAU, 'Annales Augienses', ed. G. H. Pertz, *MGH Scriptores*, I (Hanover 1826), 67–9

W. Berschin and T. Klüppel, *Die Reichenauer Heiligblut-Reliquie*, Reichenauer Texte und Bilder I (Stuttgart 1999)

'Herimanni Augiensis chronicon', ed. G. H. Pertz, *MGH Scriptores*, V (Hanover 1844), 67–133

'Ex translatione sanguinis domini', ed. D. G. Waitz, *MGH Scriptores*, IV (Hanover 1841), 444–9

RICHARD II, *Historia vitae et regni Ricardi secundi*, ed. G. B. Stow (Philadelphia 1977)

RIEVAULX, Aelred of, *Aelredi Rievallensis opera omnia*, ed. A. Hoste and C. H. Talbot, CCCM I (Turnhout 1971)

RISHANGER, William, *Chronica et annales*, ed. H. T. Riley, Rolls Series (London 1865)

ROCAMADOUR, *Les Miracles de Notre-Dame de Rocamadour au XIIe siècle*, ed. A. Albe (Paris 1907)

Rocca, A., *Opera omnia*, 2 vols. (Rome 1719)

ROME, *Codice topografico della città di Roma*, ed. R. Valentini and G. Zucchetti, 4 vols., Fonti per la Storia d'Italia LXXXI, LXXXVIII, XC–XCI (Rome 1940–53)

Rotuli de oblatis et finium, ed. T. D. Hardy (London 1835)

Rotuli litterarum patentium, ed. T. D. Hardy (London 1835)

ROUEN, Victricius of, *De laude sanctorum*, ed. J. Mulders, Corpus Christianorum Series Latina LXIV (Turnhout 1985)

ROUS, John, *Joannis Rossi antiquarii Warwicensis historia regum Angliae*, ed. T. Hearne, 2nd edn (Oxford 1741)

SALISBURY, *Breviarium ad usum insignis ecclesiae Sarum*, ed. F. Proctor and C. Wordsworth, 3 vols. (Cambridge 1882–6)

Ceremonies and Processions of the Cathedral Church of Salisbury, ed. C. Wordsworth (Cambridge 1901)

SCOTUS, John 'Duns', *Johannis Duns Scoti doctoris subtilis, ordinis minorum, opera omnia*, ed. L. Wadding, new edn, 26 vols. (Paris 1891–5)

SHARESHILL, Alfred of, 'Des Alfred von Sareshel (Alfredus Anglicus) Schrift De Motu Cordis', ed. C. Baeumker, *Beiträge zur Geschichte der Philosophie des Mittelalters*, XXIII parts 1–2 (Münster 1923)

SHREWSBURY, H. Owen and F. B. Blakeway, *A History of Shrewsbury*, 2 vols. (London 1825)

SIXTUS IV, *Tractatus de sanguine Christi* (Rome 1472, reprinted Nuremburg 1473)

SPEED, John, *The Theatre of the Empire of Great Britaine* (London 1611)

Statuta capitulorum generalium ordinis Cisterciensis, III, ed. J.-M. Canivez, Bibliothèque de la Revue d'Histoire Ecclésiastique fasc. XI (Louvain 1933–4)

SUDBURY, William of, T. Käppeli, 'Die Tabula des Wilhelm Sudbery, O.S.B., zu den Werken des hl. Thomas von Aquino', *Theologische Quartalschrift* 115 (1934), 62–85

Tabulae ordinis Theutonici, ed. E. Strehlke (Berlin 1869)

THOMAS, William, *The Pilgrim: A Dialogue of the Life and Actions of King Henry the Eighth*, ed. J. A. Froude (London 1861)

Three Chapters of Letters relating to the Suppression of the Monasteries, ed. T. Wright, Camden Series XXVIII (1843)

TILBURY, Gervase of, 'Otia imperialia', in *Scriptores rerum Brunsvicensium illustrationi inservientes*, ed. G. W. Leibnitz, 3 vols. (Hanover 1707–11)

TORIGNI, Robert de, 'Chronica', in *Chronicles of the Reigns of Stephen, Henry II and Richard I*, ed. R. Howlett, 4 vols., Rolls Series (London 1885–9), IV

TOURNAI, Simon of, *Les 'Disputationes' de Simon de Tournai*, ed. J. Warichez, Spicilegium Sacrum Lovaniense études et documents XII (1932)

TOURS, Gregory of, *Gregorii Turonensis opera*, ed. W. Arndt and B. Krusch, *MGH Scriptores Rerum Merovingicarum*, I (Hanover 1885)

TRIER, F.-J. Heyen, *Das Erzbistum Trier I: Das Stift St Paulin von Trier*, Germania Sacra neue folge VI (Berlin and New York 1972)

'Notae dedicationis S. Paulini Treverensis', ed. H. V. Saverland, *MGH Scriptores*, XV part 2 (Hanover 1888), 1275–7

Pro abbatia beati Martini Treverensis . . . de sanguine Christi corporali super terram relicto (Cologne 1514)

TRIVET, *Annales F. Nicholai de Triveti*, ed. T. Hog (London 1845)

TROIS FONTAINES, Aubrey of, 'Chronica Albrici monachi Trium Fontium', ed. P. Scheffer-Boichorst, *MGH Scriptores*, XXIII (Hanover 1874), 631–950

TYRE, William of, *Willelmi Tyrensis archiepiscopi chronicon*, ed. R. B. C. Huygens, H. E. Mayer and G. Rösch, 2 vols., CCCM LXIII (Turnhout 1986)

Valor ecclesiasticus tempore Henrici VIII, autoritate regia institutus, ed. J. Caley and J. Hunter, 6 vols. (London 1810–34)

VATICAN LIBRARY, C. Giannelli, *Codices Vaticani Graeci: codices 1485–1683* (Vatican 1950)

Vazquez, G., *Opera omnia*, 7 vols. (Antwerp 1621)

WALES, Gerald of, *Giraldi Cambrensis opera*, ed. J. S. Brewer, 8 vols., Rolls Series (London 1861–91)

WALTHAM, N. Rogers, 'The Waltham Abbey Relic-List', *England in the Eleventh Century, Proceedings of the 1990 Harlaxton Symposium*, ed. C. Hicks (Stamford 1992), 156–81

The Waltham Chronicle, ed. L. Watkiss and M. Chibnall (Oxford 1994)

WEINGARTEN, 'De inventione et translatione sanguinis domini', ed. G. Waitz, *MGH Scriptores*, XV part II (Hanover 1888), 921–3

WEISSENBURG, 'Notae Weissenburgenses', ed. G. Waitz, *MGH Scriptores*, XIII (Hanover 1881), 46

WESTMINSTER, *Customary of the Benedictine Monasteries of St Augustine Canterbury and Saint Peter, Westminster*, ed. E. Maunde Thompson, 2 vols., Henry Bradshaw Society XXIII, XXVIII (1902–4)

The Manuscripts of Westminster Abbey, ed. M. R. James and J. A. Robinson (Cambridge 1909)

Missale ad usum ecclesie Westmonasteriensis, ed. J. Wickham Legg, 3 vols., Henry Bradshaw Society I, V, XII (1891–7)

Westminster Abbey Charters 1066–c. 1214, ed. E. Mason, London Record Society XXV (1988)

The Westminster Chronicle 1381–1394, ed. L. C. Hector and B. F. Harvey (Oxford 1982)

WILSNACK, *Das Gutachten der Theologischen Fakultät Erfurt 1452 über 'Das heilige Blut von Wilsnak'*, ed. R. Damerau (Marburg 1976)

WINCHESTER, *Compotus Rolls of the Obedientiaries of St Swithun's Priory, Winchester*, ed. G. W. Kitchin, Hampshire Record Society VII (1892)

Liber vitae: Register and Martyrology of New Minster and Hyde Abbey Winchester, ed. W. de Gray Birch, Hampshire Record Society V (Winchester 1892)

WORMS, *Urkundenbuch der Stadt Worms*, ed. H. Boos, 2 vols. (Berlin 1886–90)

WRIOTHESLEY, Charles, *A Chronicle of England during the Reigns of the Tudors*, ed. W. Douglas Hamilton, Camden new series XI, XX (1875–7)

YPRES, John of, 'Chronica monasterii Sancti Bertini auctore Iohanne Longo de Ipra', ed. O. Holder-Egger in *MGH Scriptores*, XXV (Hanover 1880) 736–866

SECONDARY WORKS

Albanès, J. H., *Le Couvent royal de Saint-Maximin en Provence* (Marseilles 1880)

Alexandre-Bidon, D. (ed.), *Le Pressoir mystique. Actes du colloque de Recloses, 27 mai 1989* (Paris 1990)

Angenendt, A., *Heilige und Reliquien: die Geschichte ihres Kultes vom frühen Christentum bis zur Gegenwart* (Munich 1994)

Avala, J. G., *Canónigos del Santo Sepulcro en Jerusalén y Calatayud* (Madrid 1970)

Baldwin, J. W., *Masters, Princes and Merchants: The Social Views of Peter the Chanter and his Circle*, 2 vols. (Princeton 1970)

Barb, A. A., 'The Wound in Christ's Side', *Journal of the Warburg and Courtauld Institutes* 34 (1971), 320–1

Barbier de Montault, X., *Œuvres complètes* (Poitiers 1889–1902)

Barlow, F., 'The King's Evil', *English Historical Review* 95 (1980), 3–27
William Rufus (London 1983)

Barron, C. M., 'The Parish Fraternities of Medieval London', *The Church in Pre-Reformation Society. Essays in Honour of F. R. H. Du Boulay*, ed. Barron and C. Harper-Bill (Woodbridge 1985), 13–37

Bates, D., *Normandy before 1066* (London 1982)

Baudry, L., *La Querelle des futurs contingents* (Paris 1950)

Bautier, G., 'L'Envoi de la relique de la Vraie Croix à Notre-Dame de Paris en 1120', *Bibliothèque de l'Ecole des Chartes* 129 (1971), 387–97

Bazeley, W., 'The Abbey of St Mary, Hayles', *Transactions of the Bristol and Gloucestershire Archaeological Society* 22 (1899), 257–71

Beaune, C., *Myths and Symbols of Nation in Late-Medieval France*, trans. S. R. Huston and F. L. Cheyette (Berkeley, Calif., 1991)
'Les Ducs, le roi et le saint sang', *Saint-Denis et la royauté: études offertes à Bernard Guenée*, ed. F. Autrand, C. Gauvard and J.-M. Moeglin (Paris 1999), 711–32

Begg, E. and D., *In Search of the Holy Grail and the Precious Blood* (London 1995)

Bennett, J. A., 'A Glastonbury Relic', *Proceedings of the Somerset Archaeological and Natural History Society* 24 part 2 (1888), 117–22

Bentley, J., *Restless Bones: The Story of Relics* (London 1985)

Bernard, G. W., 'Vitality and Vulnerability in the Late Medieval Church: Pilgrimage on the Eve of the Break with Rome', *The End of the Middle Ages: England in the Fifteenth and Sixteenth Centuries*, ed. J. L. Watts (Stroud 1998), 199–233

Bethell, D., 'The Making of a Twelfth-Century Relic Collection', *Popular Belief and Practice; Studies in Church History*, 8 (1972), 61–72

Biguet, J., *La Relique du Saint-Sang de Boulogne-sur-Mer* (St-Omer 1914)

Binski, P., *The Painted Chamber at Westminster* (London 1986)

'Reflections on "La Estoire de Seint Aedward le Rei": Hagiography and Kingship in Thirteenth-Century England', *Journal of Medieval History* 16 (1990), 333–50

'Abbot Berkyng's Tapestries and Matthew Paris's Life of St Edward the Confessor', *Archaeologia* 109 (1991), 85–100

Westminster Abbey and the Plantagenets (New Haven 1995)

Bishop, E., *Liturgica Historica* (Oxford 1918)

Blaauw, W. H., *The Barons' War*, 2nd edn (London 1871)

Bloch, M., *The Royal Touch*, trans. J. E. Anderson (New York 1961)

Bocage, J. du, *Le Prix de notre salut: le très Précieux Sang de N. S. Jésus-Christ* (Paris 1970)

Bond, F., *Westminster Abbey* (Oxford 1909)

Boockmann, H., 'Der Streit um das Wilsnacker Blut, zur Situation des deutschen Klerus in der Mitte des 15. Jahrhunderts', *Zeitschrift für Historische Forschung* 9 (1982), 385–408

Borenius, T., 'The Eucharistic Reed or Calamus', *Archaeologia* 80 (1930), 99–116

Bosl, K., *Die Reichsministerialität der Salier und Staufer*, 2 vols., MGH Schriften X (Stuttgart 1950–1)

Bourbon-Parma, Prince Xavier de, *Les Chevaliers du Saint-Sépulcre* (Paris 1957)

Boureau, A., *Le Simple Corps du roi: l'impossible sacralité des souverains français XVe–XVIIIe siècles* (Paris 1988)

'Un obstacle à la sacralité royale en occident: le principe hiérarchique', *La Royauté sacrée dans le monde Chrétien (colloque de Royaumont, mars 1989)*, ed. A. Boureau and C. S. Ingerflom (Paris 1992), 29–37

Théologie, science et censure au XIIIe siècle: le cas de Jean Peckham (Paris 1999)

Boussel, P., *Des reliques et de leur bon usage* (Paris 1971)

Bouza Alvarez, J. L., *Religiosidad contrarreformista y cultura simbólica del barroco* (Madrid 1990)

Brain, P., *Galen on Bloodletting* (Cambridge 1986)

Branner, R., 'Westminster Abbey and the French Court Style', *Journal of the Society of Architectural Historians* 23 (1964), 3–18

Braun, J., *Die Reliquiare des christlichen Kultes und ihre entwicklung* (Freiburg 1940)

Breest, E., 'Das Wunderblut von Wilsnack (1383–1552)', *Märkische Forschungen* 16 (Berlin 1881), 131–301

Bresc-Bautier, G., 'Les Imitations du Saint-Sépulcre de Jérusalem (IXe–XVe siècles): archéologie d'une dévotion', *Revue d'Histoire de la Spiritualité* 1 (1974), 319–42

'Le Prieuré du Saint-Sépulcre de la Vinadière (1263–1498)', *Bulletin de la Société de Lettres, Sciences et Arts de la Corrèze* 83 (1980), 39–47

Brooke, C. N. L., and G. Keir, *London 800–1216: The Shaping of a City* (London 1975)

Brooke, R. and C. N. L., *Popular Religion in the Middle Ages* (London 1984)

Brouillet, A., 'Description des reliquaires trouvés dans l'ancienne abbaye de Charroux (Vienne) le 9 août 1856', *Bulletins de la Société des antiquaires de l'Ouest* 1st series 8 (1859), 173–83

Browe, P., *Die Verehrung der Eucharistie im Mittelalter* (Munich 1933)

Die Eucharistischen Wunder des Mittelalters, Breslauer Studien zur historischen Theologie, neue folge IV (Breslau 1938)

Brown, P. R. L., *Relics and Social Status in the Age of Gregory of Tours*, Stenton Lecture (Reading 1977)

The Cult of the Saints: Its Rise and Function in Latin Christianity, Haskell Lectures on the History of Religion, new series II (Chicago 1981)

Brückner, W., *Die Verehrung des Heiligen Blutes in Walldürn*, Veroffentlichungen des Geschichts und Kunstvereins Aschaffenburg III (Aschaffenburg 1958)

Bynum, C. W., 'The Body of Christ in the Later Middle Ages: A Reply to Leo Steinberg', *Renaissance Quarterly* 39 (1986), 400–39

Fragmentation and Redemption: Essays on Gender and the Human Body in Medieval Religion (New York 1991)

The Resurrection of the Body in Western Christianity, 200–1336 (New York 1995)

Caillaud, abbé, *Notice sur le Précieux Sang de Neuvy-Saint-Sépulcre* (Bourges 1865)

Carley, J. P., 'Melkin the Bard and the Esoteric Tradition at Glastonbury Abbey', *Downside Review* 99 (1981) 1–17

'A Grave Event: Henry V, Glastonbury Abbey, and Joseph of Arimathea's Bones', *Culture and the King: Essays in Honor of Valerie M. Lagorio*, ed. M. B. Shichtman and J. P. Carley (Albany, N.Y., 1994), 129–48

Carley, J. P., and M. Howley, 'Relics at Glastonbury in the Fourteenth Century: An Annotated Edition of British Library Cotton Titus D VII fos. 2r–13v', *Arthurian Literature* 16 (1998), 83–129

Carolus-Barré, L., 'Saint-Louis et la translation des corps saints', *Etudes d'histoire du droit canonique dédiées à Gabriel le Bras*, 2 vols. (Paris 1965), II 1087–112

Carpenter, D. A., 'What Happened in 1258?', *War and Government in the Middle Ages: Essays in Honour of J. O. Prestwich*, ed. J. Gillingham and J. C. Holt (Woodbridge 1984), 106–19

'The Burial of King Henry III, the Regalia and Royal Ideology', in D. A. Carpenter, *The Reign of Henry III* (London 1996)

Chambers, J. D., *Divine Worship in the Thirteenth and Fourteenth Centuries* (London 1877)

Chaney, W. A., *The Cult of Kingship in Anglo-Saxon England* (Manchester 1970)

Chapeau, G., 'Les grandes reliques de l'abbaye de Charroux', *Bulletins de la Société des antiquaires de l'Ouest* 3rd series 8 (1931), 101–28

Cheney, M. G., *Roger, Bishop of Worcester 1164–1179* (Oxford 1980)

Chibnall, M., *The Empress Matilda* (Oxford 1991)

Christian, W. A., *Local Religion in Sixteenth-Century Spain* (Princeton 1981)

Clayton, M., *The Cult of the Virgin Mary in Anglo-Saxon England* (Cambridge 1990)

Cocci, N., 'Le Dispute teologiche del "triduum mortis" nei secoli xiv–xv: aspetto storico e dommatico', *Sangue e antropologia nella teologia: atti della VI settimana, Roma 23 al 28 novembre 1987*, ed. F. Vattioni, 3 vols. (Rome 1989), ii 1185–233

Colvin, H. M., *The History of the King's Works I: The Middle Ages*, ed. R. Allen Brown, H. M. Colvin and A. J. Taylor, 2 vols. (London 1963)

Constable, G., *Three Studies in Medieval Religious and Social Thought* (Cambridge 1995)

Conway, M., 'The Amulet of Charlemagne', *Antiquaries Journal* 2 (1922), 350–3

Couret, A., *Notice historique sur l'ordre du Saint-Sépulcre* (Paris 1905)

Cowdrey, H. E. J., 'Pope Urban II and the Idea of the Crusade', *Studi Medievali* 3rd series 36 (1995), 721–42

Cox, E. L., *The Eagles of Savoy: The House of Savoy in Thirteenth-Century Europe* (Princeton 1974)

Crivellucci, A., *I Codici della libreria raccolta da S. Giacomo della Marca* (Leghorn 1889)

Crook, J., 'St Swithun of Winchester', *Winchester Cathedral Nine Hundred Years 1093–1993*, ed. J. Crook (Chichester 1993), 57–68

Cross, R., *Duns Scotus* (Oxford 1999)

Deér, J., *Der Kaiserornat Friedrichs II* (Bern 1952)

Delehaye, H., *Les Origines du cult des martyrs* (Brussels 1933)

Deloncle, J.-G., *La Procession de la Sanch* (Portet 1985)

Denholm-Young, N., *Richard of Cornwall* (Oxford 1947)

Deshoulières, F., 'Communication', *Bulletin de la Société Nationale des Antiquaires de France* (1916), 190–229

Dickinson, J. C., *The Origins of the Austin Canons and their Introduction into England* (London 1950)

'English Regular Canons and the Continent in the Twelfth Century', *Transactions of the Royal Historical Society* 5th series 1 (1951), 71–89

Dictionnaire de spiritualité, ascétique et mystique, ed. M. Viller, F. Cavallera *et al.*, vol. xiv (Paris 1990)

Dolberg, L., 'Die Verehrungsstätte des hl. Blutes in der Cistercienser-Abtei Doberan', *Studien und Mittheilungen aus dem Benedictiner und dem Cistercienser-Orden* 12 (1891), 594–604

Doyle, A. I., 'The Work of a Late Fifteenth-Century English Scribe, William Ebesham', *Bulletin of the John Rylands Library Manchester* 39 (1956–7), 298–325

Duffy, E., *The Stripping of the Altars: Traditional Religion in England c. 1400–c. 1580* (New Haven and London 1992)

Dupont Lachenal, L., 'A Saint-Maurice au XIIIe siècle: l'abbé Nantelme (1223–1258) et la "révélation" des martyrs de 1225', *Annales Valaisannes* 2nd series 31 (1956), 393–444

Ebersolt, J., *Sanctuaires de Byzance* (Paris 1921)

Eckhardt, A., 'Das älteste Bolander Lehnbuch', *Archiv für Diplomatik* 22 (1976), 317–44

Elm, K., 'Fratres et Sorores Sanctissimi Sepulcri: Beiträge zu Fraternitas, Familia und weiblichem Religiosentum im Umkreis des Kapitels vom Hlg. Grab', *Fruhmittelalterliche Studien* 9 (1975), 287–333

Quellen zur Geschichte des Ordens vom Hlg. Grab in Nordwesteuropa aus deutschen und niederländischen Archiven (1191–1603) (Brussels 1976)

'Kanoniker und Ritter vom Heiligen Grab. Ein Beitrag zur Enstehung und Frühgeschichte der palästinensischen Ritterorden', *Die Geistlichen Ritterorden Europas*, ed. J. Fleckenstein and M. Hellmann, Konstanzer Arbeitskreis für mittelalterliche Geschichte Vorträge und Forschungen xxvi (Sigmaringen 1980), 141–69

'Mater Ecclesiarum in Exilio. El Capítulo del Santo Sepulcro de Jerusalén desde la Caída de Acre', *La Orden del Santo Sepulcro: I Jornados de Estudio* (Calatayud and Zaragoza 1991), 13–24

Elton, G., *Policy and Police: The Enforcement of the Reformation in the Age of Thomas Cromwell* (Cambridge 1972)

Emden, A. B., *A Biographical Register of the University of Oxford to A. D. 1500*, 3 vols. (Oxford 1957–9)

Estournet, G., 'Les Origines historiques de Nemours et sa charte de franchises (1170)', *Annales de la Société Historique et Archéologique du Gatinais* 39 (1930), 207–53

Faber, F. W., *The Precious Blood: Or, The Price of our Salvation* (London 1860)

Farmer, S., *Communities of Saint Martin: Legend and Ritual in Medieval Tours* (Ithaca 1991)

Fasola, U. M., 'Il culto del sangue dei martiri nella chiesa primitiva e deviazioni devozionistiche nell'epoca della riscoperta delle catacombe', *Sangue e antropologia nella letteratura cristiana: atti della settimana, Roma 29 novembre–4 dicembre 1982*, ed. F. Vattioni, 3 vols. (Rome 1983), III 1473–89

Fayolle, M. de, 'Les Eglises monolithes d'Aubeterre, de Gurat et de Saint-Emilion', *Congrès Archéologique de France, 79ème session tenue à Angoulême en 1912*, 2 vols. (Paris and Caen 1913), II 365–97

Finucane, R. C., *Miracles and Pilgrims: Popular Beliefs in Medieval England* (London 1977)

Flint, V. I. J., *The Rise of Magic in Early Medieval Europe* (Princeton 1993)

Folz, R., *Le Souvenir et la légende de Charlemagne dans l'empire germanique médiéval*, Publications de l'Université de Dijon VII (Paris 1950)

Foreville, R., *Le Jubilé de Saint Thomas Becket du XIIIe au XVe siècle (1220–1470)* (Paris 1958)

Förster, M., *Zur Geschichte des Reliquienkultus in Altengland*, Sitzungsberichte der Bayerischen Akademie der Wissenschaften 1943 part 8 (Munich 1943)

Frolow, A., *La Relique de la Vraie Croix, recherches sur le développement d'un culte*, Archives de l'Orient Chrétien VII (Paris 1961)

Galvaris, G. P., 'The Mother of God, "Stabbed with a Knife"', *Dumbarton Oaks Papers* 13 (1959), 229–33

Geary, P. J., *Furta Sacra: Thefts of Relics in the Central Middle Ages* (Princeton 1978)

Gennes, J.-P. de, *Les Chevaliers du Saint-Sépulcre de Jerusalem, essai critique*, 2 vols. (Cholet 1995)

Gervers, M., 'Rotundae Anglicanae', *Evolution générale et développements régionaux en histoire de l'art: Actes du XXIIe congrès international d'histoire de l'art* (Budapest 1972), 359-76

'The Iconography of the Cave in Christian and Mithraic Tradition', *Mysteria Mithrae: atti del seminario internazionale su la specificità storico-religiosa dei Misteri di Mithra*, ed. U. Bianchi (Leiden 1979), 579-96

'L'Eglise rupestre de Gurat près d'Angoulême', *Archéologia* 148 (1980), 42-53

Gillingham, J., *Richard I* (New Haven 1999)

Glorieux, P., *La Littérature Quodlibétique*, 2 vols., Bibliothèque Thomiste V, XXI (Paris 1925-35)

Gould, K., 'The Sequences "De sanctis reliquiis" as Sainte-Chapelle Inventories', *Mediaeval Studies* 43 (1981), 315-41

Gouttebroze, J.-G., *Le Précieux Sang de Fécamp. Origine et développement d'un mythe chrétien* (Paris 2000)

Graham, R., 'The Priory of La Charité-sur-Loire and the Monastery of Bermondsey', *Journal of the British Archaeological Association* 2nd series 32 (1926), 157-91

Gransden, A., 'The Growth of the Glastonbury Traditions and Legends in the Twelfth Century', *Journal of Ecclesiastical History* 27 (1976), 337-58

'Antiquarian Studies in Fifteenth-Century England', *Antiquaries Journal* 60 (1980), 75-97

'The Date and Authorship of John of Glastonbury's "Chronica sive Antiquitates Glastoniensis Ecclesie"', *English Historical Review* 95 (1980), 358-63

Legends, Traditions and History in Medieval England (London 1992)

Grass, N., *Reichskleinodien-Studien aus rechtshistorischer Sicht*, Österreichische Akademie der Wissenschaften, Philisophisch-Historische Klasse Sitzungberichte CCXLVIII part 4 (1964)

Gurewich, V., 'Observations on the Iconography of the Wound in Christ's Side, with Special Reference to its Position', *Journal of the Warburg and Courtauld Institutes* 20 (1957), 358-62

Guth, K., *Guibert von Nogent und die hochmittelalterliche Kritik an der Reliquienverehung*, Studien und Mitteilungen zur Geschichte des Benediktiner-Ordens und seiner Zweige XXI (Augsburg 1970)

Haag, A., *Sanguis Christi in terra vindicatus seu discussio de sanctissimo sanguine . . . in imperiali monasterio Vinearum ultra sex saecula religiosissime adservato* (Ravensburg 1758)

Hahn, C., 'Loca Sancta Souvenirs: Sealing the Pilgrim's Experience', *The Blessings of Pilgrimage*, ed. R. Ousterhout, Illinois Byzantine Studies 1 (Urbana and Chicago 1990), 85-96

Hall, A. R., 'Studies in the History of the Cardiovascular System', *Bulletin of the History of Medicine* 34 (1960), 391–413

Hamilton, B., 'Rebuilding Zion: The Holy Places of Jerusalem in the Twelfth Century', *Studies in Church History* 14 (Oxford 1977), 105–16

'Our Lady of Saidnaiya: An Orthodox Shrine Revered by Muslims and Knights Templar at the Time of the Crusades', *The Holy Land, Holy Lands, and Christian History. Studies in Church History* 36, ed. R. N. Swanson (Woodbridge 2000), 207–15

Harrsen, M., 'The Countess Judith of Flanders and the Library of Weingarten Abbey', *Papers of the Bibliographical Society of America* 24 (1930), 1–13

Harvey, B., *Westminster Abbey and its Estates in the Middle Ages* (Oxford 1977)

Living and Dying in England 1100–1540: The Monastic Experience (Oxford 1993)

Haubst, R., *Die Christologie des Nikolaus von Kues* (Freiburg 1956)

Head, T., 'Saints, Heretics and Fire: Finding Meaning through the Ordeal', *Monks and Nuns, Saints and Outcasts: Religion in Medieval Society. Essays in Honor of Lester K. Little*, ed. S. Farmer and B. H. Rosenwein (Ithaca 2000), 220–38.

Herrmann-Mascard, N., *Les Reliques des saints: formation coutumière d'un drôit* (Paris 1975)

Herval, R., 'En Marge de la légende du Précieux-Sang – Luques – Fécamp – Glastonbury', *L'Abbaye Bénédictine de Fécamp, ouvrage scientifique du XIIIe centenaire 658–1958*, 4 vols. (Fécamp 1959–63), 1105–26, 359–61

Hirsh, J. C., *The Boundaries of Faith: The Development and Transmission of Medieval Spirituality* (Leiden and New York 1996)

Hocedez, E., *Richard de Middleton, sa vie, ses œuvres, sa doctrine*, Spicilegium Sacrum Lovaniense études et documents VII (1925)

Holtzmann, W., *König Heinrich I und die Hl. Lanze* (Bonn 1947)

Horster, M., " 'Mantuae Sanguis Preciosus'", *Wallraf-Richartz-Jahrbuch* 25 (1963), 151–80

Houts, E. van, 'The Norman Conquest through European Eyes', *English Historical Review* 110 (1995), 832–53

Hubert, J., 'Le Saint-Sépulcre de Neuvy et les pèlerinages de Terre-Sainte au XIe siècle', *Bulletin Monumental* 90 (1931), 91–100

Hudson, A., *The Premature Reformation: Wycliffite Texts and Lollard History* (Oxford 1988)

Huyghebaert, N., 'Iperius et la translation de la relique du Saint-Sang à Bruges', *Annales de la Société d'Emulation de Bruges* 100 (1964 for 1963), 110–87

Jacob, E., *Untersuchungen über Herkunft und Aufstieg des Reichsministerialengeschlechtes Bolanden* (Giessen 1936)

Jacobs, E. F., 'The Reign of Henry III. Some Suggestions', *Transactions of the Royal Historical Society* 4th series 10 (1927), 21–53

Jedin, H., *Studien über Domenico de' Domenichi (1416–1478)*, Akademie der Wissenschaften und der Literatur, 1957 part 5 (Mainz 1957)

Jones, F., 'Knights of the Holy Sepulchre', *Journal of the Historical Society of the Church in Wales* 26 (1979), 11–33

Jones, S. E., 'The Twelfth-Century Reliefs from Fécamp: New Evidence for their Dating and Original Purpose', *Journal of the British Archaeological Association* 138 (1985), 79–88, reprinted in French in *Annales du Patrimonie de Fécamp* 2 (1995), 61–71

Jordan, W. C., *Louis IX and the Challenge of the Crusade* (Princeton 1979)

Kaeppeli, T., 'Bartolomeo Lapacci de' Rimbertini (1402–1466) vescovo, legato pontificio, scrittore', *Archivum Fratrum Praedicatorum* 9 (1939), 86–127

Scriptores ordinis praedicatorum medii aevi, 3 vols. (Rome 1970–)

Kalavrezou, I., 'Helping Hands for the Empire: Imperial Ceremonies and the Cult of Relics at the Byzantine Court', *Byzantine Court Culture from 829 to 1204*, ed. H. Maguire (Harvard 1997), 53–79

Kaminsky, H., *A History of the Hussite Revolution* (Berkeley, Calif., 1967)

Kantorowicz, E. H., *Laudes Regiae: A Study in Liturgical Acclamations and Mediaeval Ruler Worship* (Berkeley 1946)

Keene, D., *Survey of Winchester in the Middle Ages*, Winchester Studies II, 2 vols. (Oxford 1982)

Kennett, W., *Parochial Antiquities Attempted in the History of Ambrosden, Burcester, and Other Adjacent Parts in the Counties of Oxford and Bucks.*, new edition, 2 vols. (Oxford 1818)

Kitzinger, E., 'The Cult of Images before Iconoclasm', *Dumbarton Oaks Papers* 8 (1954), 100–9

Knighton, C. S., 'Collegiate Foundations, 1540 to 1570, with Special Reference to St Peter in Westminster' (PhD thesis, Cambridge University 1975)

Knowles, M. D., *The Religious Orders in England*, 3 vols. (Cambridge 1948–59)

Koziol, G., 'England, France, and the Problem of Sacrality in Twelfth-Century Ritual', *Cultures of Power: Lordship, Status and Process in Twelfth-Century Europe*, ed. T. N. Bisson (Philadelphia 1995), 124–48

Kretzenbacher, L., *Bild-Gedanken der spätmittelalterlichen Hl. Blut-Mystik und ihr Fortleben in mittel- und südosteuropäischen Volksüberlieferungen*, Bayerische Akademie der Wissenschaften Philosophisch-Historische Klasse Abhandlungen n.f. CXIV (Munich 1997)

Krochalis, J., '"Magna Tabula": The Glastonbury Tablets', *Arthurian Literature* 15 (1997), 93–183, 16 (1998), 41–82

Lagorio, V. M., 'The Evolving Legend of St Joseph of Glastonbury', *Speculum* 46 (1971), 209–31

'The "Joseph of Arimathie": English Hagiography in Transition', *Medievalia et Humanistica* 6 (1975), 91–101

Lea, H. C., *A History of Auricular Confession and Indulgences in the Latin Church*, 3 vols. (London 1896)

A History of the Inquisition of the Middle Ages, 3 vols. (New York 1888)

Lefèvre, E., *Documents historiques sur les communes du canton de Nogent-le-Roi, arrondissement de Dreux*, 2 vols. (Chartres 1864–6)

Lefèvre, P., 'A propos d'une bulle d'indulgence d'Eugène IV en faveur du culte eucharistique à Bruxelles', *Hommage à dom. Ursmer Berlière* (Brussels 1931), 163–8

'La Valeur historique d'une enquête épiscopale sur le miracle eucharistique de Bruxelles en 1370', *Revue d'Histoire Ecclésiastique* 28 (1932), 329–46

Le Goff, J., 'Aspects religieux et sacrés de la monarchie française du Xe au XIIIe siècle', *La royauté sacrée dans le monde chrétien (colloque de Royaumont, mars 1989)*, ed. A. Boureau and C. S. Ingerflom (Paris 1992), 19–28

Saint Louis (Paris 1996)

Legris, A., 'Le Précieux Sang de Fécamp', *Revue Catholique de Normandie* 24 (1915), 278–89

Le Hule, G., *Le Thrésor ou abbregé de l'histoire de l'abbaye de Fescamp*, ed. A. Alexandre (Fécamp 1893)

Lemarignier, J.-F., *Etude sur les privilèges d'exemption et de juridiction ecclésiastique des abbayes Normandes depuis les origines jusqu'en 1140*, Archives de la France monastique XLIV (1937)

Lentsch, R., 'Dans le trésor des papes d'Avignon, la vaisselle liturgique contenant le sang du Christ', *Le Sang au Moyen-Age: Actes du quatrième colloque international de Montpellier Université Paul-Valéry (27–29 novembre 1997)*, ed. M. Faure (Montpellier 1999), 451–7

Leroux, A.-P., *Une tapisserie du Précieux Sang de Fécamp* (Fécamp 1927)

Lester, G. A., *Sir John Paston's "Grete Boke"* (Cambridge 1984)

Lewis, A. W., *Royal Succession in Capetian France: Studies on Familial Order and the State* (Cambridge, Mass., 1981)

Lewis, S., *The Art of Matthew Paris in the Chronica Majora* (Aldershot 1987)

Leyser, K., 'Frederick Barbarossa, Henry II and the Hand of St James', *English Historical Review* 90 (1975), 481–506

'The Angevin Kings and the Holy Man', *St Hugh of Lincoln*, ed. H. Mayr-Harting (Oxford 1987), 49–73

L'Hermite-Leclerq, P., 'Le Sang et le lait de la vierge', *Le Sang au Moyen-Age: actes du quatrième colloque international de Montpellier Université Paul-Valéry (27–29 novembre 1997)*, ed. M. Faure (Montpellier 1999), 145–62

Lincy, L. de, *Essai historique et littéraire sur l'abbaye de Fécamp* (Rouen 1840)

Lippens, H., 'S. Jean de Capistran en mission aux états bourguignons, 1442–1443', *Archivum Franciscanum Historicum* 35 (1942), 113–32, 254–95

Lloyd, S. D., *English Society and the Crusade 1216–1307* (Oxford 1988)

'William Longespee II: The Making of an English Crusading Hero', *Nottingham Medieval Studies* 35 (1991), 41–69, 36 (1992), 79–125

Longère, J., 'Les Evêques et l'administration du sacrament de pénitence au XIIIe siècle: les cas réservés', *Papauté, monachisme et théories politiques: études d'histoire médiévale offertes à Marcel Pacaut*, ed. P. Guichard et al., 2 vols. (Lyons 1994), II 537–50

Loomis, L. H., 'The Holy Relics of Charlemagne and King Athelstan: The Lances of Longinus and St Maurice', *Speculum* 25 (1950), 437–56

The Grail: From Celtic Myth to Christian Symbolism (Cardiff 1963)

Loomis, L. R., 'Nationality at the Council of Constance: An Anglo-French Dispute', *American Historical Review* 44 (1938–9), 508–27

Mabillon, J., *Lettre d'un Bénédictin à Monsiegneur l'évêque de Blois, touchant le discernement des anciennes reliques* (Paris 1700)

McGuire, B. P., *The Difficult Saint, Bernard of Clairvaux and his Tradition*, Cistercian Studies CXXVI (Kalamazoo 1991)

Macquarrie, A., *Scotland and the Crusades 1095–1560* (Edinburgh 1985)

Macy, G., *The Theologies of the Eucharist in the Early Scholastic Period* (Oxford 1984)

Treasures from the Storeroom: Medieval Religion and the Eucharist (Collegeville 1999)

Magoun, F. P., 'King Aethelwulf's Biblical Ancestors', *Modern Language Review* 46 (1951), 249–50

Mango, C., 'Héraclius, Sahrvaraz et la Vraie Croix', *Travaux et Mémoires* 9 (1985), 105–18

Manser, A., and K. Beyerle, 'Aus dem liturgischen Leben der Reichenau', *Die Kultur der Abtei Reichenau*, ed. K. Beyerle, 2 vols. (Munich 1925), I 316–417

Mantova: La Storia, ed. G. Coniglio, L. Mazzoldi, R. Giusti *et al.*, 3 vols. (Mantua 1959–63)

Marolles, M. de, *Mémoires* (Amsterdam 1755)

Marshall, P., 'The Rood of Boxley, the Blood of Hailes and the Defence of the Henrican Church', *Journal of Ecclesiastical History* 46 (1995), 689–96

Martin, J., and L. E. M. Walker, 'At the Feet of Stephen Muret: Henry II and the Order of Grandmont "Redivivus"', *Journal of Medieval History* 16 (1990), 1–12

Mayer, H. E., 'Henry II of England and the Holy Land', *English Historical Review* 97 (1982), 721–39

Mercati, S. G., 'Santuari e reliquie Costantinopolitane secondo il codice Ottoboniano Latino 169 prima della conquista Latina (1204)', *Rendiconti della Pontificia Accademia Romana di Archeologia* 3rd series 12 (1936), 133–56

Michaud, J., 'Culte des reliques et épigraphie. L'exemple des dédicaces et des consécrations d'autels', *Les Reliques: objets, cultes, symboles. Actes du colloque international de l'Université du Littoral-Côte d'Opale (Boulogne-sur-Mer) 4–6 septembre 1997*, ed. E. Bozóky and A.-M. Helvétius (Turnhout 1999), 199–212

Millet, G., *Histoire de la Sainte-Larme de Vendôme* (Avignon 1891)

Miramon, C. de, 'La Fin d'un tabou? L'interdiction de communier pour la femme menstruée au moyen-âge. Le cas du XIIe siècle', *Le Sang au Moyen-Age: actes du quatrième colloque international de Montpellier Université Paul-Valéry (27–29 novembre 1997)*, ed. M. Faure (Montpellier 1999), 163–81

Mireux, M.-D., 'Guibert de Nogent et la critique du culte des reliques', *La Piété populaire au Moyen Age*, Actes du 99e congrès national des Sociétés savantes, Besançon 1974, Section de Philologie et d' Histoire jusqu'à 1610 vol. 1 (Paris 1977), 293–301

Mislin, J., *Les Saints lieux, pèlerinage à Jérusalem*, 3 vols. (Paris 1858)

Moore, R. I., 'Guibert of Nogent and his World', *Studies in Medieval History Presented to R. H. C. Davis*, ed. H. Mayr-Harting and R. I. Moore (London 1985), 107–17

Moorman, J. R. H., *Church Life in England in the Thirteenth Century* (Cambridge 1945)

Morgan, P. E., 'The Effect of the Pilgrim Cult of St Thomas Cantilupe on Hereford Cathedral', *St Thomas Cantilupe, Bishop of Hereford, Essays in his Honour*, ed. M. Jancey (Hereford 1982), 145–52

Morin, A. S., *Le Culte du Sacre Prépuce de Jésus*, La documentation antireligieuse LXXIII (Herblay 1939)

Morris, C., 'Bringing the Holy Sepulchre to the West: S. Stefano Bologna from the Fifth to the Twentieth Century', *Studies in Church History* 33 (1997), 31–59

Muir, L. R., *The Biblical Drama of Medieval Europe* (Cambridge 1995)

Müller, M. A., *Die 'hochheilige Vorhaut Christi' im Kult und in der Theologie der Papstkirche* (Berlin 1907)

Murray, A. V., '"Mighty Against the Enemies of Christ": The Relic of the True Cross in the Armies of the Kingdom of Jerusalem', *The Crusades and their Sources: Essays Presented to Bernard Hamilton*, ed. J. France and W. G. Zajac (Aldershot 1998), 217–38

Nelson, J., 'Royal Saints and Early Medieval Kingship', *Studies in Church History 10: Sanctity and Secularity*, ed. D. Baker (1973), 39–44

Oates, J. C. T., 'Richard Pynson and the Holy Blood of Hayles', *The Library* 5th series 13 (1958), 269–77

Oblizajek, W., 'Najstarsze dokumenty bożogrobców miechowskich (1198)', *Studia Źródłoznawcze* 24 (1979), 97–108

Omont, H., 'Invention du Précieux Sang dans l'église de l'abbaye de Fécamp au XIIe siècle', *Bulletins de la Société de l'Histoire de Normandie* 12 (1913–18), 52–66

Ó Riain-Raedel, D., 'Edith, Judith, Matilda: The Role of Royal Ladies in the Propagation of the Continental Cult', *Oswald: Northumbrian King to European Saint*, ed. C. Stancliffe and E. Cambridge (Stamford 1995), 210–29

Otte, J. K., 'The Life and Writings of Alfredus Anglicus', *Viator* 3 (1972), 275–91

Owen, D. D. R., *The Evolution of the Grail Legend* (Edinburgh 1968)

Owst, G. R., *Literature and the Pulpit in Medieval England*, 2nd edn (Oxford 1961)

Park, D., 'The Wall Paintings of the Holy Sepulchre Chapel', *Medieval Art and Architecture at Winchester Cathedral*, British Archaeological Association Conference Transactions VI (1983), 38–62

Paulus, N., *Geschichte des Ablasses im Mittelalter*, 3 vols. (Paderborn 1923)

Pearce, E. H., *The Monks of Westminster* (Cambridge 1916)

Pedemonte, A., 'Richerche sulla primitiva forma iconografica del Volto Santo', *Atti della Reale Accademica Lucchese di scienze, lettere ed arti* new series 5 (1942), 117–44

Pfaff, R. W., *New Liturgical Feasts in Later Medieval England* (Oxford 1970)

Pfleger, L., 'Hostienwunder und Heiligblutkapellen im Elsass', *Archiv für Elsässische Kirchengeschichte* 8 (1933), 461–3

Piétu, A., *Neuvy-St-Sépulcre: les gloires de son passé* (Bourges 1920)

Pilon de Thury, Abbé, *Histoire et thèse sur l'insigne relique du Précieux Sang dite de la Sainte Larme* (Paris 1858)

Pincus, D., 'Christian Relics and the Body Politic: A Thirteenth-Century Relief Plaque in the Church of San Marco', *Interpretazioni Veneziane: studi di storia dell'arte in onore di Michelangelo Muraro*, ed. D. Rosand (Venice 1984), 39–57

Platelle, H., 'La Voix du sang: le cadavre qui saigne en présence de son meutrier', *La Piété populaire au Moyen Age*, Actes du 99e congrès national des Sociétés savantes, Besançon 1974, Section de Philologie et d'Histoire jusqu'à 1610 vol. 1 (Paris 1977), 163–79

'Guibert de Nogent et le "De pignoribus sanctorum". Richesses et limites d'une critique médiévale des reliques', *Les Reliques: objets, cultes, symboles. Actes du colloque international de l'Université du Littoral-Côte d'Opale (Boulogne-sur-Mer) 4–6 septembre 1997*, ed. E. Bozóky and A.-M. Helvétius (Turnhout 1999), 109–21

Pouchelle, M.-C., 'Le Sang et ses pouvoirs au Moyen-Age', *Affaires de sang*, ed. A. Farge (Paris 1988), 17–41

The Body and Surgery in the Middle Ages, trans. R. Morris (Oxford 1990)

Prestwich, M., 'The Piety of Edward I', *England in the Thirteenth Century: Proceedings of the 1984 Harlaxton Symposium*, ed. W. M. Ormrod (Stamford 1985), 120–8

Préville, Abbé, *Note historique et critique sur la Sainte-Larme de l'abbaye de Vendôme* (Blois 1875)

Ridgeway, H. W., 'King Henry III and the "Aliens", 1236–1272', in *Thirteenth Century England II*, ed. P. R. Coss and S. D. Lloyd (Woodbridge 1988), 81–92

'Foreign Favourites and Henry III's Problems of Patronage, 1247–1258', *English Historical Review* 104 (1989), 590–610

'The Ecclesiastical Career of Aymer de Lusignan, Bishop Elect of Winchester, 1250–60', *The Cloister and the World: Essays in Medieval History in Honour of Barbara Harvey*, ed. J. Blair and B. Golding (Oxford 1996), 148–77

Rigaux, D., 'Autour de la dispute "De Sanguine Christi". Une relecture de quelques peintures italiennes de la seconde moitié du XVe siècle', *Le Sang au Moyen-Age: actes du quatrième colloque international de Montpellier Université Paul-Valéry (27–29 novembre 1997)*, ed. M. Faure (Montpellier 1999), 393–403

Riley-Smith, J. S. C., 'Peace Never Established: The Case of the Kingdom of Jerusalem', *Transactions of the Royal Historical Society* 5th series 28 (1978) 87–102

Roberts, M. E., 'The Relic of the Holy Blood and the Iconography of the Thirteenth-Century North Transept Portal of Westminster Abbey', *England in the Thirteenth Century: Proceedings of the 1984 Harlaxton Symposium*, ed. W. M. Ormrod (Stamford 1985), 129–42

Rohling, J. H., *The Blood of Christ in Christian Latin Literature before the Year 1000* (Washington 1932)

Rollason, D., *Saints and Relics in Anglo-Saxon England* (Oxford 1989)

Rosin, A., 'Die "Hierarchie" des John Peckham, historisch interpretiert', *Zeitschrift für Romanische Philologie* 52 (1932), 583–614

Rosser, G., *Medieval Westminster 1200–1540* (Oxford 1989)

Rossmann, H., *Die Hierarchie der Welt: Gesalt und System des Franz von Meyronnes OFM mit besonderer Berücksichtigung seiner Schöpfungslehre*, Franziskanische Forschungen XXIII (Werl 1972)

Roth, B., *Franz von Mayronis O.F.M.*, Franziskanische Forschungen III (Werl 1936)

Roux, J.-P., *Le Sang: mythes, symboles et réalités* (Paris 1988)

Rubin, M., *Corpus Christi* (Cambridge 1990)

Runciman, S., 'The Holy Lance Found at Antioch', *Analecta Bollandiana* 68 (1950), 197–209

Russell, A. L. N., *Westminster Abbey* (London 1943)

St Clair Baddeley, W., 'The Holy Blood of Hayles', *Transactions of the Bristol and Gloucestershire Archaeological Society* 23 (1900), 276–84

    A Cotteswold Shrine: Being a Contribution to the History of Hailes County Gloucester, Manor, Parish and Abbey (Gloucester 1908)

St-Martin, R. de, *La Divine Relique du Sang Adorable de Jésus-Christ dans la ville de Billom en Auvergne* (Lyons 1645)

Saintyves, P., *Les Reliques et les images légendaires* (Paris 1912)

Saltman, A., *Theobald Archbishop of Canterbury* (London 1956)

Saul, N., 'Richard II and Westminster Abbey', *The Cloister and the World: Essays in Medieval History in Honour of Barbara Harvey*, ed. J. Blair and B. Golding (Oxford 1996), 196–218

Saxer, V., 'Les Ossements dits de sainte Marie-Madeleine conservés à Saint-Maximin-la-Sainte-Baume', *Provence Historique* 27 (1977), 257–311

Schaller, H. M., 'Der heilige Tag als Termin in mittelalterlicher Staatsakte', *Deutsches Archiv für Erforschung des Mittelalters* 30 (1974), 1–24

Schiffers, H., *Die deutsche Königskrönung und die Insignien des Richard von Cornwallis*, Veröffentlichungen des bischöflichen Diözesanarchivs Aachen II (Aachen 1936)

    Aachener Heiligtumsfahrt, Veröffentlichungen des bischöflichen Diözesanarchivs Aachen V (Aachen 1937)

Schiller, G., *Iconography of Christian Art*, 2 vols., trans. J. Seligman (London 1971–2)

Schmitt, J.-C., 'Cendrillon crucifiée. A propos du "Volto Santo" de Lucques', *Miracles, prodiges et merveilles au Moyen Age. XXVe congrès de la Société de l'Enseignement Supérieur Public* (Paris 1995), 241–69

Schöpflin, J. D., *Alsatia Illustrata Germanica Gallica* (Colmar 1761)

Schramm, P. E., 'Die Krönung in Deutschland bis zum Beginn des Salischen Hauses (1028)', *Zeitschrift der Savigny-Stiftung für Rechtsgeschichte* 55, Kanonistische Abteilung XXIV (1935), 184–332

    Herrschaftszeichen und Staatssymbolik, Schriften der *MGH* XIII, 3 vols. (Stuttgart 1954–6)

Schulte, A., *Die Kaiser-und Königskrönungen zu Aachen 813–1531*, Reinische Neujahrsblätter (Bonn and Leipzig 1924)

Schürer, G., and J. M. Ritz, *Sankt Kümmernis und Volto Santo*, Forschungen zur Volkskunde XIII–XV (Dusseldorf 1934)

Sharpe, R., *A Handlist of the Latin Writers of Great Britain and Ireland before 1540* (Turnhout 1997)

Shines, J. R., 'The Veneration of Saints at Norwich Cathedral in the Fourteenth Century', *Norfolk Archaeology* 40 (1989), 133–44

Sigal, P.-A., *L'Homme et le miracle dans la France médiévale (XIe–XIIe siècle)* (Paris 1985)

'Le Déroulement des translations de reliques principalement dans les régions entre Loire et Rhin aux XIe et XIIe siècles', *Les Reliques: objets, cultes, symboles. Actes du colloque international de l'Université du Littoral-Côte d'Opale (Boulogne-sur-Mer) 4–6 septembre 1997*, ed. E. Bozóky and A.-M. Helvétius (Turnhout 1999), 213–27

Singer, C., and E. A. Underwood, *A Short History of Medicine*, 2nd edn (Oxford 1962)

Smalley, B., 'Which William of Nottingham?', *Mediaeval and Renaissance Studies* 3 (1954), 200–38

Somigli, T., 'Vita di S. Giacomo della Marca scitta da Fra Venanzio da Fabriano', *Archivum Franciscanum Historicum* 17 (1924), 378–414

Southern, R. W., *Medieval Humanism and Other Essays* (Oxford 1970)

Robert Grosseteste: The Growth of an English Mind in Medieval Europe, 2nd edn (Oxford 1992)

Spahr, G., *Kreuz und Blut Christi in der Kunst Weingartens, eine ikonographische Studie* (Constance 1962)

Spalding, M. C., *The Middle English Charters of Christ*, Bryn Mawr College Monographs XV (Bryn Mawr 1914)

Spiegel, G. M., 'The Cult of St Denis and Capetian Kingship', *Saints and their Cults: Studies in Religious Sociology, Folklore and History*, ed. S. Wilson (Cambridge 1983), 141–68

Spinka, M., *John Hus a Biography* (Princeton 1968)

Stacey, R. C., *Politics, Policy and Finance under Henry III 1216–1245* (Oxford 1987)

'Crusades, Crusaders and the Baronial "Gravamina" of 1263–1264', *Thirteenth Century England III*, ed. P. R. Coss and S. D. Lloyd (Woodbridge 1991), 144–50

Stones, A., 'Seeing the Grail: Prolegomena to a Study of Grail Imagery in Arthurian Manuscripts', *The Grail: A Case Book*, ed. D. Mahoney (forthcoming)

Strayer, J. R., 'France: The Holy Land, the Chosen People and the Most Christian King', J. R. Strayer, *Medieval Statecraft and the Perspectives of History*, ed. J. F. Benton and T. N. Bisson (Princeton 1971), 300–14

Sumption, J., *Pilgrimage: An Image of Mediaeval Religion* (London 1975)

Swanson, R. N., 'Devotional Offerings at Hereford Cathedral in the Later Middle Ages', *Analecta Bollandiana* 111 (1993), 93–102

'Fund Raising for a Medieval Monastery: Indulgences and Great Bricett Priory', *Transactions of the Suffolk Institute of Archaeology* (forthcoming)

Tanner, J. D., 'Tombs of Royal Babies in Westminster Abbey', *Journal of the British Archaeological Association* 3rd series 16 (1953), 25–40

Tanner, L. E., 'Some Representations of St Edward the Confessor in Westminster Abbey and Elsewhere', *Journal of the British Archaeological Association* 3rd series 15 (1952), 1–12

'The Quest for the Cross of St Edward the Confessor', *Journal of the British Archaeological Association* 3rd series 17 (1954), 1–10

Tarayre, M., 'Le Sang dans le "Speculum Maius" de Vincent de Beauvais. De la science aux "miracula"', *Le Sang au Moyen-Age: actes du quatrième colloque international de Montpellier Université Paul-Valéry (27–29 novembre 1997)*, ed. M. Faure (Montpellier 1999), 343–59

Temkin, O., 'On Galen's Pneumatology', *Gesnerus* 8 (1951), 180–9

Terrinca, Natale da, *La Devozione al prez. Mo sangue di nostro signore Gesu Cristo*, 2nd edn (Rome 1987)

Thiers, J.-B., *Dissertation sur la Sainte-Larme de Vendôme* (Paris 1699)

Réponse à la lettre du père Mabillon touchant la prétendue Sainte-Larme de Vendôme (Cologne 1700)

Thompson, S., *Women Religious* (Oxford 1991)

Thomson, J. A. F., *The Later Lollards 1414–1520* (Oxford 1965)

Thomson, S. H., *The Writings of Robert Grosseteste Bishop of Lincoln 1235–1253* (Cambridge 1940)

Thümmel, H. G., 'Kreuze, Reliquien und Bilder im Zeremonienbuch des Konstantinos Porphyrogennetos', *Byzantinische Forschungen* 18 (1992), 119–26

Tillmann, H., *Pope Innocent III*, trans. W. Sax (Amsterdam 1980)

Torrell, J.-P., *Saint Thomas Aquinas*, trans. R. Royal (Washington 1996)

Treharne, R. F., *The Glastonbury Legends* (London 1967)

Tudor-Craig, P. *et al.*, *The New Bell's Cathedral Guides: Westminster Abbey* (London 1986)

Tyerman, C. J., 'Were there any Crusades in the Twelfth Century?', *English Historical Review* 110 (1995), 553–77

Vattioni, F. (ed.), *Sangue e antropologia*, Atti della settimana di Centro studi sanguis christi, 8 vols. in 21 parts (Rome 1981–)

Vauchez, A., *La Sainteté en occident aux derniers siècles du Moyen Age*, 2nd edn (Rome 1988)

Vigneras, L.-A., 'L'Abbaye de Charroux et la légende du pèlerinage de Charlemagne', *Romanic Review* 32 (1941), 121–8

Vincent, N., *Peter des Roches, An Alien in English Politics 1205–1238* (Cambridge 1996)

'Goffredo de Prefetti and the Church of Bethlehem in England', *Journal of Ecclesiastical History* 49 (1998), 213–35

'Isabella of Angoulême: John's Jezebel', *King John: New Interpretations*, ed. S. D. Church (Woodbridge 1999), 165–219

'The Pilgrimages of the Angevin Kings of England, 1154–1272', *Pilgrimage: The English Experience*, ed. C. Morris and P. Roberts (Cambridge, 2001)

'Conclusion', *Noblesses de l'espace Plantagenêt (1154–1216)*, ed. M. Aurell (Poitiers 2001), 207–14

'The Earliest English Indulgences: Some Pardoners' Tales', *Transactions of the Royal Historical Society* (forthcoming)

'Frederick II, Henry III and the Council of Lyons (1245)' (forthcoming)

Vogel, C., 'Le Pèlerinage pénitentiel', *Revue des Sciences Religieuses* 38 (1964), 113–53

Volk, W. A., 'La Festa liturgica del preziosissimo sangue', *Sangue e antropologia nella liturgia: atti della IV settimana, Roma 21–26 novembre 1983*, ed. F. Vattioni, 3 vols. (Rome 1984), III 1503–45

Walcott, M. E. C., 'The Inventories of Westminster Abbey at the Dissolution', *Transactions of the London and Middlesex Archaeological Society* 4 part 3 (1873), 313–64

Ward, B., *Miracles and the Medieval Mind* (revised edn, Aldershot 1987)

Waterton, E., *Pietas Mariana Brittanica* (London 1879)

Webb, D. M., 'The Holy Face of Lucca', *Anglo-Norman Studies* 9 (1987), 227–37

Westlake, H. F., *Westminster Abbey: The Church, Convent, Cathedral and College of St Peter, Westminster*, 2 vols. (London 1923)

Wolff, F., *Die Klosterkirche St Maria zu Niedermünster im Unter-Elsass* (Strasbourg 1904)

Wood, C. T., 'The Doctor's Dilemma: Sin, Salvation and the Menstrual Cycle in Medieval Thought', *Speculum* 56 (1981), 710–27

Woodruff, C. E., 'The Financial Aspect of the Cult of St Thomas of Canterbury', *Archaeologia Cantiana* 44 (1932), 13–32

Woolf, R., *The English Religious Lyric in the Middle Ages* (Oxford 1968)

Wülcker, R., *Das Evangelium Nicodemi in der abendländischen Literatur* (Paderborn 1872)

Zika, C., 'Hosts, Processions and Pilgrimages: Controlling the Sacred in Fifteenth-Century Germany', *Past and Present* 118 (1988), 25–64

Index

Lightning Source UK Ltd.
Milton Keynes UK
UKOW01f0917070716

277866UK00001B/48/P